NETWORKS *of* IMPROVEMENT

NETWORKS
of
IMPROVEMENT

Literature, Bodies, and Machines
in the Industrial Revolution

JON MEE

The University of Chicago Press
CHICAGO & LONDON

The University of Chicago Press, Chicago 60637
The University of Chicago Press, Ltd., London
© 2023 by The University of Chicago
Published 2023
Printed in the United States of America

32 31 30 29 28 27 26 25 24 23   1 2 3 4 5

ISBN-13: 978-0-226-82837-4 (cloth)
ISBN-13: 978-0-226-82838-1 (paper)
ISBN-13: 978-0-226-82839-8 (e-book)
DOI: https://doi.org/10.7208/chicago/9780226828398.001.0001

Library of Congress Cataloging-in-Publication Data

Names: Mee, Jon, author.
Title: Networks of improvement : literature, bodies, and machines in the
Industrial Revolution / Jon Mee.
Description: Chicago : The University of Chicago Press, 2023. | Includes
bibliographical references and index.
Identifiers: LCCN 2023001559 | ISBN 9780226828374 (cloth) |
ISBN 9780226828381 (paperback) | ISBN 9780226828398 (ebook)
Subjects: LCSH: Industrial revolution—Social aspects—Great Britain. |
Industrial revolution in literature.
Classification: LCC HC254.5 .M44 2023 | DDC 338.0941—dc23/eng/20230320
LC record available at https://lccn.loc.gov/2023001559

♾ This paper meets the requirements of ANSI/NISO Z39.48-1992
(Permanence of Paper).

CONTENTS

INTRODUCTION

Researching this book has at times felt like writing a Victorian triple-decker novel following the fates of generations of interrelated families across a restricted geographical area. Ending as it does with Elizabeth Gaskell, the analogy may seem especially appropriate, but the appearance belies a scope and method that I would like to sketch out more fully in this brief introduction. *Networks of Improvement* ranges from around 1780 to the early 1830s—roughly speaking, the period of "the shorter Industrial Revolution."[1] Geographically, it concentrates on the area long regarded as the heartland of this phenomenon, taking John Aikin Jr.'s *Description of the country from thirty to forty miles round Manchester* (1795) as its matrix. The argument of *Networks of Improvement* engages with recent claims about the "industrial enlightenment," or "the intellectual origins of the Industrial Revolution" associated with scholars such as Margaret Jacob and Joel Mokyr, displacing their model of the "knowledge economy" into a distinctive network analysis that looks at the emergence of a new structure of feeling within apparent continuities of networks and institutions traced back to Aikin's book and its connections.

Tracing this emergence requires an alertness to that slippery term "liberal." The institutions and cultural forms discussed here became familiar parts of the lived experience of nineteenth-century liberalism, not least in its celebration of free trade, open discussion, and freedom of religious opinion. Its precipitated nineteenth-century forms, where liberty of opinion included a resistance to curbs on industrial expansion and ideas of environmental codetermination hardened into "molding" human character, had a complex relationship with the "liberal" disposition found in Aikin's book and its sense a more diverse culture of "improvement" discussed in chapter 1. The transformation was a dynamic and uncertain "part of the material process itself," as Raymond Williams might have put it, whether viewed as the precipitation of something already in solution or, to my mind more appropriately, the transmutation of one structure of feeling into another within a *"pattern of recurring links."*[2] By the early 1830s, the trade union leader John Doherty could throw the word "liberal" back in the face of Benjamin Heywood's pretensions to stewardship by defining it as "averse to all reform, save that which will give him power, and additional control over the producers of the nation's wealth."[3]

Part of this historical process, as Doherty bitterly recognized, was a sharpening restriction of certain "liberal" values—including the *Oxford English Dictionary*'s "free from bias, prejudice, or bigotry; open-minded, tolerant; governing or governed by relaxed principles or rules"—to particular spheres, including spaces conceived in terms of at least formal equality akin to the eighteenth-century idea of the republic of letters, now existing inside a hierarchical world increasingly defined outside in terms of the marketplace. An idea of "knowledge" was imagined into being that could maintain the arts and the sciences at a precarious distance from political and religious strife and from moneymaking. "Useful knowledge" from this perspective was understood not, or not only, instrumentally but also in terms of what it could do for the moral order of civil society, even if in a form of "virtuous commerce" increasingly disembedded from social relations. The pairing of the "arts and the sciences," so ably described by Jon Klancher in its London context, witnessed continuous debates about the relationship between imaginative literature and other aspects of knowledge. In some powerful definitional moves, discussed in relation to Thomas De Quincey in my first chapter, this reconceptualization of knowledge involved disaggregating the "power" of literature from the broader ecology of knowledge. De Quincey's move might be regarded as a defensive gesture intended to sustain the importance of the arts against a restrictive idea of useful knowledge, but others continued to argue for literature's place within the broader paradigm. The archive offers "little suggestion," as Philip Connell reminds us, "that the rise of utilitarian radicalism made an essential impact on their pursuit of humanistic literary edification in tandem with popular scientific enquiry."[4]

One of this book's claims to originality is its focus on institutions as actants in these developments, especially the role of the formal literary and philosophical societies in the area around Manchester. I use the term "actants" here, after Bruno Latour, to draw attention to the fact that they were not simply the manifestation of the will of human actors, although most of my account of networks is human-centered, a point to which I return to later. The foundation documents and regulations of these institutions routinely lay claim to an ecumenical commitment to improvement that proved hard to sustain because of the encroachments of a variety of differences that brought with them, for instance, fractious debates about what constituted knowledge. In this regard at least, institutions displayed a relative autonomy from the hopes and desires of their founders that makes them best understood as assemblages, people and things connected in an ongoing and frequently conflicted process of organizing, rather than the solid achievements of bricks and mortar that the word "institutions" might otherwise imply.[5] I understand institutions to be in a complex relationship with networks in this regard. They may represent a consolidation of informal networks, they may represent a claim to a certain kind of authority, but they may also retain the fluidity of networks and even represent the site where two or more networks become entangled or even come into conflict over competing claims to authority, over certain ideas of "knowledge," and over a certain civic visibility felt to be all the more important because of the lack of any local institutions of higher education. Beyond but including networks of authors and texts, *Networks of Improvement* is concerned with the emergence of a particular constellation of cultural forms in the heartlands of the Industrial Revolution, although it acknowledges the controversial status of the figure of "revolution," and indeed is partly concerned with its emergence as a way of describing the deep-seated, unevenly distributed transformations that happened in its period. Rather than reading them as "expressions" of middle-class dominance, its understanding of these institutional actors shares Mitchell Dean's wariness of using "categories and concepts which it regards as products of the transformations it is seeking to analyse," even if their use is also inescapable.[6]

Networks of Improvement does not understand the development of these institutions as *driven* by any cogent preformed ideology, especially not one understood as some kind of spirit shaping the bodies of those forms. In this regard, the project has benefited from Latour's encouragement to follow "the traces left by [the] activity of forming and dismantling groups."[7] Latourian attention to connections mitigates against reducing historical processes to some kind of intention or spirit, even though these links may seem to have ultimately conformed to a singular logic something very like the "mission" that Karl Marx invoked in *Capital* in a passage following his fantasy of John Aikin rising from his grave to witness the horror of mid-nineteenth-century Manchester. Nevertheless, for all it understands institutions as actants of a sort, this project is not a directly Latourian one, certainly not in the sense that jettisons critique. Although I understand Marx's ghostly parable of Aikin rising from his grave to imply that *A Description of Manchester* cannot be reduced to an immanent historical destiny, it should be apparent from my references to Raymond Williams that I do not take this to be the same thing as abandoning the idea of determination.[8] Rita Felski believes that traditions of historical critique are necessarily deadening in their search for "hidden causes, determining conditions, and noxious motives." A major part of her project has been to use Latour's notion of letting "the actors have some room to express themselves" to stake a claim for the autonomy of textual effects. Despite the fact that she praises Latour's "modes of existence" over "cartographic metaphors" like "field and domain" because they imply "discrete and bounded spaces," this view rather downplays the relativity of that autonomy and the way that the aesthetic has always been in a complex and unresolved relationship with other kinds of knowledge (including whether it denotes a form of "knowledge" at all).[9] That question took specific forms within the institutions studied here, worth studying for the Latourian reason of not assuming the autonomy of a category prior to its connections. Why, indeed, not let the actors have a little room when it comes to debates over the relationship between the literary and useful knowledge?

The richness *Networks of Improvement* aims to recover is the richness of institutional forms that have sometimes been too easily written off as expressions or symbols of middle-class power. These institutions were actants with their own kinds of relative autonomy, which allowed them to be perpetuated in ways that were not reducible to the wishes of their members, not all of them all the time anyway, or to some higher social force. This approach has involved an understanding of these institutions as constituted out of books, lectures, meetings, and even buildings and collections as they made competing claims for what Latour would call representative authority. Societies like the Manchester Literary and Philosophical Society and their proliferation across the region provide the narrative focus of part 1, driven in many ways by a power of emulation that did not entirely coincide with the hopes of their founders (note how often the forms available to those hopes and wishes were already scripted in other books of rules and regulations). For all this formal regularity, institutions were partners in an unstable and variegated topology, full of overlaps, obstructions, and what Caroline Levine calls broken "hinges."[10] Unsurprisingly the book finds a prehistory of its own method in its objects of study, most obviously in Aikin's *Description*, but also with the medical men who brought to these institutions a sense of the entangled relations between organic bodies and their circumstances. At the forefront of these societies, especially in the 1780s and early 1790s, were a group of medical men, students of William Cullen, who shared with their colleagues recently discussed by Goodman a "recognition of abstracted causes in immediately felt effects, the presence of the remote *in* the proximate, the external world *in* the body."[11] Increasing, though, the sense of lively matter, which early on at least, extended even into papers on the perceptive power of vegetables published by the society at Manchester, narrowed into an assumption of stewardship over passive materials, whether they be items collected in museums or human beings gathered in its factories and plantations. This dark materialism may be regarded as an affordance of an earlier style of environmental thinking, I have argued, but it was neither its necessary nor only outcome.

In thinking about this project's relationship to Latour, I was drawn back to Raymond Williams's skepticism about "epochal" readings. The general method of *Networks of Improvement* is sympathetic to Williams's account of the role of the emergent, the residual, and the dominant in historical processes, if with a recognition of Levine's reservations about the ways that this method still tends toward a narrative of linear unfolding.[12] Although a powerful logic of exploitation and control emerges in these pages, sometimes hidden within the distinctively liberal idea of stewardship, it was made up of many threads, not all of which simply resolved into the dominant cultural form that Williams named "industrialism." Elsewhere I have suggested that the coinage represents a fall away from his own best practice, which was exemplary in its grasp of the complexity of social processes, the uneven way they are precipitated (a characteristic metaphor) into cultural forms, and the importance of taking this understanding into critiques of power and exploitation.[13]

The role of nonhuman things as actants has always been a significant aspect of Latour's accounts of networks, a feature particularly important to recent ecological criticism and those varieties of new materialism that paint a picture of a lively universe. Somewhat in this spirit, I have drawn attention to the entanglements of regulations, museum exhibits, books, and experimental instruments in the assemblages that were the literary and philosophical societies. The relations between these things reveal fault lines about representative authority in the societies, including fundamental questions about the way boundaries of knowledge were drawn around them. These boundaries were important because "knowledge" of certain kinds—demonstration or reading, for instance—was deemed to have relative autonomy from power as the societies purported to represent a space of equality within the outside world of differentiated hierarchies. If these issues are not immediately exhausted by questions of power, they were necessarily *determined* by them, at least in the complex sense Goodman understands the word.[14] Beyond the walls of the Manchester Literary and Philosophical Society, the emergence of the steam-factory system might very well be understood as akin to a Latourian laboratory, a network constituted from operatives, machines, even the penumbra of steam fetishism that surrounded them. There may have been benefits to *Networks of Improvement* paying more attention to the entanglement of machines and humans in the factory than it does, but to leave it there would be to ignore what was at issue between C. T. Thackrah's account of the illnesses caused by factory conditions and Edward Baines Jr.'s claim that all the demands of labor fell on the machine. For all the difficulties associated with integrating machinery into the new factories, the process produced and was produced by asymmetries that operated in the interests of some participants over others.

A distinctive aspect of *Networks of Improvement* in terms of literary studies of the Romantic period is its focus on a restricted geographical area, the area around Manchester identified by Aikin. Far from being an organic territorial unit, its identity partly depended for Aikin upon an implicit contrast with the entrenched power of London and the exclusivity of the universities at Cambridge and Oxford. Part of my project is the recovery of what I call the "transpennine enlightenment," a strategic appropriation of the "industrial enlightenment" of Jacob and Mokyr. Far from closed to global traffic, the area depended on access to wealth that flowed through Liverpool to Manchester and beyond, wealth derived from raw materials, markets, and capital generated by enslaved labor and techniques repurposed from across continents (e.g., Indian patterns and dyes), without being entirely reducible to those flows. When William Wordsworth wrote of this "inventive age" in *The Excursion* (1814), it was to distinguish between poetic creativity and the inventions associated with the Industrial Revolution and its useful knowledge. This last category is often implicitly treated by scholars of Romanticism as if it were a species of inert matter to be contrasted with the lively spirit of their inspired texts. My aim in this book has been to look at the other side of this question, to look at the ideas and forms that tumbled out of the region, whether caused by or causing the Industrial Revolution (an issue that may simply be for all intents and purposes irresolvable), and how they formed their own "literature" that could include both a pleasure in Wordsworth's poetry and a "romantic" wonder at James Watt's steam engines. When as a hierophant of Wordsworth, De Quincey decried the power of "connexion" in these same circles, he was implicitly noticing the way networks had been put to work to undermine traditional authority, even if he represented his own outrage as newly "romantic" in its defense of poetic genius. The contradictory ideological trajectory of this networked "connexion" often identified itself against traditional authority and for liberty of conscience but came to work more and more frequently against those it claimed to be liberating, whether in factories or on plantations, and for freedom of markets.

"We begin to confront the thinginess of objects when they stop working for us," famously wrote Bill Brown. These networks frequently had to face the frustration of their attempts to mold circumstance in the ways they wished, or to use circumstance to mold others. "Agency," Felski says in her defense of Latour against monocausal explanations, "is distributed, uncertain, and hard to pin down."[15] A case in point might be the specimens of the wombat and the platypus gifted to the Newcastle society in 1799. Getting the wombat to Newcastle, the first to arrive in Europe, its body preserved in a barrel of spirits, and its fate thereafter constituted a complex affair. Uncertain as to what it was, or how to classify it, the specimen was put to one side, until rediscovered in the 1820s, whereupon it was stuffed inappropriately standing on its hind legs. Here was a thing that refused, in Jane Bennett's phrase, "to dissolve completely into the milieu of human knowledge."[16] Even in a display case, it was a mockery that perhaps kept something of itself "withdrawn," as proponents of new materialism would say.[17] The wombat plays a part in a rich and complicated story, told in chapter 2, but that story cannot deny that control was exerted over the animal, social power legible in the very positioning of its body on display, even if the awkwardness also speaks of a certain recalcitrance. It remains on display today, perhaps mocking the human observer's demand for scientific accuracy, but still well and truly stuffed!

Whatever the debatable political benefits in our present emergency of shifting the anthropocentric view of agency into an interconnected world of vibrant matter, this book traces the emergence of a narrowing view of "liberal" possibilities. The project gains its urgency because this narrowed purview remains powerful, perhaps even dominant, within the world today, and seems able to reinvent itself and gain assent in the face of numerous challenges to its authority. My own experience in the archive has had its own humbling aspect, of course. Following the connections of these networks has involved dealing with destruction and decay, hard-to-read correspondence, silences in minute books just where they might have explained a decision, making sense of published accounts that seem at odds with each other and the archival record, and so on. Their richness is part of the resistance of these material objects. Had there been time and space enough, those agents in all processes of writing, it would have been well to have dwelled on more specific instances, such as the fight over the library in Newcastle, discussed at length in chapter 2, but following the connections across time makes its own demands. A global pandemic has played its own part in shaping my response, as typhoid and cholera at different times played their parts in forming and re-forming the networks described in these pages. Those answers were also shaped, as I have said, by flows of power, by capital generated from global trade, as those things have also determined my own position at a time when universities are failing to give the humanities the protection that might be expected in the face of demands for education to be narrowly focused on STEM (science, technology, engineering, and mathematics) subjects. I have had the privilege of time and space to trace these constructions of power as they shaped that world and continue to shape our own, even if, as I continue to believe with Raymond Williams, "no mode of production and therefore no dominant social order and therefore no dominant culture ever in reality includes or exhausts all human practice, human energy, and human intention."[18]

Networks of Improvement is divided into two parts. The first begins with an analysis in chapter 1 of John Aikin's *Description* as a matrix for understanding the territory explored by the book, introducing the groups that played a part in founding the Literary and Philosophical Society in Manchester, and contrasting the more familiarly "romantic" vision of De Quincey's opposition to the power of "connexion" wielded by them. Chapters 2 and 3 are more directly concerned with the forms of the societies and processes of negotiation and conflict that formed them as they spread across the region into the early decades of the nineteenth century. Networks of families, friends, and religion proved remarkably durable across fifty-odd years, but the forms and substance of the knowledge they produced mutated. If the territory imagined by Aikin in 1795 seems to be consolidated by 1830, if the vision of Thomas Percival when he set up the Manchester society seems fulfilled by societies in Leeds and Sheffield forty years later, then the formal similarities betray the emergent differences I have indicated. Part 2 of the book investigates these fissures in terms of particular debates, paying special attention to the way the belief in the environmental philosophy that everything—mental and physical—was susceptible to improvement came to power disparate ideas of relations between humans and between humans and their material environment. Chapter 4 is most directly concerned with the emergence of an environmental medicine among the Edinburgh-trained literary physicians associated with the early phase of the Manchester Literary and Philosophical Society. Their concern with the body-entangled mind opened up many avenues of inquiry, including a tradition of research into conditions in the emergent factory system. Chapter 5 looks at Hannah Greg as a case of a women excluded from the formal institution of the Literary and Philosophical Society but integral to the networks of improvement that sustained it. Her exclusion provides a case study in the gendered assumptions about space and the forms of knowledge exchange in these networks. Her own children—whom she organized into the Duodecimo Society in preparation for their graduation to the Manchester society—were educated into an idea of stewardship that her sons carried on into the 1830s, indicating a dark side to her interest in the relationship between habit, attention, and environment in the development of character. Chapters 6 is directly concerned with the retraction of the expansive environmentalism described in chapter 4 into a justification of the molding of the individual in the factory system. Chapter 7, the final chapter, looks more directly at the way the region's tradition of social inquiry shriveled into James Phillips Kay's analysis of working-class "demoralization," no longer to him a problem of environment but of the moral failings of those who suffered. These "failings" were understood as a drag on enlightened minds who advocated free trade and mechanical inventiveness, especially when they took the form of positive resistance from those classes who were the objects of reforming intentions. Edward Baines Jr. and his ilk increasingly came to view the natural world as a limitless resource at their disposal. "There are no limits," insisted his supporter the economist J. R. McCulloch, "to the powers and resources of genius."[19] Correlating the Anthropocene with liberal individualism, Dipesh Chakrabarty has suggested that "the mansion of modern freedom stands on an ever-expanding base of fossil-fuel use."[20] This book shows that this idea had a complex trajectory that contained and never entirely repressed some very different ways of understanding relations between human beings and their environment.

PART ONE

NETWORKS
and
INSTITUTIONS

CHAPTER ONE

POWER, KNOWLEDGE, AND LITERATURE

In his discussion of surplus value in *Capital*, Karl Marx gave an account of the development of the manufacturing classes in Manchester up to "the rise of machinery."[1] His main source was John Aikin Jr.'s *Description of the country from thirty to forty miles round Manchester* (1795).[2] Marx ended his account with a simple question: "What would the good Dr. Aikin say if he could rise from his grave and see the Manchester of to-day?" Marx's next paragraph inveighs against the gospel of "accumulation for accumulation's sake." This aggressive "formula" of accumulation, Marx claimed, "expressed the historical mission of the bourgeoisie," which "did not for a single instant deceive itself over the birth-throes of wealth."[3] If this sentence might imply a strong sense of bourgeois ideology as a determining force, "an *epochal* rather than a genuinely historical consciousness of ideas," to use the words of Raymond Williams, then the comments on Aikin suggest a more complex sense of the contradictions of the historical process: one potentially open to the idea that the outcomes of the Industrial Revolution were not simply present as the prior intentions of historical actors.[4] I want to start by going back to Aikin's account to place it within a distinctive networked culture of improvement more or less contemporaneous with the early decades of the Industrial Revolution—roughly speaking, 1780 to the 1830s—to begin an inquiry into the way that the liberal and progressive impulses of these networks hardened into something more like the "historical mission" described by Marx. Kurt Heinzelman has described "improvement" as "that massive cultural category that so dominated eighteenth-century century theory and practice," but exact definition is elusive for a term that operated across so many fields. Joanna Innes contrasts it with "reform" as "the ultimately unthreatening word for ameliorative change."[5] Improvement was not just a catalog of ideas but also a set of practices reinforced, if

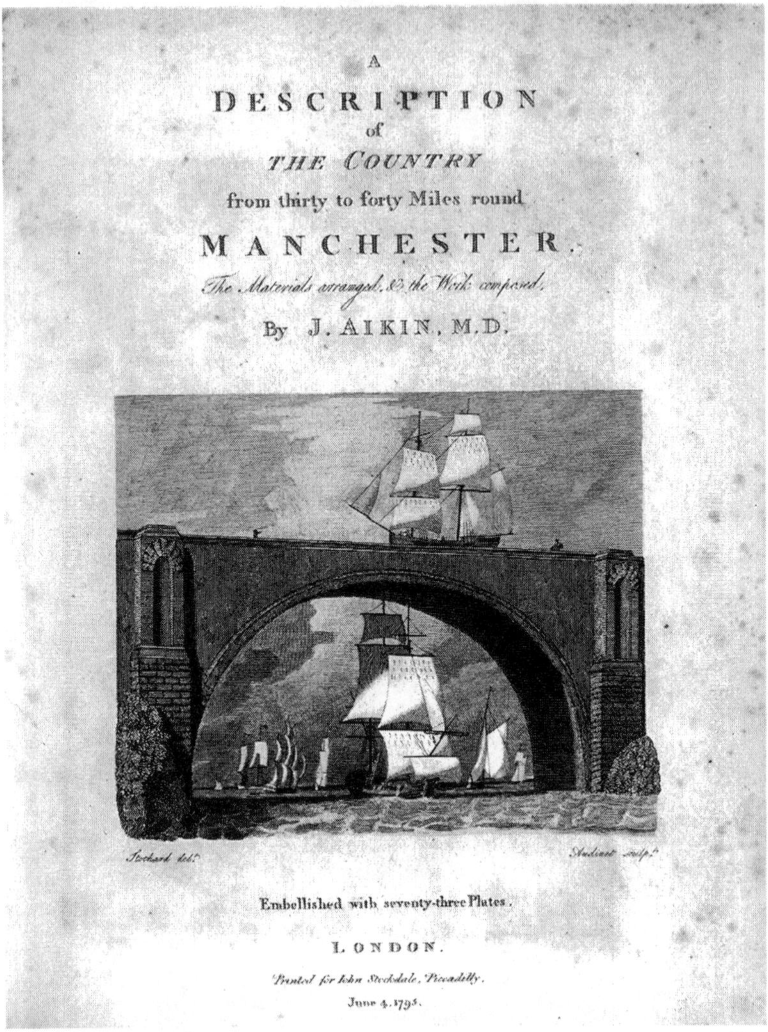

A
DESCRIPTION
of
THE COUNTRY
from thirty to forty Miles round
MANCHESTER.
The Materials arranged, & the Work composed,
By J. AIKIN, M.D.

Stothard del. *Audinet sculp.*

Embellished with seventy-three Plates.

LONDON.
Printed for John Stockdale, Piccadilly.
June 4. 1795.

FIGURE 1. Title page from John Aikin Jr.'s *A Description of the country from thirty to forty miles round Manchester* (London, 1795). Photograph courtesy of the Huntington Library, San Marino, California (RB 204522).

not learned, by many English Dissenters—Aikin included—at Scottish universities and sustained, as we will see many times in this book, by constant traffic across the border. Its synonyms could range from "reform" through to "progress," "utility," and "innovation." David Hume saw a "fermentation" in the "spirit of the age" liable to "to carry improvements into every art and science," but the word's primary association probably remained with agriculture, where it was especially linked to improving yields and reclaiming "wastes."[6] The eighteenth century was a dynamic period for agricultural improvement in Scotland, but Hume and his associates wrote on the idea across an astonishing range of subjects, avidly read by English readers. Most uses of the word "improvement" in Aikin's *Description* do appear in an agricultural context, especially in relation to reclamation schemes such as the ones at Trafford Moss and Chat Moss with which his friend William Roscoe was closely involved (as Aikin notes, 383), but the book also extended its use to mechanical innovations in the cotton trade, including the gradual introduction of steam engines, only just beginning as Aikin wrote, and especially the innovations in inland navigation associated with James Brindley discussed later in the chapter. In 1784, Richard Price believed that the "progress of improvement will not cease until it has excluded from the earth most of the worst evils," extending it into the political and religious spheres in ways that others were more wary about, especially after the French Revolution.[7] If muted on these topics compared with Price and some of Aikin's other writing, the picture of improvement painted by *A Description* is one of innovation building upon innovation—a "fermentation," in Hume's terms—that was creating a culture of ongoing development, with particular praise handed out to those who disseminated their improvements in a "liberal" manner, as he put it in relation to Brindley (145), by refusing to take out patents.[8]

A TRANSPENNINE ENLIGHTENMENT

Aikin's book was not just about the pace of change in its *time*. It is also obviously turning a geographical space into a particular kind of *place*, populated by specific kinds of historical actors connected in distinctive ways, human to human but also human to various nonhuman forms, including machines and other inventions. Aikin was identifying a certain territory—the country for the thirty to forty miles around Manchester, far from a natural organic place, divided as it was by a range of hills called the Pennines—with what would only decades later come to be described as the Industrial Revolution. Aikin's country "round" Manchester was constituted from an area that was home to diverse forms even of textile production, in terms of the raw materials—most obviously cotton, flax, and wool—and also in the organization of production. The woolen manufacture of the West Riding of Yorkshire, for instance, was still dominated by a domestic economy, described at length by Aikin, and generally regarded by his contemporaries as a morally and physically healthier form of economic organization than the factory system becoming dominant on the other side of the Pennines.[9] Aikin's spatial gambit marks a key moment in the development of a tradition that started to associate

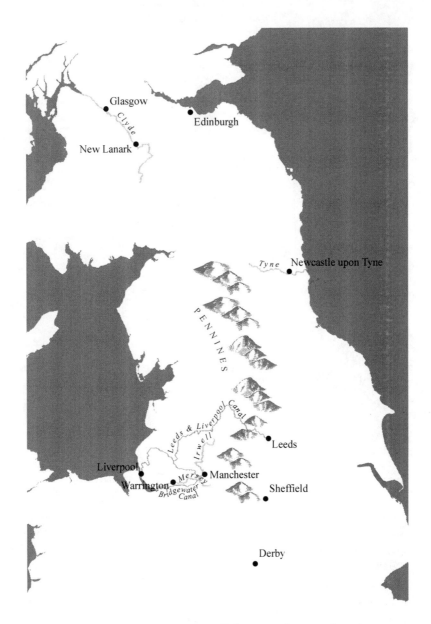

FIGURE 2. "The Transpennine Enlightenment." A map of northern England and south-central Scotland. Cartography by Julie Witmer Custom Map Design (with map data © OpenStreetMap.org contributors).

deep-seated change in the nature of human relations with this specific geographical area and to define its contours in a metaphorical "sorting process."[10] In the decades after 1795, this assemblage of networked relations was maintained and given more definition by other kinds of writing and their related associational practices, many still only emergent when Aikin wrote. In the same process, it was also transformed by them so that certain aspects of his perspective came to be discarded or, more accurately perhaps, hardened into new ideas of human being that simplified the complexity of its relations to its historical and material environments.

For many scholars, Manchester and the country around it continue to be understood, as it was understood by Marx, as the crucible of the Industrial Revolution. The trope of an industrial "revolution" has been much contested, an unstable consensus settling around the idea that there was a longer period of uneven change.[11] The neo-Malthusian account of E. A. Wrigley identified at least two phases of growth: the first based on an "advanced organic economy," derived from agricultural innovations, improvements in the division of labor described in Adam Smith's parable of the pins, and massive changes in transport infrastructure such as canals and roads. This period of Smithian growth was succeeded in Wrigley's account by a second mineral-based "revolution" that he describes as fueling a step change that confounded the steady state (and worse) anxieties of the classical economists, including most obviously the dire predictions of Thomas Malthus about excess population.[12] Aikin was writing on the cusp of this transition—however it be described—just as the steam engine was starting to be introduced in and around Manchester as the power source for recent technical innovations such as the cotton mule, but this process was an uncertain one, and the triumph of steam, despite its many advocates, was not really confirmed, so claims Andreas Malm, until the 1830s.[13] Part of my fascination with writing across this period is how contemporaries from within the region, or closely associated to it, as Aikin was, thought about and mediated this phenomenon as it was happening around them.

This writing can be understood as exerting its own productive force in shaping the changes that it might appear to be simply describing. Many of the writers discussed in the chapters that follow, for instance, influenced or at least lobbied government on the economy and related social issues. The early Victorian idea of "social reform" as a site of state and government intervention distinct from the economy as such was a product of this process.[14] James Phillips Kay, for instance, a crucial figure in my final chapter, first came to public notice with his text *The Moral and Physical Condition of the Working Classes Employed in the Cotton Manu-*

facture in Manchester (1832), which was a late product of the networks of improvement that had made Aikin's book possible. Economic historians have become increasingly interested in the determining power of ideas, writing, and related associational practices in the industrial transformation of Britain. Whereas Wrigley places his emphasis on energy sources, especially the presence of coal near the textile industry, as the primary competitive advantage for Britain, scholars such as Margaret Jacob and Joel Mokyr have made the circulation of "knowledge" the defining factor in Britain's Industrial Revolution.[15] Their work makes the communication of ideas central to the industrial transformation of Britain. "Britain's intellectual sphere had turned into a competitive market for ideas," claims Mokyr, "in which logic and evidence were becoming more important and 'authority' as such was on the defensive."[16]

Mokyr's work has tended to stress the role of a vital "select few" savants and their influence on "macroinventions" that "triggered a continuous flow of secondary and incremental inventions and improvements."[17] Other scholars see the thirst for experimental knowledge dispersed around broader networks and register the role of numberless anonymous artificers in technical developments and their dissemination. For these scholars, locations such as Birmingham and Manchester were the defining spaces of Britain's Industrial Revolution because they sustained a culture of knowledge transfer between multiple participants. Aikin's *Description of Manchester*, like John Kennedy's later "Observations on the Rise and Progress of the Cotton Trade" (1815), discussed in chapter 6, described the influence of instrument makers and other small technical innovations in the transformations taking place in their locale. More than Mokyr, whose emphasis has most often been on codification in print, scholars including Maxine Berg, Lilaine Hailaire-Peréz, and Larry Stewart have understood knowledge in the context of a networked environment that variously included print, public lectures, face-to-face exchanges on the factory floor, and debate in institutions and voluntary societies.[18]

Berg and Pat Hudson have suggested that economic revisionists such as Wrigley underestimate the depth of the transformations taking place at the end of the eighteenth century by using an aggregated national accounts framework and focusing on productivity growth. "Contemporaries," they argue, "appear to have had little doubt about the magnitude and importance of change in the period, particularly industrial change."[19] Location is important in making these judgments.[20] Berg and Hudson point out that particular locales—the area around Manchester especially—experienced deep-seated transformations that were cumulative across time and spread their effects across the country and the globe over succeeding decades. Cotton textiles quickly became the fastest-growing manufacturing industry in the world, probably supplying more than half of British productivity growth between 1788 and 1856. Stimulated by patterns of global demand to find substitutions for high-quality Indian cottons, a wave of inventions, many described in Aikin's book, preceded the steam-factory system in what has been called "the age of manufactures."[21] This response relied on a supply of raw materials from plantations in the West Indies, among other places, and, increasingly after 1800, the United States. "Never before in the history of mankind," as Giorgio Riello puts it, "had such a confined area produced for such a vast number of consumers across the world."[22] Aikin's *Description of Manchester* conveys a strong sense of a region connected to global trade without the supervening presence of London and other traditional authorities. When it comes to contemporary scholars who acknowledge the role of ideas and innovation in the Industrial Revolution, they nearly all follow Aikin—whether they use his text or not—in granting a major role to figures located outside entrenched hierarchies, constellated into flat networks, committed to experimental exchange and the distribution of useful knowledge. Most of them at least mention the Manchester Literary and Philosophical Society, founded in 1781, as the decisive knowledge institution for the boom in cotton manufactures described by Aikin (himself a member of the society from its foundation).

One question often ignored is the place of the "literary" within such societies and within the broader transformations described by Jacob and Mokyr. Was "literature" regarded as a "useful knowledge" in these circles? What delimited Mokyr's "technical knowledge" from other kinds of writing, including poetry, in its usefulness? To some extent, distinctions between the categories were solidified in this period, but they were rarely as settled as they may appear in hindsight or in theory. One famous attempt to draw boundaries was Thomas De Quincey's distinction between literatures of "power" and of "knowledge," categories that are unhelpful if they are assumed to correspond to natural kinds constituted as a binary. Before the work of Jacob, Mokyr, and others interested in the cultural origins of the Industrial Revolution, there was already a substantial body of work on the Manchester Literary and Philosophical Society by historians of science. Originally, this scholarship discussed societies like the one in Manchester as think tanks whose main purpose was the mediation of scientific discoveries into technological applications. In the 1970s, a revisionist wave argued that they might more properly be understood as institutions of eighteenth-century polite culture as it spread across provincial Britain.[23] Roy Porter, for instance, drew attention to the number of medical men involved in the societies who used their cultural activities to establish their social credentials and develop a client base. Porter was building on Arnold Thackray's "Manchester model," which placed its emphasis on the cultural role of science in a process that saw eighteenth-century "marginal men" develop into a nineteenth-century liberal elite. Both Porter and Thackray suggested that the Protestant Dissenters who featured so strongly in earlier accounts of the societies as creative outsiders were often seeking to assimilate to the dominant Anglican culture. Certainly, someone like Thomas Percival, founding member of the Literary and Philosophical Society in Manchester, seems to have accommodated himself to the Tory-Anglican medical elite in the 1770s and early 1780s, and then, in the later 1790s, to have collaborated with the evangelical loyalist Thomas Gisborne. Between these years, however, Percival had cooperated with a group that pushed for reform at the Manchester Infirmary and shortly afterward became notorious for its support for the French Revolution, developments discussed in more detail in chapter 2. To my mind, Thackray's account of the emergence of liberal hegemony is less convincing than the description of a more fraught and uncertain process found in John Seed's writing on the subject.[24]

Both Porter and Thackray did notice the importance of the "literary" in the societies, even if their accounts of "social legitimation" are somewhat reductive. Thackray understood the scientific and literary interests of the Manchester society as primarily "ornamental." Porter suggested that the literary aspects of the societies ought to be taken more seriously but spent little time discussing them.[25] Mokyr, too, pays little or no attention to the "literary" side of these societies as part of the general commitment to improvement. Literary studies and cultural history, for their part, have not really taken up this challenge, either; unsurprisingly, perhaps, since the authority of the category of "Romanticism" within the discipline, mediated by highly partisan contemporaries such as De Quincey, has defined its keys terms—especially "genius" and "imagination"—against the dissemination of knowledge and the role of networks and institutions in literary production. I'll return to De Quincey at the end of this chapter, but I'll also be suggesting that the "knowledge economy" described by historians such as Jacob and Mokyr was rather more conflicted than they allow and certainly not as unambiguously committed to accumulation as they (and Marx) imply. Their rather constrained version of "useful knowledge," familiar enough now, underestimates the inclusion of the diverse "literary" inquiries pursued in conjunction with more medical and scientific interests. Aikin, for instance, contributed papers to the Manchester society on medical and literary subjects. Literary physicians of his ilk were an especially discernible phalanx in the society and exerted a powerful influence on its direction, part of a more general traffic between aesthetics and medicine in the period, of which Erasmus Darwin, a corresponding member of the Manchester society and its successor in Newcastle, is perhaps the best-known example now.[26] Aikin and then John Ferriar, another member and honorary physician to the Manchester Infirmary, reviewed poetry and medicine in the *Monthly Review* for most of the 1790s and early 1800s.[27] The sheer volume of their output suggests that Aikin and Ferriar regarded literary endeavor as a serious part of their commitment to improvement. The fact Aikin's dual role at the *Monthly* was passed on to Ferriar also suggests something of the continuing influence in this metropolitan review of the Manchester "connexion," to repurpose De Quincey pejorative term for these circles. In this context, the "literary" is not easy to discern as an area of activity autonomous from improvement more generally construed. My general approach to these societies is concerned with this more general understanding of "improvement," the institutional forms they developed (textual and associational), and how they changed over time and under pressure from external conditions, less so with the question of causation in relation to the Industrial Revolution.[28] Societies such as the one in Manchester self-consciously operated through "networks," and—at the microlevel of organizing meetings and discussion groups but also in connections between societies—they were invested in discovering the optimal condition for transmitting, producing, and defining knowledge.

The founders of the Manchester Literary and Philosophical Society in 1781 were Aikin's fellow literary physician Thomas Percival, the dyer-apothecary-chemist Thomas Henry, and the minister Thomas Barnes, who presided over the progressive congregation at Cross Street Chapel, where the society held its meetings until 1799. Cross Street comprised a cross section of Rational Dissent that disavowed fixed dogma or even fixed forms of worship.[29] In 1789 there seems to have been a minor schism when a rival chapel was set up in Mosley Street, with its own "Manchester" liturgy. Joseph Priestley, who saw Barnes's Arianism as a block to Unitarianism proper, preached there in 1789 and 1791, but these differences don't seem to have persisted into a major division between the two congregations.[30] The leaders of the Cross Street congregation were prosperous merchants and professionals, including one or two landed gentlemen, generally oriented toward worldly issues and pleasures, including literary tastes, that distinguished them from their Puritan forebears.[31] All three of the founders of the Literary and Philosophical Society, like Aikin, were associated with the Warrington Academy, the chief center in England for the education of Dissenters from 1759 until its closure in 1784. Joseph Priestley lectured at Warrington as a colleague of Aikin's father, conducted important experiments in gases, and debated the controversial theological ideas that appeared in his *Disqui-sitions relating to Matter and Spirit* (1777). The Manchester Literary and Philosophical Society awarded Priestley a grant in the 1780s to fund his researches in Birmingham (in the laboratory destroyed by a loyalist mob in July 1791). John Aikin Jr., who was educated and later taught at the Warrington Academy before returning to practice medicine in the town, was deeply influenced by Priestley. He also worked closely with his sister the poet Anna Laetitia Barbauld. Brother and sister shared Priestley's advocacy of the abolition of the slave trade, parliamentary reform, and the civic rights of Dissenters. Barbauld's writing on "devotional taste" spoke for the general orientation of this formation away from Presby-terian puritanism and toward an affective life that included literary but also scientific interests and more worldly pleasures.[32]

Aikin's account of the area around Manchester drew on information sent in from a network of improvers who still lived in the region, many of them members of the Literary and Philosophical Society, Percival chief among them.[33] Strictly speaking only the arranger and compiler of a project that originated with the publisher John Stockdale, Aikin em-phasized the power of "connexion" that had made it possible.[34] In refer-ence to the idea of an "industrial enlightenment" associated with Jacob and Mokyr, I refer to this specifically located network as the "transpen-nine enlightenment," as it linked together the industrial and commer-cial towns on either side of the Pennines, the spine of northern England whose fast-flowing rivers drove the early water-powered textile mills. Crucial to the networked account of improvement in *A Description of Manchester* was the developing road and canal infrastructure that bound these towns into a distinctive territory in Aikin's eyes. Like the other ma-jor town's in the region covered by Aikin's book, Manchester was one of the ten most populous English towns by 1800. None of them would have appeared in a list of this kind in 1600.[35] Aikin identified the transforma-tive influence on Manchester of "the cotton manufacture; a branch of commerce, the rapid and prodigious increase of which is, perhaps, abso-lutely unparalleled in the annals of trading nations" (3). He also traced its spirit of improvement in burgeoning civic institutions, including the Literary and Philosophical Society: "an example to the provincial towns of this kingdom by . . . uniting the pursuits of science and literature with commercial opulence" (200). The four volumes of its transactions—*Memoirs of the Manchester Literary and Philosophical Society*—he took as signs of its success at home and abroad.[36] By the early 1820s, the major towns in Aikin's book all had their own literary and philosophical society. The territory of my "transpennine enlightenment" expands the matrix provided by Aikin northward to Newcastle upon Tyne as it was there that

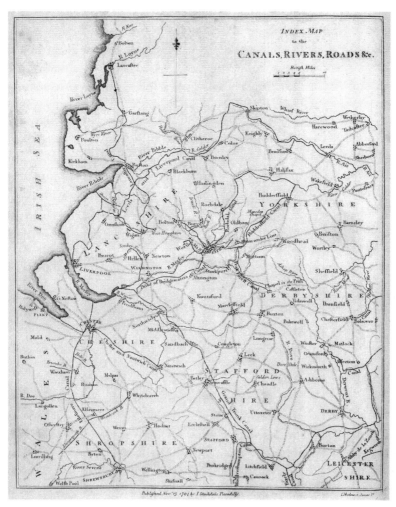

FIGURE 3. "Index Map to the Canals, Rivers, Roads, &c" from
John Aikin Jr., *A Description of the country from thirty to forty miles
round Manchester* (London, 1795). Photograph courtesy of the
Huntington Library, San Marino, California (RB 204522).

the Unitarian William Turner, predictably enough a Warrington student,
carried the flame lit in Manchester and kept alive his connections with
the area over the next forty years.

Although the unprecedented growth in the textile industries provided
the ostensible focus of Aikin's volume, transport and communications
fired his imagination equally, if not more. Canals, bridges, and turnpike
roads perfected "internal communication" (117) and opened up new mar-

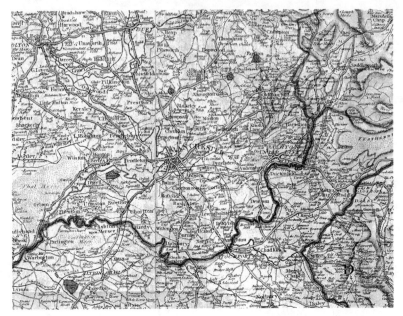

FIGURE 4. "As it were, the heart. . . ." A detail from "A New Map of the
country round Manchester," in John Aikin Jr., *A Description of the country
from thirty to forty miles round Manchester* (London, 1795). Photograph
courtesy of the Huntington Library, San Marino, California (RB 204522).

kets for the region's manufacturers on national and international scales,
in the process smoothing the way for information for his volume to reach
him in London. Wrigley claims that this kind of infrastructural improvement had taken the first "organic" phase of industrial development as
far as it could go before the steam engine (the future influence of which
Aikin's book could only dimly discern).[37] Free communication is certainly
a refrain of Aikin's book, as it is in Mokyr's *Enlightened Economy*, if there
with a narrower sense of what it was that was being circulated. Suspicious
of court and aristocracy, if in a more muted way than in some of his political writing for the London bookseller Joseph Johnson, Aikin suggested
that Manchester's status as "an open town, destitute . . . of a corporation,
and unrepresented in parliament" was "probably to its advantage" (191),
a point Jacob and Mokyr also make about the new industrial towns. Aikin
was also invested in the idea of a flat network promoting the circulation
of goods and ideas against inherited vertical hierarchies and aristocratic
hegemony: "Manchester is, as it were, the heart of this vast system, the
circulating branches of which spread all around it" (3). In Aikin's eyes,
the town becomes the most important node in a decentralized network

ranged across the Pennines and stretching to the world beyond: effectively a validation of the emergent identity of the prosperous and cultured provincial middle class against the entrenched interests of London. Appropriately for a literary physician, Aikin's disposition of his maps with their networks of roads, canals, and rivers make Manchester look like a heart surrounded by a complex network of veins and arteries.

If Manchester is the "heart" of his account, Aikin didn't render this effect as uniform in its operations or organize his book into a narrative sequence around a series of technical innovations of the kind described by Edward Baines Jr. four decades later in his *History of the Cotton Manufacture in Great Britain* (1835). Aikin's book retained the conventions of topographical writing sufficiently enough to follow the contours of the country, "consisting of the description of *particular places*" (7), as he put it, taking account of technological innovations in the context of other features of the locations he described. The heart is part of a complex web of nerves and arteries. The familiar star inventions of the early Industrial Revolution all feature without being linked in the main to any named inventor. The flying shuttle, the spinning jenny, Arkwright's water frame, and the mule all appear but not as a sequence of causes and effects driving improvement forward. The topographic structure disperses innovation around its localities, resisting any impulse to render a complex system into a unified narrative.[38]

A VIRTUOUS COMMERCE?

Strangely, Aikin's book is not referenced in either Jacob or Mokyr's discussions of Manchester's importance to the knowledge economy of the industrial enlightenment, even though its account of the town as part of an open network would seem to be grist to their mill. The reason may be Aikin's reservations about growth disembedded from social and other relations, although this aspect of his thinking is to some extent more muted in his *Description of Manchester* than elsewhere in his writing, perhaps in response to calls from friends to tone down his politics in the years just after the execution of the French monarch. Aikin did register his reservations about the moral implications of unbridled capital accumulation, as Marx understood, including, for instance, the role of the slave trade in Liverpool's affluence. He also discussed the research done by Percival and Ferriar into the conditions in and around the new machine-based factories.[39] In the immediate aftermath of the defeat of the campaign for the repeal of the Test and Corporation Act in 1790, Aikin had rallied his readers by insisting they were the natural leaders of improvement: "Your natural connections are not with kings and nobles. You belong to the most virtuous, the most enlightened, the most independent part of the community, the middle class. If this nation is ever to improve, or even if it is to retain, the freedom it possesses, to this class alone must it be indebted for the blessing."[40] The opposition of these groups to colonial slavery, often sincere enough in itself, was frequently used as a marker of their virtue, a form of "moral capital," as we will see in the following pages, but the area's improvement relied on wealth generated by the global trade, including exports of finished goods to Africa, and drew its raw materials from plantations in the West Indies and after 1800 increasingly the United States.[41] Claims to moral leadership were constantly weighed against economic consequences when it came to slavery. A boycott on slave-grown cotton as well as sugar was considered but rejected by abolitionist leader Thomas Clarkson because "it would take away the bread of a million of our fellow subjects the innocent poor of his country." He had written to the cotton merchant and political reformer Thomas Walker in 1788 to ascertain what proportion of goods made in Manchester were for the Africa trade and whether the town had flourished as much when the trade was depressed. Walker with others in these Manchester circles formed an important node in the networks that Olaudah Equiano created on his book tour for his *Interesting Narrative* (1789), as he acknowledged in a letter to the *Manchester Mercury*.[42] In Liverpool, William Rathbone III, primarily a merchant in the American timber trade, eventually became an abolitionist, for which he won Clarkson's praise. His son William Rathbone IV, a staunch friend of Roscoe, may have been the main influence in his father's conversion; even so, he made his own fortune trading in plantation-grown American cotton, starting on a small scale in the 1780s. A compromised "moral geography" plagued responses to the issue of slavery in the region. The Quaker merchant James Cropper still worried about the contradiction of importing cotton from America while calling for the abolition of slavery in British colonies in the 1820s, as his planter opponents delighted in pointing out.[43]

Aikin's confidence in the possibilities of virtuous commercial improvement waned somewhat in the course of the 1790s. His "Enquirer" essay on the prospects for "the future melioration of mankind," published in the *Monthly Magazine* for February 1799, complained that "the present system of trade" could "only be maintained by the slavery or subjugation of great numbers of mankind; and while the East and West Indies compose links in the chain of European commerce, cruelty and injustice must be the means by which it is made to hold together."[44] Like many others associated with the Literary and Philosophical Society in Manchester, Aikin's vision of middle-class virtue did not have commercial success as its ultimate goal. He subscribed still to what Karl Polanyi called "the econ-

omy embedded in social relations."[45] Likewise, speaking at the opening of
the Manchester Academy in 1786, the successor to Warrington, Thomas
Barnes had encouraged the development of literary taste as an antidote
to mere profit making and other "low debasing pleasures" he associated
with trade.[46] Nor was Aikin's version of "virtuous commerce" any more
comfortable with the idea of improvement as a form of mastery over nature, even in his *Description of Manchester*. The distributed nature of the
networks he celebrated implied a more complex set of relations with the
cultural and natural environment. Reservations about domination even
inflect his praise of the hero of his account of the transport revolution,
"the wonderful self-instructed genius" James Brindley (112): "The triumph of art over nature," Aikin suggested, "led [Brindley] to view with
a sort of contempt the winding stream, in which the lover of natural
beauty delights" (141). Aikin praised the engineer as an example of "true
inspiration, which poets have almost exclusively arrogated to themselves,
but which men of original genius in every walk are actuated by, when from
the operation of the mind acting upon itself, without the intrusion of foreign notions, they create and invent." (144). But if the description of the
"mind acting upon itself" celebrates Brindley's untutored inventiveness,
it also hints at the potential social and ecological irresponsibility of the
"enthusiast" (141), with all the negative implications of that word for
the eighteenth century. The comparison of the poet with the engineer as
"genius" is one that this book returns too, for instance, in relation to the
reputation of James Watt in the 1820s, but not, even then, simply to be
understood as a simple validation of a narrow idea of "useful knowledge"
over literary taste.

In general, Aikin did not regard poetry as useless knowledge, even if
he thought it could be improved by a dialogue with the sciences. His early
Essay on the Application of Natural History to Poetry (1777) bemoaned
the insipidity of poetry that did not keep pace with the expanding knowledge of the natural world. He corresponded about the principles of his
essay with his friends: Thomas Percival incorporated its ideas into his
own children's books, as did William Roscoe.[47] Aikin's reservations about
Brindley echoed those of Roscoe's on specialism in a paper he gave at the
Manchester Literary and Philosophical Society (discussed in chapter 2).
Their caution about narrow enthusiasm signals an ongoing issue about
the relationship between the inventions of genius—whether engineer
or poet—and their environment. Aikin's writing on biography—which
were voluminous—tended to celebrate untutored genius over privilege.
He promoted useful knowledge, which included literature, over martial
heroism and aristocratic values, but he tended to see inventions in any
sphere as the products of more general social and historical forces and

saw them as more properly directed back toward the general good rather than either personal gain or mastery over nature. This sense of innovation as a product of distributed agency is manifested in his weighty *General Biography* (1799–1815), originally compiled with his Warrington friend William Enfield, with its preference for poets and scientists over kings and generals. "How much higher does a Brindley rank," they wrote there, "directing the complex machinery which he himself has invented, than an Alexander at the head of his army!" Even when it came to useful knowledge, though, there could be "no precise line" between "invention and *improvement*": all the "great discoveries" are the product of "gradual advances given to them by successive improvers."[48]

There was a general tendency in the circles associated with Cross Street Chapel, as Herbert McLachlan noted long ago, toward the "exaggeration of the influence of external circumstances, education, and habits," that "inspired a doctrine of works, which found expression in zeal for social and political reform."[49] The tendency, identifiable enough, had a more complicated history than McLachlan's summary allows. Certainly, it did not always assume the "passive receptivity of the mind" he claims, not in the hands of those literary physicians who were such an important influence in the early life of the Literary and Philosophical Society. These physicians fully participated in the changes that witnessed the "receding influence of mechanism on medical thinking and the resurgence of environmental medicine" noted by Kevis Goodman, exhibiting a strong sense of the precarity of the relationship between any organism and its environment. An Edinburgh training, such as the one Aikin received as a pupil of its leading professor, William Cullen, prepared its students with a sense of the vitality of the body's nervous system and the complexity of its responsiveness to circumstances beyond immediate stimuli.[50] Aikin's *Description of Manchester*, like his *General Biography*, placed individual genius in a feedback loop with material networks of at least three kinds: ecological, through human interaction with the natural environment; social, through the relationship between "genius" and gradual advances made by many anonymous innovators; and physiological, in the understanding of the entangled relations between the imagination, the body, and their environment. One might add infrastructural, since Aikin viewed canals less as a communicative channel connecting two points and more as a medium in the sense discussed by Robert Mitchell—that is, as generating "something new and valuable."[51] Each of these issues and the changing nature of the relationships they describe will be important themes in this book.

Several of the early papers given at the Manchester Literary and Philosophical Society insisted on the idea that "taste" would provide a moral

framework to improvement, encouraging the "happy adjustment" between the body and its circumstances explored in the aesthetic theory
of Cullen's friend Lord Kames.[52] Literary taste was its own form of useful
knowledge from this perspective, not least in the context of a boomtown
such as Manchester, as a meliorating influence on the acquisitiveness of
the commercial spirit. What Mokyr calls "a competitive market for ideas"
was not always conceived in commercial terms, but there is less reason to
doubt his more general claims about the importance of the literary and
philosophical societies to the dissemination of knowledge, even if one is
skeptical about their causative relationship to the Industrial Revolution:
"The Industrial Enlightenment and the intellectual activities it spawned
were distinctly provincial events, located in institutions such as the scientific societies in smaller English towns or the Scottish universities of
Glasgow and Edinburgh."[53] The influence of the Scottish universities on
the ethos of the English literary and philosophical societies was palpable.
Many of its medico-literary members, including Aikin, Ferriar, and Percival, had as students enjoyed the literary clubs of Edinburgh that allowed
them to mix with luminaries of the Scottish Enlightenment. After they
relocated to Manchester and Liverpool, respectively, Percival and his
friend James Currie—another student of Cullen's—kept in close touch
with these Scottish networks, especially with their revered teacher. They
reproduced the medico-literary sociability they had experienced in Edinburgh when they met up with their friends Aikin and John Haygarth—
also educated in Scotland—in Chester and Warrington in the 1770s and
1780s.[54] Perhaps the most obvious literary monument to these Anglo-
Scottish networks of literary physicians was the edition of Robert Burns
that Currie edited with William Roscoe's assistance. Many of its values—
for instance, the idea of the genius of Burns as the product of the Scottish educational system—are akin to those found in Aikin's biographical
writing. Both "accentuated the historicity of sciences and arts and their
relation to past and present acts of institution."[55] They also suggest the
influence of the Scottish "Common Sense" tradition of Thomas Reid and
Dugald Stewart, especially on Currie, recently discussed by Nigel Leask,
with its sense of the complex relationship between volition and social
circumstance that often registered in these circles as reservations about
Priestley's emphasis on necessity.[56]

   Situated midway between Manchester and Liverpool, Warrington was
an important transport hub through which many of the ideas discussed
in this book passed, especially before 1800. Together with the Scottish
universities, the Warrington Academy was the most important academic
institution in the transpennine enlightenment described by Aikin. Its
progressive syllabus was bolstered by an extramural culture of conversa-

tion, where students could mix with tutors such as Priestley, Enfield, and John Aikin Sr. As children, John Aikin Jr. and his sister Anna reveled in this atmosphere. Its pedagogical values were disseminated in their later books for children, as they were in the various editions of Thomas Percival's *A Father's Instructions* (1776) and its follow-up *Moral and Literary Dissertations* (1784), the latter largely containing papers given at the Literary and Philosophical Society. Joseph Johnson published all these books from his shop in St. Paul's Churchyard in London, as he had, from 1767, Percival's medical essays, and the poetry of Anna Laetitia Barbauld and her brother.[57] Harking from a Baptist family in Everton, only a village outside Liverpool at the time, Johnson advertised himself as the exclusive London agent for the Warrington Academy, but he was effectively the London publisher and distributor of the wider transpennine enlightenment until his death in 1808. When Barbauld and her brother left the area in 1774 and 1784, respectively, they also acted as London agents for their friends in the north, regularly receiving guests, putting authors in touch with publishers, distributing reviewing jobs, and generally cementing the "connexion" later deplored by De Quincey.

Before turning in more detail to De Quincey's criticism of these connections, let me say more about their status as networks. In his *History and Present State of Electricity* (1767), written while he was tutor at Warrington, Joseph Priestley had suggested that the proliferation of knowledge since the formation of the Royal Society meant that it was now "high time to *subdivide* the business" into "smaller combinations." Anticipating the values of Aikin's biographical writing, Priestley insisted that their success would have more to do with the self-reliance of reasoning individuals than aristocratic or royal patronage: "Princes will never do this great business to any purpose." He was skeptical of the paternalism of metropolitan institutions, including the Royal Society, and, as Jan Golinski puts it, "their proximity to the tentacles of the government patronage machine." Golinski shows that Priestley "cultivated a network of followers and friends in other provincial circles" as the institutional corollary of a broader "democratic epistemology."[58] The Literary and Philosophical Societies of Manchester and Newcastle, directly influenced by Priestley, were "self-organizing" institutions, to use Klancher's phrase, developing out of private and informal conversation groups, with an emphasis on "small, sociable, and readily duplicable scenes of experimentation."[59] This self-organizing virus was carried by Warrington alumni when they graduated, often sent to provincial towns to minister to Dissenting congregations, just as doctors acted as leavening when they took up new posts around the country. Relationships between families and friends helped perpetuate the rollout of these knowledge institutions. After Priestley left

Warrington to become minister of Mill Hill chapel in Leeds in 1767, for instance, he started up an informal group there whose members included William Turner of Wakefield. When the Barbaulds visited their friends the Priestleys in West Yorkshire, they met Turner's son, also William, to whom Barbauld presented her poem, "Verses written in the Leaves of an Ivory Pocketbook," on the importance of early impressions to the development of the mind. Predictably enough, Turner went on to study at the Warrington Academy and join the Manchester Literary and Philosophical Society, a journey that winds its way through several chapters of this book into Turner's obituary of Barbauld—where her poem was first published in full—and, a few years later, his friendship with the novelist Elizabeth Gaskell. It is no surprise that Turner founded the Literary and Philosophical Society in Newcastle upon Tyne in 1793 or that his son played a major role in the society founded in Halifax in the early 1830s.[60]

Gaskell's novel *Mary Barton* (1848)—"A Tale of Manchester Life"—is a sign of the way that the progressive social values of Aikin (with their contradictions magnified) remained an important part of the knowledge economy well into the nineteenth century, but from at least the 1820s it was possible to see things rather differently. Looking back from 1826 on the proliferation of scientific societies in Britain and across the world over the previous four decades, the geologist Charles Lyell celebrated the role played by "the recent establishment of literary and philosophical institutions in our metropolis and many of our provinces." He identified Manchester as "the first example, in one of our provinces, of a large association of private individuals for the purpose of contributing funds for the publication of literary and scientific memoirs." Instructively, he saw it as retaining its commitment to "Physics and Belles Lettres," even complaining that its published transactions "remained almost equally divided between literary and scientific articles," but the more general thrust of his survey was to celebrate the almost miraculous survival of scientific knowledge from the wreckage of the French Revolutionary and Napoleonic Wars. Only "happy accident," he claimed, had allowed escape from "the spirit of political controversy." In this account, as Klancher puts it, the flow of knowledge had continued "almost magically free of social contradiction, public controversy, political struggle, or the complex and contingent relationship between 'knowledge' and 'practices' of many kinds."[61] The minute books, publications, and correspondence emanating from these societies shows that knowledge and its boundaries were anything but uncontested in the period.

The pages that follow here have much to say about the conflicts and contradictions masked by narratives such as Lyell's. Modern scholarship using networks analysis often suffers from a related assumption that information flows smoothly through connecting points across a smooth two-dimensional plane, where relations are open and dynamic. In practice, networks require a degree of engineering, attention to keeping valves open, and maintenance to avoid blockages and breakdown. The topology of networks, the contouring of the spaces between nodal points that determine the relations between them, is important in this regard. "What matters," Galloway and Thacker note, "is less the character of the individual nodes than the topological space within which and through which they operate as nodes. . . . To be a node is to exist inseparably from a set of possibilities and parameters."[62] This idea of topological space understands relations between points to pass through spaces formed by curves, ruins, and other disruptions rather than "stable and well-defined distances."[63] The societies discussed in this book were links—institutional nodes, they might be called—in the spread of improvement across the region and beyond, but they also constituted networks themselves, bringing together members committed to improvement, although it often turned out that tension warped the relations between them—for instance, on the grounds of religious and political differences. Moreover, those relations exceeded the boundaries of the institutions themselves to include, for instance, women excluded from formal membership: an issue explored at length in chapter 5. Questions of inclusion and exclusion in this regard exerted their own pressures on the shape and stability of any particular node and on the spread and nature of the kind of knowledge it circulated. In the process, these networks were places where a liberal middle-class identity was coming flickeringly into being.

Although the emphasis in this book is on the production of human social networks and their role in allowing us to see the emergence of certain kinds of liberal ideology, not simply expressed through them, the Literary and Philosophical Societies might also fruitfully be viewed as complex assemblages in which "lively things"—books, biological specimens, even stuffed wombats, apparatuses, and the buildings themselves—exerted their own agency, even if they could not fully resist the operations of human power.[64] Donations of books and specimens—some of which passed between societies to ease the pressure or were shared to reduce costs—could be a problem that caused individual societies to rethink their spaces, as was the case with the Philosophical Hall of the Leeds Philosophical and Literary Society soon after it was built.[65] Chapter 2 discusses the conflict over whether books or scientific apparatuses were to be granted priority in Newcastle. Purpose-built premises offered a sense of permanence but could also operate as an exclusive barrier between humans. Participants in the societies wished to create an environment to support their sense of productive exchange, but neither things nor other people were necessarily amenable to their wishes. Outside the societies, for instance, in the factory work space, improvements sometimes met resistance not just from the practical and technical problems of integrating new kinds of machinery into factories but also from the human beings who were supposed to work with these machines. Neither the new disciplines of labor nor the educational opportunities offered at the Mechanics' Institutes encouraged by the Literary and Philosophical Societies were simply accepted. Nor, of course, did slave-grown cotton come to Liverpool and Manchester without continual resistance from enslaved laborers on plantations in the British West Indies and in the United States.

If the Literary and Philosophical Societies of Manchester and New-castle with their offshoots formed nodes in the networked geography of a transpennine enlightenment, they might equally be seen as knots wherein knowledge became tangled and often transformed. Certainly, what went into them was not always what came out. The struggle to un-block the flow of knowledge could change the institutions behind the fa-cade of continuity. Listing up the spread of institutions such as theaters, assemblies, and literary and philosophical societies as signs of enlight-enment risks "blackboxing," in Latour's sense, the contested nature of their activities and makes it easier to believe they constituted a neutral zone, when they more often represented sites where hegemony was con-tinually contested.[66] There was certainly a desire among participants to engineer the smooth circulation of knowledge at every level—a feature of Aikin's writing about the transport revolution—and to create the best possible conditions for its production, but a desire for ease of flow across a level plane could not and should not be taken for granted as its outcome. Nor was the ambition neutral in itself. Aikin articulated a distinctively liberal desire for the circulation of knowledge against older hierarchies. The analogies between free-trade economics and the dissemination of knowledge, between the steam engine and the printing press, were often drawn, but in practice—as John Clennell, a local hatmaker with an ap-petite for knowledge, found out in Newcastle—manufacturers were re-luctant to share their secrets. One reviewer of Clennell's *Thoughts on the Expediency of Disclosing the Processes of Manufactories* (1807)—based on two papers he had read at the Literary and Philosophical Society— put the matter bluntly: "When public spirit shall generally triumph over selfishness, then Mr. Clennell's proposition will be adopted: but, as long as trade is carried on with views of private gain, so long will the manu-facturer, who has a profitable secret, endeavor to keep it to himself; and he will not be easily persuaded that he shall gain more by divulging it." Mokyr's "open-source" industrial enlightenment was partly blocked by the competitive ethos he sees it as espousing.[67]

Not the least of the problems facing this ambition as it developed was the way bodies in rooms could disrupt or hamper the ideal of rational debate—blushing, arguing, simply failing to engage or even turn up. Recalcitrant bodies could test the boundaries of polite exchange, a problem not without its ironies given the formal commitment to strenuous debate as a positive and generative value in these circles. Anxieties about the unpredictability of bodies meant that liberal ambition for open access always brought with it a disciplinary aspect manifested inside the societies themselves in the desire to engineer the best conditions for knowledge to flow. In these circumstances, management was as important as authorship to knowledge production. Witness the roles of Aikin and Barbauld as London fixers for the transpennine enlightenment. In a more formal institutional context, Klancher draws attention to the "administrator as cultural producer"—that is, those figures who "organized, mediated, or otherwise worked secretly or openly to 'administrate' culture."[68] Bruno Latour's contrast between "intermediary" and "mediator" offers a further nuance. Mediators "transform, translate, distort, and modify meaning," whereas intermediaries "transport meaning without transformation."[69] Few of the figures discussed in this book simply acted as intermediaries. Knowledge was rarely—if it ever is—simply transmitted across networked space or across time. The three-dimensional generational aspect of this book shows how participants transformed, distorted, and possibly degraded the knowledge they communicated.

THE DE QUINCEY "CONNEXION"

If economic historians may at times have given too much weight to the importance of the country around Manchester in their accounts of the Industrial Revolution, then literary, cultural, and even social historians have arguably been too neglectful of its importance in their spheres. Certainly, industrial Manchester has a place in Victorian historiography rarely granted to it in cultural and social histories of the late Georgian period, as Hannah Barker has pointed out in her account of the proliferation of polite institutions across the region.[70] For literary historians, it is often associated with a restricted idea of useful knowledge that functions as the defining other of Romanticism. Partly based on the responses of such major canonical figures as Samuel Taylor Coleridge, Robert Southey, and William Wordsworth, the association seriously underestimates the complex evolution of this liberal culture, which contained its own critiques of industrial capitalism, even as it also developed various kinds of intellectual justification for the steam-factory system. I end this chapter with the microhistory of Thomas De Quincey's response to the circles associated with Aikin, partly because it was a coherent and consistent—if disingenuous—account from someone born in Manchester, whose father mixed with members of the Literary and Philosophical Society of Manchester, and whose early life included encounters with figures such as Currie, Percival and Roscoe. Fresh from his success with *Confessions of an English Opium Eater* (1822), De Quincey published a series of essays as "Letters to a Young Man whose Education has been Neglected" in the *London Magazine*. Against what he saw as the rise of a mechanical system of education, De Quincey recommended education in nature and the privacy of the mind. Tellingly, he specifically railed against Isaac Watts—a major influence of the ethos of the Warrington Academy—and what De Quincey described as "the sectarian zeal of his party in religion." In the third of his letters, De Quincey gets to an early statement of his famous distinction between the literatures of "knowledge" and "power:" "All, that is literature, seeks to communicate power; all, that is not literature, to communicate knowledge."[71] His later elaborations of this idea were predicated on the categorical difference between the fine and mechanical arts: a steam engine could be superseded by a better model, De Quincey thought, but Homer could not be improved upon by Wordsworth. The contrast in itself was far from original. William Roscoe's paper on the distinction between the arts and sciences given at the Literary and Philosophical Society in Manchester in 1788 suggests that he might even have agreed with the argument in general terms. Roscoe's admirer William Hazlitt used language similar to De Quincey's in "Why the Arts are not Progressive," first published in 1814, but he did not weaponize the distinction in the way De Quincey did to suggest that the Roscoe circle was involved in an empty exercise of mechanical reproduction.[72]

Born into a prosperous merchant family just outside the town in 1785, De Quincey experienced several early traumas in Manchester, including the death of his father in 1793, that resurface in his mature autobiographical writing and its soundings of the "romantic" self. His response to Manchester, if sometimes played for comedy in his writing, nearly always appears as a foil to his sense of his own psychological and imaginative depth.[73] De Quincey's *Autobiographical Sketches* (1853) contains a vivid description of his battles with factory boys, who showered the smartly dressed De Quincey brothers with stones on their way to class. Manchester for De Quincey was identified with factories, spiritual aridity, and nascent forms of industrial conflict. From an early age he longed to escape, and he did run away from Manchester Grammar School in 1802, defying his mother Elizabeth De Quincey in pursuit of his dream of going to Oxford. Intriguingly, the family doctor in Manchester was none other than Thomas Percival, who De Quincey accepted was "a literary man, of elegant tastes and philosophic habits" in *Autobiographical Sketches*. Yet, in a typical double move, De Quincey recalled the physician's papers to the Literary and Philosophical society with an airily dismissive gesture: "These I have heard mentioned with respect, though, for myself, I have no personal knowledge of them." De Quincey then spent a few sentences relishing the story that his mother suspected the doctor of atheism because of his correspondence with French philosophes. Percival certainly had these kinds of connections, but De Quincey belatedly made hay with them by reimagining them as part of a risible clash between two empty value systems: Enlightenment free thought (Percival) and evangelical religion (his mother).[74]

Percival got off lightly in comparison with his friends in the Roscoe circle, whom De Quincey travestied as "the Liverpool coterie." Here the idea of these circles as a mere "connexion" is given its fullest strategic statement as the antithesis of imaginative "power," informed by the insider knowledge gleaned from a series of visits to Liverpool when he was a young man. His host was the banker William Clarke, Roscoe's fellow laborer in the field of Italian cultural history.[75] De Quincey's letters from his 1801 visit to the area suggest that he delighted in the company of Clarke and his daughters. In 1837, though, De Quincey mocked the literary pretensions of the Roscoe circle in an essay for *Tait's Edinburgh Magazine*, using them to demonstrate "the natural character and tendencies of merely literary society—by which society I mean all such as, having no strong distinctions in power of thinking or in native force of character, are yet raised into circles of pretension and mark, by the fact of having written a book, or of holding a notorious connexion with some department or other of the periodical press." Apart from Roscoe himself, the primary targets of his attack were James Currie, whose major edition of Burns was "just then published (I think in that very month), and in everybody's hands," De Quincey explained, and their friend William Shepherd, the Unitarian minister at Gateacre, just outside Liverpool.[76] De Quincey provided a short caricature sketch of each, carefully mixing partial acknowledgment of their achievements with satirical analysis of their shortcomings defined in relation to his romantic idea of literary genius. Roscoe he represented as "simple and manly in his demeanour" but discovered in him "the feebleness of a mere *belle-lettrist*, a mere man of *virtù*, in the style of his sentiments on most subjects." Shepherd, De Quincey simply dismissed as "decidedly . . . a buffoon . . . his grotesque manner and coarse stories, more than was altogether compatible with the pretensions of a scholar and a clergyman." Such a man, thought De Quincey, with an Oxford education behind him by the time he wrote his essay, "could not have emerged from any great university, or from any but a sectarian training." With another of his characteristic double moves, it then amuses him to think that "the pale pink of his Radicalism was then accounted deep, deep scarlet" (190–91). A pattern emerges in the essay, also found in his treatment of Percival, of acknowledging the achievements and then erasing them as the superficial accomplishments of self-important poseurs. In the process, what he seems to acknowledge as masculine virtues are implicitly feminized.[77] The climax is his account of Currie's Burns edition, whose sociohistorical analysis, he suggests, completely failed to grasp the poet's "wild and almost ferocious spirit of independence" (193). Even though the Roscoe circle had no doubt as to the poet's greatness, they measured it against criteria unacceptable to De Quincey.

De Quincey's list of their achievements scarcely seems to warrant the charge that the circle had been "petrific" (187) in its influence. In truth, he was building up the narrative to reveal his own idea of imaginative power in contrast, based on his "discovery," in their midst, as he represents it, of Wordsworth's poetry: "A grand renovation of poetic power—of a new birth in poetry, interesting not so much to England, as to the human mind—it was secretly amusing to contrast the little artificial usages of their petty traditional knack, with the natural forms of a divine art" (191). This "power" represents a "a phenomenological aesthetics of genius," to use Tilottama Rajan's phrase, where authentic reading is understood as a form of private communion between the reader and the mind of the author: it is opposed by definition to this inauthentic "connexion" and its critical method of reading texts in their circumstance.[78] De Quincey's idea of Wordsworth's "divine art" transcends "sectarian" carping and, more seriously, any kind of understanding of culture in terms of complex environmental relations (or, for that matter, as an "experiment," as Wordsworth himself described *Lyrical Ballads*, in "the history and science of the feelings").[79] Unfortunately for De Quincey, William Shepherd was still alive when the essay appeared in 1837, and he supplied a characteristically sharp retort in the press, pointing out its many distortions, especially the account of the group's attitude toward Burns, but it's worth dwelling more specifically on some of the particular terms of De Quincey's travesty, not least because his technique often identifies positive qualities before reducing them to burlesque.[80] Daniel Sanjiv Roberts has suggested that this technique reveals some of the tensions between the original scene as experienced by the seventeen-year-old and the retrospective attitudes of the mature author. De Quincey's mature critical method was predicated on "identification with the author," to return to Rajan's vocabulary, "preserving the 'inspired' text from interpersonal difference," in this case the values of discussion and debate celebrated in the Roscoe circle.[81] The irony is what Roberts calls "the prior issue of mediation"—that is, the fact that *Lyrical Ballads* had already found a ready audience in these circles. The Roscoe circle may even have been the source of De Quincey's own awareness of Wordsworth and Coleridge's collection. *Lyrical Ballads* probably was understood in these circles as an "experiment"—to use Wordsworth's word—possibly in the same vein of literary "Jacobinism" that De Quincey's mother spied in Currie's edition of Burns. Roberts suggests that the younger, more liberal De Quincey would have understood the two projects as "companion manifestos."[82]

The later De Quincey well understood the Roscoe circle to be part of a discernible networked "connexion." His journey to Everton in 1801 had seen him pass along the canal network that facilitated their dissemination of knowledge, including Wordsworth's poems. Whereas for John Aikin Jr. this traffic of improvement was active across domains that properly included both engineering and poetry, the later De Quincey represents it as a web of inauthentic social relations, opposed to the pure sympathy of mind with mind that defines his relationship with Wordsworth and, more fundamentally, his idea of the literary imagination. Furthermore, when the later De Quincey describes the Liverpool coterie in terms of "connexion," he implies that it was a kind of secret establishment, to be unfavorably compared with the freshness of his response to *Lyrical Ballads*, despite the fact, partly acknowledged in his essay, as we have seen, that its members were associated with the radical opposition and collaborated in the campaign for the abolition of the slave trade. For De Quincey in 1837, they are presented as already old-fashioned in 1801 and lacking any deeper understanding of the "spirit" of sacred texts (whether the Bible or Wordsworth). Theirs is a literature of the letter and not the life. Their "connexion" is part of a larger system of communication that carries ideas, goods, and bodies across roads and bridges in Aikin's book. De Quincey's response to Wordsworth is a transport of "the human mind:" a faculty he does not really locate in any place in the world. The "Liverpool coterie," in contrast, is defined for him by the partiality of their distinctively provincial location, despite their many European and transatlantic contacts. "Coterie" is a deliberately chosen word in his essay, effeminizing the men while eliding the presence of the women such as the daughters of William Clarke, central to the literary sociability of these circles, an issue I'll return to in chapter 5.

———————

My primary concern in this book is not with the pathologies of De Quincey's response but the complexities of the "connexion" he identifies only to dismiss. *Networks of Improvements* aims to bring back into literary, cultural, and even economic history a fuller sense of the influence and complexity of the intellectual networks emanating from the manufacturing towns of the nascent Industrial Revolution. This process of improvement was self-consciously aware of the role of mediation to its success and the allied importance of what it called "emulation." Emulation drove the proliferation of infirmaries and theaters, not to mention factories, roads, and bridges, across these towns and cities. Of central importance to this book's account is a focus on institutions of literature that provides a deliberate contrast with De Quincey's valorization of private and absorptive reading. Arguing the issues out was what these societies were about, functioning almost as a kind of extended mind for the region, and they were just as interested as De Quincey was in psychological depth, especially in the context of the medico-literary interests shared by the literary physicians discussed in this book. What makes this study more than merely "provincial" is that the process was taking place in the context of a fundamental change in human society through industrialization with global consequences. The transpennine enlightenment was increasingly conscious of its transformative position within a new kind of world economy, as the following chapters disclose. Some of the participants enthusiastically adapted their sense of human possibility to the new circumstances of the factory and the machine, a response that is still being worked out in other later industrial revolutions, including the one in which I am writing. De Quincey's distinction between power and knowledge has usually been understood as a "romantic" response to the emergence of a dark materialism willing to sacrifice the forces of life to the imperatives of technical improvement. Less often recognized is that he also deliberately travestied another side to this process that continued to struggle to preserve an idea of cultural production in networked terms, even if this way of thinking afforded a variety of more open or closed versions discussed in greater detail in the chapters that follow. De Quincey staked his version of the "literary" on a depth where the authentically human was preserved in a mental space that willed away issues of mediation and transmission. Geographically speaking, he could not imagine a literary culture flourishing in these manufacturing and commercial towns rising to view in this period. In many ways, he reinscribed the traditional places of learned authority in London and Oxford. *Networks of Improvement* offers a more decentered view of a located culture that shaped and was shaped by the networked relations of its global position.

CHAPTER TWO

THE COLLISION OF
MIND WITH MIND

Manchester and Newcastle, 1781–1823

The French Revolution cast a dampening shadow over the networks of improvement John Aikin Jr. described. Although reviews of *A Description of Manchester* agreed across the political divide that commercial and technical progress stood out against the broader picture of international and domestic turmoil, drawing different conclusions about the reasons, ideological divisions certainly impacted the development of the Manchester Literary and Philosophical Society and its imitator at Newcastle, which was founded just as the long war against republican France began. "Ideas about the proper forms of civic activity (including science), which had become common during the decades of the Enlightenment," found themselves, as Jan Golinski has shown, "subjected to conservative challenge."[1] This challenge brought a contraction in the public culture of improvement and bore down on the way that the exchange of ideas more generally was understood to best function. In the institutions discussed in this book, "the cultural centrality" of print interacted with an array of other forms of knowledge production and dissemination, including—as well as libraries of printed materials—conversation, discussion, reading aloud, museum exhibitions, scientific demonstration, and lectures.[2] Relations between these media were often fraught in ways that exposed tensions about what constituted "knowledge" and how it ought best to be created, nurtured, and circulated. This chapter follows these conflicts after the manner of Bruno Latour to disclose the processes of group formation and dissolution. A conflict between books, for instance, as a storage system of "knowledge"—useful, poetic, or otherwise—and the promotion of the lecture as a medium to demonstrate certain kinds of scientific knowledge threatened to split the society at Newcastle. Such tensions help bring to light basic assumptions about what constituted improvement. Should one invest in a library as a repository of knowledge (and perhaps private reading) or purchase a steam engine to demonstrate chemical and technological ideas? However, what may seem a straightforward contest between science-as-useful-knowledge and literature-as-books was a more complicated dispute that was as much about modes of communication and access as about its content.

Concerns about these issues stemmed from and went on to shape some basic questions about the appropriate format for intellectual and information exchange down to the level of the regulation of bodies in rooms. In this regard, the flow of ideas that these networked relations between and within societies generated, understood to be powered by a positive energy of emulation, was sometimes felt to be threatened by the material conditions of their production. The commitment to knowledge being produced and not just transmitted by the friction of debate was haunted by fears of bodies in rooms fueling conflict and, in consequence, by the question of the relationship of improvement to religion and politics as inflammatory topics. Literary and philosophical societies worked hard to find the appropriate forms—in their memberships, their regulations, and their delivery systems—to keep the lid on political and religious conflict, but foundational figures such as Joseph Priestley had suggested that improvement of whatever kind was necessarily keyed into freedom of inquiry in religion and to a more democratic politics. When these assumptions were challenged by a loyalist mob burning Priestley out of his laboratory in July 1791, there was an uneven retreat among his friends and supporters toward an idea of knowledge—literary or scientific—as beyond the claims of ideology, but it was always difficult to maintain a domain of knowledge on these terms. The rapid progress that had been promised stalled somewhat around 1800, despite the best efforts of managers such as Thomas Percival in Manchester and William Turner of Newcastle. When a revival came after 1815 (the topic of chapter 3), it brought with it a proliferation whose velocity and asymmetries—for instance, between moral and technical progress, middle-class assumptions of stewardship and working-class demands for access—seemed only to throw further doubt over the dream of an in-step march of the intellect.

PHYSICS AND THE BELLES LETTRES

Regardless of changed circumstances, those societies established in the post-1815 revival routinely granted precedence to the institution founded in Manchester in 1781. Thomas Percival's preface to the first volume of the Manchester Literary and Philosophical Society's *Memoirs* provided them with a useful statement of purpose. He had presented a European Enlightenment as the natural outgrowth of a vigorous culture of association and dissemination: "The progress that has been made in Physics and the Belles Lettres, owes its rapidity, if not its origin, to the encouragement that these societies have given to such pursuits, and to the emulation which has been excited between different academical bodies, as well as among the individual Members of each institution."[3] Closer inspection reveals a number of important features to Percival's account that are worth dwelling on further as they open up a series of issues central to this book. Although the society's published *Memoirs* began by proclaiming the encouragement of King George III, its content embodied Priestley's idea of knowledge as a relatively flat transnational network.[4] Percival's preface conceded the importance of the metropolitan center but—like Priestley in his *History of Electricity*—implies that the flow of knowledge may become silted up if its channels are not extended to "the principal towns in this kingdom." Percival gives a sense of the Manchester society riding a gathering wave in tune with Aikin's vision of the manufacturing towns and their new institutions as the lifeblood of a vigorous economy of improvement.

"Emulation" was celebrated as an almost autonomous energy shaping the institutions identified by Percival and Aikin. Percival understood it as a dynamic and generative force. These societies do not merely copy each other to disseminate knowledge; "emulation" is imagined as a positive energy that produces new discoveries out of the encounter with difference. It is not slavish imitation but what Alexander Dick calls—using a language that draws attention to the aims of its human agents— "an attempt to overcome or compete with the person or act being copied . . . but also to surpass them in accomplishments and prestige."[5] Dick's account places the term in relation to the Scottish Enlightenment, an important source for so many of the practices found in the Manchester society.[6] The gamut of extramural intellectual activity enjoyed by Aikin and Percival when they were students in Edinburgh was designed quite self-consciously to encourage "a spirit of emulation" through which "improvements become universally known; and merit receives the testimony of public approbation."[7] Emulation from this point of view is constitutive of social knowledge, as Dick explains, rather than "merely registering impressions derived from sense experience (including books), . . . the mind is already involved in a competitive social process through which those impressions become new ideas."[8]

Just how this process was understood to be competitive is moot. At least, it wasn't necessarily encouraged in the market terms used by Mokyr. For the moderate party of the Kirk in Scotland, emulation was "a theological principle," a manifestation of "the drive to praise God by working towards or improving nature and the self."[9] Most of the Unitarians active in the Manchester society had traveled a road from Presbyterian puritanism to a providential sense of virtuous commerce with the world in the name of improvement. "Association" rouses men out of "indolence," says Percival in his preface, and is in itself a means of discovery that might be lost to the individual inquirer: "Science, like fire, is put in motion by collision.—Where a number of such men have frequent opportunity of meeting and conversing with each other, thought begets thought, and every hint is turned to advantage. A spirit of enquiry glows in every breast. Every new discovery relative to the natural, intellectual, or moral world, leads to a farther investigation; and each man is zealous to distinguish himself in the interesting pursuit" (vi–vii).This passage almost certainly had its origins in Isaac Watts's *Improvement of the Mind* (1741), a Warrington textbook, and Percival echoes its claim that the benefits of privatized reading soon reach a limit if not encouraged by the spark of social interaction: "By Conversation you will both give and receive this Benefit; as Flints when put into Motion and striking against each other produce living Fire on both Sides, which would never have risen from the same hard Materials in a State of Rest."[10] Toward the end of his preface, Percival mentions unpublished papers stored in the society's archive for retrieval if relevant topics came up in discussion later (viii). Several papers that were printed in the *Memoirs* allude to their role as products of conversation aiming to stimulate further discussion inside and beyond the society through publication.[11] Percival provides a glimpse of a media ecology where read papers, print, and discussion operate together to stimulate wider networks of improvement.

Improvement in Percival's preface is explicitly understood as a matter of "Physics *and* the Belles Lettres" (my emphasis), the movement together of two spheres of inventiveness. If "useful knowledge" became a byword of the literary and philosophical societies, then a literary education was understood to have its own kind of utility.[12] The Manchester society is probably still most famous as the place where the chemist John Dalton set out his atomic theory in the series of papers published in the *Memoirs* in the later 1790s. His public lectures drew large audiences of nonmembers that included women, but Dalton first made his way into these circles through a small debating group that met in the nearby Manchester Academy—where Thomas Barnes was the principal—to discuss questions relating to philosophical materialism that were later to cause trouble for the larger society. If by the end of the period covered by this book, the arts and the sciences, not to mention moral and technological progress, could seem to be moving alarmingly out of kilter, the idea of a general improvement was never entirely abandoned by the literary and philosophical societies.

The early papers given at the Manchester society certainly insisted on the importance of works of the imagination and of science in together providing a moral framework to the activities of a commercial town. It was a topic addressed by Thomas Barnes, Charles de Polier, and Thomas Henry, among others. In several papers published in the *Memoirs*, Barnes insisted on the importance of the imagination and taste. Sir Isaac Newton, he argued in his paper "On the Influence of the Imagination and the Passions upon our Understanding," depended on a *"brilliant imagination"* to conceive of his theories of the universe. De Polier quoted from Henry Home, Lord Kames, his conviction that "a just taste of the fine arts, . . . prepares us for acting in the social state, with dignity and propriety."[13] In his paper "On the Advantages of Literature and Philosophy in general," Henry proclaimed the social benefits of knowledge of all kinds: "In proportion as a nation acquires superior degrees of it, her state of civilization advances, and she becomes distinguished from her less enlightened neighbours by a greater refinement in the manners of her inhabitants, and a departure from those ferocious vices, which mark the features of savage countries" (7). Notwithstanding the serious commercial interest in the application of chemical knowledge to dyeing witnessed in several of the papers he gave to the society, Henry insisted on the usefulness of "the English classics" as "a rich fund of entertainment and improvement" (17). In terms of contemporary writing, Henry also claimed that young men would gain from "sweet converse with the fair sex. A Montague, a Carter, a Barbauld, and a Seward, justly demand his notice," a claim that I'll return to in chapter 5. Henry's essay imagined that reading the work of these women writers would "refine . . . taste, polish . . . manners, and meliorate . . . morals" (18).

Generally speaking, then, this early group of papers asserted the importance of taste to any notion of improvement as a virtuous commerce, a social knowledge that operated beyond mere self-advancement. Promoting literary and scientific knowledge was portrayed as performing a public function requiring questions of sect and party to be put to one side for the sake of the broader community, but claims to disinterestedness were not readily credited, especially when they came from those outside the Church of England. The Manchester society presented itself as taking the step from a private conversation club into an institution with a public role in the international republic of letters. This civic role was especially important for Dissenters whose civil rights were, in theory at least, limited, but the decision to publish *Memoirs of the Literary and Philosophical Society of Manchester* invited wider scrutiny, and Percival quickly discovered there was no easy ground that could be claimed to be beyond political, religious, and other differences. In the decades to come, these societies had to continually argue for an idea of improvement that transcended differences of sect and party. In the process, the purview of what was understood to be improvable was revised and constrained.

Percival presented the origins of the Manchester Literary and Philosophical Society as a "weekly club" that met for the purpose of "literary and philosophical conversation" (vi). The step into a more public role was the consequence of various "respectable gentlemen" pushing to be involved in the more informal group. From a longer perspective, he might have mentioned the role of the Warrington Academy, but this would have been to invoke a sectarian origin at odds with a broader public project claiming the patronage of the king. He might equally have mentioned the influence of his education in Edinburgh and his convivial meetings with the region's medical men in correspondence with William Cullen, but this might have made the society seem too narrowly the child of professional interests. The early rules of the society made it quite clear that discussion was to avoid "Religion, the Practical Branches of Physic, and British Politics."[14] The regulation was a common feature of the attempt of knowledge institutions to delimit a sphere of improvement where traditional party spirit and religious differences could be set aside, but it was open to being understood as a preference for freedom of inquiry that was itself a political position, a more or less veiled preference for the liberal side of the question, especially when associated with Dissenters.

Percival was almost certainly aware that his experiment had been preceded by an attempt in Liverpool by his friend James Currie. With the Quaker William Rathbone IV and the Italian scholar William Clarke (De Quincey's host at Everton in 1801), Currie set up a society in 1778, decades before the more durable Literary and Philosophical Society founded in Liverpool in 1812.[15] Again medical men were a noticeable presence, including the Quaker abolitionist Jonathan Binns. Absent for reasons unknown was William Roscoe, despite the presence of so many of his friends. Predictably enough, the topics discussed by the Liverpool society included many that were to become important in Manchester, including "The Influence of Physical and Moral Causes," "Remarks on Laws, Police, and Government, and Hints at Reforming sundry Defects," and William Rathbone's "Reflections on the Dispositions to contain diversions generally deemed inconsistent with humanity & benevolence." Currie gave papers on biography, on hypochondria, and on "The Influence of Climation [on] human Nature." These were all questions that came naturally to a student of environmental medicine such as Currie. No doubt questions of environment also shaped discussions in these societies about which conditions would help their own debates flourish. Variously known as the Philosophical and Literary Society or the Society for Useful Knowledge, the early Liverpool society was unable to solve the question for its own survival. It was abandoned in October 1783 owing to the lack of "zeal" among its members, an issue that never entirely disappeared even in those societies that lasted for decades.[16]

Some of what zeal there was transferred to the Manchester Literary and Philosophical Society, which Currie, Rathbone, and Roscoe all joined soon after it began. Each of them contributed papers that were published in the *Memoirs*. In March 1787, for instance, Roscoe gave a paper at Manchester "On the Comparative Excellence of the Sciences and Arts," a topic that showed he was keenly aware of the issues interesting to these circles.[17] His contribution was distinctive, though, for its fear that the polite arts were in danger of being overwhelmed by commercial values and a tendency—"injurious both to our improvement and happiness" (241)—toward a disciplinary specialism associated with the sciences at odds with his idea of liberality. Science ought to be embedded, claimed Roscoe, in "that enlarged and general view of our nature and destination, by which we ought to ascertain, and arrange in due succession the proper objects of our pursuit" (242). He accepted that natural philosophy could provide such a broad view, as it was not necessarily tied to applied knowledge, but he granted preeminence to painting and poetry because they serve "to act upon our affections and passions . . . and to regulate, correct, and harmonize them" (258). There may seem little difference between the views of earlier essays in the society, which also grant the arts a regulative function within useful knowledge, but the way Roscoe firmly placed them above natural philosophy (unlike, for instance, Henry) seems to have caused sufficient stir to be registered in a lengthy and otherwise sympathetic account of the third volume of the *Memoirs* in the *Analytical Review*.[18] Restating the importance of both the arts and sciences to "the great whole or final purpose to which the pursuits of men ought to be directed," the review implies that Roscoe gave put too much faith in the principle of taste. The following month Roscoe wrote to his wife Jane from a visit to Joseph Johnson in London to tell her that even their friend Henri Fuseli had upbraided him for the essay. It left him despondent enough to hope it would "cure me of *Authorship*," but Roscoe's commercial humanism always remained on its watch against the narrowing of the category of useful knowledge, as proved to be the case in his 1817 speech at the Liverpool Royal Institution discussed in chapter 3.[19]

More generally, though, these circles were suspicious of placing too much trust in taste as a moral sense, especially where it seemed to court sentimental indulgence of the feelings. It was a note Anna Barbauld struck in a poem to Samuel Taylor Coleridge, published in her brother John Aikin Jr.'s *Monthly Magazine* in 1799, which echoed the more general concern in these circles to carefully calibrate relations between the imagination and scientific knowledge, especially when it came to questions of the public good.[20] Even the controversy going on about materialism in the Manchester Literary and Philosophical Society in these years, discussed in chapter 4, can be construed as partially a disagreement about the role of the imagination in mental processes, but these were all instances of differences of opinion within Rational Dissent against the background of a larger set of shared assumptions. Not everyone in the society, though, shared this Unitarian delicacy about freedom of conscience. Although generally speaking a friend to Dissent, De Quincey's tutor Samuel Hall—an Anglican clergyman—insisted that neither taste nor knowledge could provide a substitute for the Bible supported by the institutions of church and state in his paper "An attempt to show that a taste for the beauties of nature and the fine arts has no influence favourable to morals." His kind of worry about the orientation of the society brought resignations from Anglican members at various critical points in the first decade, culminating in a partial counterrevolution in 1792.

The question of how far the society was a creature of Dissent was certainly a sensitive one. Although the membership was mixed in religious terms, those driving its activities were strongly associated with Cross Street Chapel. Of the forty-three original members listed in 1785, fifteen were or were related to trustees or minsters at the chapel.[21] Henry had converted to Unitarianism in Manchester in the 1760s after coming to work as an apothecary in the infirmary. Barnes, who remained a staunch Arian, trained at Warrington and became minister at Cross Street in 1780. Eager to disseminate Warringtonian principles, he contributed a series of papers on education to the *Memoirs*, including "A plan for the improvement and extension of liberal education" and "Proposals for . . . a plan of liberal education for young men designed for civil and active life." In June 1783, Barnes played a key role, again with Henry and Percival, in the foundation of a College of Arts and Sciences designed to help young men transition from school to business. Percival served as president. Henry lectured on chemistry, and the respectable Anglican physicians Charles and John White offered lectures on anatomy and physiology.[22] Then in 1786 Manchester Academy was set up, taking over most of the resources of the by then defunct academy at Warrington. Together Barnes, Henry, and Percival formed a powerful bloc of opinion at the center of the Literary and Philosophical Society that was seeking to extend its influence, but their public aspirations for the society required the disavowal of any formal association between it and Dissent. The rules outlawing religion and politics from the society's debates may have been designed to protect against the suspicions of the town's Anglican elite. These were difficult to allay. Was the public good not served by the institutions of church and state? Were not educational initiatives driven by the Cross Street Chapel interest sectarian by definition? Barnes had to publish a newspaper paragraph making it clear that the Manchester Academy—an explicitly nonconformist educational institution—laid no claim to a formal relationship with the Literary and Philosophical Society.[23] The presence of a Tory-Anglican medical elite within the Literary and Philosophical Society provided a point of opposition, especially after its members resigned their infirmary posts in 1790 to protest against the reforms piloted by Ferriar and Percival (discussed in chapter 4). At least one of those physicians, Alexander Eason, wrote disparagingly of the academy to his friends: "It is to be on a small footing, and if it fails, which I think it must do, the loss will not be great."[24] Similar opposition met the College of Arts and Sciences. Thomas Henry told Benjamin Rush that "Bigotry and Party rage strove to impede our designs." Resignations followed, mainly from the ranks of the respectable rather than the talented, thought Henry: "Our loss, except in one instance, was not great. Academical degrees are not always the concomitants of well-informed and philosophic minds, and our seceders were in general Men who had contributed little or nothing to the support of our Society."[25]

Despite these controversial episodes, Henry's confidence in a project of improvement broadly conceived was justified through the 1780s and no doubt buoyed by the gathering support in Manchester for the abolition of the slave trade and the repeal of the Test and Corporation Acts. Apart from anything else, these campaigns provided a training in the organization of opinion. Thomas Cooper, James Watt Jr., and Thomas Walker (who joined the society in 1785, 1789, and 1790, respectively) were more voluble in their hopes for reform than Barnes, Henry, and Percival. The group associated with Cooper and Walker formed the Manchester Constitutional Society in 1792 to campaign for parliamentary reform. Earlier Percival seems to have cautiously cooperated with their sense of a broad remit for improvement: witness his paper on the "Principles and Limits of Taxation" in the third volume of the *Memoirs*. Cooper and Walker were campaigning together against Prime Minister William Pitt the Younger's tax on fustian (a sturdy twilled cotton fabric) at the time, a tax finally repealed in 1795, in the face of opposition from the calico lobby led by Sir Robert Peel, first Baronet and father of the future prime minister.[26] Percival's paper accepted the payment of taxation as a public duty only as long as government was properly constituted. Significantly, Cooper's "Propositions respecting the Foundation of Civil Government," read to the society in 1787, appeared in the same volume and ended with a vision of "political oppression" tottering around the globe: "Its day is far spent: the extension of knowledge has undermined its foundations, and I hope the day is not far distant when in Europe at least, one stone of the fabric will not be left upon another."[27] Republished as an appendix to his *Reply to Mr. Burke's Invective* (1792), which cannot have pleased the conservatives in the Literary and Philosophical Society, it was being weaponized in a very different context, with Cooper a protagonist in an international controversy about the French Revolution. Even at its first appearance, Cooper's paper was pushing the society's rules about topical politics to the limit.[28] Published in 1790, the third volume of *Memoirs*, where Cooper and Percival's papers appeared with Roscoe's on the arts and sciences and others by James Watt Jr. and Ferriar, was probably the high-water mark of the reform surge of these early years.

On 16 January 1788, Currie wrote to Percival to praise "the judicious and spirited" papers on the abolition of the slave trade that he and Cooper had sent to him but also sounded a note of caution: "they are not of a temporizing nature; they speak a language that admits no compromise."[29] These reservations were typical of Currie's anxieties about the abolitionist platform in Liverpool in comparison with Manchester: "My situation, as you may imagine, is delicate. Every thing I would say I cannot write." Currie was writing to Percival shortly before his friend the Unitarian minister John Yates confronted his congregation with their complicity in the slave trade. Hannah Lightbody's diary contains what may be the only description of the sermon, discussed at more length in chapter 5. Later entries record the way it dominated conversation for many weeks and months thereafter. Perhaps still feeling the reverberations of the clarion call sounded by Yates, Currie looks forward to meeting Percival in Warrington, where they could discuss the issue freely: "I have longed to converse with you; and if you can foresee any circumstance that may call you to Warrington for an evening, long enough to give me notice in time, I should have much satisfaction in meeting you there." If Currie thought the situation in Manchester allowed more freedom for progressive opinion, a few years showed him things tightening there, too. In the wake of the French Revolution, opinions such as Cooper's on the downfall of tyranny started to be subjected to intense scrutiny beyond the local contexts where they first appeared. In February 1790, Currie wrote to Percival to discuss sending delegates to a meeting in Warrington as part of the campaign against the Test and Corporation Acts but counseled the Manchester delegates against "fiery zeal."[30] Currie's letter framed his caution in relation to news of the Church and King club recently founded in Manchester: "What turn things may take here, I know not. A few days ago, there was no chance of the opposite party moving against us; but the example of Manchester, and the warmth diffused by the meeting there, may perhaps reach us."[31]

These tensions were brought to a head by events in Birmingham in July 1791 when Joseph Priestley's home and laboratory were destroyed by loyalist rioters. Priestley, as we have already seen, was an inspirational figure in these circles. He had been made an honorary member of the Manchester society early on. In a muted version of trouble ahead, various Anglican members resigned when Priestley was granted fifty pounds toward his research. Priestley was effectively the presiding deity of the confident expansion of the society in the 1780s. Manchester had both a material and a symbolic stake in the laboratory destroyed by the rioters. Currie wrote to Percival to see if he had further details of what had happened in Birmingham "for the life and safety of Dr. Priestley is an object that must interest every enlightened mind." Percival's reply seems to have contained an address prepared for the Manchester society canvassing a statement of support for Priestley: "The accounts I received of the issue of the business [of a motion in support of Priestley] you had the goodness to communicate to me, at your society, prevented me troubling you farther, as they decided me against attempting anything of the kind here. I must confess, I heard the decision at Manchester with great regret, as well as its consequences."[32] The incident exposed rifts that had been there from the beginning. Priestley himself later claimed that the address was "negatived by a considerable majority," despite the fact that it carefully excluded "any approbation of my civil or religious principles."[33] The radical group associated with Cooper and Walker resigned in protest. Although the founding generation of Barnes, Henry, and Percival were all devotees of Priestley, they remained members, as did John Ferriar, until at least 1797, perhaps reluctant to surrender to the loyalist reaction the civic space that the society occupied. John Aikin Jr., when he learned of the resignations, grieved: "If the cause of it was purely party difference, I lament that letters and science at least are not kept sacred from their intrusion." Remaining, though, meant retreat from the more expansive version of improvement found in the third volume of the society's *Memoirs*.[34]

Gatrell and others have seen these events as a watershed, part of a wide and deliberate coup against liberal opinion in Manchester culminating in the trial of Thomas Walker in 1794. Thirty-four radicals in the city were identified for possible prosecution by the Church and King club; some thirteen of these were or had been members of the Literary and Philosophical Society, including Samuel Greg, William Hibbert, George Philips, and Thomas Robinson, all of whom were Unitarians, but it would be wrong to suggest that the society simply turned to focus on Dalton's scientific inquiries.[35] Using the minute books that have since been destroyed, E. M. Fraser revealed that Robert Owen, for instance, gave papers whose titles, at least, suggest an idea of improvement still tied to social reform: "Thoughts on the connection between universal happiness and practical mechanics" and "On the origin of opinions, with a view to the improvement of social virtues." James Watt Jr. wrote to John Ferriar at the end of the year complaining that "it is the order of the day to suppress *all Jacobin innovations*." Despite his growing political notoriety, both Ferriar and Henry tried to woo him back to their society.[36]

Arnold Thackray influentially claimed that science emerged out of this situation as the main form of cultural expression in Manchester because it could be presented as a "value-transcendent pursuit."[37] Much the same perspective was offered by Lyell's review of 1826, where science is lauded as a miraculous survivor of three decades of ideological division. Both underplay the conflicted nature of the process and the fragility of its outcomes. Furthermore, Thackray's claim could and was equally made for the "literary" side of the society's activities. In the spring of 1794, Samuel Argent Bardsley, another physician in the infirmary, gave a paper on "Party prejudice, moral and political" that insists on a neutral zone of improvement beyond ideology, if now with a decidedly defensive cast. "Amidst the horrors and confusion of a revolution or a sedition," he warned, "the voice of moderation and humanity will have little chance of being heard." Was this comment meant to tell the Church and King faction within the society that it had gone too far? Or was the warning about revolution and sedition aimed at those liberals who remained? He would not have alienated the conservative Tory Party with the papers that were later published as *Critical Remarks on the Tragedy of Pizarro* (1800), where he complained that the politician-playwright Richard Brinsley Sheridan made his characters sound too much like political orators.[38] More fundamentally, though, Bardsley both retained the idea of literary topics as appropriate to the Manchester society and hoped they might open onto a domain beyond ideological difference. Katrina Navickas has seen this period as one when literary and cultural activities began to displace politics in the Roscoe circle precisely because they were a safe space, but, as Bardsley's account of Sheridan demonstrated, the literary seemed to many observers to be only too saturated with politics. Over in Liverpool, after all, De Quincey's mother told her son that Currie's edition of Robert Burns was a "Jacobin" text.[39]

For his part, in the mid-1790s, Thomas Percival seems to have entered a period of dialogue with the evangelical moralist Thomas Gisborne. Close to William Wilberforce and an important member of the Clapham sect, Gisborne's idea of the circulation of knowledge was always framed by a sense of Christian duties somewhat stricter than Samuel Hall's. A founder member of the Derby Philosophical Society, as was Erasmus Darwin, Gisborne was unlikely to have encouraged the address that the Derby society published in support of Priestley after the Birmingham riots. Charles Hope, another Derby clergyman, condemned the address from the pulpit and was expelled from the society for his troubles.[40] Gisborne's sole contribution to the Manchester society's *Memoirs* was a paper communicated via Percival in 1796, "On the Benefits and Duties resulting from the Institution of Societies for the Advancement of Literature and Philosophy," insisting that freedom of inquiry should be subservient to the moral authority of the Bible. Most of the paper is preoccupied with the dangers of science imagining itself superior to revelation: "The philosopher is sometimes found to advance in the road to infidelity in proportion as he devotes himself to scientific researches."[41] Similar comments, more specifically directed at the medical profession, appeared in his influential *Enquiry into the Duties of Men in the Higher and Middle Classes of Society in Great Britain* (1794). Although Percival's *Medical Ethics* (1803) saluted Gisborne's system of morals, Percival did not entirely defer to it, especially when it came to the place of religion by the sickbed, as we will see in chapter 4. The nuances of their relationship hints at the complexity of the accommodations made by liberal opinion in the 1790s as it attempted to keep open a route to improvement without entirely succumbing to counterrevolution.

"BOND OF UNION"

My introduction noted some of the banal difficulties of taking Latour's advice to follow "the traces left by [the] activity of forming and dismantling groups."[42] Minutes of meetings, for instance, by their nature, are often quite guarded about the conflicts that came with the collision of mind with mind. Tantalizingly, they sometimes explicitly note a decision not to give details where disagreements have grown warm. Apart from their natural guardedness about what they record, archives often survive only by happenstance: the materiality of networks is liable to decay. Even purpose-built venues do not always survive. The destruction of the Literary and Philosophical Society of Manchester's building with its archives in the Second World War means that some of the complexities at stake in the accommodation of liberal opinion to counterrevolution in the 1790s are lost to us, although insights are available in correspondence like Ferriar's and Henry's with James Watt Jr. Fortunately, extensive archives

of Manchester's most immediate offspring—the Literary and Philosophical Society of Newcastle upon Tyne—have survived and provide clearer
"traces" of the formation and deformation of these networks.[43]

The equivalent figure to Thomas Percival in Newcastle was the Unitarian minister William Turner, whose role was overdetermined, to say
the least. He grew up in the circle that surrounded Priestley after he had
moved across the Pennines to Leeds. On one of her visits to the area, Barbauld presented the young William Turner with her "Verses written in the
Leaves of an Ivory Pocketbook":

> Accept, my dear, this toy, and let me say,
> The leaves an emblem of your mind display—
> Your youthful mind, uncoloured, fair, and white,
> Like crystal leaves, transparent to the sight,
> Fit each impression to receive, whate'er
> The pencil of instruction traces there.
> O then transcribe into the shining page
> Each virtue that adorns your tender age;
> And grave upon the tablet of your heart
> Each lofty science, and each useful art![44]

First published in full over fifty years later by Turner in his obituary of the
poet, the poem is testament to the durability of those "connexions" despised by De Quincey. More to the point here, though, it was originally intended as a friendship gift that would make an "impression" on the boy's
mind, shape his character, and help him take his place in the world.[45]

Barbauld's poem provided a script that Turner followed for the rest of
his life. Predictably, he went on to become a student at the Warrington
Academy, from 1777 until 1781, where John Aikin Sr. and Jr. were among
his tutors.[46] Barbauld herself had left the area by this stage, but Turner
would surely have been aware of her virtual presence, not least via "conversation" in Thomas Henry's sense of reading. Continuing the path
laid out for him by the poet, he was made an honorary member of the
Manchester Literary and Philosophical Society in 1783, after a year at
Glasgow University. While Turner was at Warrington, John Howard was
also in residence, working with John Aikin Jr. on *The State of the Prisons in England and Wales* (1777). Its influence is explicit in the paper on
the relative merits of corporal and capital punishment Turner published
in the second volume of the Manchester society's *Memoirs*. Predictably
again, Turner argued that capital punishment was "absurd and impoli-
tic," merely repeating "those habits which are the foundations of all vicious conduct." Like many in these circles, he had a strong sense of the

role of habit and environment in shaping human conduct, "vicious" or otherwise, as set out in Barbauld's gift poem. He also shared her faith in the ability of reason to reshape these environmental influences. Echoing the principles of Aikin and Howard, Turner called for punishment to be proportionate and rational.[47]

By the time his paper was published, Turner had moved to Newcastle as minister to the Unitarian chapel at the Hanover Square, a congregation that continued to meet in the open spirit of Warrington. "A Voluntary Association," he described it in 1811, "of *Individual Christians*; each one professing Christianity for himself according to his own views of it, formed upon a mature consideration of the Scriptures, and acknowledging the minister's right to do the same belonging to no one sect and holding to no particular set of doctrines."[48] Soon after his arrival in Newcastle, he had set up a small informal conversation club. A proposal for a formal Literary and Philosophical Society followed a few years later: *Speculations on the Propriety of Attempting the Establishment of a Literary Society in Newcastle* (1792). The step from a private conversation club to an institution with civic ambitions was the one trodden by Percival and his friends in Manchester; an example Turner explicitly invoked as "eminently serviceable to that flourishing town," in encouraging, "the improvement of its extensive manufactures."[49] As might be expected of anyone educated at Warrington, Turner also subscribed to the productive collision of mind with mind. Emulation of Manchester didn't mean simply copying, of course. Turner was alert to local circumstances in the way Priestley had suggested would always benefit provincial societies and define their contribution to the common good. Newcastle already had a flourishing print culture serviced by two newspapers, and its coal industry was booming.[50] Whereas the cotton manufactures were never far away from the papers produced in Manchester, whatever their ostensible topic, Turner oriented himself toward geology and, more practically, the mineral resources of the Newcastle area, hoping to set up a registry for the area's coal mines.[51]

The practicalities of building networks through transport infrastructure were always on the minds of men like Turner, who argued that communication of "Literary Intelligence" would be particularly facilitated by Newcastle's geographical position between London and Edinburgh. As a major port, there was also a "favourable prospect . . . of being regaled with specimens of *eastern literature*; which is daily becoming more and more important in a commercial view, and which appears to be fraught with various beauties, both of sentiment and diction."[52] Intriguingly the membership did show a sustained commitment to ordering "eastern literature" for the library, at least early on. John Clennell ordered

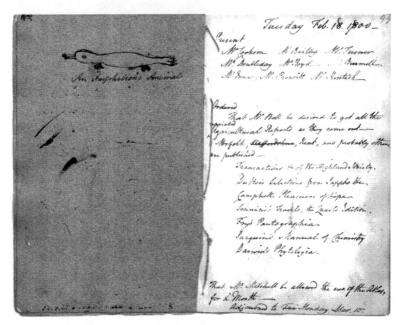

FIGURE 5. "An Amphibious Animal" (1800). Sketch from
a committee minute book. Photograph courtesy of the Literary
and Philosophical Society of Newcastle upon Tyne.

a large number of such works soon after joining the society, although the
committee sometimes balked at the cost.[53] Several evenings in 1797 were
spent discussing Clennell's paper on the relative merits of Anacreon and
Hafeez. Nor was this global perspective simply a matter of books. The new
colony in New South Wales sent specimens of a wombat and a duck-billed
platypus. A member of the committee sketched the platypus into the minute book for February 1800. The uncertain description—"An Amphibious
Animal"—and the naïveté of the drawing both suggest something of the
difficulties of incorporating such donations into the rational project of
the society: a difficulty made much more explicit by the decision—in the
1820s—to stuff the wombat standing on its hind legs.[54]

The first meeting of the Literary and Philosophical Society was held
in February 1793 at the town's dispensary. Despite the prospects enthusiastically outlined by Turner in his *Speculations*, the times were not pro-
pitious for founding a society devoted to the circulation of knowledge on
a global scale. Less than a month after Louis XVI's execution, just as Britain and France were going to war, the Newcastle society embarked on its
journey at a time when "improvement" was becoming a dirty word, and
the prospects for trade of all kinds were retarding. The following year

Turner's father's friend Theophilus Lindsey wrote to say that he was glad that Priestley had emigrated to the United States because "the prejudices against Dissenters, especially the more liberal sort, as enemies to their country because they are against the present war, are so violent."[55] Turner's role as the town's most visible Dissenter was likely to cause suspicion, something that dogged him even into the 1830s, long after he had ostensibly become one of the town's elder statesmen. His achievement, something like Percival's, was in navigating his society through these stormy waters over the next fifty years, but in the process, both by nature cautious, they also sacrificed more than a little of the radical inheritance bestowed on them by Priestley.

The committee of the Newcastle society originally contained four Unitarians, besides Turner, but also two members of the Newcastle loyalist association. Religion and politics were banned as topics from the monthly meetings—as in Manchester—and books of religious or political controversy were supposed to be excluded from the library, but these rules were a source of constant conflict, judging by the pages of the recommendation book where members could suggest acquisitions to the library or changes to the regulations.[56] Robert Doubleday, a local devotee of William Godwin, consistently ordered works associated with political reform, including *Anecdotes of the Founders of the French Republic*.[57] Ever zealous for widening the circuit of knowledge, Clennell suggested that women should be encouraged to join and also ordered books such as Mary Hays's *Appeal to the Men of Great Britain* for the library. He was also part of a failed attempt to have honorary memberships awarded to Barbauld and Hays in 1801. More than a few items requested were postponed or canceled, just as this proposal was ignored, but despite the committee's caution, Robert Hopper Williamson, recorder of Newcastle, still withdrew from the society, "fearing that such institutions, with their methods of research and enquiry, might lead to anarchy and rebellion."[58] The obituary for Robert Doubleday published in the bookseller John Marshall's *Northern Reformer's Monthly Magazine* later claimed that "the governing part of the town, the aristocracy, the established clergy, the pensioners, and dependants on the government, seeing the materials of which it was composed, and the liberal nature of the establishment, for the most part stood aloof, jealous of its prosperity, and fearful lest increasing knowledge might lead the people to dispute the claims of the privileged classes, and assert their independence of their 'natural leaders.'"[59] If inflected by Marshall's own radicalism, the description seems a reasonable account of the atmosphere of the first decade, and the relative absence of local gentry and aristocracy from its affairs, at least through the 1790s.[60]

Other tensions were less obviously political and had more to do with fears of the passions in any transmission of knowledge that involved bodies in rooms. Turner's plans for the collision of mind show a clear concern that creative exchange should not descend into conflict. A desire to avoid acrimony in debate ran through Turner's career and included an aversion to rancorous disputes over points of theological difference within the Unitarian tradition. He and Lindsey agreed that Priestley had "ever been too unguarded in things that he has thrown out to the public."[61] Early on into the life of the Newcastle society, Turner consulted with James Anderson, editor of the *Bee* in Edinburgh, on the best way to ensure constructive exchange. Anderson told him that "discussion in the society viva voce" was crucial if its energy was to be kept up: "Where meetings are confined to drily reading a paper and briefly throwing forth a few indiscriminate applause to the writer—nothing can become less interesting to its members in general—It is freedom, restrained only by the rules of politeness that calls forth the exertions of the human mind." The fear of entropy was continually balanced against the need to keep within the bounds of polite exchange. Seeking to provide a model for emulation to other societies, Anderson in turn published the society's rules and regulations. Unfortunately, the *Bee* didn't last many more issues as the political context of the war years closed the opportunities even for its modest remit of intellectual exchange.[62]

Most of the papers presented in the early months of the Newcastle society reflected Turner's interest in chemistry and geology, fulfilling his idea that the topics should suit the local situation, but they were by no means confined to these subjects. The society participated in debates about the formation of a vernacular literary canon, for instance, through the presentation at the monthly meetings of two papers by William Enfield, principal at Warrington while Turner was there. One was "An Essay on the Cultivation of Taste as a Proper Object of Attention in the Education of Youth," the topic that so engaged the members of the Manchester Literary and Philosophical Society in its early years. Enfield insisted that "to *cultivate the Taste* and *form the Heart* is at least of *equal* importance as to *exercise the understanding and judgment*." Bravely, given the political situation in late 1793, Enfield placed his inquiry in the context of "the present age of bold examination" and the "free spirit which has stript Royalty of its divine right." Marshall republished Enfield's essay in 1818, a year after he was excluded for publishing *A Political Litany*.[63] The other early Enfield paper was "An Enquiry whether there be any Essential Difference between Poetry and Prose," later published in the *Monthly Magazine* (like several other essays read at the Literary and Philosophical Society).[64] As literary editor at the *Monthly* from its inception in 1796, John Aikin Jr. continued to promote his broad idea of improvement in straitened political times. His reorientation of the language of poetry toward the vernacular in his *Essays on Song-Writing* may even have influenced Wordsworth.[65] John Guillory has shown how important the members of the group around Aikin were to this period of vernacular canon formation. Enfield's anthology *The Speaker* (1774) was a Warrington textbook that celebrated the pedagogic practice of John Aikin Sr. and contained a poem by Barbauld addressed to the academy.[66] Predictably enough, the issue of the difference between poetry and prose had been discussed in Manchester early on by Thomas Barnes, who, like Enfield, made the passions not formal qualities the basis of the distinction.

Guillory's point that *Lyrical Ballads* was "scarcely anomalous in its literary milieu" is reinforced by the Newcastle order for the volume soon after publication.[67] There were also prompt orders for Coleridge's *Poems* (1796) and *Fears in Solitude* (1798), together with Southey's *Poems* (1797 and 2 vols. 1799). The society's librarian John Marshall's bookshop—moved to Newcastle's populous Flesh Market in 1810—bridged the world of antiquarian inquiry and popular song by "the common people."[68] Even Byron's *Don Juan* was ordered for the library in 1819, but there was an objection from a local evangelical and a very public controversy followed, recently described by David Stewart.[69] Where there appeared to be a more definite boundary from early on was the line drawn at fiction. William Crawford's order for Maria Edgeworth's *Castle Rackrent* was refused by the committee because "objectionable as a novel."[70] The same objections reappeared in 1831 when a motion that there was nothing in "the spirit or letter of the rules" to prevent the purchase of the new Waverley edition of Scott's novel was rejected with the rules tightened to make it plain that "it is not the plan of this Society to admit novels into the Library."[71] What emerges from these struggles is not any simple expression of a settled middle class definition of useful knowledge, but a constant battle around its meaning.

Requests for nonfiction prose by Godwin, Hays, and Mary Wollstonecraft, including an order for Godwin's edition of Wollstonecraft's posthumous works, seem to have been successful, surprisingly given the fraught circumstances of the 1790s. Most of these recommendations were made by a group associated with Clennell, Doubleday, and Marshall, who had been appointed librarian in 1799.[72] Turner's position in relation to this group has parallels with the position of Barnes and Percival in Manchester, as they struggled to mediate between radicals such as Thomas Cooper—whose *Tracts* (1789), with its controversial discussion of materialism, Doubleday presented to the Newcastle society in October 1795—and more conservative parts of the membership, many of whom would have been suspicious of Unitarians of whatever political stripe. Turner was more successful in keeping things together perhaps, certainly when one compares the resignations in Manchester over the vote on Priestley, but in 1817 he ended up supporting Marshall's expulsion, even if he afterwards continued to provide him with work publishing some of his sermons.[73]

The group around Clennell, Doubleday, and Marshall may have shared an idea that Wordsworth's "experiment" was part of a recalibration of poetry in relation to modern vernacular knowledge going right back to Aikin's essays on songwriting. De Quincey's effective rewriting of this history was a twist in the process whereby, to use Guillory's terms, "the conservators of literature have erased its origins even in the act of writing its history."[74] On the ground in Newcastle, these developments were caught up in arguments about whether useful knowledge might be better invested in books or scientific apparatus. They were not—within these circles, anyway—primarily cast in terms of any categorical opposition between science and literature. Turner's original plan, he later insisted, made the purchase of books subservient to the discussions to the monthly meetings (whatever their topic). From this point of view, privatized reading needed to feed into the collision of mind to reap its benefits. Nevertheless, committee minute books show that a wish for "a general library" had been expressed by the members soon after the society began."[75] The minutes and recommendation book for the next few years are taken up with many of the practical details and expenses of maintaining a physical library, from the question of which texts did not fall foul of the rules against religious and political controversy to payment for a permanent librarian, first Robert Spence and then, from 1799, the bookseller Marshall.[76] The committee noted that the membership seemed to increase with the purchase of books. Turner seems to have been less sanguine about the growth of the library, which he claimed was never central to his plan. The commitment to debate seemed to wane as the books increased. Fewer papers were being offered for discussion: Turner became concerned that book buying was draining resources and diverting energy. The faction associated with Marshall, joined by another local bookseller, Eneas Mackenzie, thought otherwise: the library provided a "bond of union" between the members. The phrase suggests they viewed books as things that enabled social life.[77]

Problems relating to these differing assumptions about what constituted knowledge and how it should be communicated started to surface when Turner decided to give a lecture series in chemistry. Turner's genuine commitment to this specific aspect of Priestley's influence was palpable right from his early *Speculations*. Judging by the first volume of

"Papers read at the Society" still held in the archives, topics of this kind provided the focus for more than half the early papers. Reflecting a desire to accelerate this aspect of the society's business among other members, Turner's friend and ally Thomas Bigge proposed a lectureship in "some of the most useful branches of Natural and Experimental Philosophy." The innovation was not just about content. It was also intended to reanimate the intellectual energy of the society.[78] For other members of the society, though, the lecture series that developed into "the New Institution" represented an unwelcome diversion of funds. A paper war broke out in 1808 that included vitriolic personal attacks on Turner. The opening salvo appeared in a letter simply signed "Mentor": "The Institution is considered as a heavy burthen upon the Society, and means are now taking to prevent the funds from being diverted from the original course, in the purchase of unnecessary or useless machines, expensive printing jobs, &c."[79] The dispute that followed spilled out into squibs and pamphlets and onto the pages of the local press. Little would be known of the detail if it were not for the assiduous collecting of Anthony Hedley, who used a whole interleaved volume to gather the manuscript and print record of the dispute as it ran over 1808 and up to the general meeting of March 1809.

Turner's initial antagonists were the silversmith Ralph Beilby, "an ardent Churchman," and Henry Moises, headmaster of the grammar school and early advocate of a "general library."[80] The "Mentor" letter hints at latent resentments about the influence of a Unitarian minister in the society: "A Minister of the Gospel might be better employed than in the vain pursuits of practical philosophy; they cannot perceive, either in the conduct or the opinions of philosophers, any thing which might give them a high opinion of its efficacy in leading minds to a serious sense of the duties of religion." Early in 1809 Mackenzie and Marshall—members of Turner's congregation—began to attack from another angle, more concerned with the question of access to knowledge. Apart from the expensive outlay of resources on apparatus, the roles of Sir John Swinburne and the Duke of Northumberland in raising finances encouraged their ire. Mackenzie published a two-page broadsheet sardonically presenting himself as someone "whose business engages my attention almost unremittingly, from an early hour" ranged against self-described "gentlemen of character."[81] The committee minutes are tight-lipped apart from the brief note in November 1808 depreciating the irruption of "personalities" into the society and earnestly recommended "every Member to avoid them." The matter was finally resolved at a meeting—the day after Mackenzie's two-page broadside was published—which preserved at least the facade of unity.[82]

The distaste shown for the incident by the historians of the society rather blinds them to the complex issues it raised.[83] One interpretation of the dispute sees it as the manifestation of an ongoing tension between the development of the library and Turner's "colloquium," as Derek Orange has described it, "consisting of a small number of active members meeting regularly for discussion and exchange of scientific intelligence." This interpretation, though, threatens to collapse a complex situation into an overly neat binary between "a reading club and a scientific society." Roy Porter seems closer to the mark in his suggestion that what the members wanted was "broad access to culture rather than science *per se*."[84] The problem was the different understandings of this broad culture, its modes of exchange, and who should gain access. Turner was always concerned that the society should generate knowledge and not just become a repository of books. His correspondence with Anderson, as we have seen, shows he consulted on the best means to fire the mechanism of "literary" conversation without descending into disputatiousness. The issue of enlivening exchange still concerned him after the dispute over the New Institution was resolved. In January 1814, Turner read to the parent society a paper justifying the foundation of what he describes as a "Literary Club," whose members were committed to writing papers for discussion. The library, Turner complained again, had become so much the principal object of attention that it was extinguishing the spirit of live exchange (only two papers, he pointed out, had been submitted to the monthly meetings in the past year).[85]

Turner and his ally James Losh, a friend of Wordsworth's from the 1790s, had already started a smaller "Literary Club" within the larger society. Each member had to write (or "procure to be written") a paper. Activity was being bought by contraction. In his diary, Losh described "the first meeting of our new society for literary conversation and writing essays" as a "pleasant rational evening and such as one that promises profit and amusement hereafter." Sometimes describing it as "our Conversation S[ociet]y," elsewhere in the diary he expressed impatience when the papers were too specialized.[86] For all its seeming celebration of the coming together of diverse perspectives, the spark of conversation was usually felt to work best when those involved were in sympathy with one another to the extent that disagreement would not descend into wrangling, a feeling that may have been lost in the monthly meetings of the Literary and Philosophical Society but preserved in the smaller if more exclusive Literary Club. Social class was always an issue in the way these judgments were made. On January 30, 1815, Losh's diary mentions "a sensible well written paper" by someone from "whose appearance and manners I should not have expected any good on the subject." The question of the social complexion of knowledge haunted the Literary and Philosophical Society. It was an issue Eneas Mackenzie complained about in 1823 when it moved to the grand building it currently occupies.[87]

These episodes were never a straight fight between science (the New Institution) and books ("a general library"). A more complicated and tangled field of forces stretched between chemical lectures, library resource, and the desire for participatory exchange within disparate social limits. These differences could be understood in Latour's terms as an argument over which objects—books or apparatuses—had representative authority in the society, but they were also shaped by questions about the mode of interaction (lecture or monthly meeting) and the definition of the participating group.[88] This last question was to become increasingly complicated after 1815 in the wider context of revived political unrest on the national scene accompanied by mounting pressure from the working classes for a place in the knowledge economy. The College of Arts and Sciences in Manchester had made some moves in this direction as early as 1785 by providing free tickets for lectures to skilled workers. In Newcastle, the same spirit took the form of advice on setting up book clubs and reading societies through the weekly periodical the *Oeconomist* (1798–99). Produced by Losh and a circle of friends that included Turner, the magazine sold for only one and a half pence, much more cheaply than most magazines at the time. In its pages was a recommended course of reading and "Hints of a Plan for a Book Club."[89] In his funeral sermon for Losh in 1833, Turner described the *Oeconomist* as "one of the first attempts to enlighten the mass of the people by means of cheap publications."[90] His comments placed the magazine in the context of initiatives that included the Mechanics' Institutes of the 1820s, discussed at greater length in chapter 3. The connection also hints at an assumption of stewardship that bedeviled such initiatives. The *Oeconomist* also signaled the trajectory of the "parent" society as it retreated from the confidence of the late 1780s and early 1790s into the war years. Explicitly framed, Klancher points out, as a defense against "the political difficulties of this awful moment," the *Oeconomist* represented a form of paternalistic outreach that turned the diffusion of knowledge toward personal improvement, even if one that still maintained the forms of social reading in its advice on clubbing together over books.[91] Its emphasis on "improvability of the rational faculties" came with sharp warnings "to beware of indulging the imagination and enfeebling the understanding by books of mere amusement" that seems at odds with the more generous take on the pleasures of taste in the early papers given in Manchester, although the *Oeconomist* did published poems, including Barbauld's "Mouse's Petition" and a sonnet to Jane Roscoe by her husband.

After 1815, a new wave of working-class radicalism was increasingly taking these matters into its own hands. Mackenzie and Marshall were actively involved in radical debating societies that were starting to spring up around Newcastle. Marshall's activities probably played their part in his dismissal as librarian at a time when the society was anxious about any radical associations. In 1817, the society wrote to the metropolitan press to distance itself from Thomas Spence, whose followers had recently been involved in the Spa Fields Riots in London; it had done the same thing in the crisis year of 1798.[92] Turner also asked Losh to seek legal reassurances that the societies' meetings would not be sanctioned under the government's crackdown on seditious meetings. Mackenzie as a local antiquarian kept up a commentary on the Literary and Philosophical Society that mixed local pride with a sense of the diminished possibilities entertained by the society, especially after it sought patronage among the gentry to pay for its grand new premises, opened by the Duke of Sussex.[93] Mackenzie challenged Turner's paternalist genealogy by claiming to have been the prime mover behind the Mechanics' Institute: "I have written the resolutions and appointed the speakers. . . .] Though the yearly subscription is small, I have no doubt we shall have as much money to spend as the other society [the Lit Phil], which is daily becoming more exclusive and aristocratic."[94]

The obituary of Robert Doubleday published in Marshall's *Northern Reformer's Monthly Magazine* the year of the opening of the grand new building claimed that the Literary and Philosophical Society had "arisen, like a phoenix, out of the ashes of the old institution." This earlier Philosophical Society of the 1770s had expelled Thomas Spence for delivering the first version of his radical land plan. Doubleday's participation in both societies suggested the possibility at least of a more complex and less respectable genealogy for the town's knowledge networks than its more respectable members wished to recognize. The Doubleday obituary also echoed Mackenzie's critical account of the society's progress to its fine new building. Raising funds had meant cozying up to "the governing part of the town." "By strictly avoiding all political controversy, and a careful attention to this matter in their selection of their Library," the obituary continued, "several of the aristocratical class have been induced to become members" with the result that "its general utility diminished."[95] Useful knowledge here is understood in a much more democratic way than was often the case in the 1820s, especially in the context of the decade's drive to set up Mechanics' Institutes. In the context of these contrasting views of the development of the Literary and Philosophical

Society, Turner's "literary club" might be seen as a step in a more general process that increasingly restricted the collision of mind into specially insulated conditions, small vetted groups, and purpose-built venues, where no spark might fly out to ignite any more general conflagration. The Literary and Philosophical Society of Newcastle upon Tyne entered its grand new home in 1823. The Manchester society had entered its own purpose-built premises in 1799. Both societies had to wait for well over a decade after their inaugurations to acquire their own homes. The Philosophical and Literary Society Leeds had its Philosophical Hall within three years of its foundation in 1819. There were special conditions in Leeds, discussed in chapter 3, but there was certainly an accelerating drive toward boundaries being drawn around the free exchange that Marshall and Mackenzie understood as the bond and union of the Literary and Philosophical Society.

[CHAPTER THREE]

IMPROVEMENT REDUX

Liverpool, Leeds, and Sheffield, 1812–32

Britain and the world after the Napoleonic Wars were very different places than they had been when the Manchester Literary and Philosophical Society was founded in 1781. Contrary to Linda Colley's idea of Britons emerging from the war effort united as a nation, deep-seated differences had been incubated in the years of conflict, exacerbated by class and region, not least as those differences were rapidly reconfiguring in relation to the Industrial Revolution.[1] Among the ruling classes, still largely a landed oligarchy, the 1820s saw the beginning of the slow process of reimagining Britain as a workshop of the world that would export manufactured goods and import most of its food. The Tory administrations of Lord Liverpool and his successors, despite their traditional reliance on the support of country gentlemen hostile to reform, reacted to these changes with cautious pragmatism.[2] Liverpool and, especially, his lieutenant William Huskisson could see the importance of the cotton manufactures and the technological innovations in engineering, but they remained ambivalent enough about them to equivocate over public funding for a statue of James Watt after his death in 1819. Looking back from 1826, Charles Lyell hailed "the rise and swift growth of cities, and the sudden affluence to which commercial or manufacturing industry has raised districts hitherto insignificant and thinly peopled."[3] Provincial public opinion had certainly been feeling its strength, congratulating itself on successful campaigns against the slave trade (1807) and the restrictions of the Orders in Council (1812). The prospects of synchronous improvement in the arts and sciences together remained a pleasing prospect in such quarters, even if the terms of their relationship were far from unquestioned. Other—mainly short-lived—literary and philosophical societies had followed the examples of Manchester and Newcastle in the war years. Only the cessation of large-scale international conflict brought renewed confidence in the possibilities of emulating them on a larger scale across the region covered by this book.[4] Joseph Hunter of Sheffield, for instance, looked to the resumption of improvement after "a state of painful disunion" in 1819, and he had his wishes fulfilled when the Sheffield Literary and Philosophical Society was established at the end of 1822.[5] In Leeds, a Philosophical and Literary Society was set up in 1819 after a debate in the pages of the local liberal-Whig paper, the *Leeds Mercury*.[6] Figures such as Edward Baines Sr. and Jr., both editors of the *Mercury*; Thomas Asline Ward in Sheffield; and James Losh in Newcastle upon Tyne—all of whom took up leadership roles in the literary and philosophical societies of their respective cities—were to play important parts in agitation surrounding the Reform Bill of 1832. Roscoe had an earlier political victory when, during his brief period as member of Parliament (MP) for Liverpool in 1806–7, he helped steer the bill for the abolition of the slave trade through Parliament. The Liverpool Literary and Philosophical Society set up in 1812 was very much the product of his circle, even if financial difficulties meant he did not become active in it until 1817.

Although still devoted to the idea of a space of knowledge free from the divisive issues of party and religion, in many ways the literary and philosophical societies look like the engines of a liberal-Whig faith in reform in the broadest sense. Most of those named in the foregoing paragraph, for instance, were associated with Henry Brougham's various campaigns against "Old Corruption."[7] They tended to present this liberal vision of improvement as transcending divisions of sect and party, but others saw in it the emergence of a distinctive political and cultural phenomenon, clearly wedded to the manufacturing interest. William Cobbett, with typical vehemence, called out the elder Baines as "Brougham's grand puffer, THE GREAT LIAR OF THE NORTH, publisher of that mass of lies and nonsense called the Leeds Mercury . . . this swelled up, greedy and unprincipled puffer who has been the deluder of Yorkshire for twenty years past."[8] The proliferation of knowledge institutions might appear to be the partial payment of a peace dividend. However, any prosperity was short-circuited by the widespread unemployment of returning soldiers, a series of downturns in the trade cycle, and then a spectacular financial crash in 1825, none of which left the societies untouched. The struggle for parliamentary reform revived only to be vigorously put down by Lord Liverpool's government, most obviously in the form of the Six Acts of 1819. Freedom of opinion was a cardinal point of the faith in improvement, especially among those Dissenters loyal to the dimming memory of Joseph Priestley, but faced with an increasingly organized working class and calls for radical reform, even those who held to this inheritance became anxious about limits, an anxiety made clear in the changes at Newcastle when it sought aristocratic patronage for its grand new home it moved into in 1823.

The Peterloo Massacre of August 1819 provides a telling critical point in the disappointment of hopes for the postwar settlement, but its significance is complicated. The Manchester magistracy was largely acting in the interests of "Old Corruption" rather than the manufacturing classes, at least in any direct sense.[9] Present—it seems as observers—on the day of Peterloo were the millowner Samuel Greg and his son Robert Hyde Greg. Appalled at the conduct of the militia, they brought forward their neighbor the Reverend Edward Stanley, rector of Alderley, as a witness to the illegality of the magistrates' actions on the day. Nevertheless, their status as observers speaks of the limits to their sympathies.[10] The Manchester journalist Archibald Prentice may have placed Greg among those who had "remained true to his early principles" in the postwar period, along with the recently deceased Thomas Walker, but those principles did not readily translate into the mass platform politics of a new era.[11] A few days after the massacre, Hannah Greg wrote to her daughter Bessy that "the savage & intemperate Character of the populace will make a large party in favour of the Suppression—*the Mode of it* was the dreadful business." She ended her letter with a paranoid fantasy that "the Radicals in this neighbourhood go the full length of Equalization of property."[12]

Also present at Peterloo, probably on the platform with Henry "Orator" Hunt, was Edward Baines Jr. He too was an observer rather than a participant, reporting on proceedings for the *Leeds Mercury*, which had played a part in exposing the spy "Oliver" in the run-up to the meeting. Again, though, it campaigned against mass platform politics and radical reform. Edward Baines Sr. urged those looking for universal male suffrage to seek financial help instead or even assistance with emigration to North America.[13] Around this time, Baines father and son were also putting their energies into the creation of the Philosophical and Literary Society at Leeds. Their work there was in part an attempt to cement the cultural authority of a liberal-Whig settlement. Even within the emergent urban elite of Leeds that clustered around the institution, however, their influence was far from uncontested, especially when it came to their attempts to have political economy enshrined as a kind of master narrative. "Bainesocracy," as it came to be known in Leeds, was committed to political economy as the driving discipline of improvement, placing its greatest emphasis on the creative power of technological innovation and free trade, but the subject struggled to achieve validation, never mind hegemony, in these institutions across the 1820s. "Improvement" in the 1820s offered a landscape of shifting, grinding plates rather than any integrated new hegemony, defined as much by its differences, as by any sense of the triumph of a coherent set of values, despite every effort to present itself to the world in that aspect.

THE FLORENCE OF THE NORTH

Agitation in the Leeds newspapers to start a literary and philosophical society explicitly responded to a call to arms made by William Roscoe in his inaugural address to the Liverpool Royal Institution in November 1817.[14] A member of the Manchester society from 1784, he had praised the role of institutions in supporting provincial improvement in the arts and sciences from as early as his *Ode, On the Institution of a Society in Liverpool, for the Encouragement of Designing, Drawing, Painting etc* (1774). In 1802, speaking at the opening of Liverpool's Botanic Garden, he had argued for "the great superiority of a public institution over private collections in promoting botanical sciences," implicitly contrasting the combined powers of a commercial town against aristocratic patronage.[15] These collective enterprises, Roscoe argued, had "already excited a spirit of emulation in some of the principal towns of the kingdom, where proposals have been published for institutions on a similar plan." After the several false starts, detailed in chapter 2, Liverpool was finally rewarded with its own Literary and Philosophical Society in 1812. Surprisingly, Roscoe was not initially involved with the new society, but many of those in his circle were. The group that met to discuss founding a new society in February 1812 included his old Rathbone allies, their friend the Unitarian minister Theophilus Houlbrooke, and Thomas Traill, who had worked with Roscoe at the Botanic Garden.[16] Roscoe's close friend and staunch ally William Shepherd was a member by March 1812, as was James Currie's son and John Bostock, stepson of John Yates, whose sermon against the slave trade had rocked Hannah Greg in 1788. Shepherd successfully proposed William Henry—son of the cofounder of the Manchester society—at the May 1812 meeting. The powers of reproduction in these networks is startling. The meetings discussed "literary intelligence" and more formal papers: William Tartt, for instance, spoke on the commonsense philosophy of Thomas Reid and Dugald Stewart, always major influences in these circles.[17] Traill encouraged the young Quaker architect Thomas Rickman to give a paper on the topic of what was to become his influential *Attempt to Discriminate the Styles of English Architecture* (1817). His friend Edmund Aikin, son of John Aikin Jr., also joined the society. At the meeting that elected Rickman, a poem was presented in celebration of Roscoe's role in the city's progress. The following November he was kept in their minds by the donation of a medallion

FIGURE 6. "Liverpool Royal Institution, Colquitt Street." Drawn by
G. and C. Pyne. Engraved by F. Hay. Additional note below the title
reads, "To Wm Roscoe, Esq. This Plate Is Respectfully Inscribed,
By The Publishers. Fisher, Son & Co. London 1829." Private collection.

celebrating his achievements. Roscoe himself, struggling with financial
difficulties over this period, only applied to join in December 1817, at
which point—inevitably enough—the meeting unanimously invited him
to become president.[18]

When Roscoe opened the Liverpool Royal Institution on November 25,
1817, he celebrated the provision of a civic space dedicated to knowledge,
including rooms for the Literary and Philosophical Society, on the basis
of pledges of funding made at a public meeting back in 1814.[19] Roscoe sat
on the committee with the plantation owner Sir John Gladstone. They
had once been loosely allied in the campaigns against the town's Tory
oligarchy, Gladstone supporting Roscoe in the 1806 election on an abolitionist ticket. A decade later Gladstone had become the major spokesman
for the sugar interest after acquiring plantations in Demerara and elsewhere.[20] Nevertheless, despite these differences, including Gladstone's
initially standing in opposition to Roscoe, the broad-based support of
wealthy merchants made sure money was quickly raised, with even the
town's Common Council lending its aid.[21] The institution was intended to
provide courses of lectures for the sons of the merchant elite who did not
wish for the expense of Cambridge or Oxford, or were otherwise barred

from entry. It also supported a library and museum as well as the Literary and Philosophical Society, and it provided space for the Academy of Artists and—from 1826—for a philomathic society (for the attainment of knowledge by discussion), not to mention supporting plans for an observatory and developing a series of schools. From the very beginning, it lay claim to a broad civic role that would "diffuse a general taste for scientific and literary subjects, so as to enable the town of Liverpool to keep up with, if not excel, other populous communities, as well abroad as at home."[22] The sheer breadth of its activities suggests the hunger for a provincial higher education institution in the English regions. Its eventual downfall later in the nineteenth century probably resulted from the strain placed on its resources by trying to do too much.[23]

By 1817, Roscoe was acquiring something of the status of an elder statesman who could rise above partisan differences. His scholarly endeavors had brought international acclaim, most conspicuously through his *Life of Lorenzo di Medici* (1795) and *The Pontificate of Leo the Tenth* (1805). After the collapse of his financial interests in 1816, one correspondent told William Shepherd that even "those who disapproved of the violence of his Politics, must always have admired and loved the Scholar & the Man."[24] Early in its life, William Dixon had argued that the Literary and Philosophical Society could host "communication unclouded by Political animadversion or Sensual excess." Edward Baines Sr. later described its activities as more like "*regulated conversation* than *debate*."[25] Roscoe's inaugural address for the LRI sounded the same accommodating note about the arts and sciences advancing together under the aegis of commerce, despite the historical differences between the American and West India merchants, abolitionists and slavers, Dissenters and Anglicans, who all made up his audience. The same principle underpinned his two Italian cultural histories, wherein he presented the city-states as flourishing under a system of liberty until the Medici corrupted republican government into an oligarchy. Parallels with the situation in Liverpool where Roscoe and his friends had waged a long war against the self-perpetuating oligarchy of the Common Council were obvious.[26] Roscoe's friend John Aikin Jr. devoted a lengthy appendix to the story of its usurpation of the original rights of the freemen of Liverpool in his *Description of Manchester*, but Roscoe's 1817 address veered away from conflicts of the past to tell a story more flattering to the commercial interest as a whole. Aikin may not have been entirely tongue-in-cheek when he wrote to Roscoe soon afterward to express his hopes that one day the institution might "convert Liverpool into an Athens or a Florence."[27] The role of slavery in generating this wealth, the differences between Gladstone and Roscoe, seem laundered away in a celebration of commercial liberty guided by the LRI. *Blackwood's*, not yet quite the Tory magazine it would shortly become, likewise heaped praise on the idea, using it to browbeat the association of Cambridge and Oxford with monasticism.[28] Roscoe sent a copy of his speech to Thomas Jefferson, who wrote back to tell him "your Liverpool institution will also aid us in the organisation of our new University [of Virginia]."[29]

Where it was received rather less warmly was at the Royal Institution in London, as Jon Klancher has shown. Its new *Journal of Science and the Art* published a hostile review partly predicated on a predictable objection to provincial confidence in the alliance between trade and knowledge. Under the spell of Humphry Davy's bravura performances in its lecture theater, the Royal Institution in London was increasingly a site of aristocratic patronage. What also seems to have triggered the irritation of the London society was Roscoe's belief in the effects of historical circumstances on both the arts and sciences: "It is to the influence of moral causes, to these dispositions and arrangements in the affairs of mankind, that are particularly within our own power, that we are to seek for the reasons of the progress or decline of liberal studies" (26). There was nothing intrinsic in the development of either domain, Roscoe believed; both were equally sensitive to arrangements of power. For the *Journal of Science and the Arts*, on the other hand, there were intrinsic differences: "Painting, sculpture, poetry, music, magic, and astrology, have been peculiarly subject to these alternations of real and sometimes imaginary rise and decline." With regard to the sciences, argued its reviewer, "no person will hesitate to pronounce that the patrimony of such learning is continually improving, and sometimes increasing." Roscoe, in sharp contrast, as Klancher points out, "treated the two domains as equally" vulnerable to the rise and fall of states, and also suggested both were "fundamental to local and national prosperity."[30]

The shadow of a new kind of oligarchy haunted Roscoe's speech in the fear that manufacturers might turn into a "commercial aristocracy," to use a phrase of William Turner's.[31] Early opinion in the Liverpool Literary and Philosophical Society had been relaxed about the relationship between improvement and industry: "The enlarged state of our home Manufactures," said Dixon, "furnishes an ample field for Mathematical investigation and Chemical experiment."[32] Roscoe was rather less sanguine: "The effects of manufactures is different;" he thought, "and upon the whole not so conducive perhaps as agriculture to the formation of intellectual character" (43). Here one might see why someone with Jefferson's agrarian prejudices admired the paper. The problem for Roscoe was the division of labor and the consolidation of capital in fewer and fewer hands. Roscoe gave it an inflection that recalled the Scottish Enlightenment debates in which he was well versed.[33] In the essay he had sent to the Manchester society back in the 1780s, his reservations had been with the narrowing effects of specialism engendered by scientific studies. In 1817, his mind seems to have been turning toward the specific case of manufactures and, in particular, on the "unavoidable tendency of these employments to contract or deaden the intellect, and to reduce the powers both of mind and body to a machine, in which the individual almost loses his identity and becomes only a part of a more complicated apparatus" (43–44). The general terms of the address certainly agreed with Dugald Stewart's view, quoted in it later on, that "all the different improvements in arts, in commerce, and in the sciences," were "co-operating to promote the union, the happiness, and the virtue of mankind" (71–72). Eager to retain the nonconfrontational line developed through the lecture, he appended a note to the published version of his speech that qualified his criticism of manufactures by acknowledging that "sufficient has certainly been done, in some of our largest establishments, to prove that the comfort and respectability of this laborious part of the community may be attained not only without detriment or expence, but with great and positive advantages to those who have adopted so judicious and humane a plan" (44). Perhaps he was thinking of friends such as the Gregs at Quarry Bank, where he was a regular visitor, or even Robert Owen, whom he met and corresponded with around 1813. Nevertheless, despite their reputations as model employers, the "condition of the persons employed," as Roscoe put it, was to become an increasingly fraught issue in the 1820s that threatened the surface unity of knowledge institutions around the region.[34]

Perhaps because of the influence of Roscoe, however, political economy did not play a big part in the syllabus at the LRI. Not originally proposed as a subject for a lecture series at Liverpool, J. R. McCulloch, sometimes described as the first professional political economist, did give a series in late 1824, even offering the first gratis.[35] Although the lectures were praised by B. A. Heywood (of the banking family), Roscoe's successor as president, who described the subject as "of the utmost importance to the best interests of the nation," it still didn't catch on as a popular topic at the LRI. Mixing the report on McCulloch with news of lectures by Traill on science and others on Italian culture, even Heywood seemed most concerned with refuting critics who had accused the institution of "incongruously mixing . . . the praise of Phidias and Michel Angelo, with admiration for commercial excellence."[36] Other developments in Liverpool's institutional architecture over the decade were subject to related tensions. The opening of a Mechanics' and Apprentices' Library was celebrated with great pomp in 1823, including speeches by Sir John

Gladstone and the display of a white silken banner sent from the apprentices of New York with the name "ROSCOE" emblazoned on it.[37] "Controversial divinity" and "party politics" were, as usual, excluded from the library, but standard works on religion and "approved writings" on political economy and legislation were allowed, with even "Approved Works of Fiction" finding space on the shelves.[38] The library quickly became a School of Arts that offered classes and lectures. Traill played the same major role as he did at the LRI, encouraging a broad range of books in the library and allowing some participation of the working classes in the management committee, to the approval of Henry Brougham. Somewhat prematurely, his 1825 address claimed that "it was no longer necessary to offer any defence of a principle so generally acknowledged as the utility of the diffusion of knowledge among all classes of society," but his speech was rather less confident than these sentiments might suggest. Aware that Leeds and Manchester had chosen a much less democratic management structure, he feared that "the inexperience of the operative classes in the management of such undertakings" had sometimes directed its choices "more to amusing than to useful objects." For all the relative diversity of its library, later envied by Edward Baines Jr. in Leeds, Traill insisted that its primary aim should be "communicating sound mechanical principles to the working classes," a principle that failed to drum up the expected enthusiasm, as was the case in nearly all these initiatives.[39]

Any idea of a stable and united commercial hegemony in Liverpool were disturbed when the question of slavery resurfaced to undermine the armistice between the various factions of merchant opinion, even ruffling the surface of the minute books of the Literary and Philosophical Society. The Quaker merchant James Cropper, a foundational member of the Literary and Philosophical Society, close to the Rathbones, drew on Adam Smith's *Wealth of Nations* to advance the argument that slavery would always be driven out by the productivity of free labor. Many advocates of the abolition of the slave trade in 1807 had mistakenly assumed that slavery itself would naturally wither away with the trade, as Roscoe later admitted to Cropper.[40] Instead, emancipation had become mired in arguments about policing international waters. Cropper helped reignite the national campaign by arguing against state support of the West Indian economy through preferential tariffs. The government made encouraging noises but did nothing. In Liverpool itself, Cropper set up a local society for the "mitigation & gradual Abolition of Slavery," inviting his friend Roscoe to lend it his authority as president.[41] An acrimonious newspaper war flared in the Liverpool press between Cropper and Gladstone. Gladstone pointed out that until recently Cropper had been an importer of American cotton. Now that he had turned to become an importer of East

Indian sugar, Gladstone argued, Cropper had self-interested motives for his new campaign. Gladstone, on his side, presented his introduction of modern factory discipline to the plantations as a sign of an improving spirit, but he was attacked by hard-line planters of the old school for innovations that also included inviting missionaries onto his estates. The latter were blamed for the Demerara uprising of 1823—centered on Gladstone's estate and led by his enslaved namesake Jack Gladstone—partly because they were believed to have spread news of an imminent decree for emancipation. Whatever Gladstone's own claims to be an improver intent on meliorating the worst effects of slavery, he showed few qualms about supporting the brutal repression of the uprising. These tensions appeared at the Literary and Philosophical Society when the Rev. William Hinch presented a paper at the end of 1825 called "Reflections on Slavery among the Ancients." Classical history, as so often in these societies, circumvented the rules against topical controversies. Unusually, the minute books record something of the way the discussion went. Thomas Fletcher, an ally of Gladstone's who had gone into print against Cropper in the newspaper war, argued that the treadmill was "less severe than the flail . . . the judicious employment of this machine as an engine of punishment is neither cruel nor unjust."[42] Here was improvement from the Gladstonian point of view!

Gladstone came to believe that Roscoe, Traill, and their allies had been able to "infect with radicalism a new generation of young men."[43] Traill's memoir of Roscoe, delivered at a meeting of the Literary and Philosophical Society in the heady atmosphere building up to the Reform Bill, had no compunction about extensively detailing his active support of the French Revolution in the 1790s, including his widely circulated song, "From the vine-covered hills of France," and also warmly praised his lifelong abolitionism.[44] Whatever his radical past, Roscoe's broader vision of the cultural possibilities of commercial prosperity created a host of disciples, but many of them, as we shall see in the case of his imitators in Leeds, did not share his ambivalence about the accumulation of capital. Cropper's belief in political economy as a logic of liberty in many ways captures the new spirit of improvement in the 1820s, as Eric Williams suggested in his epochal reading of the death blow given to West Indian monopolists by the spirit of free trade and industrial expansion, but it was not economic arguments that inspired the wider resurgence of the abolitionist movement in Britain.[45] Public opinion there only really rallied to the suffering of the enslaved people after the death in prison of the London Missionary Society's John Smith. Women evangelicals played a major role in this new burst of abolitionism, including Mary Anne Rawson, who founded a Sheffield Female Anti-Slavery Society in 1825.[46] Her collaborations with

James Montgomery were powerful engines of philanthropic activism, driven by a religious energy not usually encouraged at the literary and philosophical societies fearful of the divisive power of zeal. Be that as it may, Montgomery and some of his male associates at least, Rawson being excluded on grounds of her gender, became important in the Sheffield Literary and Philosophical Society from its beginning. On the other hand, advocates of political economy as a value-neutral system of knowledge with a rightful place at the literary and philosophical societies faced battles of their own in the 1820s as they were suspected of peddling the profit-driven cant of the manufacturing interest, the formation that even from his early days at the Manchester society Roscoe had feared might pervert his vision of a virtuous union of commerce, science, and the arts.

"BAINESOCRACY" AND ITS DISCONTENTS

Across the Pennines in Leeds, finally linked to Liverpool by the completion of the Leeds-Liverpool canal in 1816, William Roscoe's 1817 speech at the opening of the Liverpool Royal Institute (LRI) threw into relief its own lack of knowledge institutions, regretted in Edward Baines Sr.'s *Gazetteer* of the town: "With the exception of those arts which have an immediate reference to Commerce and Manufactures, Philosophical researches are not much cultivated in Leeds; still less do Literary pursuits engage the attention of its inhabitants."[47] Leeds at this time was a thriving textile town, dominated by wool, worsted, and flax manufactures, as it long had been. Trailing after Manchester in terms of technical innovation, it was witnessing the early stages of a massive transformation toward the factory system led by the two major industrialists, Benjamin Gott, in wool, and John Marshall, in flax, who had started building mills on a grand scale in the 1790s.[48] These were men who had amassed enough capital to allow them to rise above the fluctuations in trade and involve themselves in cultural endeavors. Politically, the town was unreformed, dominated by a closed Tory corporation, still without a member of Parliament of its own, although Baines had started to campaign for the reform of the workhouse and other local institutions.[49] His comment in the *Directory*—reflecting his general advocacy of improvement for the town—prompted a debate in the *Mercury*, as Baines had presumably intended, beginning with a letter from "Leodiensian" (probably his son Edward), printed on September 26, 1818. The letter called for the formation of a society whose purpose would be the "discussion of subjects, historical, literary, and philosophical."[50] A note alluded to Roscoe's speech at the LRI and celebrated the institution's role in uniting "commerce" and "literature" under the same roof in order to blend "the bold, vigorous and active character of the one with the elegant accomplishments and lighter graces of the other," rather underplaying, perhaps, what Roscoe had to say about the active importance of the arts.

Much the same line was reiterated in the generally positive correspondence that followed in the *Mercury*. On October 24, 1818, one writer noted the importance of "literature as a relief to the severe and dry study of science," although more discordant voices followed. Someone using the pseudonym Juvenis, writing on October 31, expressed doubts about a provincial town sustaining this kind of cultural institution. Partly the anxiety was about the limits to improvement and the continuing fear that the collision of mind might be the harbinger of "faction and contention." Juvenis explicitly deferred to the metropolitan model being developed at the Royal Institution in London, echoing the critical tenor of the review of Roscoe's speech in the *Journal of Arts and Sciences*. Other correspondents wanted the scope of the Leeds society to be more narrowly scientific after the fashion of earlier short-lived Leeds societies that Priestley and the physician William Hey had encouraged.[51] Their opposition to the familiar rubric of "Literary *and* Philosophical" had clearly not been persuaded by Roscoe's restatement of the alliance of "Physics and Belles Lettres." Better, from these perspectives, to rely on traditional channels that operated from high to low and radiated out from metropolitan authority. Better also to avoid topics that might threaten the boundaries of "regulated conversation."

These doubters aside, the idea that the town needed such a society generated enough enthusiasm for a public meeting to be called in December 1818. The venerable Hey immediately pushed for a solely scientific focus. The consensus, encouraged by the elder Baines, argued that "the society would interest a much greater number of persons and would consequently be more useful, if it had literature among its objects, like the societies of Liverpool and Manchester."[52] Hey acknowledged that the meeting was against him, and he promptly withdrew. The conciliatory approach that was to mark the society's progress prevailed to the extent that the key terms were reversed in the title of the Leeds Philosophical and Literary Society. Still, the schedule over its first ten years did include lectures and papers on "modern literature." Thomas Campbell, the star of the London circuit, who had already lectured at the LRI, was invited, and even Coleridge (without success in either case). The passing of Sir Walter Scott was commemorated with solemnity in 1832 as a further sign of the Leeds society's seriousness about imaginative literature.[53] The usual rule excluding politics and religion spoke to its aspiration to provide a civic space beyond party and denominational divisions. R. J. Morris's detailed account of Leeds in these decades presents the society as negotiating a safe haven from party and denominational divisions. It could not, however, heal the fissures beyond its walls, nor could they be entirely stifled within them, much as the society tried to prevent notice of them reaching the outside world.

Over the first few uncertain months of 1819, the *Leeds Mercury* kept up a steady stream of encouraging reports, certainly as compared with the more tight-lipped coverage provided in its Tory rival the *Leeds Intelligencer*.[54] The *Intelligencer* was on the alert for a covertly liberal-Whig project and for years suspected the Leeds Philosophical and Literary Society of being a creature of "Bainesocracy."[55] Apart from the support gained in the *Mercury*, the short-lived *Leeds Literary Observer* published a long essay in January 1819, also probably by Edward Baines Jr., welcoming the new society and seconding the resistance to Hey's proposals. Advertised in the same day's *Mercury*, the essay looks like part of an orchestrated campaign from the Baines camp to present the society as the natural successor to a variety of smaller societies based on religious denomination. The large new "mixed" society, in which "men of different political views and religious feelings unite," thus appears as the result of a synthesis of difference from which everyone gains "a lively animation" and "that expansion which is the result of great variety."[56] This credo had been intrinsic to the vision of the literary and philosophical societies from the beginning, despite their struggles to distance it from too close an association with the freethinking of Dissent, just as the society in in Leeds struggled to escape the suspicions of the *Intelligencer* in this regard. By the 1820s, this association was becoming hardened in the minds of its opponents into the more specific idea of a manufacturing interest hostile to the traditional authority of the church and state and eager to reform institutions out of its own self-interest.

The association was strongly identified with the Baines-Marshall alliance in Leeds as they managed to steer the aristocratic Whigs of the county—centered on the seat of the Fitzwilliam family at Wentworth House—toward an alliance with the manufacturing interest. When Brougham replaced John Marshall as the county MP at the 1830 election, it appeared the fulfillment of a deep-laid plan.[57] Over the course of the 1820s, the *Leeds Mercury* consolidated its position as the most important organ of middle-class opinion across the region and beyond. T. B. Macaulay described it as "now decidedly the best and most widely circulated provincial paper in England."[58] The term "liberal-Whig" is a useful way of describing its orientation, not least because it captures its support for the new republics of Europe and South America with its growing advocacy of political economy as a knowledge system that transcended the traditional social hierarchies of party politics. The *Leeds Literary Observer* essay was

robust in its welcome of the new society's freedom from aristocratic patronage: "All cringing servility to superior rank or fortune, ought to be
most studiously avoided. If this be once permitted, it will prove the certain bane of all free and manly discussion."[59] The sentiment was echoed
throughout the early reports, although usually less polemically expressed,
as one might expect given the slight preponderance of Tory voters in the
general membership. Within this constituency, Michael Sadler formed a
"radical Tory" opposition, which aimed to prevent the society becoming
an incubator for liberal reform "in an age"—as Sadler put it to the Leeds
Pitt Club in 1819—"when it appears as though every institution amongst
us must be re-argued; when many in this country place so low a value on the
stock of wisdom treasured up for us by our ancestors." Sadler's candidacy
against Macaulay—imported from London by the Whigs—at the general
election of December 1832 was emblematic of the differences that had
churned beneath the surface of the society over the previous decade.[60]

The society was never simply the mouthpiece of the Baines-Marshall
group. Present at the first meeting in December 1818, Sadler served as vice
president and then president from 1828 to 1830 to provide a rallying point
against "Bainesocracy."[61] On the other hand, Gott and Marshall, though
Tory and Whig, worked together to fund the institution, their political
and religious differences not disabling their manufacturing interests.
Their wealth meant that from very early on a decision could be taken to
invest in a purpose-built home for the society in what became the Philosophical Hall.[62] If the society was proud of its independence from aristocratic influence, it was content to be influenced from within the ranks
of the middle classes as proof of the town's functioning meritocracy.[63]
Even in its structure, though, an internal hierarchy prevailed between
the financial influence of the proprietary members—some 20 percent of
whom were either from the Gott or Marshall families—and the professional subscription members who provided the day-to-day energies.[64] The
Baines-Marshall alliance blurs this distinction a little. Edward Baines
Sr. was a proprietary shareholder. With the elder Baines busy running
a newspaper with broader political interests, it was his son who was most
active at the society's meetings. Marshall, on the other hand, despite being a man of business, was—much more than Gott—actively engaged as
a polemicist for political economy. He gave papers "On the production of
Wealth and the Propriety of discussing Subjects of Political Economy as
distinguished to Politics" in 1824 and "On the Present State of Education
in England" in 1826. He also published a textbook, *The Economy of Social
Life* (1825), with an epigraph from Brougham: "That History, the nature
of the Constitution, the doctrines of Political Economy, may safely be
disseminated in a cheap form, no man now-a-days will be hardy enough

to deny." The triad was very much Marshall's idea of the liberal syllabus to be promoted in the Mechanics' Institutes.[65]

Unfortunately for the Baines-Marshall axis, Sadler and his allies thought political economy to be as partisan as any other belief system. Marshall gave them provocation enough when his textbook complained that there were plenty of religious books but "none which appear to me to give true ideas of the mechanism of society, of the relative bearing of the different classes of mankind, of the objects and interests of each, and in short of the rudiments of economical science."[66] His opponents in the ten-hours movement (to shorten the standard workday from twelve hours to ten) undermined his pretensions to moral leadership by exposing the employment of children in his factories. In September 1832, Marshall's son mocked Sadler's "coquetry with the Radicals" to Brougham.[67] Certainly the alliance may not have helped Sadler with Tories of Gott's ilk, but neither were Marshall and his lieutenant Baines—Cobbett's "Great Liar of the North"—easily credited as champions of value-neutral knowledge. If the acrimony generated by these disputes outside the society did not destroy it, there is certainly evidence from the minute books and elsewhere that they put pressure on the rules about avoiding political and religious topics.

The first meeting in the Philosophical Hall was in April 1821, when the society heard Charles Turner Thackrah's *Introductory Discourse* (1821), the winner of a competition to give the society's inaugural address. Thackrah was the town surgeon, recently returned from Guy's hospital, where he had been a contemporary of John Keats. Thackrah's *Discourse* places him firmly in the line of literary physicians discussed in chapter 4, although it was only later in his career that he displayed their appetite for social inquiry critical of the factory system.[68] At this stage, no impulse to ruffle the appearance of consensus appeared in his rather anodyne address. Like Roscoe, like nearly every one of these societies, Thackrah celebrated the progress of improvement with the customary recognition of the importance of association to the diffusion of knowledge. He lacked the cultural authority Roscoe could command at Liverpool—even his right to give the speech was questioned when the ballot was queried—but the general terms of his *Introductory Discourse* were not dissimilar from the address at the LRI in 1817. In that regard, Thackrah's speech stayed in key with the Leeds society's original Prospectus, which had compared its role in spreading intellectual enlightenment to the gas lighting that had recently been introduced to parts of the town. In both instances improvement was "elite led," to use Morris's phrase, by a group that assumed its influence would radiate out to those excluded from direct participation: "Thus a taste for science and literature will be gradually diffused through the different ranks of society, and literary friendships will be formed, perhaps the most durable and beneficial of any."[69] The debates certainly provided "a sounding board," as Morris puts it, for "contemporary issues and ideas" and facilitated their application in Leeds. Very shortly after the Whig physician James Williamson gave a paper on "Early Education and Infant Schools," for instance, the Leeds Infant School Society was founded. The Mechanics' Institute drew on the older society for support in various ways.[70] John Marshall Jr. kept Brougham abreast of its origins and development, explaining why Leeds had followed the Edinburgh model propounded by Leonard Horner to avoid falling into the error—as he saw it—of giving "too much of the direction of the establishment to the Mechanics themselves." It was a policy to which Brougham was generally opposed, as he made clear in his *Practical Observations on the Education of the People* (1825), despite praising the initiative at Leeds (for which he credited Gott and Marshall). Edward Baines Jr. later regretted that he let the elder Marshall persuade him that the Mechanics' Institute should not include literary material in its library. Instead it was to be dominated by technical education, and the proselytism of the elder Marshall's *Economics of Social Life*, despite the opposition on this score that his son also reported to Brougham.[71] Shortly afterward, given the opportunity at a meeting in Bradford to discuss setting up a Mechanics' Institute there, the younger Baines urged his audience not to simply encourage "scientific pursuits" but also to establish a library "to consist of works of arts and science, as well as in general literature, only excluding those on religion and politics."[72] From the beginning, he had believed that a more diversified remit was needed if the working classes were going to attend after twelve hours of daily labor.

At the Philosophical and Literary Society, the elder Marshall had not confined himself to political economy. He also gave papers on "The Relative Happiness of Cultivated Society and the Savage" (1820) and "On the Theory of the Foundations of the Earth" (1821), topics with more opportunity to provoke than the generalities of Thackrah's *Introductory Discourse*.[73] Coming from a Unitarian, discussions of the physical origins of the earth were always likely to be eyed warily by Anglicans and evangelicals. Details of Marshall's paper were leaked in the *Intelligencer*, which avoided making the obvious religious connection (it probably didn't need to) but sneered at Marshall's intellectual pretensions by suggesting that he had lifted the content from "a lecture addressed to a small Philosophical Society still in existence."[74] The Council hurriedly met to discuss the smear, concerned at the ruffling of surface unity. A regulation was passed to ban such leaks. A stiff letter was addressed to the *Intelligencer*'s editor.

Whoever was responsible for the leak may have felt that Marshall was being allowed to flout the rules on religion and politics. The *Intelligencer* continued to monitor the relationship between religion and science at the society. In February 1822, it praised a public lecture on pneumatics for "properly" concluding that the science only contributed to the admiration of the Almighty. At the end of the same year, it published an attack on Brougham's friends at the *Edinburgh Review* that might serve—whether its central pun was intended or not—as a summary of its attitude towards the Baines-Marshall group in the society, "through its prostituted pages the liberals are in the habit of feeling the pulse of the public, and of giving the watchword to their allies before they marshal their forces for any premeditated exploit of importance."[75]

The first papers Edward Baines Jr. delivered to the society almost seem designed to provoke the *Intelligencer*. Superficially in step with Thackrah's attempts to harmonize modern improvement with the achievements of classical Greece in his *Introductory Discourse*, they were in truth a barely concealed attempt to introduce the liberal perspectives of the *Leeds Mercury* as the only proper account of historical change. On April 12, 1822, Baines spoke on the "Rise of Art, Science, and Literature among the Athenians." Notebook drafts open with the idea that a "man is the creature of education." Both the intellectual and corporeal capacities of human beings, Baines argued, "allow wonderfully different degree[s] of improvement in their nature, & skill in their ['application' crossed out] employment." He goes on in familiar style to press the analogy between the numerous small trading boats in Athenian harbors and the debates of citizens in the agora, closing with allusion to the value of the debates in the society itself. His next paper, on the Elgin marbles, which he admitted never to have seen, was bolder in tracing the triumph of the fine arts in Greece to free trade between independent republics. An ending, which celebrated the Greek struggle for independence, seems to have been crossed out. Perhaps he felt he had pushed at the boundaries of the society's regulations enough. Many old-fashioned Tories were unhappy about George Canning's recognition of the new republics in southern Europe and Latin America. Soon afterward, Baines spoke on the "History of Printing." A draft begins with a note of censure against bibliomania, the fashionable taste for antique books that he sees as travestying the usefulness of the press as "a moral engine." The word "engine" prepares for the analogy drawn shortly afterward between the printing press as the power behind the Reformation and the steam engine as the animating force of a new reformation: "the history of the art of printing affords one of the strongest possible illustrations of the folly of those, who oppose mechanical improvement or intellectual cultivation—who think man is in danger with too little labour, or of becoming too wise—who would impiously reject the aid of science & the gifts of heaven—who dare to limit knowledge to the classes which at present enjoy it & in them to raise a barrier against its further advance."[76] The same defense of mechanical improvement was at the heart of his influential *Address to the Unemployed Workmen* (1826) and elaborated at length a decade later in his *History of the Cotton Manufacture in Great Britain* (1835).[77] Like Marshall, the younger Baines assumed that the proper study of political economy could persuade the unemployed working classes that machinery was not their enemy. By the end of the 1820s, working-class activists and Tory's of Sadler's ilk were uniting against this central creed of "Bainesocracy" in the ten-hours movement. Thackrah moved out from behind his general defense of improvement in his *Introductory Discourse* to provide them with ammunition aplenty.

Thackrah's *Introductory Discourse* had warned the society's members against "launching into the troubled waters *of literary contention.*" He acknowledged that "controversy has been said to sharpen the intellect and elicit truth" but cautioned that "it more frequently perverts the understanding, depraves the temper, and merges Philosophy in personal feeling" (46). Thackrah scarcely lived up to his own advice, as we will see, but Michael Sadler was particularly sharp against the emergent liberal paradigm. Always a loyal Tory advocate of the unreformed constitution, Sadler treated the society's members to a series of lectures defending the poor laws in April and May 1825, "constituting a defence of their principle in opposition to the views of some more modern political economists." The report of the council on which Marshall and Sadler both sat is tight-lipped: "Your Council are precluded, by obvious considerations giving any expression of their Opinion, or of the sentiments of the Society at large, in reference to the ability displayed by the Lectures of its own members."[78] In November 1827, Sadler returned to the fray with "On the Balance of the numbers and food of animate beings," developing the ideas of his *Law of Population* (1830), later lambasted by the Baines-Marshall ally Macaulay in the *Edinburgh Review*. The *North of England Medical and Surgical Journal* also gave them short shrift. Probably with insider information from the coeditor Williamson, an ally of "Bainesocracy," it noted that "some of them have frequently formed the subjects of debate, in the hall of the Leeds Philosophical Society." It dismissed the arguments as the products of passion rather than reason, "strong prepossessions, arising, perhaps, from some excited feelings, have misled the author in his search after truth." Sadler's paper on the author of "The Deserted Village" in the 1827–28 season was quite likely a contribution to these debates by way of literary criticism.[79]

When in 1829 the younger Baines proposed to address the society directly on "the moral influence of free trade," an objection was raised under the terms of the prohibition on religion and politics. The Baines-Marshall axis position won out at the council. Baines gave his paper. Three members resigned.[80] These tensions were to move to the center of national politics when Richard Oastler detonated his famous letter on "Yorkshire Slavery" in the pages of the *Leeds Mercury*: "Thousands of our fellow-creatures and fellow-subjects, both male and female, the miserable inhabitants of a *Yorkshire town* are this very moment existing in a state of slavery, more horrid than are the victims of that hellish system—'*colonial slavery*.'" The elder Baines claimed to be shocked by the revelations.[81] His editorial, though, threw doubts on the comparison with colonial slavery and complained at the violence of Oastler's language. In an atmosphere heated further by the controversies surrounding the Reform Bill, Baines was burned in effigy outside his newspaper office. Oastler pulled no punches in his description of the *Mercury*: "that common sewer of defamation—that cesspool of villainy and slander . . . the toads themselves would do it honour by their spittle."[82] The conventions of regulated conversation within its precincts probably kept this kind language out of the society itself, or at least out of the minute books. However, questions continued to be raised there about the moral and scientific authority of political economy. Thackrah offered to give a paper on the "Comparative Mortality of the various Professions in Leeds" in 1829. The Council Minutes record the offer and then simply show "*Rejected*" without giving any reason.[83] Edward Baines Jr. was the society's secretary at the time. Presumably the paper outlined the contents of the major book Thackrah published the following year: *The Effects of Arts Trades and Professions on Health and Longevity* (1831). When Sadler rose in Parliament to second the reading of the Ten Hours Bill in March 1832, he held Thackrah's book in his hand to quote its description of conditions in the flax industry in which Marshall had made his fortune.[84] Little wonder Thackrah's paper had been rejected in 1829, despite the society's claim to be a space of free exchange. Bainesocracy was confident that political economy was scientific knowledge that transcended religion and politics. Sadler believed that Thackrah's book placed the ten-hours movement on a footing that squared medical science with traditional morality. These were differences emerging from and being fought over on the ground, never properly resolved, which continued to unsettle the liberal idea of a march of intellect into modernity.

CLASSIC SHEFFIELD

Sheffield had been among the major towns whose improvement was celebrated by John Aikin Jr. in 1795. Like Liverpool and Leeds, it had to wait until the nineteenth century to gain its literary and philosophical society. Sheffield had been associated with metalworking, especially cutlery, from the Middle Ages onward. Daniel Defoe's *Tour of Great Britain* (1724–27) had described its smoky forges at work. In his *Description of the country from thirty to forty miles round Manchester* (1795), Aikin claimed that Sheffield had "discovered more of industry than ingenuity" (547) until the development of silver-plating techniques in the middle of the eighteenth century. From this period, Aikin noted, trade with the Continent had opened up, roads and rivers were improved, and numerous small-scale manufactures flourished. Population exploded thereafter in a town that was, like Leeds and Manchester, without parliamentary representation or even much local government. The 1790s saw it become an important center of radical opposition, perhaps the most important in England outside London, an experience that played an important part in the career of James Montgomery, who provided the Sheffield Literary and Philosophical Society—founded in 1822—with a figurehead who brought something of the cultural authority that Roscoe had in Liverpool.

Aikin's account of Sheffield was updated in Joseph Hunter's *Hallamshire* (1819). Hunter, who had a precocious taste for weighty antiquarian and topographical books, had read *A Description of Manchester* as a boy, borrowing it from the local subscription library. His own book captured the spirit of its precursor by celebrating the awakening of knowledge in the region after the war years: "We seem however to be rousing ourselves. Liverpool and Manchester have led the way; and it is hoped that the time is now arrived when the enlightened and liberal inhabitants of the town [of Sheffield] . . . will have within their reach a store of works in every department of literature" (128–29).[85] Hunter's diary from the late 1790s reveals a young man nurtured in the Unitarian networks that had provided Aikin with his information on the area, complaining that the library wouldn't subscribe to the *Analytical Review* and devouring the *Monthly Magazine*. Hunter's private reading experience coincided closely with the appetites of the social networks that subscribed to the *Monthly*'s "liberal and unshackled plan" for "mental improvement," especially the Society for the Promotion of Useful Knowledge (SSPUK), started in Sheffield in 1804, which Hunter soon joined.[86]

Fortunately, detailed archives survive of the activities of this group, which supplement Hunter's account of his private reading experiences in his diary, including summaries of and responses to the papers given there, all of which helps us see the maintenance of the spirit of improvement in the dark war years. To use Edward Baines Jr.'s terms, the SSPUK represented more of a "select" than a "mixed" society—that is, one wherein the participants could be fairly confident of a shared worldview, although the rule against religious and political topics remained, "as they might cause disputes."[87] Predictably enough, Benjamin Naylor, Aikin's Sheffield informant and Unitarian minister at Upper Chapel, was also a member. His congregation provided the nucleus of the group (seven of the first fourteen members worshipped there), with a conspicuous number of medical men also involved.[88] Less typical was Charles Sylvester, introduced to the society as "a lean unwashed artificer," Hunter later recalled. Sylvester was to become famous for designing the heating systems used for William Parry's ships on the arctic voyages of 1818–19.[89] Further along the path of celebrity at the time was the Sheffield-born sculptor Francis Chantrey, later the creator of the contentious statue of James Watt, who attended as a visitor at least once. This group—with Hunter as secretary—met every fortnight for conversation, usually focused on a short paper given by one of the members. It defined its remit as "literary and philosophical." The literary papers tended toward the medico-literary issues that could cause controversies in a more public forum of the kind explored in chapter 4. Here there was vigorous debate. A paper "On instinct," for instance, met with a denial that it was anything different from physical imitation and intellectual experience. The Quaker Robert Barnard found his paper "On taste" contradicted by the meeting's sense that it was "not more fluctuating than those principles on which our ideas of right and wrong are founded."[90]

A notable absence from these meetings was James Montgomery, all the more noticeable because he was close to many of those involved. Hunter later recalled that Montgomery refused an invitation to join. There must be at least a suspicion that the poet's growing religiosity was uncomfortable with the society's medico-scientific bent.[91] In 1804, Montgomery was just at the beginning of a journey toward an evangelicalism uncomfortable with any idea that "taste" could provide a moral sense, although, as we will see, he remained friendly with Rational Dissenters well into the 1810s and beyond. Among those friends was Thomas Asline Ward, with whom Montgomery collaborated on many projects despite their divergence in religious opinions. Ward attended his first meeting of the SSPUK in October 1804, when he heard the apothecary Hall Overend put forward the materialist argument that "irritation and sensation are the movers of mankind."[92] Originally from an Anglican family of prosperous cutlers, Ward had become a convinced Unitarian before the decade was out. The diaries and letters of Hunter and Ward provide an invaluable resource for following the growth in Sheffield's knowledge institutions. Unlike his antiquarian friend, Ward became a radical supporter of Sir Francis Burdett, eventually standing unsuccessfully as a radical candidate in the 1832 election, and always insisted on the possibility of a democratic politics of improvement: "The real cause of hostility against [Political] Unions," he told a wary Hunter, "is their showing the *March of Intellect* among the operatives, which too many of their superiors dislike. I believe there is less ignorance in them than you seem to imagine."[93] The SSPUK did not long survive Hunter's departure to train as a Unitarian minister in York in 1805, but he remained in close contact with its circle, even after he took a ministry in distant Bath. Indeed Ward's accounts of developments in Sheffield fed directly into the more contemporary sections of his *Hallamshire* book.

An ally for this group of rationally minded inquirers of truth emerged in the 1820s in the figure of Samuel Bailey, later nicknamed "the Hallamshire Bentham" by Brougham. Bailey, whose ideas have been thoughtfully discussed by Connell, was active in the meetings in the weeks leading up to the foundation of the Literary and Philosophical Society and consulted closely with Ward in devising its rules. He had only recently published his *Essays on the Formation and Publication of Opinions* (1821). In general terms, its advocacy of freedom of discussion sustained by networks of institutions is familiar enough by now in this book, not least in the frequently drawn analogy with free trade: "To check inquiry and attempt to regulate the progress and direction of opinions, by proscriptions and penalties is to disturb the order of nature, and is analogous, in its mischievous tendency, to the system of forcing the capital and industry of the community into channels, which they would never spontaneously seek."[94] He did not, though, think the boundary between productive debate and controversy should go unpoliced. In January 1824, a year into the life of the new Literary and Philosophical Society, Ward made a proposal for a rule banning discussion of religion and British politics. One wonders how Bailey and Ward had avoided including it in the original regulations, so common a feature was it in these societies.[95]

Dissenters such as Hunter and Ward relished the idea of fulfilling a narrative of free debate defying illiberal superstition, as had "Bainesocracy" in Leeds. Their relish included a sometimes self-regarding affirmation of the credentials of Rational Dissent.[96] To concentrate only on this story would be to ignore other important sources associational energy in Sheffield, not least the numerous religious societies in which Montgomery was a key figure.[97] Montgomery had started to attend Methodist meetings from as early as 1803 and returned to the Moravian church in 1814, by which time he had become increasingly active in cross-denominational

Bible and missionary societies. His stalwart collaborator Mary Anne Rawson identified 1813, the anniversary meeting of the Sunday School Union, as the point of his "coming out publicly as an evangelical Christian."[98] Across the first four decades of the nineteenth century, a great variety of philanthropic initiatives in Sheffield were associated with the so-called Four Friends: Montgomery; Samuel Roberts, an anti–Poor Law campaigner and, like Montgomery, enthusiastic supporter of philanthropic causes through poetry; the missionary traveler George Bennet; and the Anglican gentleman Rowland Hodgson.[99] No one, though, was more active than Rawson herself, who was the driving force behind the Ladies Anti-Slavery Society (1825) and the Ladies Association for the Universal Abolition of Slavery (1837).[100] The evangelical philanthropy of this group operated across a patchwork of voluntary societies, usually brought together as the branches of a national organization. They would be regularly visited from headquarters in London, but their work centered on local philanthropic initiatives, often in cross-denominational collaborations, although these could be problematic, especially when it came to cooperating with Unitarians, who were suspected of a lack of religious warmth.[101]

Only Montgomery of the "Four Friends" became active in the Literary and Philosophical Society. Rawson was excluded by her gender from any major role, although she could attend lectures there, but she may have shared a feeling with Montgomery's associates in the "Four Friends" group that "knowledge" was less important than moral activism. Although other of Montgomery's evangelical associates, including his biographer John Holland, did participate, Rawson thought the society's rooms "gloomy," presumably because she believed they lacked both physical and spiritual light.[102] Montgomery occupied a relatively fluid space that allowed him friends from across the spectrum of religious opinion in Sheffield. Even if by the 1820s Unitarian friends such as Hunter and Ward feared in private that Montgomery had "certainly been wrecked" in "the gulph of Evangelicalism," his religious faith was never tied too closely to any particular denomination.[103] Missionary activity, for instance, he described as a sphere where potentially "discordant" elements were "blended till they are lost, like the prismatic colours in a ray of perfect light."[104] "It seemed as if nothing in Sheffield," wrote Rawson, "would go well without him."

There were reasons other than his broad-based evangelical activism why Montgomery was the obvious choice to give the main speech at the Literary and Philosophical Society's first public meeting on December 12, 1822. Regularly reprinted on both sides of the Atlantic, he was the only poet whose British sales consistently matched Lord Byron's and Sir Walter Scott's.[105] The *Sheffield Iris*, the town's major newspaper, had a poet's corner, and it is remarkable how many of Sheffield's improvers published poetry there. Sheffield was a place for poetry. Even Bailey's writing, as Connell notes, "included a sophisticated defence of imaginative, morally improving literature."[106] Like Roscoe, he thought that the fine arts could give a larger moral perspective to a society increasingly driven by specialist divisions. By the 1820s, Montgomery had been editor of the *Iris* for nearly thirty years, using it as a forum to drive his moral vision in poetry and prose alike. Montgomery's longevity at the *Iris* offered an emollient relationship to the turbulence of the 1790s. When Hunter was growing up, Montgomery was "regarded as a martyr to the great cause of Human Freedom" because of his arrest and imprisonment for circulating seditious libels in 1795, an episode that seems to have affected his mental health for the rest of his life.[107] For someone with Hunter's background, Montgomery retained the aura of a patriot who had sacrificed himself for the public good. The passing of time and his celebrity as a poet broadened his appeal, perhaps especially after he started drawing a contrast between post-1815 radicalism and his own political heyday in the 1790s. Friends such as Ward may have grown frustrated with his failure to speak out on issues on which they knew he still agreed with them. Few of his earlier friends, if any, openly broke with him. Despite Ward's involvement with the rival *Sheffield Independent*, which pushed a vigorous reform platform from 1819 onward, and his qualms about his friend's vital religion, Ward managed to remain on good enough terms to act as a steward at Montgomery's retirement dinner in 1825.[108]

Kenneth Johnston includes Montgomery among those whose literary careers were warped by Prime Minister Pitt's clampdown on sedition in the 1790s. "He gradually withdrew," says Johnston, "to a much reduced posture of quietism."[109] Johnston's compressed account may need some recalibration if the various public roles I have been describing are taken into account. If Montgomery no longer wrote as a radical, he certainly continued to celebrate the diffusion of knowledge. He threw the weight of his poetry and the editorials in the *Iris* behind campaigns for the abolition of child chimney sweeps with his friend Roberts. The *Iris* frequently inveighed against "the spirit of warfare" in the years before Waterloo, especially when Britain seemed more intent on aggression than defense.[110] But no single issue occupied Montgomery's evangelical philanthropy in the *Iris* or anywhere else more than the abolition of slavery on which he worked closely with Roberts and, especially, Rawson. Montgomery used his retirement dinner to raise the issue "with peculiar emphasis" to the chairperson Lord Milton. "I sang the Abolition of the Slave Trade, that most glorious decree of the British legislature," he told the peer. "Oh! How

I should rejoice to sing the Abolition of Slavery itself by some parliament of which your lordship shall be a member!" Rawson and her female allies were disappointed at not being allowed entry to the all-male dinner. Six months earlier, the Sheffield Ladies Anti-Slavery Society had been formed under Rawson's direction. Although she always pushed him to go further in his support for a more immediate and universal abolition, Montgomery regularly provided hymns for her meetings and contributed to *The Bow in the Cloud* (1834), the anthology Rawson published to celebrate the abolition of colonial slavery.[111]

Montgomery had adopted the pseudonym "Alcaeus" for the poems he sent to various metropolitan journals and published himself in the *Iris* after 1800. Many were gathered with the title poem—about the struggle for liberty against Napoleon—in *The Wanderer of Switzerland* (1806). When the volume ran to a third edition, Francis Jeffrey wrote an outraged response for the *Edinburgh Review*. By this time, Jeffrey could acknowledge Wordsworth's eminence but fumed at the idea that uneducated provincial poets, as he saw them, took *Lyrical Ballads* as an invitation to broadcast their own ill-educated effusions. He had recently aimed the same gibe at John Thelwall, a popular lecturer in the region when Montgomery's poem came out. "Intoxicated with weak tea, and the praises of sentimental ensigns, and other provincial literati," said Jeffrey, Montgomery, Thelwall, and their fellows exploited the unformed tastes of "young half-educated women, sickly tradesmen, and enamoured apprentices."[112] Volumes of provincial poetry from the period are peppered with acknowledgments of Montgomery's help. Many of them were printed from the *Iris* office or originally in the newspaper itself. Predictably enough, John Aikin Jr. had a rather more positive view of the efflorescence of the "provincial literati" than Jeffrey, and he began a warm correspondence with Montgomery, buoyed by the poet's reputation as a martyr to liberty. Aikin's daughter Lucy published a poem defending Montgomery against the *Edinburgh Review* attack, and she too began a long correspondence with him, lasting into the 1850s. Roscoe joined the Aikins in what might be seen as part of a long-term project supportive of provincial poetry that ran from John Aikin's attacks on the insipidity of modern poetry in the 1770s, by way of Currie and Roscoe's Liverpool edition of Burns, and on to include a taste for Wordsworth and Montgomery.[113] The evangelical editors of Montgomery's memoirs played down these relationships, although they did concede that "his intimate friends at this time were Unitarians, or at least persons who knew little and cared less about vital godliness." Although their religious differences had increased, Montgomery's poetry confirmed Roscoe's sense that "the highest class of poetry is that which is founded on a simple energy of expression which strikes immediately, like an electric spark, from the breast of the writer to that of the reader." Even in the 1830s, when Lucy Aikin was puzzled why he would allow his benevolence to be "marred by his devotedness to a monstrous system of religion," she recommended his poetry along with Bailey's metaphysics as examples of "provincial genius."[114]

The choice of Montgomery to address the first public meeting of the Sheffield Literary and Philosophical Society on December 22, 1822 was surely, then, a perception of his ability to transcend denominational differences and to speak to a wide middle-class constituency, as his poetry did. In much the same spirit, his speech focused on other luminaries of the town who could claim to have achieved renown farther afield: the botanist Jonathan Salt; Hunter the antiquarian; Sylvester the chemist, and Chantrey the sculptor (whom Montgomery rated the greatest of them all). Significantly, they had all—unlike Montgomery himself—at least visited the meetings of the SSPUK. Hunter was certainly among those who regarded the new society as the fulfillment of the promise of the earlier group, but he still regarded Montgomery as the best person to recommend it to their "fellow townsmen," as he wrote from Bath on January 9, 1823 to thank him.[115] He also followed Montgomery's talk in harking back to "the men of 1794." They had, agreed Hunter, only needed encouragement from those better instructed than they were, taking a line that chimed in with Montgomery's support for the diffusion of knowledge under appropriate limits, even though they may not have agreed either on what knowledge was exactly or on what those limits ought to be.

The keynote for Montgomery's speech had been sounded by a gibe Byron had made against "classic Sheffield" in *English Bards and Scotch Reviewers* (1809). Byron lauded "Sad ALCÆUS" as a fellow victim of Jeffrey's vindictiveness, if not without throwing shade of his own:

> Nipped in the bud by Caledonian gales,
> His blossoms wither as the blast prevails!
> O'er his lost works let classic SHEFFIELD weep:
> May no rude hand disturb their early sleep.[116]

Still nettled by the condescension, Montgomery reiterated a point he had made in the *Iris* a few weeks earlier to insist that the general population of Sheffield was far in advance of classic Greece or Rome in terms of knowledge: "I speak of the relative intelligence of the whole body of the people in each of these countries, compared with the actual measure of information diffused among our own local population." He reiterated the general principle of the transpennine enlightenment when he insisted that "the aristocracy of learning has been the veriest despotism that was

ever exercised on earth." The sentiments briefly drew him into controversy with Francis Hodgson of Bakewell, near Derby, who mocked the
idea that the harangues at political and religious assemblies of manufacturing towns could have had the same uplifting effect as the speeches of
Pericles on the minds of the ancient Athenians.[117] For all his alienation
from post-1815 radicalism and despite his growing concern for vital religion, Montgomery remained unrepentant in his defense of the provincial
march of intellect. His heroes were local men whose deeds, he implied,
could be emulated from within the town's populace (a point he revisited
in the society's annual report of 1825 when he noted that all the lecturers,
bar one, had been local, and the exception was James Williamson from
Leeds).[118]

Montgomery the busy poet and hymn writer continued to be a main-
stay of the society, both as an officeholder and by contributing lectures
on the history of poetry that he gave across the region and then in the
Royal Institution in London in 1831 and 1832. The lectures took a broadly
historical line that assumed "the books of every era must resemble those
who wrote, and those who read them," an approach that loosely fits with
the environmental approach to genius typical in these circles.[119] Neil
Ramsey perceptively places Montgomery's lectures in the context of
a "condition of eventfulness."[120] "Eventfulness" was partly a product of
intense media coverage as the circulation of information more generally was intensifying in British society, not least because of the rise of
provincial newspapers like the *Iris*. For Ramsey, it also describes the
period's difficulty in securing a coherent narrative of the unfolding of
history. Hunter and others had hoped that Waterloo would allow the
history of improvement to resume, as we have seen, and in many ways,
Montgomery's participation in the Sheffield Literary and Philosophical
Society was a signal of improvement redux. However, his lectures on contemporary poetry were not as sanguine as one might expect. Like many
others, Montgomery identified "a new school," responding to the spirit of
the French Revolution, anticipated by Cowper, fulfilled by Wordsworth,
Coleridge, and Southey. Praise for their achievements was clouded by
a fear that "advancement" was coming into an unstable relationship with
moral improvement. History was in danger of going too fast into an unknown future. All the more striking because he was in general a proponent of a provincial enlightenment, Montgomery saw the "dislocation, in
fact, of every thing" as "one of the most striking proofs of the diffusion of
knowledge—and its corruption too,—if not a symptom of its declension
by being so heterogeneously blended till all shall be neutralised" (373). He
numbered not just Byron, predictably enough, but also Campbell, Scott,
Southey, and Wordsworth among those who had abandoned more tried

and trusted pathways to "scale the heights by leaping from rock to rock up the most precipitous side, forcing their passage through the impenetrable forests that engirdle it, or plunging across the headlong torrents that descending various windings from their fountains at the peak" (377). Montgomery accused all these writers of straining to "attract attention and excite astonishment" (377), a striking contrast to the more familiar idea that Wordsworth was received as a kind of spiritual "balm" in the 1820s and 1830s.[121]

"Advancement" from this point of view most obviously refers to the Industrial Revolution and the widespread anxiety that it represented a technological advance that was leaving moral questions behind. These events conjured, as Reinhard Koselleck phrases it, a troubling "aporia" opening up between "the space of experience" and "the horizon of expectations."[122] Edward Baines Jr. was lecturing about this future at the Leeds Philosophical and Literary Society just as Montgomery was giving his poetry lectures in the same venue.[123] Montgomery possibly felt the pressure of this alternate version of historical development. He was certainly deeply skeptical about scientific determinism of all kinds. Initially interested in phrenology, Montgomery reacted violently against it when it was used to suggest a biological underpinning to theories of racial difference. This kind of science threatened his belief that all races could be improved by the encounter with Christianity, the foundation of his support for domestic and foreign missionaries.[124] The Christian philanthropist in him was equally appalled by Arnold Knight's suggestion that the health risks of the dry grinding process might be displaced from free labor onto criminals.[125]

By the later 1830s, Montgomery's astonishment seems to have precipitated into something stronger. His late 1837 lecture on poetry at the Royal Institution—published in the *Metropolitan Magazine*—still registered awe at recent industrial innovations and even lamented the failure of poetry to capture "the *romance of reality* in our *un*-ideal age."[126] He praises "the inventors and employers of these wonderful creations, and the multitude who are regularly engaged in preparing and directing," and then he breaks into an antipathy against their consequences: "our present rectilinear career of all-equalizing improvements." The lecture ends with a defiant quotation from his long poem *The World Before the Flood* (1815) stating his continuing faith in "the living spirit in the lyre."[127] For Montgomery, this idea of a "living spirit" was certainly to do with vital religion. He fought many battles at the Mechanics' Institute "against fiction and infidelity," to use Rawson's characteristic conjunction. He argued against a subscription to Scott's Waverley novels in 1831 and wrote directly to the working-class members of the committee to warn them against the "loose and frothy'" allure of fiction. He refused to distinguish the rule against the acquisition of "novels and plays" from the regulation banning anything that undermined "Christian principles." Beyond this tighter evangelical sense of "spirit," however, he and someone like Bailey could agree that the extensive diffusion of knowledge needed a generous sense of the literary.[128] The progressive middle classes, as Connell rightly notes, continued to find a space for poetry within their aspirations for improvement.[129] The collaborations between Bailey and Ward might seem to mirror the Baines-Marshall axis in Leeds, but the Sheffield pair seem at once more democratic and more open to the pleasures of the imaginative life. Bailey's "Essay on the Variety of Intellectual Pursuits" had insisted that the pleasures of the fine arts were "possessed by all, the terms in which they are treated of form the common language of daily intercourse, and every mind feels itself competent to pronounce on the positions in the expression of which they are employed."[130] Connell suggests that Bailey and his fellow members of the Literary and Philosophical Society likely agreed with Roscoe that "there exists no necessity for our separating the ideas of utility and of pleasure."[131] Imaginative life was not viewed simply as an elite compensation. Instead, for those like Bailey, it opened improvement to a more general public, able, as Roscoe and the Aikins understood Montgomery's poetry, to reach more directly into the human heart.

James Montgomery's position as Sheffield's most visible proponent of popular education still seemed secure enough in 1831 for him to be nominated as the Sheffield Literary and Philosophical Society's delegate to the first meeting of the British Association for the Advancement of Science, held in York. William Turner attended for Newcastle, a connection with an older idea of improvement, but Montgomery chose not to go because the meeting was "rather *Scientific* than Literary." Interestingly, he didn't close the door on the idea that "science" might be reconstituted in its relationship to other domains of knowledge: "If they were to diversify their abstruse exercises at the ensuing meeting with some of the pleasures of the imagination," then "it would be very acceptable to some of the younger philosophers, the bones of whose hearts are not yet set, and whose blood does not yet *run* — I mean *stand* — cold in their veins."[132] Turner's decision to attend was rewarded with at least one flickering of the inheritance of provincial improvement, although not one likely to have attracted Montgomery. William Henry — son of the founder of the Manchester Literary and Philosophical Society — read a memoir of Joseph Priestley. The specter of Priestley was greeted with objections, probably because it tainted the growing ethos of professional neutrality with the political and religious controversies of the past.[133] Nevertheless, the presence of Henry and Turner shows how these networks that had set out in the 1780s endured into a new era. The year 1830 witnessed philosophical societies set up in Halifax, Whitby, and Scarborough. Turner's son played an important role at Halifax. This chapter has seen Edward Baines, father and son, at work in Leeds. Edmund Aikin joined the Liverpool society, and his father, John Aikin Jr., continued his support for initiatives in the region from his base in London.

Turner. Baines. Aikin. One could add the sons of Currie and Roscoe and their biographies of their fathers. The names persist but move around the network spatially, confirming its integrity as a system perhaps, but if the families and the forms recur, then the values associated with the improvement were subtly and unevenly shifting in the ways explored further in part 2 of this book.

PART TWO

BODIES
and
MACHINES

CHAPTER FOUR

THREE PHYSICIANS
AROUND MANCHESTER

Medical men played an important part in the early years of the Manchester Literary and Philosophical Society, especially in its debates about relations between environment, innovation, and personal and social well-being. No physicians loomed larger in these debates over its first two decades than John Aikin Jr., Thomas Percival, and John Ferriar, the subjects of this chapter. Alan Richardson's *British Romanticism and the Science of the Mind* (2001) opened a new pathway for literary scholars of this period by drawing attention to the emergence and first flourishing of "a biological science of mind." The trouble for any disinterested medical examination of biological accounts of mind-body relations was, as Richardson notes, that the idea of "an immaterial and indivisible conception of mind seemed an indispensable prop to established religious doctrine and even political stability."[1] He rightly understands the transnational nature of the inquiries that stretched across the European Enlightenment. They were sustained by networks of correspondence between doctors and scientists that we have seen linked Manchester with the latest French and German research and reached across the Atlantic to include such figures as Benjamin Franklin and Benjamin Rush (both of whom became members of the Literary and Philosophical Society). Nevertheless, Richardson's concern with "ideas" threatens to drain these networks of their social energy, ironically producing a relatively disembodied species of circulation on an abstracted plane of print. The locations of these debates, I suggest, were crucial. Networked relations facilitated their dissemination and spoke to the belief of participants in the web of "connexion" disapprobated by Thomas De Quincey. On a regional scale, the country around Manchester was part of a provincial challenge to medical authorities in London, especially the Royal College of Physicians, condemned by John Aikin as an example of the dampening powers of corporations.[2] Moreover, in the process of becoming the "shock city" of the period, Manchester was being forced to confront unprecedented practical issues about public health and the suffering body in a newly industrializing society.[3]

On a microscale, fractious relations between bodies in rooms could give debates about these issues an additional edge, as one anecdote from Robert Owen's autobiography, *The Life of Robert Owen Written by Himself*, reveals. Although not published until 1856, Owen's *Life* provided a detailed account of his early years in Manchester. Having moved to there from London in the late 1780s, Owen quickly became the manager of and soon afterward a partner in Peter Drinkwater's cotton mill, the first in the town itself to use the steam engine in the production of fine cotton thread.[4] Owen was always hungry for knowledge and quickly associated himself with the town's burgeoning cultural institutions. According to the *Life*, perhaps not always a reliable source, he spent time around Manchester Academy, where he joined the young tutors John Dalton and William Winstanley in a small discussion club. Also a likely participant was William Stevenson, Elizabeth Gaskell's father, a lifelong friend of Winstanley's.[5] Their conversations were primarily about religious belief and the physical bases of the mind. Owen articulated his lifelong antagonism to all forms of Christianity. Apparently, Thomas Barnes, principal of the Academy, got wind of their discussions and became anxious that Owen would convert his assistants to his irreligious views. Their intellectual recreations continued far enough to gain Owen a reputation as "the reasoning machine," because, as he put it, "I made man a mere reasoning machine, made to be so by nature and society."[6]

Despite this early-acquired reputation for irreligion, Owen's success in managing the new industrial processes won him an invitation to a meeting of the Manchester Literary and Philosophical Society on October 4, 1793, where—at a presentation on Persian cotton—he was "introduced to the leading professional characters, particularly in the medical profession, which then stood high in Manchester." Owen's *Life* then gives us a rare glimpse into the day-to-day functioning of the Literary and Philosophical Society itself. I'll return to the development of Owen's thinking in the context of the society in chapter 6, but my primary concern here is with the insight Owen gives into a particular debate at the society on October 3, 1794. That evening John Ferriar gave a paper "On Genius" intended, by Owen's account, "to prove that any one, by his own will, might become a genius, and that it only required determination and industry for anyone to attain this quality in any pursuit."[7] The paper was met, unusually in this lively society, with a stunned silence. Owen decided to intervene to move the evening along, if only for the edification of his guests Dalton and Winstanley. Owen rose to suggest that there must have been some error in Ferriar's thinking as, although he acknowledged himself to be very industrious, no one had ever accounted him a genius. I'll let Owen himself describe what happened next: "Dr. Ferriar rose to reply. He blushed or became so red with suppressed feeling as to attract the attention of the members, and merely stammered out some confused reply, when to relieve his embarrassment, some members began to speak, and a discussion followed." Contemporaries, even friendly ones, noted that Ferriar was prone to "warmth."[8] Involved in several controversies at the Manchester Infirmary, caustic at times, fond satire of a learned variety, but also given to identification with the suffering of others, Ferriar was a man for whom the experience of embarrassment figured in his flushed face provides a handy symbol of the interest he shared with many others in the society in the entanglements of mind and body discussed in this chapter.

The version of Ferriar's essay later published in his *Illustrations of Sterne* (1798) suggests some deep-seated differences with Owen, rather travestied by the account in Owen's *Life*. Owen's materialism, as Owen himself boasted, was of a mechanical kind that made mental experience the product of proximate causes. Ferriar had a more complex view of relations between mind and body, as one might expect of a student of William Cullen's.[9] His essay on genius begins by pointing out problems caused by the stickiness of "our early reading even among those who boast an emancipation from all prejudices of education." Among the prejudices passed on through studying classical literature, of which Ferriar was a serious student himself, the essay criticizes the occult idea of genius as "a kind of magic splendor over the heads of men of talents, which the herd of metaphysicians has beheld with awe."[10] The parallels with John Aikin Jr.'s *General Biography* are obvious. Genius is not a kind of magic but the product of complex influences, like the early impressions of reading mentioned by Ferriar, talent—of the kind Aikin's self-tutored hero Brindley showed—being one among them. Owen likely thought Ferriar's paper smacked too much of voluntarism. Ferriar's writing, for its part, was always wary of the search for final causes and tended to mock signs of "medical essentialism" among his colleagues.[11] Like Aikin and Thomas Percival, the two other medical men discussed at length in this chapter, Ferriar was committed to the imaginative life, as the fact that he published *Illustrations of Sterne* suggests, a life understood as the product of complex relations between mind and body and, in its turn, as much a determinant on mental and physical well-being as any more direct circumstance.

The informal discussions about mind-body relations held by Owen and his little group at Manchester Academy were part of a broader debate also being pursued at the grander Literary and Philosophical Society. "The phenomena termed mental," as Thomas Cooper reminded the members, "are a frequent topic of discussion in this society."[12] These discussions were bound up with developments in Manchester's medical institutions and the interventions by physicians such as Ferriar and Percival in public health reforms that had far-reaching consequences. The rapid socioeconomic transformation of Manchester forced physicians early on to confront relations between humans and their environment of the kind later tabulated in Charles Turner Thackrah's *Effects of Arts, Trades and Professions on Health and Longevity*. Writing about the public health reforms that Ferriar helped inaugurate in Manchester, John V. Pickstone contrasted his approach with those liberal reformers of the 1830s, especially the physician James Phillips Kay, discussed in length in chapter 7, who conceived of the poor in terms of the "abstract, law-governed operations of an environmental system including and determining the conditions of men and women." Pickstone represents Ferriar, in contrast, as the product of a medical training which "stressed the sensibility of all body parts, and especially the nervous system." "Sensibility," of course, was much more than a medical term in this period. Pickstone says nothing about Ferriar's interest in Laurence Sterne, perhaps the most obvious literary figure associated with sensibility in the period, or the other literary topics that occupied him.[13] This chapter aims to supply this deficit and, more broadly, to argue that the literary interests of Manchester's medical men in this period, far from being "ornamental," in Arnold Thackray's terms, were integral to their version of improvement. In their hands, the commitment to Percival's "Physics and the Belles Lettres" showed a particular fascination with such medico-literary concepts as "imagination," "taste," and "sensibility," interrogated in the interests of understanding the relationship between environment, mental life, and health more generally.

JOHN AIKIN'S MEDICAL NETWORKS

Physicians in this period produced a variety of writings that could switch between medical and literary discourse and also inhabit a hybrid generic space populated by case histories, medical biographies, and educational tracts. No one was more conspicuous in this varied field than John Aikin Jr., whom Kathryn Ready has described as "among the first to think seriously about the literary physician as a historical phenomenon." Ready points out that in a period usually associated with the professional narrowing of medicine, Aikin regularly blurred the boundaries between "medicine, morality, and politics." In this regard, he was far from unusual among his fellow members of the Literary and Philosophical Society. In 1786, Aikin published an essay in the *Gentleman's Magazine* under the title "An Apology for the Literary Pursuits of Physicians." Perhaps responding to the intensification of professional expectations, he was apologizing for a phenomenon that he played no small part in bringing into view, not least by editing medically oriented poetry, including John Armstrong's *The Art of Preserving Health* (1795, orig. 1744) and Matthew Green's *The Spleen* (1796, orig. 1737). Earlier, his *Biographical Memoirs of Medicine* (1780), completed at Warrington, was effectively, as Ready notes, "a record of Aikin's thoughts on the historical phenomenon of the literary physician." Generally speaking, *Biographical Memoirs* presented physicians as integral to the inquiring spirit of the Renaissance. They were "literary" because they were part of a diverse world of learning rather than narrowly medical in their outlook. Aikin's own writing frequently combined and moved across the roles of "physician, naturalist, and divine."[14] His educational work with his sister Anna Laetitia Barbauld, who praised the combined power of his "healing hand and pitying eye" in her poem "To Dr. Aikin," put an emphasis on learning through a practical engagement with nature and science.[15] His influential essays on songwriting and on the importance of natural history to poetry, discussed in previous chapters, had promoted the values of observation and experiment. For the poet no less than for the natural philosopher, he argued, these Baconian principles were key to breaking with exhausted tradition. Modern poetry was falling into insipidity, thought Aikin, because its ignored nature's "minuter distinctions and mutual relations." Overreliance on outworn models was "only to be rectified by accurate and attentive observation, conducted on somewhat of a scientific plan."[16]

Aikin was starting to play a role in the medical enlightenment around Manchester as he wrote these literary-critical works. He had trained in the Warrington Academy's liberal syllabus, like Thomas Percival, before following him to Edinburgh in 1764, where Aikin studied under William Cullen. Both Aikin and Percival imbibed the Edinburgh faculty's fascination with "the extent and nature of the mind's interaction with the body," especially as mediated by the sensibility of the nervous system, if always with the sense that these relations were not simply determined by anatomy.[17] To further develop his professional skills, Aikin in 1766 returned to Manchester, where he became a pupil of Charles White. Lucy Aikin later described her father's decision as a "renewed sacrifice of that independence which he had enjoyed under the free system of a Scotch university."[18] The apprenticeship with White compensated him with ac-

cess to the infirmary in Manchester, the opportunity to conduct medical research, and contact with his old friends in the region's flourishing
Unitarian community. To complete his training, Aikin spent a further
few months as apprentice to William Hunter in London before returning closer to the area around Manchester, first in Chester, where he be-
friended John Haygarth, before moving his practice to Warrington in
1771. Almost inevitably, he began lecturing at the Warrington Academy
on medical subjects in 1774 and re-created something of the "free system"
of the Scottish universities with his friends Currie, Haygarth, and Percival in the informal gatherings that count among the precursors of the
Literary and Philosophical Society.[19]

Aikin's *Thoughts on Hospitals* (1771) was dedicated to Haygarth,
despite their "marked opposition both of political and religious sentiments," and contained a preface written by Percival, who had revised the
manuscript. Its ideas on the importance of ventilation that influenced
John Howard's *The State of the Prisons in England and Wales*, first published in Warrington in 1777, were part of a broader affinity between these
two texts.[20] After the philanthropist's death, Aikin played an important
part in the creation of the idea of Howard as a "true hero," deploying
his characteristic contrast between aristocratic martial virtues and the
more useful heroism of the improver. The key to Howard's philanthropy
was the reformation of character through the manipulation of circumstances translated by Aikin into a series of principles: strict and constant
superintendence; close and regular employment; religious instruction;
rewards for industry and good behavior; penalties for sloth and auda-
ciousness; distribution into classes and divisions according to age, sex,
delinquency, and so on; and even occasional solitary confinement. The
disciplinary regime was intended to operate within limits set by a recognition "that men, partaking a common nature, have certain claims
upon their fellow-creatures, which nothing can entirely abrogate." At
this stage, as least, the disciplinary aspect of environmental science was
not abstracted from natural limits, not extended into "complete domination," to adapt a distinction of Michel Foucault's.[21] Aikin reported that
Howard "lamented that the plan of reformation seemed, of all parts of his
system of improvement least entered into or understood in this country"
and stressed that any disciplinary tendency was always "tempered by the
real demands of human nature, and sanctified by a regard to the best interests of offenders themselves."[22] The principle of physical and mental
improvement at the heart of their networks had not yet frozen into what
Alison Twells calls "the semi-industrial language of moulding, solidifying
and creating stability among a 'mass.'"[23]

There were perhaps signs enough of this formation apparent in the educational programs that Aikin and his sister began in the 1770s and extended to the *Evenings at Home* series (1792–96).[24] They are discernible, too, in the lines on the ivory tablet that Barbauld gave to William Turner, whose mind remained impressed—literally and metaphorically—by the gift. David Hartley's *Observations on Man* (1749), at the core of the associationism of these circles, took the view that "children may be formed or moulded as we please." Literary criticism is familiar with the romantic resistance to the language of "impressions" expressed in Charles Lamb's distrust of "the cursed Barbauld crew." Joanna Wharton has usefully redressed the balance by contrasting the flexibility of the "domestic materialism" of Barbauld and Aikin, for instance, with R. L. Edgeworth's belief that learning through play "weakens and dissipates the mind."[25] Barbauld's poem to Turner, in contrast, had praised "the softer influence of the polish'd muse." Generally speaking, like Ferriar, she presented environmental influences as sticky in ways that could be difficult to control, unlike the slate her poem was written upon, which—she noted—could be wiped clean with water. Compared to Owen's idea of the man-machine, she and her brother tended to identify "circumstance" as a mix of proximate and remote influences, something "of infinitely more consequence to the habit, than that which is direct and apparent." "This education goes on at every instant of time," she explained, "it goes on like time; you can neither stop it, nor turn its course. What these have a tendency to make your child, that he will be."[26]

Aikin and his medical friends showed the influence of their teacher William Cullen in their tendency to trust observation and the cautious and flexible marrying of principle to context over theories that trusted to final causes.[27] The demise of the Warrington Academy "scattered this little knot of literary friends." Aikin moved to Yarmouth to further his career after a period in Leyden, but his political opinions cost him his medical practice there. By early 1792 he had resettled in London, where friends in the faculty at the Hackney Academy, the circle of authors that surrounded Joseph Johnson, not to mention his sister, offered a more robust network of like-minded writers. Nevertheless, Aikin remained keenly and regretfully aware of what he had left behind in the Manchester region.[28] Chapter 1 suggested that Aikin, with his sister, ought to be regarded as agents of the transpennine enlightenment in the metropolis. He certainly exerted considerable influence on its behalf in the reviews, often promoting and publishing his friends from the Manchester region, including the summaries of several of the papers from the *Manchester Memoir* in the short-lived *Memoirs of Science and the Arts* (1793). Among them was John Ferriar's paper on materialism discussed later in this chapter. At the end of the decade, he passed on to Ferriar his mantle as reviewer of poetry and medicine at the *Monthly Review*.[29] By this time, Aikin was busy at the *Monthly Magazine*, explicitly founded on a "liberal and unshackled plan" to protect "mental improvement" in the face of the reaction against the French Revolution. De Quincey's later complaint about the power of this "connexion" seems justified at least in terms of the disproportionate influence of these circles in the reviews. The region's medico-educational writing also loomed large in Joseph Johnson's publishing list, not least in the person of Thomas Percival, who was at the center of Manchester's vigorous institutional innovations of the 1780s and early 1790s that ran from the Literary and Philosophical Society, the College of Arts and Sciences, and the Manchester Academy to developments at the Manchester Infirmary and the new Board of Health that came into being in 1796. Institutions for Percival seem to have been integral to a vision of creating positive environmental conditions for physical and mental improvement.

PERCIVAL'S PRECARITY

Thomas Percival's approach extended to his investigations into the effects of the new industrial conditions being created in and around the cotton mills. Treatment was understood not just in terms of medicines but also questions of a larger regimen of life. This viewpoint extended to the care taken over ventilation and cleanliness in his writing with Aikin on hospitals, for instance, but they also encompassed broader questions of culture and custom, social relations, and economic conditions. Historical inquiries such as William Roscoe's into the relationship between conditions of political liberty and broader forms of improvement should be understood in this light. They certainly fed into Roscoe's collaboration with James Currie on the biography of Robert Burns. Relations between body and mind from this point of view were comprehensible as a network whose various parts communicated through the brains and nerves into, as Cullen described it, "our connexion with the rest of the universe—by which we act upon other bodies, and by which other bodies act upon us."[30] It was a perspective that lent itself to something like the idea of extended mind that Wharton has seen at play in Barbauld's object-oriented pedagogy.[31] Percival extended his investigations to the perceptive life of vegetables and concluded that it was unimaginable that "such profusion of life subsists without the least sensation or enjoyment": "Let us rather, with humble reverence, suppose that vegetables participate, in some low degree, of the common allotment of vitality."[32]

Humility wasn't always the order of the day. Neither Aikin nor Percival was free from assumptions about their power to control others in

the name of scientific inquiry. Aikin voiced his frustration at "the unrea-
sonable prejudice" among poor patients against "rational experiment."[33]
Percival's *Medical Ethics* (1803) counseled against sharing theoretical
discussion in the consulting room, quoting Lord Mansfield to a recently
appointed governor to the West Indies: "When you decide never give reasons for your decision." The quotation and its source may be a strange
choice for someone who devoted a great deal of his energies to the abolition of the slave trade, but it was part of a calibration of the likely effects
on the sensibility of the patient of such information.[34] More generally,
Percival's ideas on shaping behavior—whether in a medical context or
otherwise—tended to attend to Cullen's sense of precarity, if arranged
under a providential sense of the possibilities of improvement: "as relations, employments, offices, and ranks are multiplied, the connections
or collisions of duty and interest are also multiplied: And combinations
of the principles of action are formed, unknown in the primeval state of
man; giving him fresh energies; and casting his character, as it were, in
a new and larger mould."[35] Published by Joseph Johnson in several editions over three decades, *A Father's Instructions* set out an educational
plan that placed the child's ethical development within a network of "connections or collisions." "Sympathy, friendship, generosity, and benevolence" are dynamic qualities that "acquire vigour by exertion, and energy
by being uncontrouled." "Uncontrouled" here does not imply unsuper-
vised. Percival understood the success of his book to depend on "the capacity of the parent or tutor to explain the terms; point out the analogies,
and enforce the reflections, which are here delivered." His educational
program, as M. O. Grenby points out, was "in effect, a collaboration between the author who produced the text and the adult supervising its use";
one might add into the mix the many objects the child was encouraged to
exercise their "powers of understanding and imagination" upon.[36]

In his *Moral Dissertations* (1784), also published by Johnson, Percival
was more explicit about the complex physical laws of habit and association that determined moral behavior: "The strongest tint in the complexion of the human character, may be sometimes formed by a circumstance,
or event apparently casual; which, by forcibly impressing the mind produces a lasting association, that gives a uniform direction to the efforts
of the understanding, and the feelings of the heart."[37] If he encouraged
parents to create the right circumstances for reading and learning, the
acknowledgment of "casual" circumstances hints at the difficulties of fix-
ing the proper environment. As with Aikin and Barbauld's educational
writing, it brought with it a recognition of a need for tolerance, partly
in the engineering sense, that could at least approach a kind of humility
about the refusal of things "to dissolve quickly into the milieu of human

knowledge." The calculus of proximate and remote causes was not amenable to mathematical precision, and Percival remained closer to the spirit of Cullen in this regard than some of his other students.[38]

Most of the papers collected in *Moral Dissertations* had been given at the Literary and Philosophical Society. They were prefaced by a Socratic dialogue—originally privately published on its own—that investigated some of the delicate issues of calibrating freedom of opinion with an ethos of benevolence.[39] Percival's educational writing explicitly favors the dialogue form—"freedom of conversation"—against "rigid adherence to the precise rules of system." A taste for polemic for its own sake is to be avoided because of "the tendency of this habit of altercation to create indifference." Unlike Ferriar, who often displayed a caustic manner, Percival showed no desire to emulate Diogenes.[40] Many of Percival's essays are concerned with the development of taste and the cultivation of a kind of reader response that makes "every grove a sacred fane," to use the line that Percival initially quoted from James Thomson and then subsumed into his own phrasing in later editions.[41] After his death, there was a minor controversy in Dissenting circles about whether Percival had been too "accommodating" to the Church of England. His correspondence with such figures as William Paley and Richard Watson, Bishop of Llandaff, makes it clear that he favored a national church only if it guaranteed freedom of belief. Percival's writing may not be anticlerical as such, but there was a consistent defense of freedom of conscience in religion that might cause alarm to Tory-Anglicans, as it did to De Quincey's mother.[42]

A spirit of accommodation might be traced at work in *Medical Ethics*, completed just before Percival's death, not least because of its acknowledgment of the evangelical Thomas Gisborne's *Enquiry into the Duties of Men in the Higher and Middle Classes of Society* (1794) "as the most complete system, extant, of PRACTICAL ETHICS."[43] Percival had sent an early draft to Gisborne sometime after 1792, as he did to several others, including Aikin and Ferriar. The evangelical minister used it extensively in his own book's discussion of the duties of physicians, stressing what they owed as Christians to their calling and toward their patients. Percival's work on the fever outbreak in the cotton mills in the 1780s came in for special praise. Gisborne had gained his reputation with an influential rebuttal of William Paley's utilitarian ethics in *Principles of Moral Philosophy Investigated* (1789), which drew on Bishop Butler's *Divine Analogy* to insist on the primacy of conscience and revelation. Percival's son Edward later acknowledged the role of Butler's work in saving his father from the influence of David Hume's "Essay on Miracles," but this confluence does mean that Percival broke with his inheritance in the Scottish Enlightenment.[44] *Medical Ethics* was a palimpsest, its earliest version written immediately after the "infirmary revolution" in Manchester (discussed in the next section). It was rewritten to give professional advice to Percival's son James, whose early death delayed publication and may be responsible for some of the gloomier aspects of the published version.[45] The final version was also, as Pickstone notes, the product of the retrenchment after the sustained period of reforms in the Manchester Infirmary. Percival's relationship with Gisborne needs above all to be understood in the context of his accommodating tendency toward an ecumenical sense of public-spiritedness, sympathetic to the idea of a national church, if not to the doctrines of the Church of England, as a forum for bringing people together, where adapting to circumstance was understood to be a key principle of healthy living.

Gisborne himself was a more complex figure than the label "evangelical" may suggest to some readers, quite possibly as influenced by Percival as influencing him. An important member of the Clapham Sect, close to Hannah More and William Wilberforce, he was very active in the Society for the Bettering of the Condition of the Poor, which reported positively on Ferriar and Percival's initiatives in public medicine.[46] Gisborne was an outspoken critic of aristocratic decadence and sharply critical of capitalist moneymaking, even if loyal to the existing political order. This paternalist tendency was not unsympathetic to the improving spirit of the literary and philosophical societies as long as it was set on firmly Christian principles guided by the Bible. Gisborne's "On the Benefits and Duties resulting from the Institution of Societies for the Advancement of Literature and Philosophy," communicated to the society by Percival in 1796, makes clear from its first page the importance of "authority" and "sanctions."[47] Most of its emphasis is on the conditions that might impair learned societies from this perspective, especially the tendency of medical men toward infidelity. One recalls the anxieties of Samuel Hall about any notion that the moral senses might be the product of taste or sentiments.

Whatever Gisborne's belated influence on *Medical Ethics*, Cullen's remains palpable in its developed sense of the "complicated and multifarious" skills required of a physician, including a "knowledge of human nature and extensive moral duties" (vii). "*Feelings* and *emotions*," remote causes of disease, Percival believed, "no less than symptoms need to be understood" (10). Politeness is encouraged as the basis of relations with the patient and with other medical practitioners: "Observance of the duties which they enjoin, will soften your manners, expand your affections, and form you to that propriety and dignity of conduct, which are essential to the character of a GENTLEMAN" (ix). Ultimately Percival's idea of proper medical conduct will, he says, "unite tenderness with steadiness, and condescension with authority, as to inspire the mind of their patients with gratitude, respect, and confidence" (9). These are qualities as "important to the comfort and relief of the sick poor," wrote Percival, as to "the rich under such circumstances" (10). These principles are united under a sense of a benign and rational Creator rather than Gisborne's starker emphasis on sanctions. Gisborne was concerned that moral purpose should precede narrowly medical interests—for instance, when it came to medical experiments, but especially regarding the traditional association between physicians and freethinking. Percival's career had been devoted to the idea that medical therapeutics had a moral purpose, but this did not come with Gisborne's emphasis on the physician's duty to worship in the Church of England. In a lengthy discussion of Gisborne's opinions on this topic in his notes, Percival carefully affirmed the value of "social worship," a phrase that may signal his association with the Barbauld-Aikin circle and carefully distinguish his beliefs in this regard from the Churchman's.[48] Percival, unlike Gisborne, could understand that "scruples respecting doctrines and forms, [might be] sufficient to produce an alienation from the sacred offices of the temple." When it came to treatment of the dying, too, a topic on which John Ferriar had already written an important essay, Percival firmly rejected a role for the priest in the treatment room: "The character of the physician is remote either from superstition or enthusiasm: And the aid which he is now exhorted to give, will tend towards their exclusion from the sick wards of the hospital . . . where their effects have been known to be not only baneful, but even fatal" (12). Ferriar had been even more robust: "While the senses remain perfect, the patient ought to direct his own conduct, both in his devotional exercises, and in the last interchanges of affection with his friends."[49] In both instances, practical medical matters hold a line against evangelical piety.

John Pickstone has given more weight to the origins of *Medical Ethics* in the infirmary revolution of 1789–90 than Percival's Edinburgh training, leaving it somewhat like the jetsam in a receding tide of reform.[50] In certain respects, Percival's characteristic preference for accommodating to his environment can be seen in his relations with the infirmary hierarchy before the years of reform that peaked with the third volume of *Memoirs*, when he worked with the Tory-Anglican hierarchy that dominated medicine in Manchester. Only from the middle of the 1780s does a more clearly progressive impetus seem to manifest itself in his association with Thomas Cooper and Thomas Walker, and their medical ally Ferriar. Critics and historians often describe this group as "radical," sometimes in comparison with the more cautious Percival. I have been unable to trace any public statement on political matters from Ferriar.

He does not seem to have joined the Manchester Constitutional Society, for instance, although he was reputed to have helped his friend George Philips draft his *Necessity of a Speedy and Effectual Reform in Parliament* (1793).[51] Ferriar also continued on friendly terms with Cooper and Walker after their politics had made them notorious, but his own radicalism really resided in his insistence that all parts of society shared a common experience in the body.

THE INFIRMARY REVOLUTION

Ferriar's biopolitics becomes apparent in the so-called infirmary revolution that coincided with his rising role in Manchester medicine in the expansive years of reform from the late 1780s to early 1790s, the period when he was also most active in the Literary and Philosophical Society. The infirmary had been controlled by Tory-Anglican gentry families from its inception in the 1750s. Charles White, a young surgeon at the time, was its main architect. At midcentury, infirmaries represented the newest and most fashionable form of civic philanthropy. They were organized on a joint-stock company principle, controlled by the votes of subscribers, who usually elected a management committee from among their own number. Patients were admitted on the recommendation of a subscriber in the familiar way of eighteenth-century patronage. "In a small town of growing affluence," Pickstone notes, "these easily-bought rights of patronage were attractive."[52] A matron and domestic help with an apothecary who cared for the patients usually did most of the actual work, while the honorary physicians looked to their more lucrative clients.[53] White was well placed to develop this system when local opinion in Manchester decided it ought to follow the recent example of Liverpool.[54] The son of a Manchester attorney, White had built his reputation as a man-midwife partly on the prestige of having studied in London with William Hunter, but neither White nor his patrons can have expected the population explosion that made the traditional structure of the infirmary untenable by the last decade of the century.

Infirmaries were never really intended as serious public health resources: their regulations excluded many kinds of patients, including those "suspected of having smallpox, itch, or other infectious distemper."[55] These diseases were usually treated on an outpatient basis at dispensaries, but the demographic influx to Manchester and the surrounding towns soon put this system under acute pressure. Aikin, Haygarth, and Percival were alert to the situation early on through their research interest in medical statistics. Unlike Thomas Malthus, another Warrington Academy graduate and Johnson author, they encouraged relief on behalf of the urban poor if the public benefits of industrial expansion were to be sustained.[56] It was a position Percival's ally Thomas Henry presented to members of the Literary and Philosophical Society in 1786 in a paper on mortality bills: "A contagious fever has proved very destructive, and its virulence has been, probably, increased, by the crowded and uncleanly manner, in which the poor people have been lodged . . . great towns, it must be allowed, are unfavourable for the duration of human life."[57] In the background to these remarks must have been the experience of the typhus outbreak in Radcliffe, near Bury, where Percival was called in by the local magistrate to investigate. The inauguration of a tradition of social inquiry among the physicians of the transpennine enlightenment was a product of a training in environmental medicine that encouraged them to look "beyond the confines of the individual frame into the space between bodies."[58] Henry's report identified overcrowding and bad sanitation brought on by the factory system as among the remote causes—in Cullen's sense—of the fever. The local mill owners—Sir Robert Peel (1st Baronet) among them—bitterly resented the report as an encroachment on their private business.[59]

These events form the backdrop of the "infirmary crisis" of 1790. There had been some muttering about a monopoly dominating appointments to the infirmary in the 1770s that didn't get very far.[60] In 1786, the newly qualified Thomas White, eldest son of Charles, was elected physician to the Infirmary. With Charles and Richard Hall, also father and son, four of the six honorary physicians were from two established Tory-Anglican families. The power of the traditional monopoly had been extended, but there were signs of change.[61] John Ferriar arrived in Manchester around 1785. With Thomas White's appointment, he was the only experienced physician in town without a position at the infirmary.[62] At the end of 1788, George Philips, Thomas Walker, and Thomas Cooper spearheaded a push to appoint their friend. The Quarterly Board proposed that the rule limiting the size of the honorary staff be rescinded, with a view to an election to be held in March 1789, despite protests from the Whites. The reform group already had plenty of campaign experience, not least on the Manchester committee against the slave trade, where they worked with Henry and Percival. Ferriar contributed an adaptation of Aphra Behn's *Oronooko* under the title *The Prince of Angola* (1788).[63] The battle in the infirmary spilled over into newspaper controversy through the winter of 1788–89 as supporters of the old order presented the proposed changes as part of a larger reformist conspiracy. One letter dated March 17, 1789, and signed by "A CONSTANT READER," painted the reformers as proposing "a Medical Republic of the worst kind, untried and unknown in the Government of those Hospitals with which we are acquainted."[64] In this heated atmosphere, the trustees negatived the proposals at the annual meeting. A motion to appoint two home physicians did succeed with the support of evangelical Anglicans and Methodists convinced of the urgency of the problems facing the urban poor. Philips proposed Ferriar and George Bew for the new posts.[65] When these appointments were confirmed in October, the honorary physicians resigned their responsibilities for home patients. Charles Este wrote to the London newspaper the *World* to defend their reputations, denying that any change was needed, a position undermined when typhus broke out in 1789.[66] Ferriar was effectively left in charge of the fever victims disbarred from treatment in the infirmary. Further reforms were pushed through in 1790: a new ward for inpatients; the building of a new dispensary; and the extension of the home-patient service to poor women in labor.

Pickstone and Butler show how this last development—proposed by the man-midwife William Simmons, only recently arrived in Manchester—constituted a direct threat to the interests of the Hall and White families.[67] They had dominated obstetrics in the town and decided to defend their position in a fashionable market by creating their own new charity outside the infirmary. The newspapers were again full of the dispute, which ended with Eason and Charles White resigning from their infirmary posts. White's resignation letter, published in the *Manchester Mercury*, complained at "the attempts . . . very unjustifiable . . . to overturn the constitution as originally established." On the same day, August 10, the newspaper also announced Ferriar's appointment as honorary physician. When Charles and Richard Hall also resigned, the way was cleared for vigorous institutional reform with Ferriar and Percival in the vanguard. Reporting again to the London press, Este represented the resignations as the result of "the same wild system" that had expanded the service to the home patients. A flourishing charity would be left as "a theatre of experiment for boys, just stepping from the pestle and mortar."[68]

The next decade only partially justified Este's fear that a broader set of reforms would follow. New rules for the infirmary were circulated to demonstrate its "universal benefit to our fellow creatures."[69] Ferriar began to advertise to the lay public the advice he had been giving to the town's Police Committee. Attention was being drawn to the state of cellar dwellings and filthy lodging houses that migrant workers were being forced to occupy. As part of this campaign, Ferriar also presented an essay on the "Origin of contagious and new Diseases" at the Literary and Philosophical Society. His intention was to present "a motive for active benevolence . . . little considered before" (1:xii). The essay was published in his *Medical Histories and Reflections* (1792), a volume dedicated to Percival as "its natural protector, a medical philosopher, zealous for improvement" (1:iii–iv). It followed the course set by Percival and Henry to argue that new diseases were being produced "among the poor of great cities" (1:222). More radical was the idea of a "secret" relationship between the diseases of luxury and those of "wretchedness": "The poor are indeed the first sufferers, but the mischief does not always rest with them. By secret avenues it reaches the most opulent, and severely revenges their neglect, or insensibility to the wretchedness surrounding them" (1:241). Ferriar's sense of the biopolitics of the situation insisted on a shared animal exis-tence. Moreover, it was a suffering body that Ferriar took to be mindful even where it seemed most abject, even where "wretchedness" seemed to narrow down to the utmost failure to live up to any idea of "the clean and proper body."[70] John Phillips Kay's usage of the term "social body" in the 1830s to denote an abstracted aspect of biological life at the heart of my final chapter could hardly have been more different from Ferriar's sense of a precarious and dispersed network linking the population of the industrial city.

Ferriar's detailed accounts of the suffering of his patients renders them as feeling subjects rather than simply objects of sympathy. The payoff was his insistence that the charitable institutions in place could not cope with the situation. He identified a series of problems behind the typhus epidemic, including the filthy state of lodging houses, "where the master of the house is totally regardless of the misery before his eyes" (1:137), the scandal of people being forced to live in cellars, the continu-ing problems with conditions in the factories themselves, and the general want of food and clothing. Nor did he take these problems to be simply physical, a problem with the functioning of the animal machine. They were exacerbated by "the constant action of depressing passions on the mind": "I have seen patients in agonies of despair," he continued, "on finding themselves overwhelmed with filth and abandoned by everyone who could do them any service; and after such emotions I have seldom found them recover" (1:139). Ferriar always saw mental and physical states as entangled, a situation complicated further by the emergence of "new, unexplained categories of disease" in the unprecedented circum-stances of the Industrial Revolution.[71] Refusing any simple distinction between body and mind, Ferriar insisted that the poor suffered in their bodies—and suffered more than any fine person—because they felt the hopelessness of their condition.

Around this time, Ferriar also drew up a circular—*Advice to the Poor*—directly addressing the laboring classes, later published as an appendix to the third volume of his *Medical Histories* (3:211–19). Although the pub-lished version darkly mentions the Board of Health obstructing its circulation, he reprinted it in the hope it might be taken up in other expanding towns. It soon circulated nationally by the Society for the Betterment of the Condition of the Poor. Fifty years later, Edwin Chadwick appended it to his *Report on the Sanitary Conditions of the Labouring Population* (1842).[72] George Rosen's charge that Ferriar failed to address the economic causes of distress seems harsh given the pace of change in this "shock city."[73] Moreover, it neglects Ferriar's indictment of "luxury" as one of the causes of the evil. Nor did he blame the poor in the way Kay and his allies in the 1830s would do later for a congenital improvidence. Ferriar encouraged the poor to take measures to improve their domestic economy without accusing them of any inherent tendency toward dissipation. His paper to the Literary and Philosophical Society made it clear that there was a shared responsibility, which included an opportunity for the privileged "to do for ourselves, in disarming the virulence of animal poisons, by increasing the happiness of our fellow creatures" (1:248). Maria Edgeworth later noted the way he had appealed to "the selfish as well as the humane by shewing how infectious fevers which spread often to the rich are generated in the squalid lodgings of the poor."[74]

The Board of Health and the House of Recovery were the most visible products of Ferriar's efforts. Set up at a public meeting in December 1795, under the direction of the sympathetic magistrate and stalwart member of the Literary and Philosophical Society, Thomas Butterworth Bayley, the greatest achievement of the Board was the establishment of a Fever Hospital near the Infirmary in 1796 (a model followed soon elsewhere, including London). There was again opposition from entrenched medical opinion and the inhabitants of wealthy streets around the hospital worried about contagion. "House of Recovery" was adopted as a less ominous name than Fever Hospital. Ferriar's more radical ideas about the inspection of lodging houses were beaten back. The main lesson of the epidemics for Ferriar, as Pickstone sees it, was the need for a redistribution of wealth that would lift the majority of the poor out of the "interstitial" conditions that forced them into old and filthy subdivided houses.[75] Ferriar's paper to the Literary and Philosophical Society on the origin of contagious diseases ends by addressing the excesses of the rich not simply in their consequences for the individuals involved: "when voluptuous habits induce him to withhold his real superfluities from the indigent, he contributes to the diseases and destructions of thousands" (1:247). His criticism of "voluptuous habits" had more to do with the redistribution of wealth than any program of moral restraint that held the body to be an object of disciplinary suspicion of the sort found in such successors as James Phillips Kay.

FERRIAR'S EMBODIED MIND

John Ferriar's strictly medical writing is continuous with the more exploratory thinking he started to develop at the Manchester Literary and Philosophical Society, where he had quickly made his way after joining in April 1786, probably with the patronage of Thomas Percival.[76] My main interest here is with Ferriar's engagement with debates surrounding philosophical materialism, always a fraught topic, but especially so in the years after the French Revolution, when the society struggled to retain an atmosphere open to debate. Ferriar originally debated the issues with his friend Thomas Cooper, who on January 17, 1787, gave a paper at the society that sparked a controversy noticed far beyond Manchester. The clash between Ferriar and Owen in 1794 was probably a more local instance of the ripples of trouble the topic caused. Although Cooper and Ferriar were friends, agreeing about the importance of material circumstances to mental phenomena, they ultimately differed—as Ferriar and Owen differed—around the question of mechanism and medical essentialism.

In his original paper, Cooper described himself as "singular in my sentiments," aware that his position made him an outlier even in a society generally interested in Priestley's materialism.[77] His most immediate point of disagreement was with "our worthy secretary" Thomas Barnes, who early in the society's activities had given a paper "On the Influence of the Imagination and the Passions upon our Understanding," which argued for a positive view of imagination as one of several mental modes that together made up the mind as "ONE UNCOMPOUNDED ESSENCE, continually in motion."[78] Cooper was carefully respectful to Barnes, if insistently skeptical about anything that might look like "immaterialism" being introduced to Priestley's thinking on matter and spirit.[79] "Materialism" in Cooper's definition is *that Opinion which makes the Phenomena termed MENTAL, depend on the Properties necessarily resulting from one Organization, without the Assistance of a distinct immaterial Principle.*[80] Unsurprisingly given its candor, Cooper's paper was not published in the society's *Memoirs* but in *Tracts Ethical Theological and Political* (1789), printed by William Eyres at his Warrington press for Joseph Johnson (and later ordered for the Literary and Philosophical Society in Newcastle). Most of the essays in *Tracts* had been read to the Manchester society, but others could not "from the nature of the subjects treated."[81] Presumably these included his "Summary of Unitarian Arguments," which would hardly have gone down well with those Anglican members who harbored suspicions that the society was a Unitarian front. One wonders how those in the room reacted, if they attended the paper on materialism. For his part, Cooper was bullish about truth being the only reasonable standard of judgment for any argument and dismissive of claims that there was any tendency in his ideas subversive of religion (a point on which even Priestley had his doubts).[82] Aside from Cooper's relatively polite mentions of Barnes, his style is punchily contemptuous of the broad sweep of what he calls "immaterialism," including recent medical defenses of vitalism and the "common sense" philosophy of James Beattie and "the Scotch doctors." He gets close to his hero Priestley's *History of the Corruptions of Christianity* (1782) when he ascribes Christian immaterialism to the influence of Platonism, stopping himself going further, he said, in deference to the society's rules on theological controversy.[83]

Some of those who listened to his paper at the society must have thought Cooper had jumped that fence from early on in his talk. Even so, less than a month later, the topic was revisited when his dismissive comments on vitalism were expanded upon by Ferriar. The physician defined "vitalism" as the idea of "a living power independent of the mind," tracing it back to Plato's notion of "plastic nature," dismissed by Cooper as a mystical "soul of the world." Ferriar saw the error as stemming from a need to explain the "reciprocal action of the soul and body on each other," a metaphysical problem that his essay gives little space.[84] Ferriar's main business was with Alexander Monro and John Hunter, two of "the Scotch doctors" Cooper had handled roughly. Monro's *Observations on the Nervous System* (1783) had identified, in Ferriar's words, "a living principle, pervading the universe." John Hunter had offered a specific site for the vital principle in the blood. There, Hunter claimed, could be discovered "a power of forming and renewing parts . . . almost to a degree of rationality." Resisting explanations that might remove the issue of the vital principle beyond the physical into an occult domain, Ferriar insisted, on the contrary, that the brain was the "source of sensibility and irritability." If at first glance, this sounds like a straightforward defense of Cooper's materialism, Ferriar's conclusion is more reserved: "I have uniformly considered the action of the mind and brain on the body as identical without reference to the question of materialism, because with respect to our facts, and indeed to all medical facts, this notion is sufficiently complete." He doesn't underwrite Cooper's confidence that "the mind is the brain" (to use the phrase Cooper quoted from Richard Price's debates with Priestley). Ferriar took the view that "it is of more consequence to examine one opinion, which is said to be supported by facts, than either to reject or advance many plausible hypotheses." His final sentence simply echoed Cooper's care not to transgress the society's rules on religious controversy: "I have purposely omitted to consider the application of a vital principle to pathology, as the subject would lead to disquisitions inadmissible to the rules of the society."[85]

"Pathology" here is being used in the sense of "the study of *dis*ease and its multiple causes" recently discussed by Kevis Goodman: Ferriar's refusal to reduce these to a monocausal mechanism was made clearer when he turned to his differences with Cooper in his "Argument against the Doctrine of Materialism," read to the society in November 1790.[86] Ferriar's "soft materialism" resisted not only occult notions of mind extracted from the material networks of the body, on the one hand, but also the materialist axiom that the brain simply was the mind, on the other.[87] Ferriar's "Argument against Materialism" is primarily concerned with the implications of cases of serious brain damage where some form of consciousness is retained, "almost demonstrating that the Brain is the instrument only, not the Cause of the reasoning Power." The "almost" here is not to be glossed over. Nor is the tone of the essay, which teases "Metaphysical" doctrine with "facts." Ferriar's writing is nearly always suffused with genial skepticism that manifests as a distinctive mixture of Baconian trust in observation and learned wit against metaphysical system building. His conclusion that "something more than the discernible organization must be requisite to produce the phenomena of thinking," suggesting the importance of "remote" rather than simply physiological causes, is framed as an amiable riposte to "my good friend." He ends with a sophisticated pun drawn from Lucian, a favorite author, to present himself as Diogenes the Cynic rolling his tub up and down the hill "so that he should not seem to be the only idle man" (the pun is on the homophone between an area of Corinth and the Greek word for the skull, appropriate as Ferriar had been rolling his tub—as it were—around the skull in search of the mind).[88]

Cooper himself later generously accepted that Ferriar had "rendered it dubious how far the sentient principle ought to be confined to the brain," only noting the open nature of the physician's conclusions that did nothing to support "the common hypothesis of a separate soul, acting by means of the body."[89] If an amiable relationship was preserved between the two protagonists, the broader reception of their exchange was more complicated, not least because the version published in the fourth volume of the Manchester society's transactions was engulfed by the firestorm directed against Cooper's support for the French Revolution. Ironically, the problem was caused partly by the society's success in attracting national and international coverage of its debates. The *British Critic*'s review of the volume at the end of 1793 misrepresented Ferriar's paper as an expert refutation of French atheism. By this stage, attacked by Edmund Burke in Parliament, Cooper was widely known to have visited the Jacobin Club in 1792 with James Watt Jr. The reviewer in the *British Critic* refused the *Memoir*'s denial of responsibility for opinions expressed in its pages as not "equally justified in every proceeding." Freethinking was allowable in "matters of experiment, and hypothesis purely philosophical," but prohibited when "matters of morality and metaphysics" are circulated "which may prove injurious to society." This position precisely contradicted Cooper's claim that the only measure of an argument was whether it was true or not. The review presented Ferriar's case histories as "the testimony of facts, opposed to the speculations of theory," ignoring the fact that Ferriar refused to draw positive conclusions from them in favor of religious orthodoxy. Against Cooper's belief that "the brain is . . . a mechanical organization of fibres, so delicately curious, that the result of it is mind," as the reviewer put it, Ferriar is celebrated as "a man of much learning, and no small share of taste and judgment." Ferriar's jokey closing allusion to Lucian is read as a sign of cultural literacy weighed against Cooper's base materialism. The review scarcely does justice to either the tone or content of Ferriar's essay, flipping his skepticism about mechanistic accounts of mind into a positive affirmation of the doctrine of spirit.[90]

The febrile political atmosphere of the 1790s tended to force complex medical ideas into this kind of crude binary. The same tendency—if from the other side politically—produced a scathing attack on Ferriar by the Liverpool physician William Tattersall in *A brief view of the anatomical arguments for the doctrine of materialism; occasioned by Dr. Ferriar's argument against it* (1794), another Joseph Johnson pamphlet. Tattersall took Cooper's materialism to be "the only rational foundation for the doctrine of resurrection," and he strongly suggested that Ferriar was a defender of Church and King.[91] Seemingly appalled by this construction, Ferriar replied in the second volume of his *Medical Histories*, reiterating his admiration for Cooper, as "a man of great knowledge and splendid talents," a brave enough position given that his friend had by now been driven into exile in the United States. He also insisted that he had not anywhere mentioned "the doctrine of spirit" (2:248, 253). Hardly a ringing endorsement of orthodoxy, especially given the pressures of those times!

Ferriar described Tattersall's position as "the boasted mechanical theory of thinking" (2:254). Like his teacher Cullen, he was suspicious of reductively monocausal explanations, a suspicion that extended from his more general thinking on mind to his reservations about the experiments into the medical value of "fixed airs" being pursued by Thomas Beddoes.[92] James Watt Sr. had begun to produce an apparatus to deliver Beddoes's pneumatic therapy from 1794.[93] Told about the development

by Cooper, Ferriar asked for details from the younger Watt, who encouraged the physician to test the apparatus in the infirmary, confiding in his
letter of reply that Sir Joseph Banks had refused his support because of
"Beddoes's cloven Jacobin foot and it is the order of the day to suppress
or oppose all *Jacobin innovations* such as this is already called."[94] Ferriar
was more open-minded about Beddoes, but his initial enthusiasm for
the pneumatic therapy cooled quite quickly, to Watt's disappointment.
"I expect to be able to recommend it," he told Watt, but also sounded
a skeptical note: "the most splendid theories are not admitted to the
highest honours, till they have been confirmed by those humble observers, whom Dr. Beddoes has chosen to abuse."[95] By September 1795 the
elder Watt, traveling through Manchester, confirmed Ferriar's lack of
progress, writing to his son that "at the Infirmary they make a bungling
hand of the preparation of the airs, leaving that to a parcel of ignorant
boys."[96] Ferriar only moved slowly toward making his doubts public,
suggesting he didn't want a public break with Beddoes and Watt Jr. The
second volume of *Medical Histories* (1795) gave conditional support:
"I shall, therefore, continue to use the pneumatic medicine but only in
those disorders which prove intractable to common remedies, till I can arrive at certain conclusions respecting it. For I think it wholly inexcusable,
to hazard the life of a poor patient, by substituting uncertain remedies,
for those which experience justifies us in directing. But I confess that
I shall proceed in my trials, with hopes much reduced, and with eagerness
greatly abated" (2:242). The third volume, published in 1798, finally made
a decisive statement against the treatment, although it noted that "the
science of medicine would suffer equally, by an illiberal discouragement
of speculative opinions, or by too ready an acquiescence in them." The
problem, he suggested, was when any theory aimed "to reduce the causes
of disease and death to one or two." Predictably enough, the *British Critic*
was delighted at "the manly and decisive tone in which he finally delivers
his own opinion on the subject of pneumatic medicine," as if it had been
impatiently waiting for him to stamp on the cloven foot of Jacobinism.
No such political disavowal of Beddoes ever came.[97]

APPARITIONS OF THE MIND

Ferriar fully participated in the resurgence of environmental thinking
that witnessed the receding influence of mechanistic explanations, despite the contrary tendency found in Cooper and Owen. As early as the
preface to the first volume of his *Medical Reflections*, Ferriar had inveighed against the tendency of "medical writers to form systems" (1:ix).
So far, I have traced this disposition in Ferriar in its more critical aspect,

but there is a more affirmative side to his skepticism about the mono-causal explanations of medical essentialism, perhaps most apparent in his literary criticism, especially in his *Illustrations of Sterne* (1798), whose origins lay in his "Comments on Sterne," read to the society in January 1791. There the figure of François Rabelais looms large, often as a source of "general satire on the abuse of speculative opinions" celebrat-ing what another student of Rabelais, M. M. Bakhtin, called "the gro-tesque body."[98] Bakhtin's grotesque body is open to the messiness of the world around it—that is, part of a mesh of remote and proximate causes, in Cullen's terms. Ferriar's literary criticism participates in the version of aesthetics as *aisthesis* recently recovered by Goodman from the late eighteenth-century traffic between medicine and aesthetics. Central to Goodman's analysis is the contrast between nosology—the system-atic study of symptoms abstracted from their causes—and pathology as the study of the development and origins of disease.[99] Ferriar seems to have been drawn to Sterne by the way the novelist was concerned with the pathology of hobbyhorses in so far as they could be traced back—only ever uncertainly—to the history of the body in its physical and remoter circumstances.

Specifically concerned with tracing the origins of some of Sterne's ideas to Rabelais, Robert Burton, and other Renaissance satirists, *Illus-trations of Sterne* has earned Ferriar a place of dishonor among scholars of Sterne (at least in their footnotes). Despite often being portrayed as a killjoy, Ferriar was quite clear about his veneration for the novelist: "I do not mean to treat him as a Plagiarist: I wish to illustrate, not to degrade him."[100] The general tone of his response is a celebration of the use Sterne makes of his sources: "the dexterity," as Ferriar puts it, "with which [Sterne] has incorporated in his work so many passages, written with very different views by their respective authors." Incorporation is a useful idea here. Ferriar effectively details the long history of using the exigencies of the body to poke fun at speculative systems (a key strategy of his favorite Diogenes). Ferriar used the device in the printed version of the essay on genius that had sparked the dispute with Owen: "I know not whether weakness or pride contributed more to those delusions, which appropriated a divinity to preside over the most usual, and the least dig-nified of our natural functions, but if the ancients supposed themselves to be supernaturally assisted on such occasions, it is not wonderful that they should lay claim to superior protection, in the bright and enviable moments of literary success." This learned lavatory humor may well ac-count for the stunned response from the audience for the paper in 1794. Ferriar's literary writing—and, I would suggest, his professional medical writing and practice—was actively hostile to ideas of genius as a "distinct power of the mind," as he put it, but equally resistant to replacing it with any idea of man as machine.[101]

Likewise, Ferriar's writing on "medical demonology," on the face of it an exercise in medical disenchantment, is in fact a nuanced part of his debate with Cooper on "the phenomena termed mental." Cooper's essay on materialism dismissed "the vulgar notion of apparitions" as a prop of immaterialist superstition.[102] Ferriar's "Of Popular Illusions, and particularly Medical Demonology," read to the Literary and Philosophical Society a few months earlier in May 1786, agreed in substance, perhaps, but showed a characteristic relish for his materials to the point where his paper arguably shows rather more tolerance for folk superstition than for the illusions of the educated elite. "Errors are imputed to ignorance," he wrote, "which, however they arose, were supported in the most enlightened times, and by writers of the greatest knowledge and acuteness." Enlightenment has its own pathologies: "even the present century, notwithstanding the boasted improvements of reason, has proved fruitful in illusions of the most ridiculous nature."[103] Ferriar's medical duties at the lunatic asylum, close by the infirmary, were to give ample experience of treating mental disorders and delusions of many kinds. Leonard Smith suggests that Ferriar regarded mental illness as "closely aligned with physical disorders," as one might expect given his sense of the entanglement of mind and body.[104] His system of care allowed the patient to "minister to himself." It might not cure, Ferriar accepted, but it would "soften the destiny" of those in his care.[105] His experiences in the hospital provided some of the case histories in his *An Essay Towards a Theory of Apparitions* (1813), otherwise effectively a full-length elaboration of his papers on medical demonology and occult ideas of genius.

Ferriar's *Essay* does not address insanity as such. Instead, he provides an explanation of the role of remote causes in the experience of "spectral impressions" by those otherwise in control of their faculties, opening with the striking claim that "the forms of the dead, or absent person have been seen and their voices have been heard, by witnesses whose testimony is entitled to belief." Apparitions are not spiritual interventions for Ferriar, but products of the mind that appear as hallucinations. The aim of the essay is to discern "whether the improved state of physiology affords any glimpse of light on this subject, . . . from the known laws of the animal oeconomy, independent of supernatural causes." A characteristic mix of clinical cases with historical material, the essay does not quite fulfill its self-protective claim to keep to "profane history and to the delusions of individuals only," discussing, for instance, examples drawn from the English Civil War.[106] Hallucinations are traced to a series of physical causes, among them digestive problems, diseased nerves, circulatory irregularities, or a "peculiar condition of the sensorium." Rather than simply operating as proximate causes, these and other physical problems inflamed the brain and renewed previous visual or auditory impressions, sometimes recombining them into new forms. Renewed impressions then appeared in the brain as if they were external objects. They did not depend on proximate physical causes, as in more mechanistic theories of relations between the mind and the body. General times of crisis, like the English Civil War, and intense reading experiences, Ferriar noted, could also trigger them. True to the tradition of environmental medicine in which he had been trained, as Goodman describes it, "custom, memory, imagination, and discourse were considered to act upon men and women just as effectively as present persons and objects."[107]

Ferriar's preface sent an invitation to a literary readership that had precipitately, it drily suggests, granted Beddoes "the honors due to the inventor of a new pleasure" with his beguiling "Gas of Paradise" (v), a reference to his notorious experiments with nitrous oxide. Rather than place himself above "readerly pleasure" by jovially taking up the position of medical disenchanter, Ferriar appeared as a Gothic magician: "Take courage, then, good reader, and knock at the portal of my enchanted castle." Understanding how the mind worked, Ferriar suggested, would make available "to the makers and readers of such stories, a view of the subject, which may extend their enjoyment far beyond its former limits" (v–vi).[108] Numerous novelists and poets responded to the invitation. Copies of the *Essay* were owned by Samuel Taylor Coleridge, Walter Scott, and William Wordsworth. William Godwin seems to have read it carefully, and Percy Bysshe Shelley made at least one reference to the essay.[109] Helen Groth argues that Ferriar "urges his readers to relax their vigilant application of the machinery of rational explanation and embrace the inexplicable phenomena of dreams, hallucinations and apparitions of various kinds."[110] Perhaps it would be closer to the truth to say that rational explanation and playfulness go hand in hand in the essay, as elsewhere in his writing. He mocked physicians, like Beddoes, when he thought they put too much trust in monocausal explanations. He was equally dismissive when novelists such as Ann Radcliffe used such contrivances as secret passageways to explain away phantoms of the mind: "It has given me pain to see the most fearful and ghastly commencements of a tale of horror reduced to mere common events at the winding up of a book." Sliding panels, waxwork figures, and "other vulgar machinery" are given short shrift (vi). Ferriar effectively predicted the destiny of Gothic in psychological terror produced from the internal workings of the mind, a direction James Hogg took up for his *Memoirs and Confessions of a Justified Sinner (1824)*, although, to be fair, they are scarcely neglected in Radcliffe.

Ferriar showed general concern with the way that dramatic spectacle engaged the mind through the embodied affections. In October 1786, he had given a paper to the Manchester society on the plays of Philip Massinger, later picked up and developed in Coleridge's dramatic criticism.[111] Ferriar imputed the success of Massinger's plays to his ability to "interest our feelings." Drawing a distinction between plays that attracted the "taste" rather than the "understanding," Ferriar identified Massinger's greatness with his ability to prevent any "faint sense of propriety to dwell on the mind." Instead, Massinger "inflames or soothes, excites the strongest terror, or the softest pity, with all the energy and power of a true poet."[112] A similar idea of dramatic effects depending on a response located in the senses was also at heart of John Aikin Jr.'s "On the Impression of Reality Attending Dramatic Representations," which argued that emotions raised inside and outside the theater, the interplay of remote and proximate causes felt on the body, "are precisely the same in nature, and only differ in degree of intensity." For Aikin, "the identity of the sensation is proved by the sameness of the corporeal effects" and extends to the experience of solitary reading, taking as his example the experience of Sterne's much anthologized story of Le Fevre from *Tristram Shandy*: "Now will anyone fairly consult his feelings, assert that in such a case he weeps merely from the reflexion on possible human calamities; and that Le Fevre is not for the first time a real person in his imagination."[113] Physical impressions caused by intense reading could outlast the encounter with the printed page. The book as a material object is effectively understood as part of an extended mind in the way some of Aikin's work with his sister had imagined the interaction between the child and the child's environment.

When it comes to the belief in apparitions, Ferriar takes a similar line to Aikin on drama by insisting that the forms of the dead are physically seen in hallucinations. In other words, these may be illusions, but they are seen and heard as physical experiences. "Impressions on the eye," as he puts it, "are more durable than the impression's cause" (13 and 16). Hallucinations are a "waking dream" (19), to use his anticipation of John Keats, with origins in a kind of dreamwork: "When an object is presented to the mind during sleep, while the operations of judgment are suspended, the imagination is busily employed in forming a story, to account for the appearance, whether agreeable or distressing" (17). Distancing himself from "theological discussions," he insists that neither the "horror" of the vulgar nor the disdain of the skeptic are appropriate responses to phenomena he regards as a valuable source of physically pleasurable experiments on the self (ix). Both Aikin and Ferriar located literary pleasures in physiological responses. "Illusion" is seen as part of a complex economy of sympathy and pleasure, of proximate and remote causes, part of a means of making sense of the universe that encompasses those who believe in apparitions and the audience for drama, not to mention everyday psychological experience.

Ferriar's *Theory of Apparitions* celebrated such experiences as a source of pleasure; "a great convenience will be found in my system; apparitions may be evoked, in open day . . . Nay, a person rightly prepared may see ghosts, while seated comfortably by his library-fire, in as much perfection, as amidst broken tombs, nodding ruins, and awe-inspiring ivy" (viii). Conjuring embodied images for his readers is what Ina Ferris thinks Scott gained from reading Ferriar. His literary writing certainly did not assume the superiority of his medical gaze over popular forms of knowledge, whether folk traditions or modern novel reading. "Attraction to apparition narratives," as Ferris acutely notes of his influence on Scott, "speaks as much to the roots of such narratives in ancient medical 'lore,' with its links to local tradition (tales, gossip, anecdote), as to the ambitions of a modern medical 'science' anxious to classify and systematize the phenomena that were the subjects of such narratives."[114] Ferriar's satire at Beddoes's expense hints that medical science could get just as tangled up in such illusions as the uneducated. His suggestion that "delusions of the imagination," as he called them, helped explain the influence that "the doctrines of Plato have exerted, in this respect, even since the establishment of Christianity" hinted that the same tendency persisted in the church (99–100). Nevertheless, his essay was generally well received, if sometimes with a lingering sense that he had failed to acknowledge that there might be a genuinely religious kind of visionary experience.[115] *Blackwood's* declared its "decided *anti-ferriarism*" in the same number that contained its notorious attack on Keats as a Cockney poet. Ferriar had, it feared, sacrificed the "noble faculty of our souls, the imagination" to a "decisive victory of the genius of physiology."[116] I've suggested that Ferriar never saw this issue in binary terms. His idea of mind was more concerned with reenchantment than the disenchanted version of a human being as a "reasoning machine" found in Owen. Both ought to be viewed as competing affordances of the pursuit of useful knowledge in the Manchester Literary and Philosophical Society.

CHAPTER FIVE

HANNAH GREG'S DOMESTIC MISSION

The liberal circles associated with the Manchester Literary and Philosophical Society were generally encouraging to the education of women, at least partly because as mothers they were deemed to be crucial to the creation of an early environment that would provide a strong foundation to the character of the individual. "Home was always the theatre of my exploits," Hannah Greg claimed, "and the boundary of my views and prospects."[1] Greg was not simply confining herself to a private sphere. Not only did she educate her children in liberal principles—boys and girls alike—for a broader world, she used printed and manuscript circulation to disseminate her ideas, and also developed them—for better or worse—with the apprentices next to her home at Quarry Bank House. Hers was a domestic mission. Her education in the circles of Rational Dissent had given her every encouragement to take these steps, within certain limits. Joseph Priestley had argued that "the minds of women are capable of the same improvement, and the same furniture, as those of men."[2] Nevertheless, Warrington Academy, where Priestley taught, did not admit women students, despite providing the original context for his friend Anna Laetitia Barbauld's achievements. Thomas Henry's presentation of the Literary and Philosophical Society as a venue where young men would be able to experience "sweet converse with the fair sex" was primarily metaphorical, at least in terms of what happened in the society's rooms, even if plenty of his friends had met and talked with Barbauld elsewhere. No woman was elected a member of the society until Winifred Faraday in 1900.[3] They could visit the institution to hear lectures, but they could not take part in the collision of mind with mind at the monthly meetings that were understood to be its engine room.

Where women had an increasingly active institutional life in these circles was in philanthropic societies, especially from the 1810s. They were not simply helpmeets. Women organized committees and ran institutions whose remit went far beyond the confines of the home. Catharine Cappe's *Thoughts on Charitable Institutions* (1814), with its "address to females of the rising generation," was a palpable influence in this regard across the transpennine region.[4] This terrain of philanthropic activism admitted no simple distinction between public and private, although some judgments were made on this basis. Mary Anne Rawson's home outside Sheffield, as Alison Twells has shown, was a center for the dispersion of philanthropic activity in the 1810s and 1820s, but William Wilberforce had reservations about her antislavery activism when it came to door-to-door visiting.[5] During Joseph Hunter's time at Manchester College, York, Cappe invited students to her home for intellectual gatherings: "I valued the privilege of visiting her. I liked the conversation & have met with few people whose conversation I thought equal to her." Others complained that she interfered and brought the College "under Petticoat Government." Better disposed than some, Hunter still wished her autobiographical writing had not revealed "her motives and feelings in the undisguised manner" and thought she was governed by an "*ill regulated desire of being useful*."[6] Even in their philanthropic activities, Cappe and other women operated under "a complex mix of permission and prohibition deriving from their sex," as writers, and in their networked and institutional relations.[7]

DELICACY, AGENCY, AND PARTICIPATION

Women's participation was intrinsic to the strength of the knowledge networks described in this book, as should have already been apparent, but their participation in the institutional nodes that formed within them depended on complicated norms surrounding their "delicacy," to use the word chosen by the committee of the Literary and Philosophical Society in Newcastle. These norms were understood to make their participation in vigorous debate undesirable. In this light, David Livingstone's suggestion that this period assumed "female corporeality rendered women unsuitable for intellectual pursuits in general and for science in particular" needs to be qualified by taking the mode of exchange into account.[8] As a young woman, Hannah Greg had been able to participate in the debate on materialism when it was restaged in her home. Her daughter Elizabeth (known as Bessy to the family) could attend John Dalton's lectures at the Literary and Philosophical Society. However, the monthly discussions of his ideas held in the same venue were closed to her.[9] William Turner's daughter Mary experienced the same prohibitions with regard to the society in Newcastle upon Tyne, despite her father's encouragement of her intellectual abilities. Anxieties about the disposition of bodies in rooms, questions of where and how debates took place, and not simply their subject matter, helped form these barriers and complicated the role of women in the networks of improvement discussed here.

If Hannah Greg was excluded from formal participation in the Literary and Philosophical Society when she moved to Manchester after her marriage, she seems to have enjoyed some secondary access to their debates when Thomas Percival and other members "used to adjourn to her house for supper after their meetings and she made the most of the society around her (including the Heywoods and Philipses)."[10] Percival and his circle did not share Thomas Gisborne's sense that women lacked powers of "close and comprehensive reasoning." They certainly did agree that the female sex constituted the source of "the most amiable tendencies and affections implanted in human nature."[11] Thomas Henry's confidence that contact with the improving minds of women, at least via their writing, was shared by other members Greg knew. When John Ferriar published *The Prince of Angola* in support of the campaign for the abolition of the slave trade, he made a point of celebrating the role of women in the moral education of commercial society, "which every man of a right heart will be proud to obtain."[12] If Ferriar and Henry figured women as a softening influence on male manners, Manchester's sense of their capabilities was also evolving into "a lively, even if highly contested, conversation on the rights of women."[13] In March 1787, when Ferriar's friend Thomas Cooper read his "Propositions respecting the Foundation of Civil Government," he suggested that assumptions about "self-direction" for "unmarried women at years of discretion" appeared "to be inequitable," a situation that extended "perhaps indeed to the married." Republished as an appendix to his *Reply to Mr. Burke's invective* (1792), Cooper added a lengthy note on "the Rights of Woman." The note complains that women's "Minds and [...] Persons are kept in Subjection," praising the work in particular of Barbauld, Anna Seward, and Mary Wollstonecraft as evidence against "the present and most iniquitous and most absurd notions on the Subject of the disparity of Sexes."[14] George Philips called for women to be given the vote in his *The Necessity of a Speedy and Effectual Reform in Parliament* (1793), although he later recanted these "wild enthusiastic hopes" as "unattainable," blaming his earlier enthusiasm on the influence of Cooper and Ferriar.[15]

Support for the education of women was part and parcel of the intellectual traffic that flowed between Manchester and Liverpool in the 1780s and early 1790s, especially among these Rational Dissenters. The lifelong collaboration with his sister that had begun at Warrington, although she was excluded from formal participation in the academy, was a foundation of John Aikin's career as an educational writer. "Virtue, wisdom, presence of mind, patience, vigour, capacity, application," he argued, "are not *sexual* qualities: they belong to mankind."[16] When the young William Turner moved from Warrington to Newcastle in 1784 to take up his ministry at Hanover Square, he took these principles with him. He was someone who had directly experienced converse with Barbauld when she presented him with her "Verses written in . . . an Ivory Pocketbook." Barbauld made sufficient impression on Turner for him to remember her as one of the greatest writers of either gender in the obituary he wrote for the *Newcastle Magazine* in 1825. Further following the poetic script Barbauld had given to him as a boy, he supported the education of women in rational principles, encouraging his daughter, Mary, to read Wollstonecraft's *Vindication of the Rights of Woman* (1792) and to attend science lectures at the Royal Institution in London.[17] Late in her life, Mary Turner fondly remembered visiting the Aikins and the Barbaulds on a trip to London. These reminiscences came after a long marriage to John Gooch Robberds, pastor at Cross Street Chapel, whom she had met on a visit to Catharine Cappe in York. The same networks drew in Elizabeth Cleghorn Stevenson, who lodged with Turner and his family before she married William Gaskell, copastor at Cross Street, in 1832.[18]

Harriet Martineau was another woman who seems to have been encouraged by Turner in her intellectual ambitions. She visited Newcastle regularly as a young woman, and her *Autobiography* recalls "good Mr. Turner of Newcastle, my mother's pastor and friend before her marriage." She remembered him as the first clergyman "who took any direct notice of me." Although he turned her away from questioning her brother about foreknowledge and free will, his rebuke was really about his sense of the uselessness of inquiry into "what he took for granted to be an unknowable thing," more a comment on theological controversy than a gendered statement of what was appropriate for women to know.[19] Unlike Manchester, the question of women's actual membership of the Literary and Philosophical Society at Newcastle was at least raised rather than simply assumed to be unthinkable. In 1798, shortly after ordering the posthumous works of Wollstonecraft for the society's library, John Clennell got wind of a discussion of female membership at the committee. He wrote a note in the recommendation book asking after the committee's intentions, to which he received a rather disingenuous reply:

> Ladies are and always have been admissible as members, by the way set down in the Rules of the Society; what was suggested, was, whether some mode less revolting to their delicacy could not be adopted; but as that

required an alteration of, or addition to the Rules, it was necessarily deferred till the anniversary meeting in March.[20]

What was being proposed by the committee was effectively a form of passive membership: the "reading membership" agreed by the committee in March 1799. It allowed for privatized study, borrowing books from the library, but not for participation in the collision of minds at the meetings. By 1810, only two women had taken up the opportunity, which may reflect on the limited scope for participation it afforded. Back in the 1790s, Clennell suggested that the decision about the new form of membership should at least be advertised in the newspapers, "as the first to admit Ladies into its circle," so that other societies might be encouraged to follow its example. The response in the recommendation book was unenthusiastic: "The Committee does not think any information of this sort is necessary." Women did attend Turner's lectures on chemistry, held under the auspices of the society but open to paying nonmembers, repeating the pattern found in Manchester at around the same time. The situation suggests a nuance to Livingstone's claim that "scientific space, by and large, was masculine space."[21] "Space" in these societies was being implicitly defined in relation to female "corporeality" but moderated by assumptions about practices and modes of knowledge exchange, wherein, for instance, a lecture was assumed to be, up to a point, a more passive form of intellectual participation, more appropriate to female "delicacy," than a meeting where the collision of mind with mind might and often did grow heated.

Mary Turner helped prepare the diagrams for her father's lectures on chemistry in the rooms of the Literary and Philosophical Society. "As I could do them privately before the lecture," she wrote, "there could be no objection, & I quite enjoyed the work; it also enabled me better to understand the lecture."[22] "Privately" is a word that communicates the frisson that surrounded women's "public" access to knowledge, a porous boundary, policed by scattered roadblocks, not always applied in the same ways in each place. In Newcastle, for instance, Barbauld and Mary Hays were nominated for honorary membership on July 14, 1801. There were six proposers, including Clennell, but not William Turner, for whom the whole episode may have been a personal embarrassment given his long family association with Barbauld. The male candidates were all elected the following month. The minutes are simply silent on the two women.[23] The same resistance remained present elsewhere in the region. Twenty years later, in the early burst of correspondence surrounding the Philosophical and Literary Society in Leeds, "Di. Vernon"—taking her name from the hunter heroine of Walter Scott's *Rob Roy* (1817)—wrote to call for women to be allowed to attend lectures at least. The letter—dated 17 February 1819—begins by mentioning Lord Byron's sarcasm toward "literary women" before proceeding to the fact that women were allowed to attend lectures at Liverpool and Manchester. On February 17, 1819, a letter of support expressed surprise at their exclusion and added a precedent from the Birmingham Philosophical Society, where every Monday night there meets "an assemblage of the most respectable Ladies of that town and neighbourhood." Mentioning various scientific topics, the letter asks, "What is there in these subjects that directly or indirectly, remotely or proximately can prove injurious to the mind, or offensive to the modesty of any lady?" Despite further supportive correspondence on the issue, it was decided that women would not be admitted, a decision confirmed in 1828 when the matter was reopened.[24]

After Clennell left Newcastle for London around 1807, he took the opportunity to encourage women into a series of local knowledge institutions, none of which lasted very long. "A respectable number of ladies" attended the inaugural meeting of the Hackney Literary Institution and Subscription Library at the Lamb Tavern in 1815. The first book proposed for purchase was Wollstonecraft's *Rights of Woman*. Women also participated in the meetings that convened—initially in Clennell's home—to discuss papers given by members. The society struggled to keep its membership much above seventeen, but at least two women can be identified as active participants: Miss Williams and Miss Wafford. The latter "politely attended" a committee meeting in December 1816 to indicate her intention to remain a subscriber, but there is no mention of her speaking. On March 6, 1817, a Mr. Lumby—who had proposed Miss Williams as a member back in 1815—gave a paper on "the character of the female heart," at which "some ladies expressed disapprobation." One wonders what Lumby said, but the meeting was adjourned. A scribbled final note in the minute book says the society was dissolved in May 1817. It is hard not to grant this final episode some symbolic import. Moving from Newcastle to Hackney, Clennell had continued to seek the active participation of women, but other men—however progressive their aspirations may have been about female "conversation"—struggled to find a way to conduct themselves when faced with the active and embodied participation of women.[25]

"A WOMAN OF SENSE AND TASTE"

These unevenly applied gendered norms then excluded Hannah Greg from direct participation at the Literary and Philosophical Society in Manchester, although she was very much an active part of the broader intellectual networks on which it relied. From an early age, when she was Hannah Lightbody, born into a prosperous family of Liverpool merchants, she had been encouraged to participate in the vibrant intellectual culture of Rational Dissent. Her father had died when she was twelve. Her mother, Elizabeth Lightbody, retained a formidable presence amid the congregation of John Yates at Kaye Street chapel. There she cultivated a strong network of like-minded women, most notably Anna Cropper, who died in 1791, and her sister Arabella Nicholson. Hannah Lightbody was sent to school in Stoke Newington, then just outside London, where she stayed with her cousins in the wealthy banking family of Thomas Rogers, whose son grew up to be the poet Samuel Rogers. There she met the celebrated minister of the local chapel Richard Price, and possibly Mary Wollstonecraft.[26] She certainly got to know Barbauld, generous host of visitors from the north. Hannah's diary records them meeting on a visit back to London 1787, when Barbauld recommended Hannah read *Vathek* and *The Castle of Otranto*.[27] The diary had been started a few months earlier on her return from Stoke Newington. There are several points where Hannah records the kind of experience of God in nature that suggests a familiarity with the religious sublime found in Barbauld's "Address to the Deity." On June 1, 1788, for instance, she reflected that in the "tranquillity of the Country your thoughts rise without interception to the creator of that Beauty so liberally spread before you—every surrounding object is an Auxiliary to their assent, and you throw off for a time the incumbrance of a connection with the world." Revealing her precocious interest in the science of the mind, encouraged by Barbauld in her educational writing, she described the diary as "a sort of Register of those actions which have left a trace behind them by impressing my mind, and of those sentiments and feelings that have led to or accompanied such actions, that by occasionally perusing an abstract History of my own heart I might remark thereby learn to avoid every circumstance, situation or pursuit that had proved unfavourable to its virtue or peace."[28] Twenty years later, when as Hannah Greg (having married Samuel Greg in 1789) she was running her own home at Quarry Bank, Barbauld was effectively a household deity.[29]

When Hannah Lightbody had returned to Liverpool in 1786, her precocious gifts had been further encouraged by the improvers of the Roscoe circle with whom her mother mixed in the Octonian club, sometimes hosted in her home. Hannah became especially close to James Currie and William Rathbone IV and his wife Hannah. Both men were members of the Literary and Philosophical Society at Manchester, and the same lines of connection frequently took Hannah Greg to stay with Thomas Percival's family.[30] Liverpool's social and cultural advantages over Manchester at this early stage depended in large part on its role in the Africa trade, vigorously supported by the Common Council that governed the city. For all their enlightened views, many Dissenters had prospered from involvement in the slave trade, as we have seen; even the abolitionist William Rathbone IV derived much of his commercial success from importing slave-grown sea-island cotton from the Carolinas. John Yates confronted his congregation at Kaye Street Chapel with its complicity in a sermon delivered on January 28, 1788, widely circulated in manuscript afterward. The account in Hannah Lightbody's diary records the shock to her system, but she can hardly have been unaware of Liverpool's role in the trade, not least because her sister Elizabeth had married Thomas Hodgson, who had a major financial stake in it.[31] Nevertheless, the diary describes the sermon's words in searing detail: "Did we but follow that short and comprehensive precept of our Great Master—Do to others &c. this inhuman traffic, this oppression of our brethren could never have taken place—he was unhappy to say that 2/3rds of the Slave trade carried on by Britons was by his Townsmen." The same afternoon, Yates followed up by preaching the virtues of self-examination that produced several days and nights of conversation and reflection recorded in the diary. A few weeks later Currie and Roscoe collaborated in writing the "The African," which Currie had privately printed for rapid cheap circulation in the London newspapers. Hannah discussed the poem with Currie on a day she found it difficult to be attentive in chapel. They also discussed Roscoe's *The Wrongs of Africa* on the day it came out a fortnight later.[32] The young woman was at the heart of the debates about the most difficult moral issues facing her community.

For his part, Currie relished the conversation of women and never seems to have thought such serious matters any threat to his young friend's "delicacy," but then they were not exchanging their thoughts in a public debate.[33] He spent a lot of time discussing her commonplace book and recommending challenging reading such as Thomas Reid's *Essays on the Active Powers of Man* (1788), which he had reviewed for the *Analytical Review*. Her diary also contains some vivid accounts of her involvement with the members of the Octonian Society, "who," she wrote, "bring together in their various characters, Learning, Science, Vivacity, Seriousness and solid worth. In their conversation the heart and head share profit." When she met Currie on February 2, 1787, they discussed the controversy between Clara Reeve and Anna Seward in the *Gentleman's Magazine* on the right of women to choose and interpret literature for themselves.[34] A few months later Currie also made sure that his friend Thomas Christie, editor of the *Analytical Review*, visiting on a tour of the intellectual life of the area, saw a lot of his young protégé.[35] Even when she still lived in Liverpool, this bright young woman was certainly alert

to controversial topics exercising the Literary and Philosophical Society at Manchester. A diary entry from February 1787 shows that a Mr.
Nicholson, probably Matthew Nicholson, had visited and discussed "the
dispute between Mr. Cooper and Dr. Barnes on Materialism" explored in
chapter 4. A few months later the issue caused a quarrel over the dinner
table: "Dr. Currie and Mr. [Richard] Godwin dined with us and had an
argument on materialism on which Dr. C shone very much—Mr. Godwin
was a very liberal defender of this doctrine." Richard Godwin, William
Shepherd's predecessor at Gateacre Chapel, evidently took the side of
Cooper against the Arian compromise of Barnes.[36] Currie's opposition
fits with recent accounts of his allegiance to Dugald Stewart when it came
to "physiological theories concerning the mind that have made so much
noise of late." More to the point here is that these debates were not regarded as improper topics for the Lightbody dinner table, anticipating
the kind of outcome that the *British Critic* had feared would result from
the papers being published.[37]

Among Hannah Lightbody's supportive network of female friends
from her mother's generation, there were those who thought her appetite for such issues was a distraction from traditional female duties.
Anna Cropper feared that her young friend was endangering her marriage prospects by ignoring "the accomplishments peculiar to the female
province in domestic life." The lengthy account of their exchange in the
diary shows that the younger woman gave a firm reply: "A woman of Sense
and taste was likely to apply those faculties to whatever duties her situation presented, and that the minutest & vulgarest occupation of ordinary life would certainly be better performed when their performance
was under the direction of a cultivated mind."[38] Marriage, when it came,
was to prove a challenge to this independence of mind. Hannah Lightbody's marriage to Samuel Greg reinforced the links between a "charmed
circle" of commercial families, but it was not a straightforward match.[39]
Her husband-to-be had fast become one of the major cotton spinners,
shifting the family business from trade to manufactures. He had set up
his water-powered mill at Quarry Bank in 1784, near the village of Styal
in the Cheshire countryside south of Manchester, building on the capital
accrued through his Irish merchant family and its commercial contacts
in the Lancashire textile business. The Greg family also had extensive
investments in plantations in the West Indies inherited by Samuel in
1795.[40] They were bound into the broader nexus of slavery and cotton,
which, as we have seen, appalled his new wife. The integration of the new
technology into the factories and workshop also brought new forms of
work-time organization that became the center of nationwide debate in
the 1820s, discussed in chapter 6. Suffice to say here that they emerged

partly from a desire for employers to have more powers of surveillance over their workers. For the first two to three decades of the firm, Greg lived in the center of Manchester, away from the mill, where he could attend to other aspects of the firm's business, and relied on a manager at Quarry Bank. Development there was relatively slow until 1796, when the talented engineer Peter Ewart became a partner. Only in 1815 did the family move out to Quarry Bank House from the increasingly smoky town.[41]

Even before their marriage, Hannah encouraged Samuel to worship at the new chapel on Mosley Street, which adopted the progressive liturgical forms used by Yates in Liverpool.[42] Hannah joined her minister and other members of his Liverpool congregation in crossing to Manchester to celebrate the opening of the new chapel on May 10, 1789. She also took the opportunity to visit Manchester Academy. The following evening, she dined with the Percivals, where she saw Samuel Greg and his sister during the day. It is usually assumed that she also encouraged her husband to join the Literary and Philosophical Society the following year, but he was not very active when he did, never giving a paper or holding any office there.[43] His wife's experience of married life in Manchester was not a happy one, judging by the diary and correspondence from the 1790s. Even when marriage was still only an indistinct prospect, her diary entry for March 11, 1787, recorded her fears about losing "my favourite system of single blessedness—independence &c." After her move to Manchester, she chafed against the "constant rain confinement and constraint."[44] William Rathbone understood her "wish to be unfettered by the *common offices cares & employments that form a woman's province.*" Her daughter Ellen imagined her in these years "under the surveillance of her husband and aunts, so strict and formal about all the conventionalisms of society."[45] The shift into a restrictive domestic life was exacerbated outside the home by the loyalist reaction after 1792. The defeat of the campaign for the abolition of the Test and Corporation Acts, the stalling of the campaign for the abolition of the slave trade, and then the loyalist attacks on Manchester's Dissenting chapels of 1792 coincided with the restrictions of married life to produce a much-diminished horizon of possibilities. Samuel was among those associates of Thomas Walker brought before the magistrate under suspicion of seditious activity in 1794. In July, she told William Rathbone that it was "the want of Candour, Charity, and Trust in the Society that turned me back (as it always does) to the Remembrance of those friends and that society where they all abounded."[46]

The Greg family's Irish connections added to the sense of embattlement in these counterrevolutionary years. Returning from a visit to Ireland in 1794, she concluded that "one must be infected with indignation when in contact with this oppressed and engaging people." Her indignation could reach an apocalyptic note: "Certain will be the day of retribution . . . the crimes of this country and the crimes of old France are crying out and will be visited . . . to be Irish has always been sufficient to make anything obnoxious to the English Government."[47] Sometimes the depth of her feeling about British colonialism alarmed her friends in Liverpool in its ferocity: "Surely in Ireland, in India and in Africa the English name must be for ever odious—expressive of injustice, arrogance and cruelty."[48] The sense of being surrounded intensified back in Manchester when her sister-in-law Jane Greg came to seek sanctuary with them after she had been accused of seditious correspondence in Belfast in 1797.[49] In April 1798, Hannah Greg told the Rathbones of her sense of enemies closing in on the family: "We are teazed with perpetual reports one friend and acquaintance and another being taken up in the next street."[50] Toward the end of her life, writing to her nephew Tom Pares, she could still remember how dark and dangerous these years had been for her: "I have lived thro' the French Revolution and the Irish Rebellion, and tho' it may sound absurd for an obscure Female to say that I became almost personally versed in the tumults of the national interests . . . in the busiest period of it, and even in my own family, I was called to think and feel—if not to act upon subjects that seldom fall much into a woman's way."[51]

By 1809 Hannah Greg had given birth to thirteen children and regularly reported on the draining demands of her domestic duties to the Rathbones, "those middle years when household cares—bearing, feeding, clothing, teaching young children brought me down from the skies."[52] On top of these demands she was often asked to take care of Samuel Greg's business affairs when he was away, an area wherein she showed herself more than capable. Despite these demands and pressures, the inquiring young woman of the 1780s did not simply disappear into married life. She continued her intellectual exchanges with James Currie and the Rathbones in Liverpool. In 1794, she had told William Rathbone, who was doubting his own faith in the prospects for improvement, that they should "hold fast our Enthusiasm whatever betide and I believe it is at least one means of holding fast our Integrity." In reply, he seems to have encouraged her to channel her energies into her educational ideas, recommending she read the Edgeworths' *Practical Education* as "the best mental medicine."[53] She started to develop her own ideas for a book based on maxims drawn from her readings that she had discussed with Currie. A letter to Rathbone from 1797 made clear her anxieties about going into print: "My expectations respecting my little book are really so moderate . . . and my utmost hope has been to supply what to my immediate experience is a want, and were it even to have been published, as well as printed, my ambition would have been more than gratified to have seen it in the use of schools, and to have ranked with some of the Editors of 'Reading made easy.'" Currie recommended that she should write her own preface and not "deprecate or apologise too much."[54] Initially printed privately as *Virtue made Easy* (1799) for circulation among friends and family only, it was soon expanded, printed by John M'Creery, with whom Roscoe worked, and published as *A Collection of Maxims, Observations, etc,* (1799) and *The Moralist* (1800), and then reedited and published again as *The Monitor* (1804).[55]

These collections combined her own reflections with her quarry of extracts from other sources. "My book does not exhibit so much queer reading as Dr. Ferriar's," she told Currie, probably referring to his *Illustrations of Sterne*, "but I believe I have quoted as many old books."[56] Many of them echo the simple sense of a benign deity transcending any particular creed that had often found expression in experiences of nature echoing Barbauld's poetry in her diary. It was crystallized in *The Moralist* by a quotation from the veteran reformer John Jebb: "Morality is the sum and substance of this religion: when we are rational we are pious; when we are useful, we are virtuous; and when we are benevolent we are righteous and just."[57] Typically of Greg, though, this simple faith is explicitly supported by further reading from the Scottish Enlightenment. *A Collection of Maxims* included excerpts from Reid's *Active Powers of the Mind*, in one instance using Currie's review in the *Analytical Review* as a source, as well as a selection from Wollstonecraft, although the latter was dropped from *The Moralist*.[58]

Jane Rendall has shown the importance of Reid and his disciple Dugald Stewart to women of "moderate liberal backgrounds," including the novelists Maria Edgeworth and Elizabeth Hamilton, both of whom Greg knew. Many of these women became philanthropic activists.[59] Reid and Stewart were also important influences on Hannah Greg, for whom their influence readily merged with Barbauld's. Stewart's *Elements of the Philosophy of the Human Mind* (1792–1827) developed a system of practical morality out of Reid's response to David Hume's skepticism that placed great importance on early education. Key was the idea of "watching over the impressions and associations which the mind receives in early life, to secure it against the influence of prevailing errors; and, as far as possible, to engage its prepossessions on the side of truth."[60] This strain in Stewart's thinking reinforced the role of the mother in the early development of her children to which women readers seem to have responded warmly. In *Outlines of Moral Philosophy* (1793), originally intended for his students, Stewart imagined the development of "a science of the mind not inferior in certainty to the science of body."[61] Greg was proud that she had read Reid's and Stewart's "large works," and she told Rathbone that *Outlines* was just the restorative she needed when ill: it would provide her with "a text book for conversation," a phrase which hints at her interactive approach to educating her own children.[62] "My advice and instruction (in relation to the education of daughters) will be," she told William Rathbone IV, "in the notion of their being individual and rational and immortal Beings."[63] She disseminated these principles to other families. Mary Ann Roscoe, writing to her family from a house party at Quarry Bank in 1807, gave a catalog of gifts Hannah Greg had prepared for them. She had received "six volumes of scientific dialogues," probably Jeremiah Joyce's *Scientific Dialogues* (1800–1805).[64] Hannah Greg's dedication to her daughter at the start of her collection of maxims shares Stewart's faith that early measures would cement "the natural alliance between our duty and our happiness."[65] Addressing Bessy as a "beloved companion" to be influenced by "esteem and confidence" rather than simply "filial duty," Greg encouraged the regular perusal of her maxims to "strengthen their impression on your mind" so that they will "more readily occur to you on the several occasions of application which your progress through life will supply.'"[66]

Rathbone's recommendation of *Practical Education* evidently encouraged Greg to go on to read Maria Edgeworth's novels. Not uncommonly in these circles, Greg was cautious about the moral status of fiction but certainly more willing to entertain its benefits than her husband was. Although he joined the committee of the Portico Library with John Ferriar and others in 1810, he told his son Tom a few years later: "Avoid novels—prating Books & books for prating upon." "Your first study be a knowledge of man," he went on, "know your own country, its history, commerce and manufacture, for England is indebted to them & to her marine for all her consequence. Next the history & polity of other countries."[67] Hannah Greg herself encouraged habits of attention, judgment, and self-command in her children, as one might expect of a devoted reader of Stewart, but, like the Scottish philosopher, she could see the possibilities of the novel as a medium of moral education, as she told Rathbone: "Reading novels has all the good effects of going into the countryside without the restraint and trouble of it—they dissipate thought and exhilarate the spirit." Their discussion moved naturally to her belief that "*perpetual observation by older persons* is particularly necessary in reading Novels to young people," and then on to the merits of Edgeworth's fiction itself.[68] When the Edgeworths visited the area in 1813, Hannah Greg hurried to meet her, disappointed only that the father continually talked over his daughter.[69] Like Barbauld, Edgeworth offered a model of the powers of the female mind of the kind that Greg celebrated unequivocally in her maxims: "Nature has, perhaps, made the sexes mentally equal, but fortune and man, seem to have established an oppression which degrades woman from her natural situation." Hannah Greg encouraged her daughter Bessy to act on the principle that women were "rational, accountable, individual human beings."[70] Bessy attended John Dalton's lectures in Manchester and fully participated with her brothers in the children's version of the literary and philosophical society Hannah Greg set up in 1811.

The idea of a children's debating society seems to have owed something to the "juvenile budget" that appeared in Aikin and Barbauld's *Evenings at Home*. The Percival household may have provided her with another example. She described its more immediate origins to her nephew Tom as "a little institution formed over the fireside last winter where a domestic Literary & Philosophical was instituted, officers appointed, rules drawn etc. & all on the spot, in the true spirit of youthful precipitation all in ½ an hour & being 12 little people we christened it the *Duodecimo*." The children were encouraged not only to interact with one another but also to take their ideas seriously with visitors, who included Theophilus Houlbrooke, shortly to be elected president of the new Literary and Philosophical Society at Liverpool. For Hannah Greg, the parallels with the Literary and Philosophical Society in Manchester were quite explicit. She hoped it would give her son Robert "the opportunity of feeling his way with papers intended for the Manc'r Society—but should it bear no fruit, but merely scatter flowers round the idea of home, it may be salutary to the Youth who may be wandering through the Earth, the Wilds of America, the plains of Mexico, or the City of London."[71] Although she adopted a stance of self-effacing dutifulness in relation to her aspirations for Robert and the others, there is something more than self-depreciating irony in her presidential address:

> To none can it be more difficult thus to speak than to your President, who having been elected as it were by acclamation . . . she must not decline saying a few words in her new Character . . . But, my dear Children!, you to whom it has always been so easy to me to write individually, and at a distance—how strange, how unnatural, and above all how formidable a task is it thus to address you viva voce—in your collective capacity! As a Corporate Body—a Literary and Philosophical Society![72]

Her presidential role, like the title of the last version of her collection of maxims, also implies the monitorial aspects of her position as an educator. In a letter probably written in 1795, William Rathbone told her that "you would have been distinguished and mankind benefited if the fates had decreed you to have been a female Preacher, and who will say that this may not yet be the character for which you are destined?"[73] The delight she showed in the conversational mode was often in tension with her persuasion "that a few quaint maxims, or striking verses . . . serve to engrave a truth more deeply on the mind."[74]

"USEFUL LEGACY"

Virtue made Easy seems to have been designed with a view to teaching the apprentices at the mill and not only for her own circle. The preface defines proverbs as a popular form, suited to those "whose laborious lives exclude study and reflection."[75] Barbauld's use of affective objects in her educational writing may have influenced Greg's suggestion that maxims might be "rendered popular and familiar, by being painted as mottoes on common jugs, cups, &c; those that are too long for this purpose might be printed on handkerchiefs, or used for writing copies in charity schools, where they might likewise be learnt by heart." "The Eye is too much neglected in the business of Education," she thought, "I would have a schoolroom, nay a whole house hung with prints of heroic and virtuous actions so that youth could not lift up its eye without receiving a useful and wholesome impression."[76] Presumably the picture of George Washington over the fireplace at Quarry Bank House was meant to encourage this sense of social duty in her family. The darker aspects of his surveillance prevailed when it came into materials for the education of the workers at Quarry Bank: "Under such forms, little is required of the reasoning faculties, and the moral lessons they contain are generally most strongly impressed, easily remembered, and readily applied."[77] The direction of travel from the family circle to work-time discipline with a benevolent face was clear enough: *A Collection of Maxims* introduced a section called "Time and Industry," retained in all the other versions of the book.[78]

Colony mills like Quarry Bank had little by way of local population they could draw on as labor. The Greg mill relied on a large quota of apprentice children, imported from as far away as London in some cases, retaining the practice much further into the nineteenth century than many other mills.[79] From as early as 1797, possibly after a visit to Quarry Bank, William Turner of Newcastle described the wagons bringing the apprentices to the cotton mills as "slave vessels upon wheels," the perverted product of a "commercial aristocracy."[80] While other women, including Mary Anne Rawson in Sheffield and Greg's own daughter Bessy Rathbone over in Liverpool, were developing the domestic and foreign missions that were becoming a key aspect of middle-class philanthropy in the 1810s and 1820s, Hannah Greg made the local factory colony into her own "laboratory of virtue," with all the ambiguities entailed on that phrase.[81] Only after 1815, in what has been described as the golden age of the firm, did the Gregs spend more time at Quarry Bank than in their King Street house, and it was in this period that the business developed a village around the mill with a school, shop, chapel, and more extensive accommodation for the workers.[82] The mill workers worked a six-day week every week of the year, until the 1820s, when time off at Christmas and a few days in the summer were allowed. Twelve hours was the usual working day. The 1802 Factory Bill did little to improve regulation of the industry, notwithstanding Ferriar and Percival's researches, besides making church attendance compulsory.[83]

James Currie, like many other Rational Dissenters, believed that the rising middle class had a social duty to the laboring classes. A letter he published in the *Liverpool Advertiser* in August 1789 told its readers that "the labouring poor demand our constant attention. To inform their minds, to repress their vices, to assist their labours, to invigorate their activity, and to improve their comforts—these are the noblest offices of enlightened minds in superior stations."[84] When he visited David Dale's cotton mills in New Lanark in 1792, Currie sent a detailed account to Hannah Greg and his other friends in Manchester, describing the mills, "five in number, each calculated for six thousand spindles," as "wonderful objects." He was particularly interested in the conditions of the "nearly two thousand souls" who worked there. With a physician's eye he praised "the utmost cleanliness, health, and order, pervaded the whole manufactory." The children he thought "cheerful and happy, with rosy cheeks and chubby countenances;" the product of "excellent regulations established for health, morals, and knowledge," which Robert Owen built upon when he took over at New Lanark.[85]

When the Gregs started to develop a village community around their factory, Hannah Greg looked again to New Lanark, discussing the merits of "Owen*mania*" and "Owen*phobia*." She thought highly of Owen's "excellent schemes." Her husband did not support her, she told their daughter, indulging in the "free expression of his prejudice . . . which had arisen from the impression of his *early* character," presumably based on his knowledge of Owen's ideas on the man-machine from their time together as members of the Literary and Philosophical Society in the 1790s.[86]

Conditions at Quarry Bank were not as grim as in many other mills, although far from the "charitable institution none could surpass" celebrated in the family's self-mythology.[87] Hannah Greg is usually credited with meliorating her husband's commercial imperatives to bring about improved conditions: the cottages built in the 1820s; the education offered to the apprentices and then the children of the village; the committees of operatives that ran the shop; the Female Society and debating

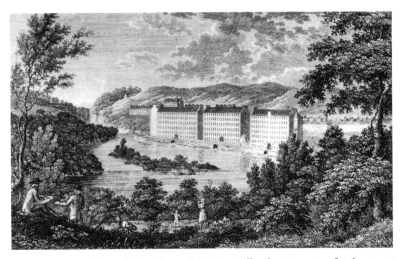

FIGURE 7. Robert Scott, "Lanark Cotton Mills, the Property of Robert Owen Esq. And Co." (1799). Photograph © City Library, Edinburgh. Reprinted by permission of Historic Environment Scotland.

club. At the end of her life, she recalled that she had "pleaded hard" [to her husband] for an Institution for securing and paying interest for what could be saved from wages."[88] Be that as it may, her own science of mind could translate into a rather mechanical idea of the inculcation of virtue, even when it came to her own children. She had told her son Tom in a letter that "development of character" depended on "a system of *habits*, not a mere collection of *actions*—and every day even in the life of a humble manufacturer supplies opportunity of habitual practice of the sublime virtues of self-command, self-denial & fortitude & benevolence."[89] She could sound equally harsh even with her beloved Bessy when it came to her "*indolent* habit." "Long sensible of this defect, this serious defect, a defect that if not counteracted threatens the destruction of both virtue and happiness," she wrote unsparingly. She thought of sending Bessy to Turner's school to inspire "energy" through "emulation," even if only because she would have to study with others, "mechanically as it were, because *necessarily*."[90]

The Monitor's prescriptions about "Time and Industry" did come with some sense of what was owed to those who worked in the mills, set out in a section on "Social Affections" that at least looked "to see the poor adequately rewarded, to prevent exertion from exceeding strength or extinguishing spirit, to suppress the deficiencies occasioned by sickness, to procure for the mothers of families the ease necessary for rearing healthy children—to afford hours of pleasure and relaxation to the young, and years of cheerful inactivity to the old."[91] Her posthumously published *Practical suggestions towards alleviating the sufferings of the sick* (1828) was remembered decades later by John Morley for "its delicate consideration and wise counsel for the peculiar mental susceptibilities of the invalid" (111). Hannah Greg understood, like Ferriar, that the sick poor suffered in their feelings no less than the rich. Nevertheless, her sermons to the apprentices steadily inculcated the doctrine of forming character through the close management of habit: "We have all much to do, many bad habits to conquer; much, very much to learn. Some have pride, ill-temper, disobedience; and discontent to correct. Others have idleness, of thoughtlessness, of untidiness, and of waste to conquer."[92] Owen's schemes, she told Bessy, could not easily be fitted to the necessities of business: "His talents are more applicable to some public or National benefit, than to a concern of Business that requires constant attention, faculties & time, mind and anxiety, of its possessors to keep it from ruin."[93] The section on "Social Affections" in *The Monitor* ended with the modest aspiration that "the rich should use their fortune and should consider themselves but as stewards, appointed by their Creator, for the management of terrestrial affairs in behalf of the rest of mankind."[94] This idea of stewardship was to have a powerful influence on her sons, in whom it translated into a strong sense that the poor had few rights of self-determination. Hannah Greg felt that the protests at Peterloo had in part been caused by a failure to listen to the poor: "The wants ought to have been relieved & the minds conciliated before they were ripened into despair and desperation—at least they should have been attended to—and not disregarded and disbelieved." But in the wake of the massacre, as we have seen, she was haunted by fears of "the savage & intemperate Character of the populace."[95]

Hannah Greg may have defined her mission in domestic terms, but her reputation spread around the networks described in this book and beyond, partly through the circulation of manuscripts and commonplace books. Jane Roscoe admired the advice she gave to her son Tom and encouraged her to copy it to share with others. Her ambition to have her collections of maxims used in schools was met when it was used in Lant Carpenter's Bristol school attended by some of her children.[96] In the language of social network analysis, Hannah Greg's degree centrality was high. Henry Holland recommended her to Lucy Aikin in 1809: "I do not at this moment recollect whether you know anything of this Mrs. Greg of whom I have spoken. She is a woman whom I greatly esteem & admire—if I had no other mode of recommendation to you, it would be sufficient to say that she was one of Dr Currie's most intimate friends & correspondents."[97] Eliza Fletcher, herself an important hub of intellectual sociability in Edinburgh, credited Hannah Greg with raising the aspirations of improvement in her community beyond merely commercial matters: "We stayed a week with them and admired the cultivation of mind and refinement of manners which Mrs. Greg preserved in the midst of a money-making and somewhat unpolished community of merchants and manufacturers." The Gregs' sons benefited from these connections when they studied in Edinburgh, as did Henry Holland, but even at home Hannah Greg did not have a free hand with her children's education.[98]

Samuel Greg favored a prompt entry into the business world for his sons. He apparently harbored a "general disapprobation of Schools."[99] Although all the children were sent to progressive provincial schools such as Lant Carpenter's in Bristol and James Tayler's in Nottingham, Thomas was quickly forced to learn the trade at a London insurance-broking firm in part to rectify what his parents saw as "defects in character." "Cultivating too much the Fancy & the Imagination," his father warned him, "certainly weakens the mind."[100] Even John's tuition by the local hero John Dalton could be sidelined by the demands of business, as his mother complained to Bessy: "Yesterday on his asking leave to have Mr. Dalton's instructions this summer, your Father told him he must learn his business. I said nothing of course then, but ventured to remonstrate for this one vacation to allow John to procure Learning while 'the iron is hot.'"[101] Ominously, Robert told his mother he would return from his European travels "ready to be manufactured into any thing . . . be shipped off to Spain, Portugal or Mexico, any where every where—to do any thing every thing . . . with as much *common sense* as if he had never opened a book but the ledger."[102] Thinking especially of her influence on her two younger sons, John Morley described Hannah Greg as a "woman of strongly marked character . . . with a literary capacity of her own . . . who cared eagerly for the things of the mind" (110), but she had her own doubts about fancy and the imagination. She reproached herself with encouraging Thomas's literary tastes: "I often blame myself as one cause of your having cultivated a love of poetry &c (so sadly too much my own taste), beyond the more manly studies, living on which . . . rather than on the more solid nourishment of the mind that induces strength and power, but I trust it is not too late." She was glad to hear that he had more recently taken a liking to reading Stewart.[103] Her admiration for Roscoe's address at the opening of the Liverpool Royal Institution in 1817 was tempered by a wish that "space allotted to the Fine Arts had been given to the closing Subject—and his taste & elegance had illustrated still farther &

dwelt longer on the relation between cultivation of mind taste &c & Moral Worth & religious excellence."[104]

On the other hand, she worried that as Unitarianism solidified as a denomination, its ministers were becoming overly invested in the "understanding" rather than a simple religion of the "heart."[105] Her "rational" religion, like William Turner's, distinguished freedom of inquiry from nitpicking over points in theology. She took pains to make sure that the new minister at Mosley Street, John James Tayler, who succeeded William Hawkes in 1821, was not too doctrinaire. Tayler's letter in response to her "candid enquiry" made clear his opposition to "ultra-Unitarians— those *radicals* of *Christianity*." His belief that "rational Christianity" should not be "ostentatiously brought forward as doctrine" was to cause him problems down the line. When he preached at Mosley Street in 1828 on "communion with unbelievers," he found himself under attack from within his own community as an "apologist of infidelity."[106] Tayler went on to gain a reputation for developing a new more spiritual and "romantic" Unitarianism under the influence of William Channing, one of the presiding deities at Quarry Bank, but he also contributed to the drive for social inquiry into the condition of the working classes discussed in chapter 7. Whatever was romantic about Tayler's sermons, they still blended a sense of "spiritual egalitarianism and philanthropic obligation," as Howard Wach describes them, with "adherence to social hierarchies," or, more to the point, a strong desire to order the lives of the poor after his own image of improvement.[107]

Hannah Greg certainly encouraged a thirst to improve themselves and others in her children.[108] Bessy spent several summers with the Rathbones in Liverpool as a girl, sending home a firsthand account of the violent reception William Roscoe received after the passing of the bill to abolish the slave trade. Nor was the manufacturing side of her inheritance ignored. She learned about the Rathbone's cotton-broking business and visited factories as her mother had done.[109] She married William Rathbone V in 1813 and carried her mother's sense of mission out into Liverpool, reporting back to Quarry Bank on the "satisfactory amendments in conduct" brought on by her Bible association. She also recommended Cappe's pamphlet *On the Desireableness and Utility of Ladies Visiting* (1817) to her mother, whose typically self-deprecating response suggested the frustration she had felt at not being able to take her own reforming zeal out into a wider world: "It does me good to hear of your prisons, Bible society &c doing no good to any body myself it is like a compensation."[110]

Cast much more in the improving image of their mother than any of their brothers were the two youngest sons, Samuel Greg Jr. and W. R. Greg. Both retained her "simple Unitarian Christianity under the influence of which [their] character was formed."[111] Educated at the University of Edinburgh, both benefited from her range of intellectual contacts. Samuel enjoyed the Fletcher household there, commenting on the women's "enthusiastic liberal opinions on social and political subjects." Perhaps more strangely, he also retained "a romantic affection" for Quarry Bank, not just to his home but also "the consistent musical whirr of its machinery, and the sight and sound of the workpeople, passing to and fro at their regular hours each day."[112] He went on to build a model factory at nearby Bollington. In a series of letters to the factory inspector Leonard Horner, Greg claimed to have learned from the mistakes of the Mechanics' Institutes that "want of resource and recreation is not to be supplied by mere intellectual pursuits."[113] Music and singing, flower shows, even political debate at the community's social clubs were introduced, but the factory started to amass debts. When strikes greeted the introduction of new machinery in 1846, Greg suffered a nervous breakdown. Elizabeth Gaskell entertained the idea of basing a fictional character on his travails: "He knew that he was watched in all his proceedings by no friendly eyes, who would be glad to set down failure in business to what they considered his Utopian schemes. I think he, or such as he, might almost be made the hero of a fiction on the other side of the question."[114] The inherited sense of domestic mission struggled to survive its encounter with the difficult reality that the working classes did not necessarily want to be improved on its terms.

"The cottage system makes slaves of the operatives," maintained Engels after visiting Quarry Bank in the 1840s, "[the manufacturer] uses the school to train children to subordination."[115] What Hannah or Samuel Greg thought of the fate of the enslaved workers on the family's plantations in Dominica isn't known. Their son Samuel Greg Jr. was mortified by the family's involvement in slavery, as he confessed to his former teacher Lant Carpenter in 1823: "My father has a large estate in Dominica, which I wished belonged to anyone else, except that I hope the slaves are better treated than on some other plantations." He was sufficiently self-aware to see the horror of slavery as irreducible: "interest biases the mind, it is too apt to pervert good principles."[116] Nevertheless, the family took compensation after abolition. Such contradictions continued to bedevil the Greg sense of stewardship as it contributed to a range of new institutions in the 1820s and 1830s designed to improve the working classes they employed. Their frustrations only grew, however, as they discovered, like the younger Samuel at Bollington, that their materials were resistant to being molded to their idea of improvement, a frustration that became very apparent in W. R. Greg's notorious review of Elizabeth Gaskell's *Mary Barton*, discussed in the closing pages of this book.[117]

CHAPTER SIX

AN INVENTIVE AGE

The machinery-based factory system was only just starting to be powered by steam when John Aikin Jr. described its presence around Manchester. By the following decade, the system was perceived to have such deep-seated moral and social consequences that it warranted government intervention. Limited measures with regard to the working hours of pauper apprentices were introduced by the Health and Morals of Apprentices Act (1802), brought in by Sir Robert Peel (1st Baronet), now converted from his earlier resistance to intervention in the governance of factories.[1] Poets such as Robert Southey and William Wordsworth became involved in the national debate. Wordsworth in book 8 of *The Excursion* represented the period as one where labor-saving inventions seemed to herald the overthrow of a natural moral order:

> An inventive Age
> Has wrought, if not with speed of magic, yet
> To most strange issues. I have lived to mark
> A new and unforeseen Creation rise
> From out the labours of a peaceful Land,
> Wielding her potent Enginery to frame
> And to produce, with appetite as keen
> As that of War, which rests not night or day,
> Industrious to destroy![2]

Southey published a series of influential articles in the *Quarterly Review* attacking the dislocating social effects of the manufacturing system.[3]

This chapter is concerned with the work of an altogether different kind of writing that emerged from the heart of the manufacturing experience around Manchester shaped by debates in the literary and philosophical societies. Running through this seam was an attempt to make sense of the manufacturing system in terms of the relationship between circumstances and character. First comes Robert Owen's *A New View of Society* (1813), greatly influenced by his experiences in Manchester in the 1790s, both as an industrialist, where he had played a part in managing the transition to large-scale machine-driven factories, and as a participant in debates about the "man-machine." The transition to the machine-factory system and its effects on labor were among the topics addressed by the "knowledgeable" industrialist John Kennedy in a series of papers read at the Manchester Literary and Philosophical Society after 1815.[4] Like Owen, with whom he had done business in Manchester in the 1790s, Kennedy in his writing claimed the authority of the participant-observer to make larger claims about the social consequences of the manufacturing system. Kennedy's observations became an important source for Edward Baines Jr.'s landmark *History of the Cotton Manufacture in Great Britain* (1835), still much in use today by economic historians. My concerns with it are rather different from theirs, more "literary," if you will, and to do with its rewriting the narrative of improvement traceable back to Aikin's *Description of Manchester* (which it cites). Contrary to Wordsworth's vision of "an appetite . . . Industrious to destroy," Baines presented the steam-driven factory system as a "romantic" triumph for the arts of peace. Building on the papers he had given at the Philosophical and Literary Society of Leeds in the 1820s, he appropriated the language of liberty associated with Protestant Dissent to a millenarian vision of limitless growth and a gospel of capital accumulation that was very different from Aikin's sense of the complexity of environmental constraints.

OWEN'S LIVING MACHINES

Robert Owen's ideas in *A New View of Society* have often been traced back to his "formative years" in Manchester.[5] At this stage, there were very few large factories in the town of the kind Richard Arkwright and Jedediah Strutt had made famous in exploiting the waterpower of secluded valleys. Samuel Greg's large water mill was out in the countryside at Styal.[6] Kennedy and Owen both began their involvement in the cotton trade adapting the new machinery to small workshops in an urban environment.[7] Owen had first moved to Manchester to take up a job in supply and distribution with a draper, but, alert to the emerging possibilities of applying technology to the booming cotton trade, he set up a partnership with a wire maker, who possessed the engineering skills Owen lacked. His new partner had told him of the "great and extraordinary discoveries that were beginning to be introduced into Manchester for spinning cotton by

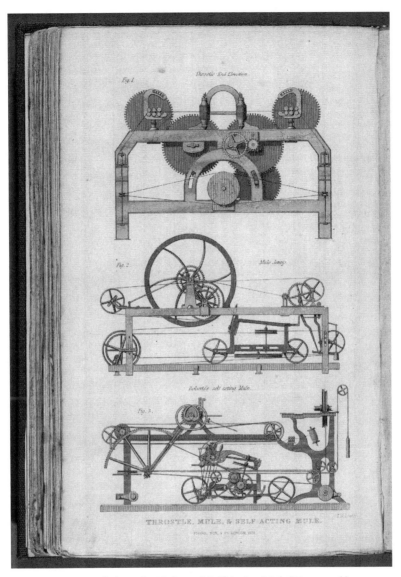

FIGURE 8. "Throstle, Mule, and Self Acting Mule." Engraved by J. W. Lowry. Plate from Edward Baines [Jr.], *History of the Cotton Manufacture in Great Britain* (London, 1835). Photograph courtesy of the Huntington Library, San Marino, California (HD 9881.5.B2).

new and curious machinery." Late in 1790 or early in 1791, they opened
a workshop for making frames to produce rovings (thicker cotton threads
that could then be spun into yarn). The workshop was also large enough to
accommodate a small number of spinning machines. Among their sup-
pliers was the firm of M'Connel and Kennedy. Kennedy's own trajectory,
discussed at greater length in the next section, had not been dissimilar,
aside from the important difference that he had machine-making skills
of his own. In this period, steam technology was just beginning to be
adapted to inventions such as the jennies and mules originally intended
for other power sources. The Boulton and Watt company's steam engines
were expensively protected by patents, so their introduction jostled with
local piracies and attempts to adapt older atmospheric engines to the new
spinning machines.[8]

Owen's early success attracted the attention of Peter Drinkwater,
who wanted him to manage his new state-of-the-art spinning mill where
a Boulton and Watt engine was being installed. Drinkwater had begun to
use some of the capital he accumulated as a textile middleman to set up
as an industrial capitalist over the course of the 1780s. Accommodating
the expensive new steam engines to the factory system was proving to
be a struggle.[9] Owen's achievement had to do with the management of
the production process, through which he was able to improve the quality of the yarn produced and, especially, to integrate the workforce and
machines into a factory system. Owen later claimed that his success at
New Lanark was an application of principles tested at Drinkwater's.[10]
So successful was Owen that he was offered a future partnership in the
firm and invited to participate in the Literary and Philosophical Society,
probably by Thomas Percival. The first talk he attended was Percival's
presentation of Matthew Guthrie's "Some Account of the Persian Cotton
Tree," on October 4, 1793. Percival invited Owen to comment on Guthrie's paper because he was already "well known for his knowledge in fine-
cotton spinning"; that is, on the basis of the reputation he had achieved
at Drinkwater's. By the following month, Owen was a member in his own
right, making his first contribution with "Remarks on Improvement
in the Cotton Trade" and, shortly afterward, his paper on the "Utility
of Learning." Within a year, he was clashing with John Ferriar on their
differing ideas of genius, as described at the beginning of chapter 4. The
physician's wariness of mechanistic forms of determinism was very much
at odds with Owen's lifelong faith that "any character might be formed by
applying the proper means."[11] Although Owen claimed that Ferriar never
spoke to him again after the incident at the Literary and Philosophical
Society in 1794, they did serve together on the Board of Health shortly
afterward in the period when it was extending its inquiries into factory

conditions. A set of questions was sent to David Dale, whose enterprise at New Lanark already had a reputation for philanthropy that drew admiring visitors, including James Currie, as we have seen, also attracted by its romantic situation near the Falls of Clyde. If Owen didn't already know Dale through connections in the cotton industry, he probably knew his responses to the inquiries of the Board of Health, which were also published in the *Monthly Magazine*.[12]

Owen, then, was at the center of Manchester's intellectual life as it began to explore the social and moral consequences of emergent machine capitalism. He left Drinkwater's around 1795 and became a founding partner of the Chorlton Twist Company. With two of the other partners, he visited New Lanark for himself in 1799, on the lookout for investment opportunities. By January 1800, he was in place as managing partner, having married Dale's daughter Caroline, and started to deploy the system that had won him a reputation at Drinkwater's. Initially, it seems, he encountered a fair degree of resistance to his attempt to install the sanitary and educational regime encouraged by the Board of Health within a strict work-time discipline. His key principle, though, in a Howardian manner, was not punishment but "kindness" in the creation of circumstances he believed would engender an atmosphere of cooperation. Within the factory, he used such devices as the silent monitor, small, wooden pyramids hung next to each worker, each side displaying a different color to indicate the worker's performance. Black indicated "bad" behavior; blue "indifferent," and so on. A superintendent turned the monitors each day with the results recorded in "books of character." Often credited to similar methods in Joseph Lancaster's educational system, to which Owen was an early adherent, it seems like a sinister twin of the object-oriented pedagogy of John Aikin Jr. and his sister Anna Laetitia Barbauld.[13] Outside the factory, Owen had started to adopt similar principles in the education of the factory children, innovations that attracted Hannah Greg. Owen's doctrine of "circumstance" may seem more rigid than Aikin and Barbauld's pedagogy. He lacked their flexible idea of the relationship between the body and the mind, but he did subscribe to their sense of the educational value of play. There was always latitude in Owen's system, even if some critics came to see his "play" as a species of puppeteering.

Owen was nothing if not a talented publicist, and these principles were first laid out in his *Statement regarding the New Lanark Establishment* (1812) with its proposal that he develop a *"New Institution"* that would serve as a "general education-room and church for the village." Ostensibly an attempt to reconfigure the partnership that ran the mill, confirming the central role of his innovations in work organization and education, the *Statement* proclaimed "the simple and evident principle, that any characters, from the savage to the sage or intelligent benevolent man, might be formed, by applying the proper means, and that these means are to a great extent at the command and under the control of those who have influence in society." Two aspects of the document are distinctive to Owen's writing of this period: first, the naive confidence that he could appeal directly to those with "influence in society" rather than, for instance, any organization drawn from among the workers; and second, his belief that he could easily contrive circumstance to produce a new kind of benevolent person.[14] Even in this delimited business plan, the aspiration to reach a much wider audience is apparent, with New Lanark taking on "the appearance of a national benevolent institution," to use Hannah's Greg's distinction, rather than simply a "manufacturing works."

The third of the four essays Owen published as *A New View of Society*, originally appearing at the end of 1813, came with an address to "the superintendents of manufactories," men like himself, on behalf of the "living machines" they employed. The phrase makes a rhetorical point to his addressees, but it also speaks to the mechanical nature of Owen's ideas on the relationship between character and circumstance.[15] Michael Ignatieff was not the first to note that "Owen's faith in discipline ... harked back to the intellectual ambience of the Manchester Literary and Philosophical Society." For Ignatieff, "Owen's ruling principle that people's characters are formed for them, not by them, in their encounter with education and environment, was a product of the Hartleian materialism of that milieu."[16] This summary rather underestimates the complexity of the "milieu" as tracked in this study so far, not least the reservations of medical men such as Ferriar about mechanistic materialism that may have informed his clash with Owen at the Literary and Philosophical Society in 1794. Owen assumed a near perfect competence in his ability to match environmental causes and effects, offering the profitability of the New Lanark business as validation for his ideas: "extensive experience for upwards of twenty years . . . proved by multiplied experiments." His experimental remolding of character, he claimed, could produce "any language, sentiments, belief, or any bodily habits and manners, not contrary to human nature." If, like Barbauld and Aikin before him, Owen accepted in theory that "human nature" was a limit to the fungibility of character, his writing conveys little sense of anything being beyond his control. Whereas Aikin and Barbauld accepted that habits could form in ways not easily controlled by the educator, Owen espoused a doctrine of perfectibility: "For that Power which governs and pervades the universe has evidently so formed man, that he must progressively pass from a state of ignorance to intelligence, the limits of which it is not for himself to define." Society as it was, claimed Owen, punished those it "trained to commit crimes." Echoes of the Howardian principles so important in Manchester's liberal circles segued into a deeper-seated critique of inherited institutions, especially religious ones, which caused unease even among his supporters. Predictably enough, these sentiments attracted William Godwin, whose ideas on necessity had provoked Ferriar to write a satire published in *Illustrations of Sterne*. Given Ferriar's sense of the complex relationship between character and circumstance, it is no surprise that he disagreed with both Godwin and Owen on the issue. Godwin's sense of the possibilities of disinterested reason as a driver of human action was much more congenial to Owen, and the two began collaborating in London on the later essays issued in *A New View of Society*.[17]

Owen's promise that the "privileged" could meet their moral obligations "without domestic revolution—without war or bloodshed—nay, without prematurely disturbing any thing which exists" (38) also drew the attention of the government, aristocratic philanthropists, and leaders of provincial opinion alike. Edward Baines Sr. joined a deputation from Leeds in 1819, only days after Peterloo, to examine the innovations at New Lanark.[18] William Hazlitt, who later mocked Owen as the classic "man with only one idea," thought his respectable support would drain away when the consequences of his ideas for property rights became clearer.[19] This proved to be correct, although the process was accelerated by the doubts of those who feared his antagonism toward religion. Ironically, as these antagonisms developed, his own language developed an increasingly prophetic register. A prose style always based on the mechanical repetition of a key idea ratcheted up to millenarian exhortation. Popular radicalism was familiar enough with this register in its own circles, but in 1817 its leaders repudiated Owen for his refusal to affirm their parliamentary-reform agenda. William Cobbett famously attacked his famous "Plan" as "parallelograms of paupers," while Robert Wedderburn, the child of an enslaved West Indian, interrupted a meeting held at the City of London Tavern in August 1817 to accuse Owen of offering "nothing but an improved system of slavery."[20]

Robert Southey came to similar conclusions from another route without ever entirely abandoning his hopes for the possibilities of Owen's plan. Southey blamed the manufacturing system for the crisis in poor relief. For a while, after Owen visited him in London in 1816, he entertained the possibility that Owen's plans represented a paternalistic alternative to the factory system. A return visit to New Lanark in 1819 decided him that "Owen in reality deceives himself." "Kind looks

FIGURE 9. "Mr. Owen's Institution, New Lanark (Quadrille Dancing)."
1825. Photograph courtesy of the Robert Owen Museum.

and kind words" Southey judged to belie "the perfect regularity" of the
performances of the children, such as quadrille dancing, in the Institution for the Formation of Character: "So I could not but think that these
puppet-like motions might, with a little ingenuity, have been produced by
the great water-wheel, which is the *primum mobile* of the whole Cotton-
Mills." The end result, Southey believed, differed "more in accidents
than in essence from a plantation: the persons under him happen to be
white, and are at liberty by law to quit his service, but while they remain
in it they are as much under his absolute management as so many negro-
slaves."[21] The analogy had haunted the factory system from early on—it
was made in 1797 by William Turner when he investigated the picture
painted by Aikin's *Description*—and exploded in the "Yorkshire Slavery"
controversy at the end of the 1820s. Southey, though, continued to entertain the possibility that Owen's schemes might contribute to a rebirth of
English society. His *Colloquies on the Progress and Prospects of Society*
(1824), later mocked by W. R. Greg, praised its possibilities, if—a crucial qualification—they were to be underwritten by an education in the
religious principles and feelings Owen despised. Otherwise, without the
animating spirit of religion, Southey thought "among persons so trained
up, moral restraint is not to be looked for, and there is little prudential
restraint." Nor would Owen be able to sustain the warm support that Bible

societies had won among the better off for a scheme that was "as cold as Unitarianism."[22]

The continuing attraction of some variant of Owen's "Plan" for someone of Southey's intellectual temperament was the counterweight it offered to the gaining influence of Thomas Malthus. Owen implied that overpopulation was a chimera that could be driven away by a reordering of society and its resources. The Malthusian view that population was driven by biological forces too fundamental to be mitigated by policy arrangements took its time to find acceptance among those long invested in improvement. Thomas Percival and his allies had proceeded on the basic assumption that population was a measure of national wealth. Barbauld's "Thoughts on the Inequality of Condition" (1807) brought a brusque common sense to the argument about overpopulation: "We always use the phrase of a numerous poor, a burdensome poor, a country overstocked with poor, whenever, from any accidental overflow, they happen to exist in greater numbers than we can conveniently use."[23] James Currie was more troubled and registers something of the challenge Malthus made to long-held assumptions in these circles. Malthus effectively reduced the complexities of environmental medicine to a single bodily driver. In 1804, Currie wrote to his son, studying in Edinburgh, to see if he could find out Dugald Stewart's response. Currie had read Malthus's *Essay on Population* "with attention; and I confess to you, not without some painful impressions," and feared that his son's faith in the meliorating power of "policy" had not fully understood its implications: "The human race are sunk in ignorance, and the stimulus to sexual intercourse is so strong, the connection between the sexes will be regulated rather by brutal impulse than by rational conversation." Currie thought Malthus had carried "the application of his principles too far" but sorrowfully conceded that the English economist had identified "an effectual bar to any permanent amelioration of the condition of the great body of our species." Famine, war, and disease now appeared as if they might be "the system of Providence for keeping the numbers down to the level of subsistence."[24]

Currie's struggled to find any real blessing in a prospect so at odds with his long-held faith in improvement. Others celebrated Malthus for offering what Mitchell Dean describes as "a providential discipline for the labouring poor."[25] Out of the population principle would come a new kind of laborer made fit for the market by the demands of prudence and foresight. Influential in this sea change in opinion was the Scottish evangelical Thomas Chalmers, Malthus's "disciple, the arch-parson," as Karl Marx described him in *Capital*.[26] Chalmers started a vigorous campaign against the English system of poor relief in a series of articles in the *Edinburgh Review* over 1817–18. Those who thought state provision of poor relief a duty misapprehended the principles of Christian charity. Self-reliance and a moral obligation to compete in the marketplace were the Chalmers gospel.[27] Personal charity was one thing; it was among the duties of those who had to atone for their wealth, bringing moral benefits to both sides of the equation. Public interventions were likely only to reproduce the problems they aimed to alleviate, not least by detracting from the laborious virtues taught in the stern school of the population principle. From this perspective, Owen's schemes, initially attractive to manufacturing towns as a way of dealing with economic distress, looked—at best—increasingly like a misguided reinvention of relief as the natural right of those who received it. "We certainly do not mean," explained Chalmers, "to advocate either the potato system, or the cow system, or the cottage system, or the village system of Mr. Owen, or any system that promises to alleviate poverty through an ingeniously constructed method of positive administration."[28]

The free market had to be left to do its work, Chalmers believed, supported by vigorous policy of church building and moral persuasion of the kind he had experimented with in the Glasgow parish of St. Johns. His "prophetic fury in the pulpit," as Hazlitt described it, fueled a personal crusade over the next decade bolstered by the authority of his monumental *Christian Economy of Large Towns* (1821–26) and numerous shorter publications. In Liverpool, his charisma worked almost equally on adversaries such as John Gladstone and James Cropper. The *Leeds Mercury*, recovered from its front-page interest in Owen's "Plan," was celebrating Chalmers as "eloquent and enlightened" by 1827.[29] The final two chapters of Malthus's original *Essay* presented the struggle of life as "the instruments with which the Supreme Being forms matter into mind."[30] In truth, this perspective rarely granted the laboring classes anything more than the status of "living machines." The drive of such institutions as the Manchester Statistical Society in the early 1830s, discussed at length in chapter 7, used Chalmers to develop an idea of labor defined by self-reliance in the marketplace, sexual restraint in the bedroom, and frugality in domestic economy.[31] On the Statistical Society's committee was John Kennedy, by this stage an elder statesman of the manufacturing interest. He had not always been a convinced Malthusian, if he ever was. His earlier writing about the development of the machine-factory system in the 1810s and 1820s, the focus of the next section, placed less emphasis on biological determinism or religious proselytism and more on the ability of work-time discipline to create a new kind of machine-tooled laborer. The problem of the limits to growth identified by Malthus would be solved by the genius of technical innovation.

JOHN KENNEDY'S OBSERVATIONS

From very early on, John Kennedy had played an active role in developing the steam-factory system that commentators such as Southey blamed for the crisis in poor relief. Estimates suggest there that there were not many more than 30 Boulton and Watt steam engines in Manchester in 1800.[32] By 1825 there were nearly 250. Engineering skills were at a premium in this period of rapid innovation, and men who had them, like Kennedy, had profitable opportunities to transition away from machine making to become spinning masters. Initially involved with adapting old Savery engines, M'Connel and Kennedy ordered their first Boulton and Watt engine in 1797. In 1802 they bought another factory, known as the New Factory, where a few years later they installed gas lighting that allowed the machinery to run beyond the time between dawn and dusk.[33] The system that made the steam-powered machine the arbiter of the rhythms of labor in the cotton industry was coming into shape. Kennedy and his partner, Margaret Jacob has argued, were able to apply their technical knowledge to win a place at the forefront of these developments. To use her striking distinction, he was "knowledgeable, and not simply striving." Jacob understands Kennedy's career as the product of "networks based upon values and knowledge," including what she calls "the Unitarian ethos." Here she traces "the seeds of innovation in cotton manufacture."[34]

Initially, though, Kennedy was not part of the tight-knit group around the Gregs, Henrys, and Percivals, although he became so, eventually marrying his daughter to John Greg. Arriving in Manchester in the 1780s, he came to the Literary and Philosophical Society relatively late, only after his business was established as one of the largest in the town. By the 1810s, unlike Samuel Greg, who seems to have remained a relatively passive presence, Kennedy was giving papers that shaped debates beyond the walls of the society.[35] The "Observations on the Rise and Progress of the Cotton Trade" that Kennedy delivered to the Literary and Philosophical Society in November 1815 presented a defense of the steam-factory system against the diverse claims of Owen, Southey, and others that it was causing deep-seated moral harm.[36] Although the firm of M'Connel and Kennedy was the biggest one producing fine yarn at the time, Kennedy did not, unlike many others, simply point to the contribution to national wealth made by his industry. Instead, he provided a sketch of a conjectural history of the cotton trade, a "hypothetical history," as Maxine Berg describes it, organized around the division of labor, and culminating in the appearance of the steam engine as an instrument of social restructuring.[37] Although Kennedy claimed that his paper was confined "chiefly to facts and circumstances that have taken place within my own experience and observation" (115), there is little of the local detail that distinguished Aikin's *Description of Manchester*. Instead, Aikin's networked account, with its generic debts to topography, gives way to a bare narrative sequencing in Kennedy's. Comparing Kennedy's treatment of the train of technical advances in cotton spinning to Aikin's, one might see at the outline of Mary Poovey's "more general process of generic differentiation, the gradual elaboration of sets of conventions and claims about method that were intended to differentiate between kinds of writing."[38] The generic differences between Aikin and Kennedy are thrown into greater relief by the ostensible similarities in their immediate intellectual context.

Kennedy attended the Unitarian chapel in Mosley Street where the Gregs worshipped in a knot of other prominent manufacturers, including his business partner James M'Connel. In line with the emergent traditions of social inquiry already traced in these networks, "Observations" was less about the technical application of science as the social relations that flowed from it.[39] Kennedy may not have had the University of Edinburgh education of Aikin and his literary friends, but the interest in "metaphysical and theological questions" he declared later is discernible in his development of the commerce-and-culture argument associated with the Scottish Enlightenment toward a new kind of industrial history.[40] "Observations" not only records a shift to large-scale urban enterprise powered by steam like that of M'Connel and Kennedy, it also presents it as its inevitable outcome, despite the contingencies of his own experience as a machine maker–turned–cotton master who began a small enterprise in rented rooms in the 1790s. Those contingencies are repressed in "Observations" in favor of a narrative he deemed compelling enough to answer "the frequent complaints, both in public and private, against the manufacturing system" (115). Among those pressing at the question of the social consequences of the emergent manufacturing system was Parliament itself, whose inquiry into the conditions of child laborers, chaired by Sir Robert Peel (1st Baronet), at Owen's prompting, investigated M'Connel and Kennedy among the larger concerns in Manchester and Salford. The firm considered the commission's inquiries to be "a very dangerous interference" and a threat "to all large Manufacturers of every description." Jacob if anything understates the case when she notes of this letter, "The Unitarian emphasis on personal freedom could cut in decidedly self-serving ways."[41] Increasingly the ethos of Protestant liberty dear to the self-image of Dissent underwrote a narrative of the factory system as a new Reformation.

Kennedy adopted a measured tone in the paper he presented to the society. Criticisms of the cotton mills, he suggested, "demand an impartial investigation, and none are more called upon to take a part in such discussions than those who are interested in manufactures" (115). He certainly was not a disinterested observer, but he did think seriously about the social consequences of the growth of the cotton manufactures beyond any mere tabulation of their economic value. Accusing Kennedy of bad faith or partiality, well-founded though the accusation would be, risks ignoring the distinctive form he gave his answer. Whereas Aikin's account of the growth of the cotton trade took on a wide geographical area, retaining a sense of its diversity, Kennedy's presents a series of structural changes in "a retrospect of 50 of 60 years" (115). Central to it is the calibration of changes in social relations against changes in modes of production.

An initial emphasis on "the division of labour, and small improvements made by workers to hand implements" (118) does not sound like the opening bars of an anthem to the heroes of invention. Kennedy's purposes are less individual and build up an argument from its own small steps. The familiar inventive quartet of John Kay, James Hargreaves, Richard Arkwright, and Samuel Crompton are named as steps within a series of incremental changes, including the application of water as an energy source to inventions originally powered by hand. In certain respects, this approach anticipates the recent revisionist accounts of the Industrial Revolution, at least in the incrementalism of the idea of "an age of manufactures" as opposed to a steam-driven big bang. It also retains something in common with Aikin's sense of dispersed agency operating in the region, but Kennedy writes with a gathering sense of a necessary fulfillment of distinct stages in a historical process. With each incremental improvement, Kennedy registers new forms of work organization, of the kind that Berg has made central to her analysis of the Industrial Revolution, and registers their consequences for social relations. Adam Smith had famously acknowledged the potentially damaging psychological effects of the division of labor: "that drowsy stupidity, which in a civilized society, seems to benumb the understanding of almost all the inferior ranks of people."[42] Kennedy admits the dangers of the laboring classes losing "their attachment to rural employment," the clarion call of Southey and Wilberforce, "being united by slender ties to their new employers, they became unsettled, and more indifferent than formerly to the good opinion of their neighbours; and consequently became less respected by them." More unusual in this period is the development of an upside to a situation where "all were compelled to exert themselves to procure a livelihood, having no claims on their employers unless they did so" (125). The loss of social ties becomes an opportunity for self-definition clinched by the punctual arrival of James Watt's steam engine with "its inexhaustible power, and uniform regularity of motion" (128). The threat that change might stall or even go into reverse—the specter of Smith's stationary state, always present in Aikin's book, not to mention Malthusian limits to growth—is overcome by this new power in the land: "Had it not been for this new accession of power and scientific mechanism, the cotton trade would have been stunted in its growth, and, compared with its present state, must have become an object only of minor importance in a national point of view" (128).

In terms of the organization of work and its social consequences, Kennedy paints the effects in equally positive terms. Eliding his own role in the rise of the steam engine as the power source for the new spinning machines by using the passive voice, he describes Watt's invention as bringing new regularity to factories and the people who worked in them: "Larger establishments were erected, and order, system, and cleanliness in their arrangement and management, became more necessary and more generally cultivated. This has been attended with good effects on the habits of the people. Being obliged to be more regular in their attendance at their work, they became more orderly in their conduct, spent less time at the ale-house, and lived better at home" (129). All this was predicated on the mobility of the steam engine as a source of power: "Instead of carrying people to the power, it was found preferable to place the power among the people" (127). Populous towns rather than secluded river valleys were becoming the key sites of production. Andreas Malm has recently claimed that Kennedy's portentous statement reveals that the move to steam power had more to do with the relations of production than the resource scarcity and cost-effectiveness emphasized by economic historians such as E. A. Wrigley. "*In spite of water being abundant, cheaper and at least as powerful,*" Malm argues emphatically, steam-driven factories allowed their owners a ready supply of labor that supplied its own maintenance costs and could be easily hired or dismissed.[43] Kennedy implicitly displaces the trouble of disciplining so-called free labor onto the machinery itself. Discipline is at the center of Kennedy's narrative, presented as a benefit for both worker and capitalist, supplying a new spirit of belonging to the operatives to compensate for their loss of rural attachments.

Kennedy's paper was surely responding, if only indirectly, to his old colleague Robert Owen's recent *New View of Society* (1813). Critics such as Owen blamed the social dislocation acknowledged by Kennedy for the alarming increase in poverty and the crisis in provision of relief. The first *Report from the Select Committee on the Poor Laws* (1817) revealed the growing influence of Malthusian ideas, placing reform squarely on the parliamentary agenda, even if it had to wait until 1834 to be fulfilled.[44] Kennedy entered this debate in the next paper he gave to the society,

"An Inquiry into the Effects of the Poor Law," read in March 1819, but he showed no enthusiasm for the Malthusian tenets recommended by Chalmers that started to grip these circles around this time. Intriguingly, at this stage at least, Kennedy's take on the issue retains an embedded sense of economic relations that accepts an original social contract to provide the poor with relief. Parochial relief, Kennedy argued, kept a trained labor force available for times of economic recovery: "By this they are relieved, until the cause of their depression is removed. The elasticity of their minds is thus preserved, and their spirits remain un-broke" (436). In practice, this kind of response was often accepted by manufacturers when faced with poverty and social unrest.[45] Kennedy, though, went rather further and provided a most un-Malthusian defense of parochial relief as a social right—if a limited one—justified by the role of labor in producing the profits of capital, "a capital, indirectly arising out of their own former labour, and upon this capital they have a claim, until, by the revival of trade, their industry and activity are again called forth unimpaired based on the rights of the workers to the fruits of their labour" (436). The sentiments would not have been out of place in Owen's writing in this period. More ominous, if less surprising, is the metaphor Kennedy offers for a new disposition of society as a whole, coming to a sense of a new body politic emerging from industrial transformation: "The evil, however, does not rest with the debasement of the lower class; for this class may not unaptly be compared to an indispensable part of a moving piece of mechanism, of which, if the form or situation be altered, the whole machine is deranged" (435). In fact, the idea of a "body" is precisely what is displaced here by the trope of society as a machine. If Kennedy retained a sense of the rights of labor that might be found, for instance, in Aikin or Roscoe's thinking, his sense of the importance of technological innovation had penetrated deep enough into his psyche to displace their idea of society as a complex organic entity made up of interconnected living beings. This way of thinking—the idea of the machine as the model for a new kind of social order—was at the heart of Edward Baines Jr.'s *History of the Cotton Manufacture*, a book explicitly indebted to Kennedy.

Before turning to Baines, it is worth reiterating the status accorded Kennedy's essays in and beyond the transpennine region. B. A. Heywood quoted from Kennedy's "Observations" in his address to the Liverpool Royal Institution's proprietors of 1824, the same year the institution invited J. R. McCulloch, who proved an important supporter of Kennedy's ideas, to lecture on political economy.[46] Through the 1820s and beyond, McCulloch regularly used the developmental history provided by Kennedy's essay to justify the authority of political economy as a discipline, not least his claim about the importance of the mobility of the steam engine: "The work that is done by the aid of a stream of water, is generally as cheap as that which is done by steam, and sometimes much cheaper. But the invention of the steam-engine has relieved us from the necessity of building factories in inconvenient situations merely for the sake of a waterfall. It has allowed them to be placed in the centre of a population trained to industrious habits."[47] Possibly McCulloch had first become aware of Kennedy's "valuable paper," as he called it, from reading Edward Baines Sr.'s *The History, Directory and Gazetteer of the County Palatine of Lancaster* (1824–25) which had made use of both Aikin's *Description* and Kennedy's "Observations."[48] In his review of this compendious tome, McCulloch urged that the sections dealing with the cotton industry, in fact written by Edward Baines Jr., should be published separately to provide the cotton industry with its first proper history. McCulloch's encouragement—with Kennedy's "Observations" behind it—helped produce the ambitious *History of the Cotton Manufacture in Great Britain.*[49]

VAST AND COMPLICATED CONCERNS

Chapter 3 showed that Edward Baines Jr. became a voluble presence at the Leeds Philosophical and Literary Society in the 1820s on such topics as free trade and political economy. Always keen to plug these issues into a longer historical perspective, he made the flourishing of Greek democracy the product of free trade in the Aegean. The influence of the printing press on the Reformation he made into an augur of the role of the steam engine in the Industrial Revolution that rebutted "the folly of those, who oppose mechanical improvement or intellectual cultivation."[50] In his *History of the Cotton Manufacture*, this analogy became the hinge around which to articulate a parallel between the Industrial Revolution and the Reformation as world-historical events with consequences that to his mind were far from being merely technical or simply commercial.

Baines retained his references to Aikin and Kennedy when he wrote up his *History of the Cotton Manufacture*, thanking the cotton master directly in his preface (8).[51] The debt serves to throw into relief the differences among these three texts as descriptions of the development of the Manchester cotton boom. More forcibly than Kennedy, who defensively balances his sense of the gains of work-time discipline against the dislocations brought by social change, Baines insisted that the steam-powered factory emerged as a turning point in a universal history of progress, a perspective partly established by the account of cotton spinning in the East Indies in his early pages. Whereas in India there was no change, ef-

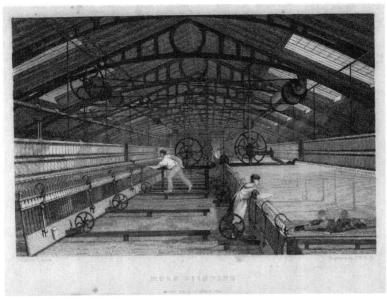

FIGURE 10. "Mule Spinning." Drawn by T. Allom. Engraved by
J. W. Lowry. Plate from Edward Baines [Jr.], *History of the Cotton
Manufacture in Great Britain* (London, 1835). Photograph courtesy
of the Huntington Library, San Marino, California (HD 9881.5.B2).

fectively no history, according to Baines, British cotton manufacture was
defined by the rapid succession of inventions: "The following document
furnishes superabundant proof how a manufacture which has existed
without a rival for thousands of years, is withering under the competition
of a power which is but of yesterday" (81). The apogee and guarantee of
this triumph for Baines was the steam-factory system, "this new accession of power and scientific mechanism," quoting Kennedy, but relegat-
ing his claims about the advantages of its mobility to a footnote (228).
The many incremental changes that Aikin and Kennedy had made part
of their narratives are acknowledged and recounted by Baines, certainly,
but more fully sublated into what Malm calls "steam fetishism."[52] "Without the steam-engine," writes Baines, "Manchester and Glasgow could
not have approached to their present greatness." (227). The steam engine
effectively saves *The History of the Cotton Manufacture* from any need
to engage with Malthus's gloomy predictions about the limits to growth:
"AMAZING as is the progress which had taken place in the cotton manufacture prior to 1790, it would soon have found a check upon its further

extension if a power more efficient than water had not been discovered to move the machinery. The building of mills in Lancashire must have ceased, when all the available fall of the streams had been appropriated" (220).

Global historians of cotton, such as Giorgio Riello, now routinely distinguish between two world cotton systems. The first—organized around India—was centripetal, sensitive to local demands in taste, and catering for diverse and dispersed export markets. Baines acknowledged the fine quality of the product that this system had produced. His self-appointed task was to hymn its replacement, centered on "the confined area" around Glasgow and Manchester, that now exerted its power to determine the supply of primary resources and dictate demand around the world.[53] Baines represented this shift as the overthrow of ancient and outmoded practice by a new form of rapidly self-improving modernity. This comparison was not based on technical progress alone, far from it; he was too much a product of the transpennine enlightenment not to aim at a broader perspective. As one might expect of someone with the wide range of interests discussed in chapter 3, Baines identifies a more general spirit of improvement that goes beyond Jacob and Mokyr's account of Industrial Enlightenment to include the imaginative literature of James Beattie, Oliver Goldsmith, and Samuel Johnson with the inventiveness of Arkwright and Watt.

The steam engine drives this spirit of improvement to a horizonless future in his narrative, although the presiding deity of his book, perhaps surprisingly, is not really James Watt. It is instead Richard Arkwright's portrait which faces the title page. Like many other accounts from the time, including Aikin's *General Biography*, Baines (147) is critical of Arkwright's attempts to assert intellectual property rights over his innovations. His importance for Baines was in "arranging a comprehensive system of manufacturing and in conducting vast and complicated concerns," including innovations that "enabled the master spinner himself to superintend every stage of the manufacture" (194, 185). The achievement is celebrated by a lengthy quotation from Erasmus Darwin's *The Botanic Garden* (1791) describing "the wonders of Arkwright's establishment on the Derwent" (186). Arkwright is the architect of the "laboratory" for factory discipline described by Malm that the steam engine could exploit and bring to a perfection "far beyond the limit which it could otherwise have reached" (227).[54] In a phantasmagorical elaboration, possibly derived from Darwin, Baines places the steam engine "in the same relation to the spinning machines as the heart [stands] to the arms, hands, and fingers, in the human frame; the latter perform every task of dexterity and labour, the former supplies them with all their vital energy" (227).[55]

The machine appropriates the human form of the workers whose labor it now directs.

It was precisely this sublation of human relations that was the objection to the factory system at the heart of Michael Sadler's and Charles Turner Thackrah's arguments with Baines at the Philosophical and Literary Society in Leeds. Thackrah's critique forces itself into notice in Baines's *History* in his late chapter on the "Condition of the Working Classes," where he explicitly mocks Thackrah's inquiries by claiming that Thackrah set his standards for the health of factory workers by the "high vigour" required of competitors in the Olympic Games rather than "their necessary subjection to the toils of trade and handicraft in an age of severe commercial competition" (460). "Subjection," though, sounds a false note within the more general impression Baines projects of factory discipline as a distinctly Protestant form of liberation. Whereas Sadler and Thackrah emphasized the enslavement of the operative to the intolerant demands of machine time, Baines insisted that the steam engine abridged the burdens of labor: "All the precision, power and incessant motion belonged to the machine alone; and the work-people have merely to supply them with work, to oil their joints, adjust their slight inaccuracies, and piece the threads broken by the mechanical spinner." (460). But the image of the machine as servant to the operative is rather undercut by the anthropomorphism of those passages representing the steam engine as a "vital force" or "heart." More fundamentally, the idea of the machine as a servant is also at odds with the techno-determinism that drives forward his narrative, even if the narrative wants to proclaim its outcome as a new kind of properly free individual, freed from the limits imposed by organic sources of power, and liberated into a limitless future of economic growth. The machine remains in place as the governing circumstance of a new kind of human character that has transcended its vulnerability to the bodily drives at the heart of Malthus's analysis.

The need to respond to claims about the "tyrant power" (452) of the steam engine certainly ruffles the sense Baines projects of an inheritance in Protestant Dissent superior to the immemorial customary knowledge of India, on the one hand, and aristocratic privilege closer to home, on the other. His later biography of his father described him as "self-harnessed to the car of progress," a warrior in "memorable struggles for the amelioration of our laws and institutions," struggles that include parliamentary reform, Catholic Emancipation, and the abolition of colonial slavery. The use Baines makes of Aikin's *General Biography* in his *History* helps illuminate his attempt to harness the legacy of liberty claimed by Protestant Dissent to his narrative of industrial superiority.[56] The cotton manufactures are aligned with the arts of peace to be contrasted with aristocratic militarism: "To trace the origin and progress of so great a manufacture, with the causes of that progress, is more worthy the pains of the student, than to make himself acquainted with the annals of wars and dynasties, or with nineteen-twentieths of the matters which fill the pages of history" (5–6). Nowhere does Baines invoke the radical potentialities of this inheritance—and the spirit of Aikin—more clearly than when he suggests that Britain was more indebted to Arkwright and Watt than Nelson and Wellington: "The genius of our mechanics repaired the errors of our statesmen. In the long and fearful struggle which followed the French revolution, this country was mainly supported by its commerce; and the largest though the newest branch of that commerce was furnished by the cotton manufacture" (503). The contradiction that emerges in such passages is the fact that the steam engine both represents the arts of peace and underwrites Britain's victory in the French Revolutionary and Napoleonic Wars.

Nevertheless, the idea of the cotton industry as an economic improvement to be weighed with more general cultural progress was an important strand of Baines's argument. His own book is presented as one of the fruits of this advance. The fact that there had not previously been a history of the cotton manufactures is "discreditable to the literature of the country which is the birthplace of so many admirable inventions" (7–8). These judgments are brought to rest again on the parallel between the steam engine and the printing press: "Within the memory of many now living, those machines have been brought into use, which have made so great a revolution in manufactures as the art of printing effected in literature" (6). This idea of this change as a "revolution" (53) appears several times in the book. As a description of technological advances, the revolution trope was not unusual even in the eighteenth century. Baines pushes it much further toward the ideas of a fundamental reordering of society.[57] Aikin's sense of a mixed ecology of improvement is swept away by a narrative of economic growth that makes machinery the driver of history, bringing with it a newly punctual—"free"—form of human being.

In the same year that Baines provided the cotton manufacture with his definitive history, Andrew Ure provided it with a "philosophy" that identified a new system of factory discipline arrayed around a "prime mover" as a pattern for society more generally. Generally less concerned with historical detail than Baines, Ure did echo the heroic status he granted Arkwright: "To devise and administer a successful code of factory discipline, suitable to the necessities of factory diligence, was the Herculean enterprise, the noble achievement of Arkwright."[58] Arkwright was Hercules not as warrior, or even inventor, but as manager. Writing in 1795, Aikin praised Arkwright for developing the inventions of others without making him any kind of demigod. For Baines and Ure, the inventive "genius" Aikin had seen dispersed around Manchester was manifested as an ironclad steam-powered spirit of the age that would spread an ethic of "vigilant superintendence" (483) around the globe: "from a country at the head of civilization" to what Baines called "the less enlightened parts of the earth" (531). British power seemed about to transcend the limits set by the organic economy: "We see no ground for apprehending that England will lose her present manufacturing pre-eminence. All the natural and political causes which originally made this a great manufacturing and commercial nation, remain unimpaired. The exhaustless beds of coal and iron-stone, the abundance of streams with an available fall of water, the inland navigation and well-situated seaports, the national tranquility, the security for person and property" (505–6). Correlating the Anthropocene with liberal individualism, Dipesh Chakrabarty has suggested that "the mansion of modern freedom stands on an ever-expanding base of fossil-fuel use."[59] Certainly it was a relationship to which Baines and his allies could see no end. "There are no limits," insisted McCulloch, "to the powers and resources of genius."[60]

Edward Baines Jr. believed that the Industrial Revolution had already exceeded "all that the most romantic imagination could have previously conceived" (112). That is hardly a version of improvement his precursor John Aikin—with his anxieties about the moral limits to commercial expansion—would have claimed for his own, as Marx seems to have recognized. Nevertheless, if Aikin's complex idea of improvement was displaced by a narrative techno-determinism in *History of the Cotton Manufacture*, the messianic message Baines preached was to find its encounter with messy reality as chastening as Aikin might have predicted. The ten-hours movement, for instance, continued to struggle against the power of the steam engine to set the rhythms of the industrial process. Sadler and Thackrah joined together with working-class radicals who refused to accept the liberal philosophy of history Baines proposed. The Mechanics' Institutes at Leeds, of which Baines was an important architect, found similar recalcitrance among a working-class membership that rejected an unappetizing diet of political economy and technical education.[61] Chapter 7, the final chapter, looks at the way that social reformers in the 1820s and 1830s invented the idea of "the social body" as a space where they could intervene to make good the inherited promise of improvement around Manchester. The Gregs, Heywoods, and Kennedys all reappear in a project where the rights of stewardship ultimately floundered on their own asymmetries and forgot that relations between bodies and their circumstances may need to take account of multiple agencies.

CHAPTER SEVEN

LIVES, DAMNED LIVES, AND STATISTICS

The repeal of the Test and Corporation Acts in 1828, Catholic Emancipation in 1829, the establishment of the British Association for the Advancement of Science in 1831, the Reform Bill of 1832, the Factory Acts of 1833, the abolition of colonial slavery in 1833, the Poor Law Amendment Act of 1834: the raft of legal and institutional reforms that marked the late 1820s and early 1830s might seem the natural fulfillment of the spirit of improvement traced in this book. James Losh, the great ally of William Turner at the Literary and Philosophical Society in Newcastle, celebrated the abolition of the Test and Corporation Acts as a glorious demonstration of "the progress of knowledge and liberal sentiments and the decay of Toryism more strongly than anything which has hitherto occurred."[1] Losh and Turner with many other of the names that have recurred in these chapters contributed directly to the campaigns to bring about these changes. Intergenerational continuities, though, mask important differences that cast doubt on any view of them as the necessary fulfillment—for good or ill—of the sense of social mission present from the earliest days of the transpennine enlightenment.

Chapter 4 examined the role of a fraternity of physicians in the Literary and Philosophical Society in Manchester who drew upon broadly materialist assumptions about mind-body relations, always a fraught issue, especially so in the heated atmosphere of the 1790s. Generally speaking, those physicians approached mind-body relations as part of an ecology of improvement that assumed the precariously interlinked nature of the material world. The first decade or so of the Literary and Philosophical Society provided an institutional home for habits of mind comfortable, if to differing degrees, with granting agency to relatively open and distributed networks made up of people and things, society and nature, history and culture. They celebrated Manchester as the center of an "inventive age." They were also watchful about the detrimental effects of industrial growth on the health of the working classes and on a natural environment taken to bind together all forms of life. By the 1820s the machinery question had become an issue that was understood to define the future direction of the country as a whole. For polemicists such as Edward Baines Jr. in Leeds, it mapped out a future not just for Britain but for global history. A way of thinking about relations between external environment and character narrowed to a machine-tooled future. The punctuality and dynamism of the steam factory and its perceived ability to transcend the limits to growth were increasingly underwritten, in some quarters at least, by the authority of political economy as a value-neutral knowledge. Equally, political economists such as J. R. McCulloch used the growth of the cotton industry, understood as the product of independent genius operating in line with general laws, to push against social oligarchy and the traditional hierarchies of knowledge. Mechanics' Institutes and other educational institutions encouraged by the Literary and Philosophical Societies in the 1820s and 1830s were regarded as the appropriate conduits to diffuse this knowledge so that workers might better understand where their real interests lay. In practice, workers frequently resisted both the patronage on offer at the institutes and the intellectual diet on their menus.

Even within circles that celebrated Manchester as the metropolis of the emerging industrial system, there were those who demurred at the paradigm of society as a machine. They reconfigured an older imaginary of society as an organic body, if with little of the sense of an open ecology found in John Aikin Jr. and others. Increasingly, instead, they thought of society and its knowledge formations as tessellated domains that included "the social body" described by the Manchester physician James Phillips Kay in his *Moral and Physical Condition of the Working Classes employed in the Cotton Manufacture in Manchester* (1832). "The social body cannot be constructed like a machine," argued Kay, "on abstract principles which merely include physical motions, and their numerical results in the production of wealth. The mutual relation of men is not merely dynamical, nor can the composition of their forces be subjected to a purely mathematical calculation."[2] Passages such as these confirm Kay as the heir of John Ferriar or Thomas Percival, not only in his resistance to mechanism but also because of the focus on public health in the industrial city. James Phillips Kay is often treated as the harbinger of the "*the condition of England*" question that dominated national discussion in the 1840s. This book has aimed to make visible a longer trajectory for the tradition of social inquiry and reform in the industrial heartland and this chapter to place Kay within it.[3]

In this context, it comes as no surprise that the substance of Kay's most famous work was first given as a paper at the Literary and Philosophical Society advertised in the local press at the end of March 1832. The date of the advertisement shows that Kay's pamphlet predated the cholera epidemic—often mistakenly taken to be its occasion—that hit Manchester a few months later.[4] Kay, who wrote poetry as a young man, quoted Percy Bysshe Shelley's "Mask of Anarchy" on a political platform in the early 1830s, and finally retired into novel writing in the 1860s, deserves to be understood in the line of literary physicians traced in this book. At the same time, he transformed this inheritance in specific ways.[5] His friends such as the younger Gregs, if anything more deeply imbricated in the area's traditions of improvement, shared in the transformation. Taken together as a group, these friends and allies were "mediators" in Bruno Latour's sense. They transformed—hardened, we might say, and narrowed—what they transmitted as their networked relations morphed across generations. In this regard, for all that they differed in their social imaginary, they shared something with Edward Baines Jr., not least in the way Kay used his writing on public health to argue against "enormous taxation and a restricted commerce" (9) and refused to countenance the idea that the factory system had anything to do with the terrible conditions he described. Instead his analysis took the problem to inhere in the culture of the working class; "another world," as John V. Pickstone puts it, "remote from the experience even of local manufacturers; an under-world which has to be uncovered by special techniques, by social statistics."[6]

THE SOCIAL BODY

James Phillips Kay was born into the Lancashire textile industry. His father, Robert, was a Congregationalist millowner in Rochdale, now in Greater Manchester, who also owned warehouses in the town itself. Kay's mother was the daughter of a Birmingham Unitarian family close to Joseph Priestley's. Robert Kay became very wealthy very quickly but found himself haunted by his prosperity, turning to itinerant preaching and chapel building. He educated his sons at a Manchester school built to meet the needs of the newly wealthy excluded from the English universities, regularly warning them about the dangers of mammon. His fellow Congregationalist Edward Baines Jr. was sent across the Pennines to the same school. Both families had both found prosperity in the transpennine enlightenment, Baines from the diffusion of knowledge in the provincial press, as we have seen, but neither was part of the Unitarian intellectual elite associated with Cross Street Chapel.[7] Despite their many collaborations with Unitarians on social issues, Congregationalists like Baines and Kay could find working with heterodox anti-Trinitarians uncomfortable. Even after the repeal of the Test and Corporation Acts in 1828, Unitarians were treated with suspicion by Trinitarian nonconformists and the Anglican establishment alike, tensions that could blight interdenominational philanthropic initiatives. In 1837, by now a Poor Law Commissioner in Norfolk, Kay felt it necessary to call on Thomas Chalmers to clear him from any guilt by association.[8] In Manchester, the disproportionate influence of Unitarians in local politics and civic affairs continued to bring resentment into the mid-nineteenth century and beyond, not least because of the effectiveness of their social networks that Thomas De Quincey had complained about. William Gaskell, on the other hand, contended that he and his fellow Manchester Unitarians had been "stigmatized as blasphemers, enemies of the cross of Christ, and deniers of the Lord who bought us."[9] Kay experienced the exclusive side of Gaskell's tight-knit community when he lost out to W. C. Henry in an election for the post of honorary physician at the Manchester Infirmary in 1828. Before the estrangement caused by the contest, Henry and Kay had been firm friends on the well-beaten path from Manchester to medical school in Edinburgh.[10]

On his way to Edinburgh, Kay had also been helped from within his own denomination. James Williamson, the Congregationalist physician allied to "Bainesocracy" in Leeds, advised him on which lectures to attend and other professional medical matters. After Kay's graduation, the two collaborated to found the short-lived *North of England Medical and Surgical Journal* (1830–31).[11] By this stage, Kay had been compensated for his defeat in the infirmary election by an appointment to the new auxiliary dispensary in the rapidly expanding industrial area of Ardwick and Ancoats, "chiefly inhabited," as Kay put it, "by a dense mass of pauper population."[12] There he witnessed poverty on a scale that would have been unimaginable to Ferrier and Percival as the town's population was in the process of quadrupling between 1801 and 1851 to 300,000.[13] Kay joined the Literary and Philosophical Society in January 1829 to swell a new generation of medical men continuing its long interest in the consequences of urban growth.

Despite the fact that it repeatedly stressed its strictly medical and professional purview, the *North of England Medical Journal*'s final issue, published in May 1831, included a review of W. W. Currie's recently published biography of his father. Regretting that it had not been written by a stylist like William Roscoe, the review celebrated James Currie as "the uncompromising champion of liberal principles" but concluded "that the qualities of his mind fitted him rather for the discursive pursuits of literature, than for the more severe, and matter-of-fact investigations of science."[14] If the judgment suggests something of the narrowing of the medical mind, more broadly the *Journal* did not neglect the question of the living and working conditions of the working classes that had occupied Currie's generation. The *Journal* opened with an essay by Edmund Lyon—continued over two issues—on the medical topography of Manchester. The second part included a history of the town's medical institutions, with details of the infirmary revolution—"a complete revolution," Lyon claimed—and the role of Ferriar and Percival in setting up the Board of Health and House of Recovery. "Revolution" it may have been in certain regards, but Lyon framed it as a shift toward medical modernity rather than a political story.[15] Kay himself supplemented his strictly medical essays with one on the conditions in the neighborhood of his infirmary, which fed directly into *The Moral and Physical Condition of the Working Classes*, and another on the effects of cotton factories on the health of the workers, a theme rather downplayed in his famous pamphlet. The *Journal* had also published a brief and revealingly unenthusiastic review of Charles Turner Thackrah's *The Effects of Arts, Trades, and Professions on Health and Longevity* that complained of its being of so "general and popular a nature." More explicitly hostile was the review of Thackrah's ally Michael Sadler's lengthy anti-Malthusian treatise *Laws of Population* (1830). Probably written by Kay, the review anticipates his later attack on "exaggerated and unscientific accounts of the physical ailments to which [factory children] are liable" (*Moral and Physical Condition*, 70). Although it opened with a pledge to "ever be the last to pollute the weapons of the profession of which we are humble members, by wielding them, as partizans, in the strife of political sophists," it made no bones about averring that "a physician may confer important benefits on political economy—a science which contemplates the happiness of the human race."[16] The contorted efforts to distinguish political economy as a scientific endeavor distinct from political conflict is one familiar from the 1820s. Kay was already well on the way, as his friend and colleague Williamson feared, to sacrificing his medical career in its service.

Even before *The Moral and Political Condition of the Working Classes* was published, Kay had become embroiled in the fraught political debates leading up to the passing of the Reform Bill. His *Letter to the People of Lancashire concerning further Representation of the Commercial Interest* (1831) was a fierce no-holds-barred attack on Tory oligarchy and "Old Corruption." Posing as a venerable nonconformist, Kay voiced his strong support for the liberal candidate Benjamin Heywood, nephew of Benja-

min Arthur Heywood. By this stage already a key figure at the Literary
and Philosophical Society and the main patron of the town's Mechanics'
Institute, Heywood became an important ally of Kay's in the Statistical
Society, an institution discussed at length in the next section. Kay's *Letter*
offered a program with which Heywood could readily agree: free trade,
the abolition of slavery, and a version of commercial society "which in-
creases the comforts and luxuries of life, and rapidly assists the progress
of civilization: which, supported alone by mutual good faith, is the enemy
of rapacity and violence." On the face of it, the liberal creed that "the
dissemination of wealth, scatters also the seeds of knowledge, and of the
arts" seems close to Roscoe's speech at the Liverpool Royal Institution
in 1817, not least in its celebration of the town's "monuments of fertile
genius and successful design." Kay, though, displayed a more explicitly
partisan scorn for Manchester's Tory-aristocratic hierarchy and, even
more tellingly, showed none of Roscoe's doubts about the social consequences of the manufacturing system. Kay only touched on the question
of the condition of the working classes in the image of "that multitude of
the labouring population, which for the present, lies like a sleeping giant
at their feet," a tableau that Elizabeth Gaskell revisited in an arresting
passage in *Mary Barton* discussed at the end of this chapter.[17] The circles
in which Kay was moving at this time were already busy developing their
inquiries into the state of this sleeping giant, although it soon enough
showed sufficient signs of wakefulness to scorn their pretensions to moral
leadership.

Kay's *Moral and Physical Condition* was a key statement in the development of a new mode of social inquiry. An earlier Stranger's Friend
Society, which had supported Ferriar and his allies in the infirmary, had
divided Manchester into districts to enable them to distribute aid to the
town's swelling population as the system of parish relief buckled. Their
immediate purpose, as their name indicates, was to provide succor to
those who had no right of settlement in Manchester. They also pioneered
the use of volunteer inspectors, each taking responsibility for a district in
the town to decide on where their help was needed, directly distributing
food, clothing, coals, and money.[18] Where the earlier initiatives differed
from those of Kay and his allies, as Pickstone points out, was that they did
not aim for "the systematic penetration of the urban mass; their mission
was to seek and to save those who were peculiarly lost."[19] Kay's "social
body" described a distinct domain, disembedded from the economic and
the political, disentangled from the more complex sense of social being
implied by the older idea of the body politic or, more particularly, from
the tradition of medical thinking about the precarious ecology of life in
general. Identified as a distinct domain, it became the object of proto-

cols of observation derived from natural philosophy that were then transformed into uniform statistical quantities. "Empirical observation," as Poovey describes it, was superseded by "abstraction, generalization, or theory, which displaces actual bodies."[20] The "social body" of Kay and his allies represented a domain separate from the factory system and the laws of supply and demand. Instead it was concentrated on the "social" issues of education, crime, and sanitary conditions in ways that are not unfamiliar today. The "domestic economy" of the working classes became the key area of investigation and intervention.

Kay's abstraction was partly enabled by a change in the social geography of Manchester and other industrial towns. The expansion of the city intensified the impoverishment of working-class areas as the movement of manufacturers away from their factories accelerated. Investigation became a more deliberate process of crossing boundaries between disparate worlds. These boundaries shaped an underlying assumption that the worlds were inhabited by creatures alien to each other. Kay staked the authority of his pamphlet on statistics and their ability to transcend mere impressions. Many of the admirers garnered by *The Moral and Physical Condition of the Working Classes* — Friedrich Engels among them — were equally if not more impressed by his descriptions of poverty.[21] Those descriptions would seem to owe at least something to accounts like this one from Ferriar's *Medical Histories*:

> The floor of this room is often unpaved: the beds are fixed on the damp earth. But the floor, even when paved, is always damp. In such places, where a candle is required even at noon day, to examine a patient, I have seen the sick without bed-steads, lying on rags; they can seldom afford straw. This deplorable state of misery becomes frequently the origin, and certainly supports in a great degree the progress, of infectious fevers. I have been able, in many instances, to trace the infection from cellar to cellar, and to say where it might have been stopped, by prudent management on the part of the infected family.[22]

The whole mise-en-scène, not least its emphasis on oozing filth and atmospheric degradation, was repeated by Kay, with important differences, most notably a pervasive sense of the distance between the polite observer and the revolting condition of the poor (32):

> A whole family is often accommodated on a single bed, and sometimes a heap of filthy straw and a covering of old sacking hide them in one undistinguished heap, debased alike by penury, want of economy, and dissolute habits. Frequently, the inspectors found two or more families

crowded into one small house, containing only two apartments, one in which they slept, and another in which they eat; and often more than one family lived in a damp cellar, containing only one room, in whose pestilential atmosphere from twelve to sixteen persons were crowded. To these fertile sources of disease were sometimes added the keeping of pigs and other animals in the house, with other nuisances of the most revolting character.

In Ferriar's analysis, certainly as Pickstone sees it, factory owners and their workers were still perceived as part of the same social and biological universe. In Kay's descriptions of urban deprivation, the objects of his investigations are merged with into the filth that surrounds them and implicitly in contrast with the supervening and impersonal "inspector."

Ferriar, Percival, and their allies in the 1790s also investigated conditions in the new cotton factories. Kay acknowledged the negative health effects of repetitious factory work in a powerful paragraph early on in his pamphlet (24):

They are drudges who watch the movements, and assist the operations, of a mighty material force, which toils with an energy ever unconscious of fatigue. The persevering labour of the operative must rival the mathematical precision, the incessant motion, and the exhaustless power of the machine.

In this passage at least, the causes of working-class "demoralization" (21) emanate from the factory system to hollow out the moral economy of domestic life (25):

Hence, besides the negative results—the abstraction of moral and intellectual stimuli—the absence of variety—banishment from the grateful air and the cheering influences of light, the physical energies are impaired by toil, and imperfect nutrition. The artisan too seldom possesses sufficient moral dignity or intellectual or organic strength to resist the seductions of appetite. His wife and children, subjected to the same process, have little power to cheer his remaining moments of leisure. Domestic economy is neglected, domestic comforts are too frequently unknown.

Baines's *History of the Cotton Manufacture* had laid this passage side by side with one from Thackrah to complain that both were "highly coloured." However, only Thackrah's was mocked (for his Grecian ideas of health).[23] Kay's faulty description—as Baines saw it—was mitigated by the current in *The Moral and Physical Condition* running in the opposite direction: "the natural tendency of unrestricted commerce, . . . is to develop the energies of society, to increase the comforts and luxuries of life, and to *elevate the physical condition* of every member of the social body." The condition of the lower orders was attributable only to "*foreign and accidental causes*" (77–8). Kay traced the problem of working-class demoralization to a failure to provide education and moral instruction. Enough political economy, supported by a diet of religion and morality, would make them understand that their interests lay in supporting capital. Enough domestic economy would make them take care of their persons in preparation for the rigors of the "free" labor market.

Faced with the problem of explaining how the creation of a great industrial city had brought about only squalor, filth, and political disaffection, Kay shifted the blame onto the contagious example of Irish migrants. John Kennedy a decade earlier had imagined that the rise of the factory would be a natural civilizing force in the shape of work-time discipline: it was the tune later picked up and played by Baines. But how could this be squared with the pauperism Kay discovered? Work-time discipline has failed to provide a durable foundation in times of hardship, Kay implied, because the Irish had brought with them the contagious example of a subsistence existence ignorant of the benefits of the industrious revolution. Compared to industrial man in his healthy aspect, the Irish migrant was "a barbarian." In a passage added to the second edition, the subliminal case for Protestant modernity was reinforced by a reference back to pre-Reformation social welfare: "the gross and indiscriminate bounty of ancient monasteries" (45). There followed a sustained attack on the principles of the old poor law that showed none of the professional restraint—such as it was—found in the review of Sadler in the *North of England Medical Journal* (47–48):

> Fearful demoralization attends an impost whose distribution diminishes the incentives to prudence and virtue. When reckless of the future, the intelligence of man is confined by the narrow limits of the present. He thus debases himself beneath the animals whose instincts teach them to lay up stores for the season of need.

In the first edition, this passage has a footnote to the paper on the poor laws Kennedy gave at the Literary and Philosophical Society discussed in my previous chapter.[24] Unsurprisingly, Kay dropped it from the second edition. Kennedy's defense of relief during downturns of the trade cycle was a poor fit to Kay's conviction—intensified in the second edition— that "a rate levied on property for the support of indigence is, in a great degree, a tax on the capital, from whose employment are derived the incentives industry and the rewards of the frugal, ingenious, and virtuous poor" (45–46). Probably building on annotations Chalmers supplied to the first edition, the second—prefaced by an introductory letter to the Scottish evangelical—develops into a furious Malthusian sermon on the idea that the poor laws "create the poor which they maintain."[25]

Brief mentions of Henry and Percival apart, removed after the first edition, Kay ignored the pioneering work of the Board of Health in 1796, despite the fact that as recently as September 1830, when the Manchester Infirmary had applied for royal patronage, the names of Percival and Ferriar were listed chief among those officers "who had attained, by their writings and practice, high and deserved public eminence."[26] He would, of course, also have known Lyons's account of their work from the *North of England Medical Journal*. But to have mentioned their names in his *Moral and Physical Condition* would have been to provide unwelcome evidence that the problems described—in essence, if not in scale—might be intrinsic to manufacturing towns. Kay implied that new problems required new tools of analysis and novel forms of social inquiry. In June 1832, Kay had told Chalmers that he had been subjected to bitter attacks from those who were "easy" about the state of the town. By November, "the inconsiderate hostility which was at first raised by a few of those capitalists, who considered themselves attacked" had been "almost entirely assuaged." Within a few weeks, he was working with John Kennedy and the sons of Hannah Greg in the Manchester Statistical Society.[27]

NEW INSTITUTIONS

There might have been an even more intimate relationship between James Phillips Kay and the Kennedy clan had John Kennedy's niece Helen accepted Kay's proposal of marriage in 1834. After several years of courtship, her mother decided—as James Williamson feared—that Kay's financial prospects were being made uncertain by interests beyond his medical practice. Whatever the personal and emotional toll for the couple, it seems not to have impeded the early years of the Manchester Statistical Society, founded in 1833 as the new institutional form for interventions into the social body. In truth, John Kennedy was something of an anomaly there anyway, the representative of an older generation of manufacturers who still lived in Manchester itself and perhaps only a reluctant Malthusian. The impetus for the Statistical Society was mainly from the younger group who had been very active in the Reform Bill campaigns and shared strong views on political economy and poor law reform. A walking trip to the Peak District that Kay shared with the young Greg brothers, Samuel and William Rathbone (W. R.), seems to have been the origin of the idea.[28]

The brothers naturally were products of the serious concern with social issues showed by their mother at Quarry Bank. They been taught at progressive Unitarian schools in Bristol and Nottingham, and then by Thomas Traill of Liverpool before—inevitably—going on to Edinburgh University. Their teacher in Nottingham was the father of John James Tayler, who became pastor at Mosley Street and later joined the Statistical Society. The Greg brothers traveled widely in the 1820s after Edinburgh, their taste for Lord Byron guiding their route, and published a book of poetry together in Paris. W. R. Greg presented papers on the ruins at Sardis and Mycenae at the Literary and Philosophical Society on his return.[29] A glimpse of his thinking on his travels is given in a letter to Kay written on Christmas Eve 1831. Replying to Kay's "shocking account of the state of affairs at home, and . . . gloomy forebodings," Greg seems relatively open-minded about the prospects for change: "I hope I may yet be in time for the Revolution you predicted, but I intend first to observe the state of a Revolutionized People in Greece, and a despotic government in Turkey and Austria, that I may be better able to take my choice of the two evils."[30] This relatively open disposition was also evident in a pamphlet he had published before his European tour.

An Enquiry into the State of the Manufacturing population (1831) had claimed the authority of "individual observation." Greg insisted that individual proprietors like his family had always had the welfare of their workers at heart.[31] Confident that "the benefits resulting from the establishment and extension of manufactures, are intrinsic and essential," he acknowledged that inquiries such as Robert Southey's into the condition of the working class were all too rare but dismissed the *Colloquies* as mere "poetical declamation": "We shall not conclude, like Mr. Southey, that the houses of the manufacturing poor must be the abodes of wretchedness and immorality, because, instead of being surrounded by gardens, and embowered by creepers, they are built 'naked, and in a row.'"[32] Nevertheless, at this stage at least, his position on the factory question differed markedly from the one Kay was soon to lay out in the *Moral and Physical Condition*. Greg made it clear that the "most important" thing that could be done to improve the condition of the working classes was the restriction of labor to ten hours a day. Unthinkable government interference in Kay's eyes, Greg saw a reduction in working hours at this stage as "absolutely necessary." Without the time for rest, relaxation, and reflection, argued Greg, "all plans and exertions for ameliorating the moral and domestic condition of the manufacturing labourer, can only obtain a very partial and temporary sphere of operation." Sounding rather like Southey in this regard at least, he argued that "the *present* unwholesomeness of large manufactories" was obvious to anyone "who has seen children enter them at ten or twelve years of age, with the beaming eye, and the rosy cheek, and the elastic step of youth; and who has seen them gradually lose the gaiety and light-heartedness of early existence, and the colour and complexion of health, [. . .] under the withering influence of laborious confinement, ill oxygenated air, and a meagre and unwholesome diet."[33] Kay's pamphlet accepted such descriptions to a degree, as Baines complained, but refused any idea their causes could be traced directly to factory conditions.

Greg claimed that "intense fatigue" wore out the "the sensorial power" of the worker: "he has no energy left to exert in any useful object, or any domestic duty; he is fit only for sleep or sensual indulgence."[34] Kay was more skeptical about there being any power of mind in the working classes. *The Moral and Physical Condition* opened with a famous exordium on the fact that society, unlike the "animal structure," lacked any "sensorium" that could make "every order immediately conscious of the evils affecting any portion of the general mass" (17–18). Without such a sensorium, it was necessary for techniques of social inquiry to make these evils known, and for minds like his to act on the results. Writing later in his pamphlet *The Factory Question* (1837), Robert Hyde Greg dismissed his little brother's early pamphlet as "little more than a college thesis, written before he had any experience, and scarcely any acquaintance with factories, or factory population, and he imprudently adopted as facts, the misrepresentations of a heated partizan of the 'Ten Hours Bill.'"[35] Needless to say, working-class leaders were delighted with the younger Greg's pamphlet. John Doherty's *Misrepresentations Exposed* (1838) made hay by pointing out that the younger brother had hardly been a neophyte: "As his father was a cotton spinner, one would think he had pretty good opportunities of witnessing the effects of factory labour." For Doherty, the leading trade unionist in Lancashire, the panacea of education promoted by the Statistical Society could not explain to female operatives how "educating *them* will prevent *him* from working them either for more than 9 or 12 hours, as they case may be." It was a direct hit on the way that these groups proposed educational goals *for* the working classes but resisted any suggestion that their own economic power might be curtailed, or even—for a good while at least—that the operatives might have much to say in the management of any educational program set for them.[36]

Doherty had earlier crossed swords directly with W. R. Greg himself in the pages of the *Voice of the People*, the newspaper of the National Association of United Trades for the Protection of Labour, in ways that help reveal the limits to the younger Greg's sympathies even in 1831. Greg had written to the paper to point to the unparalleled prosperity brought by machinery. Doherty agreed on the "folly and absurdity . . . of opposing the employment of machinery." The difference was that he urged his readers to unite and gain "A FULL SHARE OF THE PRODUCE OF EVERY MACHINE."[37] By the time W. R. Greg joined with Kay to inaugurate the Statistical Society, any dissonance between them on these issues seems to have disappeared. One of the society's earliest acts was to constitute W. R. Greg and Samuel Greg Jr. as a subcommittee to prepare a digest of the report of the Factory Commissioners. Their response, made public in the newspapers, insisted that there was little in the report to justify the charges against the factory system: "The health and morals of the people employed in the mills are at least equal to that of those engaged in other occupations in the towns in which they are situated; and the long hours of labour do *not* fatigue the children."[38]

The truth is that there were probably always more similarities than differences between W. R. Greg and Kay. The open-mindedness of Greg's letter from Naples at the end of 1831 is more properly to be seen as an expression of optimism about who would come out as the leaders of any "revolution." More often Greg brooded on the possibility that men like Doherty—with "inflammatory speeches, public and private, and by their monotonous complaints"—would disrupt the transition: "I write to induce the people to leave politics to wiser heads, to consent to learn and not endeavour to direct or teach," he told his sister in September 1830, anticipating the tone of his correspondence with the *Voice of the People*.[39] This same attitude came out strongly in his report to the Statistical Society on the evidence given to the Factory Commissioners. One hostile witness, he told the society in horror, "commenced his evidence by refusing to take the oath—declares that he does not believe in a God—that he formerly lived with [Richard] Carlile and the Rev. Robert Taylor—and that nevertheless he is a moral character!"[40] In many ways more liberal than the Congregationalist Kay in matters of religion, where he increasingly tended toward a very agnostic Unitarianism, Greg shared with his friend a conviction that avoiding revolution depended on sympathetic relations between classes, if on the understanding that they would always be based on deference to "wiser heads."[41]

The decision to set up the Statistical Society was made at the home of Benjamin Heywood, whose candidacy for the 1831 county election Kay had supported. As might befit the grandson of Thomas Percival, Heywood was already playing an important role in the range of institutions that emerged from the civic ambitions of members of the Literary and Philosophical Society in the 1820s, especially the Mechanics' Institution, where he was president from its foundation in 1825 to his retirement in

1840. His several *Addresses* to the institution over this period—published together in 1843—give a good sense of the kind of education that he thought would benefit the working classes.⁴² Always making his working-class audience aware of the opposition that still existed to any form of popular education as a seedbed of political unrest, Heywood's addresses, certainly early on, defined the Mechanics' Institute in terms of teaching the scientific principles behind useful knowledge, so that practical skills might be developed toward new inventions. James Watt, as usual, provided the primary example of the fruits of such a policy (13–14).⁴³ Like Baines in his *History of the Cotton Manufacture*, Heywood further illustrated his point by distinguishing the supposedly merely imitative skills of Indian craftsmen from the changes brought in the cotton industry by the inventiveness of the Industrial Revolution. Behind the distinction was also the familiar contrast between Protestant modernity and "adherence to the same practice from generation to generation, to which, by their superstition, these poor Indians are bound" (4). Heywood's plans for Manchester, initially at least, showed more of "the liberality of a gentleman" (np), as the editors of his *Addresses* (1843) put it, and less of the missionary zeal for political economy promoted by the Marshalls in the Mechanics' Institute at Leeds.⁴⁴ Nor did any explicitly religious education have a conspicuous role at this stage, a feature common to many institutions associated with Brougham that tended to confirm the suspicion of churchmen about godless Unitarians and their ilk.

When it came to the management structure of the Mechanics' Institution, though, the limits of Heywood's "liberality" were clear enough. Despite the displeasure of Brougham, voiced in his *Practical Observations*, Heywood followed the model of Leonard Horner at the Edinburgh School of Arts by excluding any working-class involvement in the running of the institution. Subsequent promises that there would be changes in governance only came about after the shock of Rowland Detrosier's breakaway New Institution, founded in 1829.⁴⁵ Changes in the syllabus were also made with some reluctance. Heywood's initial faith in the power of science and technology to attract an audience had wavered after the crash of 1825. Political economy started to appear in the lecture series in an attempt to explain what had happened. "Mortified and disappointed" (35) that this still failed to attract a working-class audience, his 1830 address declared the answer to be "more moral improvement" (37). The change in tack was somewhat against the grain of traditional Unitarian methods, with their suspicion of proselytism, perhaps reflecting the creeping influence even in these circles of Thomas Chalmers. Be that as it may, religion did not bring the working classes flocking to the doors of the Mechanics' Institution.⁴⁶ Eventually and unevenly over the course of the next decade or so, Heywood bowed to a demand for more accessible and entertaining fare: nonscientific books became a majority in the library; lectures diversified, starting with travel and poetry; newspapers were allowed in the reading rooms; and musical events and excursions were added to the fare to provide some kind of relief for exhausted working people.[47]

Heywood's experiences at the Statistical Society followed a similar pattern. Its first report made it clear that its origins lay in "a strong desire felt by its projectors to assist in promoting the progress of social improvement in the manufacturing population." Its first resolution was to meet "for the discussion of subjects of political and social economy, and for the promotion of statistical enquiries, to the total exclusion of party politics."[48] The last regulation was somewhat redundant given that they were nearly all liberal supporters of the manufacturing interest with strong connections to religious dissent.[49] The intimacy of friendship and family ties extended beyond the initial nucleus to include most of the early members, many of whom were members of the Literary and Philosophical Society, including John and James Kennedy and James and Henry M'Connel. John James Tayler joined early on. Samuel Robinson, Heywood's brother-in-law and John Kennedy's son-in-law, was another early member. These connections not only show that the Statistical Society was another engine of social reproduction, though it surely was, but also indicate how claims to scientific principles belied the networked nature of this knowledge, even if in its restricted form of family and denominational relations. Despite the overlap in membership with the Literary and Philosophical Society, the newer organization did not pretend to share its broader cultural and civic ambitions or its formal inclusivity.[50] Instead, the first report explained, "it was considered desirable to unite the members as closely as possible by the attractions of an agreeable social intercourse."[51] Soon afterward it limited its number to fifty. Some of its meetings took the form of a "soiree" such as the one members were invited to at the York Hotel in Manchester the day after Christmas 1834, where they heard a paper by Kay "On the means existing for Religious Instruction in Large Towns."[52] The society represented a liberal-minded elite coming together to achieve specific social goals (within the limited sense of the "social" discussed by Poovey). Above everything else, as M. J. Cullen puts it, the society was intended to "provide a coherent justification of the factory system, at least in its more humane forms."[53]

This endeavor was closely tied from early on to the campaign in favor of the New Poor Law finally introduced in 1834. One of the Manchester Statistical Society's earliest reports was Kay's *Defects in the Constitution of Dispensaries* (1834), originally read at the third meeting in November 1833. Kay not only dismissed the role of medical charities in the complex landscape of poor relief that Ferriar and Percival had helped extend in the 1790s as inadequate to the rapidly expanding population, he also presented them as doing positive harm: "The universal interference of an officious benevolence creates a reliance on assistance, and a craving for support, whose demands it will ultimately be unable to supply." Although *Defects in the Constitution of Dispensaries* was also part of a larger nationwide movement on behalf of medical professionalism, it was originally a shot fired on behalf of manufacturers and their allies in their campaign against "the perversion of the Poor Laws, which has created a population bound like slaves to toil, but having a right to be maintained— unwilling to work, yet demanding the wages of labour." The Statistical Society, in Kay's words, provided "the means of penetrating beneath the surface of society, and of observing the habits and manners of the poor, stripped of disguise."[54]

In the same way, Kay's *Moral and Physical Condition* (66–67) also praised the work already being done by Manchester's Christian instruction societies after the example of the Boston Unitarian Joseph Tuckerman.[55] The meeting of the British and Foreign Unitarian Association held at Cross Street Chapel in 1830 had passed a series of resolutions in favor of setting up city missions on the model of Tuckerman's.[56] His influence was probably deeper and more congenial to the Unitarians in the Statistical Society than the Chalmers material Kay circulated.[57] Although the two streams fed each other in the early 1830s, the Unitarian tradition tended to stress social action and sympathy more than the distribution of tracts. Coals, bedding, and infirmary tickets were given out by Unitarian city missionaries along with advice. Part of the same stream were the many charities already being run by women such as Elizabeth Rathbone, sister to the Greg brothers. The Greg children also had the direct example of their mother's mission at Quarry Bank, where, as Morley pointed out, Tuckerman's friend Channing was a strong influence.

Taken with the Statistical Society's own mission, the energies thrown into this campaign of surveillance are startling, but it was more difficult in practice to penetrate beneath the surface of things than was initially imagined. The Statistical Society collected data about the number of shared beds through to distinctions, left to its agents to draw, between houses that could be described as *"well furnished"* (with "a table and chairs, a clock, a chest of drawers, and a fair stock of necessary utensils") and those deemed *"comfortable"* ("clean, neatly arranged, and protected from the external air, even when somewhat bare of furniture"). These categories were acknowledged to be "vague" and difficult to render into "tabular form." Despite the confident general thrust of its rhetoric, the Statistical Society was forced to admit to various blind spots, even in the large survey of the region's working population proudly delivered to the British Association for the Advancement of Science in 1837. One problem was the obstruction and the resentment of the population, "jealousy and suspicion as to the objects and motives of the enquirers." "A disposition to mislead, or to resent enquiry" was manifested most strongly in relation to the question of wages and the hours of labor. Consequently, these questions were omitted, because "it was feared they could lead to no direct results," which it is difficult not to translate as a fear that they might lend succor to the ten-hours movement.[58] Some members of the established clergy simply found inquiries into religious provision "impertinent," a response that may have stemmed from suspicions of the Unitarian influence.[59] Kay's hoped-for "permanent links between the different orders of society" were not readily created by intrusive methods.[60] There was, above all, as Cullen neatly puts it, "a tension between moralism and environmentalism in their ideology, a tension between a moralistic attitude of condemnation of laziness, lack of self-reliance, and improvidence, and an environmentalist appreciation of the effects of lack of education and atrocious living conditions."[61]

The reports of the Unitarian domestic mission in Manchester from this period reveal a similar mismatch between the confidence of the supervising committee and the experience of their agents in the field.[62] John Ashworth made more than 3,500 visits between January and November 1834. He reported that he was initially met with suspicion, which he answered by pointing to his role as someone "whom the rich have made a mediator between rich and poor." Ashworth, like his successors George Buckland and John Lahye, shared the basic assumptions of the wealthy committee members, in that "whenever I visit a more than ordinarily wretched habitation, I feel a suspicion that vice must be there." However, what they saw forced on them an awareness of the difficulty of any moral or intellectual improvement for those who had little leisure for reading or reflection. There was often barely enough food even for the "frugal and industrious."[63] "I confess," Buckland told his superiors in the *Sixth Report* (1840), "that I often feel much perplexed in the endeavour to ascertain the real causes of the destitution which I so frequently find to exist: the whole matter is often so complicated a nature, that it becomes next to impossible to understand it thoroughly." Faced with cellar dwellings crammed with the bodies of the dead and dying, the corpses of children propped against unemployed looms, Buckland found himself "at a loss what to say, or what to recommend."[64]

By the early 1830s, working-class opinion was increasingly organized and articulate. Political unions, worker's organizations, and newspapers like the *Voice of the People* exposed the limitations of the vision of improvement provided by "wiser heads." A column on "Mr. Heywood and the Working Classes" in Doherty's *Voice of the People* (July 16, 1831) mocked Benjamin Heywood's claim to be a man of the people, pointing to his record at the Mechanics' Institute, "where he has always resisted the repeatedly urged claims of the subscribers to possess the entire management of the institution." What followed provided a sharp definition of a "liberal": "Mr. Heywood is a 'liberal,' and like most of that class, averse to all reform, save that which will give him power, and additional control over the producers of the nation's wealth." Doherty had meted out similar treatment, as we have seen, to the Gregs in the pages of the *Voice of the People*. The Gregs and the Heywoods had prided themselves on a heritage of reform and rational improvement over two generations. They were finding that their pretensions to leadership were not to be uncontested, circumstances were not simply to be molded to their wishes, and those they sought to improve increasingly had their own ideas on what they understood reform to be.

A MANCHESTER TALE

Strictly speaking, Elizabeth's Gaskell's *Mary Barton: A Tale of Manchester Life* (1848) is beyond the period remit of this book. My concerns with it are less with its synchronic relations to "the hungry forties" than the diachronic perspective that connects it to the networks of improvement explored in the previous chapters. More particularly, W. R. Greg's well-known hostile review of Gaskell's novel discloses many of the contradictions and tensions within the idea of improvement I have been discussing. Elizabeth Stevenson, as she was then, was born into the heart of the networks traced in this book. After the early death of her mother, she lived with her widowed aunt in Knutsford, near Quarry Bank. She is said to have accompanied her maternal uncle, the physician Peter Holland, on his rounds at the mill. Her biographer even speculates that she may have attended the Duodecimo Society. Gaskell's personal copy of Hannah Greg's *The Monitor*, inherited from her aunt, still exists in Knutsford Library, signed by the author.[65] The connection was strengthened further via William Turner of Newcastle, who married a sister of Peter Holland's first wife in 1799, the same year that Henry Holland, the physician's son, began attending Turner's school in Newcastle.[66] William Stevenson, Gaskell's father, was elected to the Newcastle Literary and Philosophical Society in 1804, probably through the connection with Turner, who baptized the first child of his second marriage in 1815.[67] Before her marriage, Elizabeth Stevenson lodged with Turner and his family in Newcastle, where she heard him lecture at the Literary and Philosophical Society on a variety of scientific subjects.[68] Turner's eldest daughter, Mary, had married J. G. Robberds, minister at Cross Street Chapel, in 1811. William Gaskell was appointed under Robberds at Cross Street in 1828. He and Elizabeth married in 1832. Mary Robberds and Elizabeth Gaskell shared the experience of the demands made on a minister's wife, a subject on which they both corresponded with William Turner.[69]

J. G. Robberds and William Gaskell both served on the committee of the Unitarian city mission. It was an initiative that became woven into Elizabeth Gaskell's daily life.[70] She certainly knew the reports of the Ministers to the Poor—the agents in the field—in some detail. *Mary Barton* makes direct use of John Lahye's 1842 report on more than one occasion. The earlier reports of Ashworth and Buckland also seem to have been a source.[71] The novel's descriptions of the filthy, damp traditions in which the poor were forced to live developed a strain of writing that stretched back through the Ministers to the Poor to Ferriar, repeating its recurrent emphasis on the "ooze" that to the later generation at least seemed to corrode proper distinctions between forms of life:

> The smell was so foetid as almost to knock the two men down. Quickly recovering themselves, as those inured to such things do, they began to penetrate the thick darkness of the place, and to see three or four little children rolling on the damp, nay wet brick floor, through which the stagnant, filthy moisture of the street oozed up; the fire-place was empty and black.[72]

This passage was one of many W. R. Greg chose to quote in his review of the novel, but its contents would have been already familiar enough to him.[73] Familiar too would have been the institutions that the region's tradition of Unitarian stewardship had helped put in the place—the Mechanics' Institution and the Manchester Infirmary—that play their own important parts in the plot. By the 1840s, Gaskell could represent the institution, where Mary's friend Margaret Jennings sings folk songs, as a place that had adapted itself toward working-class pleasures, but the barriers placed around medical charities remained dependent on the grace and favor of the masters and play their part in John Barton's alienation.

Gaskell used almost verbatim Lahye's claim about "the feeling of alienation between the different classes of society" from the *Eighth Report* (1842).[74] The novel form enabled her to cast the commonplace into dramatic life in encounters such as George Wilson's attempt to get an order for the infirmary from the factory owner Henry Carson (68):

"Davenport—Davenport; who is the fellow? I don't know the name."

"He's worked in your factory better nor three year, sir."

"Very likely; I don't pretend to know the names of the men I employ; that I leave to the overlooker. So he's ill, eh?"

"Ay, sir, he's very bad; we want to get him in at the fever wards."

"I doubt if I have an in-patient's order to spare; they're always wanted for accidents, you know. But I'll give you an out-patient's, and welcome."

In terms of what went on in the factories, Gaskell offers little by way of description, but she did give some sense of the struggles to improve factory conditions through working-class organization (perhaps the greatest bugbear of Greg's review). She told her publisher Edward Chapman that she would be "amused to read the manufacturing novel you tell me is forth-coming;. . . . It is a large subject, & I think it ought to be written upon."[75]

What she did develop, as many commentators have pointed out, was a sense of interiority and depth to working-class experience, especially in relation to domestic life, a sense of self and solidarity not lost in the ooze of their living conditions. Poovey suggests that *Mary Barton* reveals that the "mode of representation epitomized by political economy may have rendered aspects of the social domain visible as never before, but in so doing it also erased other facets of contemporary life." The novel's elaboration of feelings attempts to connect readers to the struggles of the Bartons through the generic resources of the novel, something Ashworth and Buckland had at least attempted in their reports. Ferriar's accounts of "patients in agonies of despair on finding themselves over-whelmed with filth" might be understood as written before the disaggregation described by Poovey. The sense of embattled but sympathetic interiority that Gaskell developed in relation to both male and female characters in the novel was increasingly coming to be seen, Poovey argues, as a gendered domain specific to the remit of the novel. Important in this regard is the novel's emphasis on the domestic and its complex relationship with the social in its largest sense: they remain entangled in *Mary Barton*, but arguably the novels makes the social recede as the domestic and interior life is elaborated.[76]

These were aspects of the novel that W. R. Greg admired in his review. He was certainly confident that it was "very palpably [. . .] the production of a lady" (403) at least partly because of its emphasis on the domestic. The same reasons accounted, as he saw it, for the failure to give John Barton any awareness of "the first principles of commercial and economic science" (412). Acknowledging that the author "has actually lived among the people she describes" (403), Greg confirmed that "mutual helpfulness and unbounded kindliness towards each other" (406) was a striking aspect of working-class life as he had witnessed it. Gaskell was echoing one of the key sentiments of the domestic missions sponsored by Greg and their ilk when she called for greater knowledge of the poor by the rich. Greg and his brother Samuel had worked hard to bring this about in the 1820s and 1830s, as Gaskell acknowledged in her letters, but the review sounds a note of disillusion about the Greg family's philanthropic inheritance: "the rich can never have the same knowledge of the troubles and difficulties of the poor, which the poor have of their own. Their paths lie apart. However much they may endeavour to visit among them, to become familiar with their circumstances., and acquainted with their griefs,—they can do all this, from the very nature of the case, only very imperfectly (410)." Perhaps to be viewed as a welcome modification of the middle-class will to knowledge, Greg's modesty curdles into a series of intensifying diatribes against of working-class moral failings, as if the failures in the domestic missions reported by Ashworth and Buckland led him to double down on the old complaint about "improvidence," a word which echoes through his review. John Barton's problem, as Greg saw it, was that he remained "utterly unconscious, even to the last, of his own improvidence and of its sinister influence on his condition" (413).

Sinister to Greg was John Barton spending "his time and money on trades' unions when both child and himself are unsupplied" (413). Refused the status of self-reliance or forethought, from this perspective working-class organizations are simply instances of "an inability to resist evil counsel" (423). The Statistical Society's rejection of any questioning of "the regularity or the remuneration of their work" (421) remains resolutely in place. The solutions offered by his form of social activism had been rejected by the poor, Greg believed, and now they should look to their own inner strength, except "the power of *will*" (422) to resist improvidence, as he defines it, is inevitably lacking. In this situation, the "signs and elements of progress towards a social and moral emergence, distant yet, and very lofty, but nevertheless within their reach" (404), outlined at the beginning of his review, are doomed to be always deferred in a short-circuiting of any form of improvement in which its objects— the working classes—have any agency.

Greg acknowledged that *Mary Barton* had "higher pretensions than an ordinary novel" (410) but refused to accept that his class had played any role in creating the condition that he complained about. In one of the best-known passages in the book, not quoted by Greg, Gaskell offered a very different, if conflicted and even contradictory, perspective which, partially at least, recast the stewardship relationship in terms of one between culpable creator and embittered creature: "The actions of the uneducated seem to me typified in those of Frankenstein, that monster of many human qualities, ungifted with a soul, a knowledge of the difference between good and evil" (165). The idea of the mute appeal of the dumb monster seems familiar enough from the various reports discussed in this chapter, but the complicity of the improvers in the situation they aimed to reform was less often acknowledged in these circles: "The people rise up to life; they irritate us, they terrify us, and we become their enemies. Then, in the sorrowful moment of our triumphant power, their eyes gaze on us with a mute reproach. Why have we made them what they are; a powerful monster, yet without the inner means for peace and happiness?" (165).The reproaches of Doherty and his comrades had scarcely been mute or even inarticulate, but Gaskell extended her engagement with Mary Shelley's novel by remembering that its creature did have a voice. Within its "wild and visionary" articulations, the possibility at least of "a sort of practical power, which made him useful to the bodies of men to whom he belonged" is granted to Barton. Something that W. R. Greg found almost impossible to accept flashes—if only temporarily— into view. John Morley's penetrating account of Greg's career presented him as "one of the best literary representatives of the fastidious or pedantocratic school of government. In economics he spoke the last word, and fell sword in hand in the last trench, of the party of capitalist supremacy and industrial tutelage."[77] Delving behind this public persona, Morley created a picture of a sensitive man, especially influenced by his mother's tastes, caught between loyalty to the industrial classes and a more imaginative and inquiring mind, a fervent reader of Byron, who was also reading William Godwin and Jean-Jacques Rousseau at Edinburgh in the 1820s, aiming to contradict both Malthus's and Sadler's theories on population. Quoting from his travels to Europe and Turkey published in the early 1830s, Morley presents Greg as open-minded, eager for improvement, brought up in an ethos of service where "the genial side of the patriarchal system was seen at its best" (113). Like his brother Samuel, a relationship delicately touched on by Morley, the frustration of his life was that he could not bend circumstances to create the improvements that he wished. His materials—including the workers he wished to help— had proven intractable.

Morley provided an astute commentary on the emerging asymmetries of stewardship that this book has traced. By 1830, as Morley tells it, Greg was already "poisoned by the conception that haunted him to the end": "When the people complain, their complaint savours of rebellion. Those who make themselves the mouthpiece of popular complaint, must be wicked incendiaries. The privileged must be ordained by Nature to rule over the non-privileged. The few ought to direct and teach, the many to learn" (115). Greg may have been brought up in a household whose idea of "taste" was formed by Anna Laetitia Barbauld, as Morley noted, but little of the flexibility of her idea of circumstance was carried forward into his thinking. Instead character was to be molded by the assumed authority of Greg and his friends at the Mechanics Institute and in the Statistical Society. The echoes of John Aikin's sense of the social mission of the middle classes are palpable here, but where those remarks were primarily directed against the traditional oligarchy's rejection of religious and other freedoms, now the claim to moral authority was oriented more toward command; "an aristocracy," Morley described it, "of education, virtue and public spirit" (124).[78]

It would be easy to see this new "aristocracy" as the inevitable result of the idea of improvement explored in this book, rather than simply as an affordance of it. I have suggested that it represented a disciplinary strain always bound up with more imaginative and flexible ideas of relationships between humans and their environment, between character and circumstance, and between the different domains of knowledge that emerged over the period. Power, wealth, and self-interest may have narrowed these perspectives into a righteous "mission," to use Marx's word. Increasingly precipitated into a distinctive "liberal" structure of feeling they may have been, but countercurrents swirled still within the solution. These played their part in movements such as Owenism—always in a complex relationship with its begetter—and the challenges that figures such as Detrosier and Doherty made to the narrowing version of a creed of improvement. They have remained an important part of social reform and progressive politics in Britain, including the suffragist and welfare reformer Eleanor F. Rathbone, great-granddaughter of Hannah Greg, even as they have also constantly been prey to the assumption of a right to control others in the name of the public good.[79] These networks of improvement had no simple-minded attitude to the power of circumstance. They were rarely as mechanical as their opponents and later critics made out, and their writing, practices, and institutions deserve attention as part of the broader literary and intellectual culture of the pre-Victorian period, even if they are routinely conjured—without much investigation—as the enemy of a more familiar Romanticism. They had their own visionary gleam, as Morley noted of the Gregs, if one that could be as excited by the "romantic" growth of the cotton industry as by the power of nature or poetry (which they, like Edward Baines Jr., also certainly felt). Ironically, perhaps, where it became most visionary and most "romantic" was often also where this improving ethos withdrew from an encounter with the messy reality of its environment—whether in human or natural terms—to assert its own power to shape circumstance to its own ends. Within this formation, even in its later versions, there was far from being any simple rejection of the imaginative life. My own circumstance of writing is one in which the arts and humanities are increasingly seen, even in universities, as extraneous to improvement. This book may usefully recall us to the fact that, even in the heartlands of the Industrial Revolution, often held up today, at least in the United Kingdom, as a space and time of positive growth and useful knowledge, there was a continuous emphasis—if on various terms—on the relevance and even necessity of the humanities to any form of improvement worth having.

ACKNOWLEDGMENTS

Anyone interested in networks ought to have a sense of how much their own work depends on collaboration. This book has certainly been the product of a widely distributed agency, all the more necessary because of the restrictions caused by the pandemic that began in 2020. If it had not been for the support of any number of archivists and librarians, amazingly generous of their time when it came to responding to inquiries, chasing up references, and scanning documents, it would have been several more years in the making. They also made in-person visits a special pleasure when places started to reopen after pandemic restrictions eased. I would particularly like to thank Alkestis Tsilika and the staff at Quarry Bank, who supported the project from the beginning. Kay Easson, librarian of the Newcastle Literary and Philosophical Society, has been tremendously helpful throughout, especially early on when I had no idea what I was asking to see. Thank you for the several invitations to speak at the Lit Phil. It has always been a pleasure. I'm also very grateful to Caroline Grove for scanning the platypus from the minute books. I gained immeasurably from Paul Gailiunas's wealth of knowledge about the Lit Phil.

The staff at Special Collection of the Brotherton Library, Leeds, were fantastically helpful in providing scans when it was impossible to visit the archive itself, close by York though it is. Janet Douglas invited me to speak at the event celebrating the bicentenary of the Philosophical and Literary Society of Leeds in 2019. As with Newcastle, it's always great to visit these still-thriving institutions. At the Leeds event, I had the great pleasure of meeting Bob Morris in person. Somewhat late in the day, on the recommendations of Jane Corrie and Megan Coyer, I appealed to the Royal College of Physicians of Edinburgh for confirmation that John Ferriar had been a student of Williams Cullen's. Estela Dukan generously sent me scans of letters from the archives of the RCPE that are mentioned in chapter 4. In Sheffield, the staff of the City Archives were unfailingly generous and helpful. The only distraction was the pleasure of listening to the inquiries about local history going on around me, many of them deeply moving, others very funny. I had much the same experience in Liverpool and Manchester in the search rooms at the two central libraries. Liverpool University Library staff in Special Collections were incredibly helpful when it came to my ordering and reordering the many Hannah Greg letters from the Rathbone Papers. Similarly, the John Rylands Library was endlessly accommodating, both with personal visits and some slightly strange archival access via Zoom that I'm not sure I ever really mastered. From early on, Susan Killoran, and right at the end, Kate Alderson-Smith, of Harris Manchester College, Oxford, were generous and patient with my importunities. I also received gracious assistance from the Bodleian Library, the Royal Commonwealth Society Library at Cambridge University, Special Collections at the Sheffield University Library, Special Collections at the University of Edinburgh, the Warwickshire County Record Office, and the West Yorkshire Archives Service. The British Library, both in nearby Boston Spa and London, were as patient and supportive as ever. Katie Sambrook of Special Collections at Kings College London helped me start to trace some Ferriar-Keats connections in the library of the Physical Society, which I hope to take further.

Time to gather the research of many years together and to write the book was provided by a British Academy Senior Research Fellowship from 2019 to 2020, generously extended to take account of the difficulties caused by the pandemic. The award of the R. Stanton Avery Distinguished Visiting Professorship at the Huntington Library from 2016 to 2017 gave me one of the best years of my life and the opportunity to fully map out the territory I wanted to cover in this book. Thanks to Steve Hindle and Kevin Gilmartin for making it happen, and for the conviviality and support of all the fellows, especially Steve Hahn and Fuson Wang. Helen Deutsch, Michael Meranze, and Saree Makdisi each helped make Los Angeles great fun and gave me plenty of food for thought. During this period, a trip to Vancouver organized by Alex Dick and Michelle Levy gave me the valuable opportunity to air some of these ideas at the University of British Columbia and Simon Fraser University. I had a similarly fruitful experience at the University of Notre Dame a few weeks later, thanks to Greg Kucich, Ian Newman, and Yasmin Solomonescu.

I have been the beneficiary of many conversations with colleagues across many areas of this project, going right back to the Networks of Improvement Leverhulme project that formed its roots, including Sarah Auld, Mike Brown, Alexandra Buchanan, Tom Duggett, Georgina Green, John Gardner, Daisy Hildyard, Ian Inkster, Felicity James, Roseanna

Kettle, Caleb Klaces, Declan McCormack, Kirsty McHugh, Chris Murray, Alice Rhodes, Virlana Shchuka, John Seed, Mark Steadman, David Stewart, Nick Thurston, Rebecca Tierney-Hynes, Jon Topham, Mark Towsey, Christopher Webster, Jo Wharton, and Bob White. I've gained immeasurably from collaborations with Matthew Sangster on the two collections of essays—*Institutions of Literature, 1700–1900* and *Remediating the 1820s* from Cambridge and Edinburgh University presses—funded by Arts and Humanities Research Council and Royal Society of Edinburgh Network grants, respectively. I'd like to thank all the participants in the networks and the contributors to the books. Jon Klancher has been an inspiration for the whole project and unfailingly helpful when it came to details, especially about lecturing networks and the relationship between networks and institutions. I was flattered and delighted when he and Jonathan Sachs invited me to contribute to the special issue of *Romantic Circles Praxis* on Raymond Williams and Romanticism. Paul Keen's hospitality in Ottawa gave the whole project a wonderful convivial warmth that Jon Sachs just kept topping up. I'm grateful to Cassie Ulph and Andrew McInnes for inviting me to speak at the first session of the Transpennine Research Network and to the invitation from Greg Dart and David Duff to the London-Paris Romanticism seminar shortly afterward. Thanks also to Mark Towsey for the opportunity to speak about the Scottish influence on the transpennine enlightenment at the Eighteenth-Century Scottish Studies Conference in Liverpool in July 2022. A keynote at the Romantic Studies Association of Australia conference in Melbourne in 2015 helped me clarify what I was trying to say about De Quincey. Thank you very much to Deirdre Coleman and Peter Otto for the invitation, and to Susan Conley and Clara Tuite for their hospitality. At the 2019 RSAA in Canberra, I heard Kevis Goodman speak about environmental medicine in the period. Since then, she very graciously sent me the proofs to her wonderful *Pathologies in Motion*. It really helped me pull together my thinking in chapter 4, and the methodology of this book more generally.

Closer to home in York, I'm very grateful to Katie Crowther for sharing transcriptions of Hannah Greg letters. Katie was one of several students from my Literature, Medicine, and Modernity module who keep showing enthusiasm for the topic even when they had heard me go on about John Ferriar a million times. I am grateful to my colleagues in the Department of English at the University of York who struggled through all the difficulties of hybrid and online teaching that I came to only belatedly and in relatively benign forms. It felt good to be back in a classroom without a mask, for most of 2022 at least. Helen Smith, Nicola McDonald, Cathy Moore, Anne Chantry, and Helen Barrett all gave invaluable practical support. My colleagues at the Centre for Eighteenth-Century Studies were helpful as ever; Mary Fairclough, Catriona Kennedy, Jane Rendall, Gillian Russell, and Jim Walvin all shared their knowledge on particular issues with characteristic generosity. I'd also like to thank Steve Newman at the Minster Library. John O'Halloran and Kenneth Clarke were wonderful supports all through lockdown and after, as was everyone connected with the Pig & Pastry.

Parts of this book have been published in other places. Some of the material in chapter 2 was discussed in an article written with Jennifer Wilkes that appeared in the *Journal for Eighteenth Century Studies* in 2015. A later article in the same journal from 2019 helped me work out my thinking on Hannah Greg, and parts of it duly appear in chapter 5. The essay I contributed to the *Romantic Circles Praxis* issue helped sharpen my thinking about Williams and Latour, and various parts of the essay are dispersed around this book. Siobhan Carroll, Jeremy Davies, Eric Gidal, and Nigel Leask were wonderful to work with on the special edition of *Studies in Romanticism* from 2022 devoted to Romanticism and the Industrial Revolution, parts of which appear in chapter 6. I'm grateful to Jeremy for the chance to speak on the "Land and Society" at the joint British Association of Romantic Studies/North American Society for the Study of Romanticism conference held in Edge Hill in 2022.

Finally, I am very grateful for the love and support of my family: Mum, Dad, Chris, and Bec. My daughter Sharmila has had to put up with endless Zoom calls where she probably caught my eye wandering to a footnote somewhere else on the screen. Likewise, Jane Huyg, my wife, has lived with my anxieties about everything from digging out lost references to finding train tickets for archival visits when I should have been thinking about her. I hope that you both know how much I love you!

ABBREVIATIONS

DRO	Derbyshire Record Office
HG	Hannah Greg
HMCO	Harris Manchester College Oxford
JRL	John Rylands Library, University of Manchester
LRO	Liverpool Record Office, Central Library
LPLS	Leeds Philosophical and Literary Society
LRI	Liverpool Royal Institution
LUL	Liverpool University Library
MCL	Manchester Central Library
MLPSM	*Memoirs of the Literary and Philosophical Society of Manchester*
MM	*Monthly Magazine*
NLPS	Newcastle Literary and Philosophical Society
QBA	Quarry Bank Archive, National Trust
SCA	Sheffield City Archives and Local Studies Library
SDUK	Society for the Diffusion of Useful Knowledge
SLPS	Sheffield Literary and Philosophical Society
SSPUK	Sheffield Society for the Promotion of Useful Knowledge
WCRO	Warwickshire County Record Office
WYAS	West Yorkshire Archives Service

NOTES

INTRODUCTION

1. See C. Knick Harley's review of Mokyr's *Enlightened Economy*. I am indebted to the discussion in Davies, "Introduction: Romantic Studies and the Shorter Industrial Revolution." Full citations of these and most other sources appear in the bibliography.

2. Raymond Williams, *Marxism and Literature*, 61; Manuel DeLanda, *A New Philosophy of Society*, 60. Using Williams's familiar trope of precipitation here might be taken to imply that the later formation emerges as the "real" meaning of the earlier, whereas I'd suggest the second formulation is truer to "the complex relation of differentiated structures of feeling to differentiated classes" (134) as middle-class identity changed across this period.

3. Chapter 7 provides more detail regarding the clash between Heywood and Doherty.

4. Philip Connell, *Romanticism, Economics, and the Question of "Culture,"* 107.

5. See the definitions of "institution" offered in Jon Mee and Matthew Sangster, introduction to *Institutions of Literature*.

6. Mitchell Dean, *The Constitution of Poverty*, 4.

7. Bruno Latour, *Reassembling the Social*, 29.

8. Kevis Goodman, *Pathologies of Motion*, 16–17.

9. Rita Felski, *Limits of Critique*, 12; "Latour and Literary Studies," 737, 739.

10. Caroline Levine, *Forms*, 120–21.

11. Goodman, *Pathologies of Motion*, 25.

12. Levine, *Forms*, 62–63.

13. Jon Mee, "Raymond Williams, Industrialism, and Romanticism, 1780–1850."

14. Goodman, *Pathologies of Motion*, 16–26.

15. Felski, "Latour and Literary Studies," 739.

16. Jane Bennett, *Vibrant Matter*, 3.

17. See, for instance, Timothy Morton, "An Object-Oriented Defense of Poetry," 4.

18. Williams, *Marxism and Literature*, 125.

19. J. R. McCulloch, "Rise and Progress of the Cotton Manufacture," *Edinburgh Review* 91 (June 1827): 17.

20. Dipesh Chakrabarty, "Climate of History," 208. This idea is discussed more fully in chapter 6.

CHAPTER ONE

1. Karl Marx, *Capital*, 557.

2. References to Aikin's book are given in the main text from this point onward.

3. Marx, *Capital*, 558.

4. Raymond Williams, *Marxism and Literature*, 67.

5. Kurt Heinzelman, "The Last Georgic," 177. Joanna Innes, "Reform in English public life" 77, suggests that the word "improvement" was bound to a scientific-technical sphere that could define itself as transcending religious and political differences. The rules against religious and political debate at the literary and philosophical societies discussed subsequently are a part of this complex history, as is the attempt to widen its ambit to political matter in some quarters.

6. David Hume, "Of Luxury," in *Essays and treatises on several subjects*, 23.

7. See Richard Price, *Observations on the Importance of the American Revolution*, 110, where he extended the prospects of improvement to the extirpation of vice, war, and even death.

8. Christine MacLeod, *Inventing the Industrial Revolution*, 104–5, discusses Brindley and patents.

9. Alan Hardy, *Origins of the Idea of the Industrial Revolution*, 118–19.

10. Manuel DeLanda, *A New View of Society*, 13.

11. E. A. Wrigley, *Continuity Chance & Change*, 3, is one of many disavowals of the Industrial Revolution as a "cumulative, progressive, unitary phenomenon." See the useful survey of recent debates within economic history in Emma Griffin's *A Short History of the British Industrial Revolution*.

12. Wrigley's *Energy and the English Industrial Revolution* gives more explicit emphasis to environmental consequences. See also Fredrik Albritton Jonsson, "The Industrial Revolution in the Anthropocene."

13. See Andreas Malm, *Fossil Capital*, which also discusses Wrigley's use of the word "organic" (38).

14. This abstraction of "social reform" is central to the otherwise contrasting accounts in John V. Pickstone, "Ferriar's Fever to Kay's Cholera," and Mary Poovey, *Making a Social Body*, discussed further in chapter 7.

15. See Margaret Jacob, *Scientific Culture and the Making of the Industrial West*; Margaret Jacob, *First Knowledge Economy*; Joel Mokyr, *Gifts of Athena*; Joel Mokyr, *Enlightened Economy*.

16. Mokyr, *Enlightened Economy*, 31.

17. Joel Mokyr, "Intellectual Origins of Modern Economic Growth," 300; Mokyr, *Enlightened Economy*, 81.

18. See the special issue of *History of Science* 45, no. 2 (2007) discussing Mokyr's *Gifts of Athena*, including Maxine Berg, "The Genesis of 'Useful Knowledge,'" 123–33; Lilaine Hailaire-Peréz, "Technology as Public Culture in the Eighteenth Century," 135–53; and Larry Stewart, "Experimental Spaces and the Knowledge Economy," 155–77.

19. Maxine Berg and Pat Hudson, "Rehabilitating the Industrial Revolution," 26.

20. John Langton, "The Industrial Revolution and Regional Geography of England."

21. N. F. R. Crafts, *British Industrial Growth*, 85, 151. See the discussion of other revisionist analyses in Maxine Berg's *Age of Manufactures*, 3–6, 14–19; as well as Berg and Hudson's "Rehabilitating the Industrial Revolution." Even a revisionist such as Crafts

suggested that in the "glamour" industries such as cotton textiles there was "spectacular growth that licensed the 'Revolution' trope" (*British Industrial Growth*, 8).

22. Giorgio Riello, *Cotton*, 228. See also, more recently, Riello, "Cotton Textiles and the Industrial Revolution in a Global Context."

23. A. E. Musson and E. Robinson, *Science and Technology in the Industrial Revolution*, and R. E. Schofield, *The Lunar Society of Birmingham* represent the societies as mediating science into technological applications. This position was critiqued in Roy Porter's "Science, Provincial Culture and Public Opinion," drawing, especially on Arnold Thackray, "Natural Knowledge in Cultural Context."

24. See, for instance, John Seed, "Unitarianism, Political Economy and the Antinomies of Liberal Culture" and "Gentleman Dissenters." Seed acknowledges the influence of Raymond Williams on his idea of this "liberal culture" as "a contradictory field of discourses structured in a highly localized network of practices, institutions and social relations" ("Antinomies," 2–3). Chapters 2 and 4 discuss the relationship between Percival and Gisborne.

25. Thackray, "Natural Knowledge," 678, 685; R. Porter, "Science, Provincial Culture," 25.

26. John Aikin Jr., "An Apology for the Literary Pursuits of Physicians," 667. See the excellent account in Kathryn Ready's "'And make thine own Apollo doubly thine'" and Lucy Aikin's *Memoir of John Aikin, M.D.,* for details. The papers Aikin gave at the society included "On the Impression of Reality Attending Dramatic Representations," discussed in chapter 4. The first volume of *MLPSM* carried his "Remarks on the different success with respect to Health, of attempts to pass the Winter in High Northern Latitudes."

27. Derek Roper discusses Aikin's and Ferriar's tenures at the *Monthly Review*; see Roper, *Reviewing before the Edinburgh*, 88–92 and 105–10, respectively.

28. One does not need to see "knowledge" as the primary driver of economic change to believe that it was important, at least in compounding and even influencing its direction. See C. Knick Harley's review of Mokyr's *Enlightened Economy*.

29. Percival's career is discussed at length in chapter 4. On Henry and Barnes, see W. V. Farrar, Kathleen Farrar, and E. L. Scott, "The Henrys of Manchester Part 1: Thomas Henry," 183–208; A. E. Musson, "Early Industrial Chemists: Thomas Henry," 231–51; obituary of Thomas Barnes, *Monthly Repository of Theology and General Literature*, 5 (August 1810): 56; Thomas Baker, *Memorials of a Dissenting Chapel*, 47–50.

30. G. M. Ditchfield, "Early History of Manchester College," 83–84. On October 8, 1789, Priestley confided to Theophilus Lindsey that Barnes "cannot conceal his jealousy of Mr. Hawkes's Unitarian Chapel," *Theological and Miscellaneous Works*, 1, pt. 2: 35. Priestley nevertheless stayed with Percival in Manchester in 1791. The following year Barnes signed the Unitarian petition, while William Hawkes, intimidated by loyalist attacks, did not: see Theophilus Lindsey to John Rowe, 6 March 1792, in Theophilus Lindsey, *Letters of Theophilus Lindsey*, 2:171.

31. Seed, "Gentleman Dissenters," 302–3; Baker, *Memorials of a Dissenting Chapel*.

32. Felicity James, "Religious Dissent and the Aikin-Barbauld Circle," and Daniel E. White, *Early Romanticism and Religious Dissent*, 50–55, discuss the Aikin-Barbauld collaborations. Barbauld's "Thoughts on the Devotional Taste" was first prefixed to her *Devotional Pieces* and then published again in John Aikin Jr. and Anna Laetitia Barbauld, *Miscellaneous Pieces in Prose.*

33. Aikin thanked Percival for "the communication of various papers, as well as for

many judicious hints and remarks towards the execution of the design" (*Description of Manchester*, vii). Thomas Walker also contributed materials: John Aikin Jr. to Thomas Walker, 2 May 1795, Add MS 88955, f. 11, Letters Addressed to Thomas Walker, British Library.

34. On the publishing background and its reception, see Mee, "'All that the most romantic imagination could have previously conceived': Writing an Industrial Revolution," 235–37.

35. Wrigley, *Continuity Chance & Change*, 15.

36. The many overseas corresponding members included Philadelphia physician Benjamin Rush, whose membership certificate—dated December 22, 1784—is in the Rush Family Papers, Library Company of Philadelphia, Unbound Correspondence, Box 2, Folder 31, with his correspondence with Percival and Henry.

37. Wrigley, *Continuity Chance & Change*, 75.

38. John Kay is only mentioned as the inventor of the flying shuttle in the section on Bury (267); neither James Hargreaves (the jenny) nor Samuel Crompton (the mule) are mentioned with the inventions usually associated with their names; Arkwright is discussed in various locations and with some doubts cast on his intellectual property claims.

39. Aikin's *A Description of Manchester*, 338-39, is guardedly critical of the slave trade: "Concerning the slave trade, for which Liverpool has since become so distinguished, it is difficult to speak with the coolness of discussion that belongs to commercial topics in general. One the one hand, it has been warmly arraigned by the friends of justice and humanity, and, indeed, by the common feelings of the uninterested part of mankind; on the other hand, it has been warmly defended by those who are ardent in the pursuit of every extension of individual and national wealth . . . Some, however, are of opinion that it pushed this adventurous spirit beyond all due bounds; has introduced pernicious maxims and customs of transacting business; has diverted to itself the capital and attention which might have been better employed on other objects; and has occasioned a great waste of lives among the seamen." Aikin quotes from Percival on factory conditions (456) and Ferriar on housing (192–93). In *Capital*, Marx picked up on Aikin's allusions to "the earlier infamies of the factory system" (710) and Liverpool's dependence on the slave trade (711). See L. Aikin, *Memoir of John Aikin*, 1: 64–65, for the recommendation that Aikin should tone down his politics.

40. John Aikin, Jr., *Address to the Dissidents of England on their Late Defeat*, 18.

41. Christopher Brown, *Moral Capital: Foundations of British Abolitionism*.

42. Clarkson's views on the cotton boycott are reported in "Diary of Katherine Plymley," March 1792, 1066–6 (24 Feb 1792–5 Mar 1792), Shropshire Archives, in a discussion of an untraced pamphlet by the Unitarian minister Theophilus Houlbrooke, a friend of Roscoe and the Rathbones. Thomas Clarkson to Thomas Walker, 3 April 1788, Add MS, 88955, f. 67. Equiano acknowledged the assistance of Walker and the magistrate Thomas Butterworth Bayley. See Equiano, *The Interesting Narrative*; John Bugg, "The Other Interesting Narrative," 1430.

43. See Brian Howman, "Abolitionism in Liverpool," 281; David Lascelles, *Story of the Rathbones*, 34–35, 45–46; Lucie Nottingham, *Rathbone Brothers*, 21–22; Eleanor F. Rathbone, *William Rathbone*, 8, 11. Thomas Clarkson praised William Rathbone III for not allowing "any article to be sold for the use of a slave-ship" in Thomas Clarkson, *History of the Abolition of the African Slave-Trade*, 1:413–14. See also Richard Huzzey, "Moral Geography of British Anti-Slavery Responsibilities"; James Cropper to Joseph Sturge, 14 July 1827, in James Cropper, *Extracts from Letters of the late James Cropper*, np.

44. *MM* 7 (February 1800): 12. Identified as Aikin's in his daughter's account: L. Aikin, *Memoir of John Aikin*, 2:297.

45. Karl Polanyi, *Great Transformation*, 60.

46. Thomas Barnes, *Discourse Delivered at the Commencement of the Manchester Academy*, 23–24, usefully discussed in Gregory Claeys, "Virtuous Commerce."

47. John Aikin Jr., *Poems* (1791) included lines addressed to his sister, to Priestley, and to his friend William Enfield. There are also addresses to heroes of Aikin's brand of Dissent such as John Howard, Richard Price, and George Washington. Aikin's *Essay on the Application of Natural History to Poetry* (1777) is discussed illuminatingly in Stephen Daniels and Paul Elliott's "John Aikin's Geographical Imagination." Thomas Percival refers to it in his *Moral and Literary Dissertations*, 227. Aikin wrote to Percival to thank him: see [Edward Percival,] *Memoirs of Thomas Percival*, xcv–xcvi. On Aikin's relationship with Roscoe, see Henry Roscoe, *Life of William Roscoe*, 2:300–301. Thomas P. Miller, *Formation of College English*, 107–8, discusses Percival's reservations about imaginative literature.

48. John Aikin and William Enfield, *General Biography*, 1:4.

49. H. J. McLachlan, *Essays and Addresses*, 106.

50. Goodman, *Pathologies of Motion*, 6.

51. Robert Mitchell, *Experimental Life*, 149. See also Eric Gidal, "Industrial Transport and Political Economy."

52. Kames, *Elements of Criticism*, 1:179, discussed in Goodman, *Pathologies of Motion*, 54–56.

53. Mokyr, *Enlightened Economy*, 48.

54. R. D. Thornton, *James Currie*, describes Currie's involvement (157), and his correspondence with Cullen (135). Jan Golinski, *Science as Public Culture*, discusses Percival's relationship with Cullen (38, 58, 112). See also John Thomson, *An Account of the Life, Lectures, and Writings of William Cullen*, and the digital edition of Cullen's correspondence in the Cullen Project (http://www.cullenproject.ac.uk/).

55. Jon Klancher, *Transfiguring the Arts and Sciences*, 156.

56. Leask, "Robert Burns and Scottish Common Sense Philosophy," esp. 70–87.

57. G. P. Tyson, *Joseph Johnson*, 66; Helen Braithwaite, *Romanticism, Publishing and Dissent*, 20, 61. Johnson placed unusual faith in William Eyres of Warrington for "a country printer": *Joseph Johnson Letterbook*, lxii.

58. Joseph Priestley, *History and Present State of Electricity*, xiii–xv; Golinski, *Science as Public Culture*, 70, 63.

59. Klancher, *Transfiguring the Arts and Sciences*, 129, 130.

60. Turner's career and his relationship with Gaskell are revisited in subsequent chapters. Halifax Literary and Philosophical Society's *Centenary Handbook*, 8–9, describes his son's role there.

61. See Charles Lyell, "Scientific Institutions," 167, and Klancher's discussion in *Transfiguring the Arts and Sciences*, 148.

62. Alexander R. Galloway and Eugene Thacker, *The Exploit*, 40; see also Galloway and Thacker, "Protocol, Control, and Networks."

63. Michel Serres, *Conversations on Science*, 60–61.

64. See Jane Bennett's *Vibrant Matter*, viii, on "lively things."

65. Mark Steadman, "History of the Scientific Collections," 23, discusses its "largely uninvited influx of new objects."

66. Latour's *Pandora's Hope*, 304, uses "black box" to describe "the way scientific and technical work is made invisible by its own success. When a machine runs efficiently,

when a matter of fact is settled, one need focus only on its inputs and outputs and not on its internal complexity. Thus, paradoxically, the more science and technology succeed, the more opaque and obscure they become."

67. *Monthly Review* 56 (July 1808): 336. The phrase "open-source" comes from the description of Mokyr's project in Jonsson's "Industrial Revolution in the Anthropocene," 681.

68. Klancher, *Transfiguring the Arts and Sciences*, 51.

69. Bruno Latour, *Reassembling the Social*, 39.

70. See Hannah Barker, "'Smoke Cities.'"

71. Thomas De Quincey, "Letters to a Young Man," in *Works of Thomas De Quincey*, 3:54, 71. H. J. McLachlan, *Warrington Academy*, discusses the influence of Watts there (51, 66). De Quincey's famous elaboration appeared in a review of the reissue of an edition of Pope originally edited by Roscoe. De Quincey offered his distinction as a categorical difference between the fine and the mechanical arts, especially the improvability of the steam engine as opposed to the singularity of "power" as the expression of "sympathy with the infinite" (*Works*, 16:337). See also Thomas De Quincey, *Confessions of an English Opium Eater*, in *Works*, vol. 2.

72. William Hazlitt, "Why the Arts are not Progressive," in *Complete Works*, 4:160–64. As a boy, Hazlitt spent time in Liverpool, where he was tutored by the Unitarian minister John Yates. Hazlitt judged Roscoe, whose portrait he painted, "an excellent man, and a good patriot" (*Complete Works*, 9:241). See George Chandler, *William Roscoe of Liverpool 1753–1831*, xxxv.

73. De Quincey writes amusingly of his guardian, the Reverend Samuel Hall, whose contribution to the Literary and Philosophical Society is discussed in chapter 2, as the representative of a class "who sympathise with no spiritual sense or spiritual capacities in man; who understand by religion simply a respectable code of ethics—leaning for support upon some great mysteries dimly traced in the background" (*Works*, 2: 113).

74. De Quincey, *Works*, 19:75.

75. Clarke helped in the research for Roscoe's *Life of Lorenzo de Medici* (1795). See Chandler, *Roscoe*, 88. De Quincey's mother sent him detailed instructions on how to get from Manchester to Liverpool by canal and coach via Warrington for his 1801 visit. Elizabeth De Quincey to Thomas De Quincey, 20 May 1801, HM 37708, ff. 1–2, De Quincey Correspondence, Henry E. Huntington Library.

76. De Quincey, *Works*, 10:187, 192. De Quincey uses the phrase "the Liverpool coterie" (10:191), having referred to the Roscoe group as "a well-known coterie" a few pages earlier (187). Subsequent quotations from this essay are given in the main text from this edition. The diary is at 920 MD 424, Liverpool Record Office (LRO).

77. De Quincey's correspondence with his mother bears out his later claim that she suspected Currie of being a Jacobin: "I am reading Dr Currie's Life of Burns, not without a jealous Eye to the Doctor's Jacobinism." HM 37708, f. 2.

78. Tilottama Rajan, *The Supplement of Reading*, 18.

79. William Wordsworth, *Prose Works*, 1:118, and his note to "The Thorn," in William Wordsworth and Samuel Taylor Coleridge, *Lyrical Ballads*, 351. On the relationship of Wordsworth's project to the tradition of environmental medicine discussed earlier, see Goodman, *Pathologies of Motion*, chap. 4.

80. Shepherd's reply was published in *Tait's Edinburgh Magazine* 4 (May 1837): 340.

81. Rajan, *Supplement of Reading*, 38, 103.

82. On the possibility that *Lyrical Ballads* was influenced by Currie's edition, see

Daniel Sanjiv Roberts, *Revisionary Gleam*, 71, 82. Carson Bergstrom, "Literary Coteries," notes the overlap between the early papers given at Manchester and the preface to *Lyrical Ballads*. Roberts suggests that Wordsworth's preface was influenced by Currie's biography of Burns (*Revisionary Gleam*, 82).

CHAPTER TWO

1. Jan Golinski, *Science as Public Culture*, 156.

2. Multigraph Collective, *Interacting with Print*, 3. The essay "On Public Lectures on Works of Imagination at Literary Institutions," *Blackwood's Edinburgh Magazine* (November 1819): 162–67, anticipating the manner of De Quincey's "Letters to a Young Man," defended the hermeneutics of immersive reading for works of imagination against the encroachment of lecturing on literary topics. The defensive posture suggests the encroaching popularity of literary lecturing in the period, which has recently encouraged a series of excellent studies, including Jon Klancher, *Transfiguring the Arts and Sciences*, Mary Helen Dupree and Sean Franzel's *Performing Knowledge* collection, and Sarah Zimmerman, *The Romantic Literary Lecture in Britain*. On the itinerant networks of science lecturers that preceded and overlapped with the literary and philosophical societies, which sometimes hosted them, see Jon Klancher, "Lecturing Networks and Cultural Institutions, 1740–1830."

3. [Thomas Percival,] "Preface," *Memoirs of the Literary and Philosophical Society of Manchester* [hereafter *MLPSM*], 1 (1785), v. References to Percival's "Preface" are given in the text from this point onward.

4. Benjamin Rush's "Result of some Observations during his Attendance as Physician General of the Military Hospitals of the United States" appeared in the second volume of *MLPSM*; his "An Account of the Progress of Population, Agriculture, Manners, and government in Pennsylvania" in the third, with an essay on the production of saltpeter (potassium nitrate, an ingredient used in medicine, fertilizer, and gunpowder) that discussed its abundance in India. The next volume contained an essay on famine by Percival himself that discussed agricultural conditions in India. The exchanges on dyeing that run through the first three volumes identify Egypt as the origin of the art and make extensive use of current French research on the topic.

5. Alexander Dick, "'A good deal of Trash,'" 6.

6. Edward Percival's *Memoirs of Percival* discusses his father's friendship with Hume and William Robertson, xiii and xiv. Percival's renewed his acquaintance with Hume in Paris after leaving Edinburgh and kept up a warm correspondence with Robertson, for instance, on the plans for a Manchester Academy and the town's committee for the abolition of the slave trade.

7. This was the intention of the Select Society of Edinburgh's plan to award premiums for improvements in arts and manufactures. See David McElroy, *Scotland's Age of Improvement*, 49.

8. Dick, "'A good deal of Trash,'" 6.

9. Dick, "'A good deal of Trash,'" 6, 7.

10. Isaac Watts, *Improvement of the Mind*, 42–43. I discuss the influence of this passage in Jon Mee, *Conversable Worlds: Literature, Contention, and Community*, 68–74.

11. Thomas Barnes hoped his paper "On the Nature and Essential Characters of Poetry" would serve as the basis of "further discussion in the society" (*MLPSM* 1 [1785]: 63).

12. Thomas Henry's "On the Advantages of Literature and Philosophy in general"

claimed that the natural tendency of "polite learning" was to "enlarge the field of useful knowledge" (*MLPSM* 1 [1785]: 7–29, at 8). References to Henry's essay are given in the main text from this point onward.

13. Barnes, "On the Influence of the Imagination and the Passions upon the Understanding," 387; De Polier, "On the Pleasure which the Mind receives from the Exercise of its Faculties," 133.

14. Rule VIII, *MLPSM* 1:xiii.

15. Materials relating to the earlier society are held in the Holt and Gregson Papers 942 HOL/10, ff. 489–567, Liverpool Record Office (LRO). Others on the printed "List of Members" (at f. 491) include the antiquarian upholsterer Matthew Gregson; John Knowles, later biographer of Fuseli; Thomas Nicholson; Edward Rogers; and the clergymen Henry Barton, George Gregory, and John Yates. Intriguingly, given the absence of women in most of the formal societies, there is also "Miss S. Heywood."

16. R. D. Thornton, *James Currie*, 64, suggests that there were two separate societies in this period, but the fluidity of naming leaves this as conjecture to my mind. The president wrote to the members on October 6, 1783, to inform them that it had been agreed to dissolve the society. Its property was to be auctioned, the proceeds to be repaid as a dividend (HOL/10, f. 567). Various printed notes in the archive attest to difficulties in securing attendance and active participation. On July 17, 1782, the secretary reminded members of their duty to attend and announced the intention that in the future "every member in rotation be obliged to propose a subject and deliver a written paper upon it." Printed and written invitations to hear the various papers mentioned in this paragraph are held in Holt and Gregson 942, HOL/10, ff. 497–567, LRO. A blank is left on the printed forms for the insertion of the particular evening's topic.

17. William Roscoe, "On the Comparative Excellence of the Sciences and Arts." *MLPSM* 3 (1790): 241–60. References to Roscoe's paper are given in the main text from this point onward.

18. *Analytical Review* 9 (March 1791): 266.

19. William Roscoe to Jane Roscoe, 4 April 1791, 920 ROS, 3506, LRO.

20. Anna Laetitia Barbauld, "To Mr. S. T. Coleridge," in *Poems*, 132–33, originally published in *MM* 7 (1799): 231–32.

21. See V. A. C. Gatrell, "Incorporation and the Pursuit of Liberal Hegemony in Manchester," 33.

22. Thomas Barnes, "Constitutions and Regulations of the College of Arts and Sciences in Manchester," 42. Lectures covered chemistry with reference to arts and manufactures; the history of fine arts; the origin and progress of arts, manufactures, and commerce; and moral philosophy. Henry's lectures on chemistry have been credited with informing the wider community about "the techniques of applied art as well as textile manufacture" by C. P. Darcy, *Encouragement of the Fine Arts in Lancashire*, 97. Because some tickets were made available to artisans, the college is sometimes seen as a precursor of the Mechanics' Institutes: Charles Webster and Jonathan Barry, "Manchester Medical Revolution," 172–74.

23. The newspaper paragraph in the *Manchester Mercury* of March 15 read: "Whereas an Inference has been drawn from a Passage in the first Page of the Report of the new Institution, now called, or intended to be called the MANCHESTER ACADEMY, that this Society, *as such*, favour the Principle and Design of that intended Academy. Resolved, that this Society having, at their first Institution, totally disavowed, and still continuing to disavow all Bias toward, or Intercourse with any Religious Opinion, or Sect whatever, do hereby declare their Independence; and that they do not mean to afford any Patron-

age to the above named Academy." Ralph Harrison in *A sermon preached at the dissenting chapel in Cross-Street, Manchester,* identified himself as a member of the Literary and Philosophical Society on its title page. Barnes did the same on his appended discourse, also published separately as *A Discourse Delivered at the Commencement of the Manchester Academy* (1786), acknowledging "that the LITERARY AND PHILOSOPHICAL SOCIETY have avowed a generous zeal to foster rising genius, to incite emulation, and to give energy to the powers of the mind, by calling them forth in early exertion; and that it may be presumed, they will admit the senior Academics, to attend the more instructive discussions" (2). He presumed too much given the opposition that followed.

24. Alexander Eason to Charles Macintosh, Manchester 1784, in George Macintosh's edited volume Charles Macintosh, *A Biographical Memoir of the Late Charles Macintosh,* 3. Eason's role in the infirmary crisis is discussed in chapter 4.

25. Thomas Henry to Benjamin Rush, Manchester, 10 May 1784, vol. 7, Rush Family Papers: Correspondence, Library Company of Philadelphia.

26. Frida Knight, *Strange Case of Thomas Walker,* 26–34; Thackray, "Natural Knowledge," 693. Percival wrote to Walker on April 7, 1794, after Walker was finally acquitted of a charge of treasonable conspiracy, to congratulate him on "the honourable termination of the iniquitous prosecution, which has been carried on against him." Add MS 88955, f. 310, LRO.

27. Thomas Cooper, "Propositions respecting the Foundation of Civil Government," 509.

28. Burke had attacked Cooper and James Watt Jr.'s visit to Paris, ostensibly on business for James Watt Sr., because they also appeared at the Jacobin Club as representatives of the Manchester Constitutional Society. Dumas Malone, *Public Life of Thomas Cooper,* 35–40.

29. James Currie to Thomas Percival, 16 January 1788, in W. W. Currie, *Memoir of the Life of James Currie,* 2:50.

30. James Currie to Thomas Percival, 7 February 1790, in *Memoir of James Currie,* 2:57.

31. Currie to Percival, 7 February 1790, 2:58.

32. James Currie to Thomas Percival, 17 July 1791, and Thomas Percival to James Currie, 12 November 1791, in *Memoir of James Currie,* 2:67, 69.

33. Joseph Priestley, *Appeal to the public, on the subject of the riots in Birmingham, part II,* 105.

34. Ferriar's name is absent from the list of members given in *MLPSM* 5 (1798): viii–x, although he was still vice president in 1797 according to Manchester Literary and Philosophical Society, *Complete List of the Members & Officers,* 10. Possibly he was simply too busy at the Board of Health to carry on at the society, although he may also have started worshipping at an Anglican church around this time (see the discussion in chapter 4). Aikin's sentiments were expressed in a letter to Percival of December 17, 1791, quoted in Ian Inkster, "'Under the eye of the public': Arthur Aikin," 128–29.

35. Gatrell, "Incorporation and Liberal Hegemony," 33. See also Katrina Navickas, *Loyalism and Radicalism in Lancashire,* 9.

36. James Watt Jr. to John Ferriar, 19 December 1794, MS 3219/6/7/F 20–21, James Watt and Family Papers, Library of Birmingham. Henry told Watt: "The society which perhaps you left too abruptly, prospers much this winter—I wish you would not forget you had been a member of it, & that you have many friends in it, who love and respect you—send us a peace offering, [w]rapped in the form of a communication, & I think I may venture to say that we shall reinstate you graciously, in our favour." (MS

3219/6/2/H/49). The details of Owen's papers are given in E. M. Fraser's "Robert Owen in Manchester," written in 1937–38, before the archives were destroyed.

37. Arnold Thackray, "Natural Knowledge," 693.

38. Samuel Argent Bardsley, "Cursory Remarks, Moral and Political, on Party-prejudice," 10. Bardsley's *Critical Remarks on Pizarro* [iii] describes the paper as written "on the spur of the occasion, to fulfil a duty imposed on the Author as Member of a Literary Society. They were read and discussed at two meetings of that Society, at a time when provincial curiosity (which had stood on the tiptoe of expectation) was first gratified with the representation of Pizarro."

39. Navickas, *Loyalism and Radicalism*, 89.

40. Paul A. Elliott, *The Derby Philosophers*, 98–100.

41. Thomas Gisborne, "On the Benefits and Duties," 86.

42. Bruno Latour, *Reassembling the Social*, 29.

43. The extensive archives at Newcastle Literary and Philosophical Society (NLPS) are uncataloged. I refer to them in the notes that follow by the individual item name. Research is further aided by two grangerized collections of the society's reports made by members Rev. Anthony Hedley (11 vols.) and John Fenwick (9 vols.). I have referred to these collections by name and volume number.

44. Barbauld, *Poems*, 27–28. Turner published the poem in *Newcastle Magazine*, 4 (April 1825): 185–86. The obituary continued into the next number. Turner published an excerpt from the poem at the end of "Memoirs of Mr. Turner's Life and Writings" appended to William Wood's *Sermon Preached on the Death of the Rev William Turner*, 56.

45. Joanna Wharton, *Material Enlightenment*, 31–34.

46. Stephen Harbottle, *William Turner*, 15–20, provides details of Turner's education.

47. William Turner, "An Essay on Crime and Punishments," 312, 319.

48. William Turner, *A Short Sketch of the History of Protestant Nonconformity*, 29, discussed in Harbottle, *William Turner*, 21–24.

49. William Turner, *Speculations on the Propriety of Attempting the Establishment of a Literary Society in Newcastle*, 2.

50. Kathleen Wilson, *Sense of the People*, 324, 289.

51. Turner was frustrated in his hope that mine owners would share information via the society (see Harbottle, *William Turner*, 58–59), just as Clennell's call for the free exchange of information on manufacturing processes foundered.

52. Turner, *Speculations*, 9, 11.

53. The date John Clennell joined the society is not recorded in the monthly minutes, but he appears in the published members list for 1798 (Hedley 1). He proposed more members and recommended more books for purchase than anyone else. He often recommended books with Crawford, who proposed that the society purchase *Lyrical Ballads*. Clennell presented seven papers at the monthly meetings between October 1797 and his move to London in 1808. See Paul Gailiunas, "Women during the Early Years of the Newcastle Lit and Phil," for details.

54. John Hunter, governor of New South Wales from 1795 until his recall in 1800, is listed as an honorary member in the *Rules of the Literary and Philosophical Society of Newcastle upon Tyne*. Hunter's letter describing the settlement at Port Jackson in New South Wales was read to the society at a monthly meeting in 1799. In its first year, the society was also read Thomas Clarkson's "Account of the New Settlement at Sierra Leone" (from a letter sent to the society July 9, 1793), and Edward Laing gave a paper on the colony at Port Jackson. "Papers Given to the Society," vol. 1, NLPS archives. Depictions of

the platypus and the wombat were included—with descriptions from Hunter's letter—in the addenda to Thomas Bewick's *History of the Quadrupeds* (1800), 521–25, probably written by Ralph Beilby, whom the minute book records as present when the sketch was made. Bewick's *Memoir*, 111, 123, records Bewick's admiration for Turner and Robert Doubleday, who had tried to resolve the dispute with Beilby over which could claim to be the book's "author." Beilby later opposed Turner in the dispute over the New Institution.

55. Theophilus Lindsey to William Turner, 10 June 1794, *Letters of Lindsey*, 2:295. From 1791, Lindsey kept up a constant flow of intelligence about Priestley's movements in his letters to Turner.

56. See Harbottle, *William Turner*, 55.

57. "Character of the Late Mr. Doubleday," *Northern Reformer's Monthly Magazine*, March 1, 1823, 88–92, noted that Doubleday had addressed verses to William Godwin on the publication of *Political Justice* (90).

58. Richard Welford, *Men of Mark Twixt Tyne and Tees*, 3:639. James Losh's diary entry for March 12, 1800, describes Turner's fast day sermon at Hanover Square as "evidently on the side of liberty." "Diary of James Losh," MSS, Carlisle City Library.

59. "Character of Doubleday," 91.

60. Marshall first appears in trade directories in 1801 as a bookseller, a stationer, and the proprietor of a circulating library in Gateshead. By 1811 he had moved to Newcastle itself, where he started to print and sell chapbooks and collections of songs. His business failed in 1831. Frances M. Thomson, *Newcastle Chapbooks*, 11–123. Paul Gailiunas, "John Marshall: Printer, Librarian and Radical," 5–36, suggests that radical texts only became a significant part of Marshall's output after he was expelled from the society.

61. Lindsey, *Letters of Lindsey*, 2:451–52. Turner was a devoted memorialist of Warrington Academy, but even he was concerned over the potential of freedom of inquiry in religion to degenerate into rancorous disputation. See William Turner, *Warrington Academy*, 12, 19. This useful book collects the essays Turner wrote on the academy for the *Monthly Repository*.

62. James Anderson to William Turner, 18 June 1793, "Correspondence Book 1," NLPS. See also Jon Mee, "The Buzz about the *Bee*," 67–68.

63. Thomas Miller, *Formation of College English*, 109, quoting from Marshall's 1818 edition, claims these sentiments "mark a sharp departure from the more utilitarian orientation and Calvinist traditions of Enfield's predecessors." The evidence from Manchester and Newcastle suggests this break was not as unusual as Miller implies. Enfield's paper was read on November 12, 1793. The transcription is in "Papers Read at the Monthly Meeting," vol. 1, NLPS. Enfield's essay was included when the Newcastle society finally published its transactions in 1831.

64. "Enquirer No. VI: 'Is Verse Essential to Poetry?" *MM* 1 (July 1796): 453–56.

65. David Sampson, "Wordsworth and the 'Deficiencies of Language,'" 55.

66. John Guillory, *Cultural Capital*, 101–3.

67. Guillory, *Cultural Capital*, 126.

68. See, for instance, *A Collection of Songs, Comic, Satirical, and Descriptive, chiefly in the Newcastle Dialect, and illustrative of the language and manners of the common people on the Banks of the Tyne and neighbourhood* (1827), published by Marshall, and often known as *Marshall's Songs*.

69. David Stewart, "The End of Conversation: Byron's Don Juan at the Newcastle Lit & Phil."

70. "Books Recommended to be Ordered," vol. 1, NLPS, contains the request and the committee's response.

71. "Monthly Minutes" for February 1831 and the report on the debate in the *Tyne Mercury* March 8, 1831. The rule against novels was affirmed in *The Thirty Ninth Years Report* (1832), 12. I am grateful to Paul Gailiunas for giving me access to his spreadsheet referencing the recommendations book, the catalog of additions to the library in the annual reports, and dates of committee meetings when accession was agreed.

72. In July 1799, Turner, with Prowitt, and Clennell, had proposed Marshall for the new category of membership "honorary with privileges," introduced for those who could not afford the full subscription. Gailiunas, "John Marshall," suggests that Turner may have been Marshall's teacher. Clennell and Marshall seem to have been among the Unitarian Baptists who joined Turner's congregation with their minister Edward Prowitt in 1797, only to secede around 1811, events discussed in Eneas Mackenzie, *Descriptive and Historical Account of the Town and County of Newcastle upon Tyne*, 376–78.

73. Gailiunas, "John Marshall," 26–27.

74. Guillory, *Cultural Capital*, 133.

75. The original rules stated that "it be left to the future deliberations of the Society to determine what, or whether any, measures shall be taken for obtaining the establishment of a general Library." *Plan of the Literary and Philosophical Society of Newcastle Upon Tyne* (1793), 15. The committee minutes for December 26–27, 1793, show that Henry Moises wrote to Turner to encourage the idea. A committee was appointed on which Moises and Turner served with Ralph Beilby, the major protagonists in the dispute over the New Institution a decade later, but it was unable to resolve a way forward, primarily because of issues about ownership of the books. Later annual reports comment on the success of the library but express concerns about attendance at the monthly meetings typical of Turner: "Committee Minutes 1793-4" and *Proceedings relative to the Establishment of the Library of the Literary and Philosophical Society*, 1–4; privately printed, this latter document is bound in Hedley 1 as is the printed *Plan* quoted earlier. After Doubleday complained about recent orders for work by Ralph Cudworth, David Hume, and William Paley, the committee ordered that books of religious controversy were to be removed.

76. The committee ordered the librarian to root out any book deemed "improper." Debate also went back and forth about the fate of the society's journal subscriptions. Decisions were influenced by which were already widely subscribed to by the members, but political beliefs seem to have played their part. The *British Critic*, no friend to the *Monthly Magazine*, the journal in which several members published, was discontinued on March 17, 1795, but then brought back into the fold in mid-December, only to be dropped again in June 1798, when the committee decided it was "a work inferior in merit to the rest." "Committee Minutes 1794 to 1806" and "Books Recommended to be Ordered," vol. 1.

77. Mackenzie's phrase appears in his *Descriptive and Historical Account*, 467. Variants appeared in the earlier debates about the New Institution described subsequently.

78. Thomas Bigge read a paper on "establishing a lectureship in Chemistry or Nat. Philosophy in Newcastle" in May 1802. Losh proposed it should be referred to the committee. Bigge then published *An Address to the Public from the Literary and Philosophical Society of Newcastle upon Tyne* for consideration at the General Meeting of June 2. See the accounts in Harbottle, *Turner*, 67–68, and Derek Orange, "Rational Dissent and Provincial Science," 215–19.

79. The original manuscript letter dated January 14, 1809, is pasted into Hedley 4.

80. The description of Beilby comes from Welford, *Men of Mark*, 1:229. See note 54 on the dispute between Beilby and Bewick over authorship of *History of the Quadrupeds*.

81. Mackenzie, *To the Ordinary Members of the Literary and Philosophical Society of Newcastle upon Tyne*, in Hedley 4.

82. Turner's allies were victorious, although not without making some concessions. Use of the library was disallowed for the lectures, and the money given to the institution was kept for apparatus and other expenses rather than Turner's remuneration. Moises resigned immediately (Harbottle, *Turner*, 83, who reproduces his angry letter to Turner written after the vote). Moises probably had a hand in the original "Mentor" letter attacking Turner.

83. Harbottle, *Turner*, 80, and Robert Spence Watson, *The History of the Literary and Philosophical Society of Newcastle upon-Tyne*, 219.

84. Orange, "Rational Dissent and Provincial Science," 213; R. Porter, "Science, Provincial Culture," 34.

85. Turner's paper was printed as *Address to the Monthly Meeting of the Literary and Philosophical Society*, found in Hedley 5.

86. James Losh, *Diaries and Correspondence of James Losh*, 1:30, 31, 34.

87. The description of the library as "a bond of union" was made in the context of Mackenzie's criticism of the costs of the new building creating a barrier to "easy access" that would make it "merely a fashionable lounging place for the opulent classes of society." Mackenzie, *Descriptive and Historical Account*, 468.

88. Latour, *Reassembling the Social*, esp. part 1.

89. "On a Plan of Reading," *Oeconomist* 23 (November 1799): 325–29; "Hints of a Plan for a Book Club," *Oeconomist* 24 (December 1799): 350–57. "The Diary of James Losh," MSS, Carlisle City Library, for 1798–99 shows that he and Bigge were the principal contributors. Essays were published anonymously, but Turner contributed at least two essays, both on the provision of food for the poor: Harbottle, *William Turner*, 48. The issue attracted debate in the Literary and Philosophical Society in the late 1790s as reported in *MM*, 4 (December 1797): 487.

90. Turner, *Resignation and Submission*, 21. Turner's *Introductory Address*, 6, described the Literary and Philosophical Society as the "parent" of the Mechanics' Institute. Losh's diary records attending Turner's sermon on the importance of the education of the poor on December 15, 1799.

91. Jon Klancher, *Making of English Reading Audiences*, 43, quoting the magazine's "Concluding Paper" (December 1799, 374), a baleful discussion of the pains being taken in the country to prevent the flow of knowledge.

92. Documents relevant to the 1798 claim are gathered in Hedley 1, including a printed copy of Spence's original lecture. A denial of any link was published in *MM* 7 (June 1798): 415. The later letter was published in the *Quarterly Review* 15 (Jan 1817): 546–47. See also Gailiunas, "John Marshall," 10, 12–13. The committee meeting of April 22, 1817, decided to write to Losh on the subject of the recent Act of Parliament respecting "suppression of Seditious Meetings." The December meeting recorded that Sir John Swinburne had promised to inquire into the situation among "London Literary Institutions." See "Committee Meetings, 1806–1817" and "Committee Meetings 1817–1825." Through the early months of 1817 the issue of Marshall's dismissal was also rumbling on, first in relation to his post as librarian and then as to whether he should remain an ordinary member.

93. Mackenzie remained committed to the conversational model for the diffusion of knowledge and collaborated with Marshall in setting up a society for literary and philosophical debate in 1816: "A Proposal for a New Philosophical Institution," dated October 23, 1816, and signed "John Marshall," in Hedley 6. Marshall and Mackenzie

were involved in public meetings to protest the Peterloo Massacre and a few years later in support of Queen Caroline. See Harbottle, *William Turner*, 99; Gailiunas, "John Marshall," 12–14.

94. Quoted in Welford, *Men of Mark*, 3:117.

95. "Character of Doubleday," 91.

CHAPTER THREE

1. Linda Colley, *Britons: Forging the Nation*. For a regional perspective on the period, see Donald Read, *The English Provinces c. 1760–1960*, 35–77, and Katrina Navickas, *Loyalism and Radicalism*, esp. 13–42. Christine MacLeod, *Heroes of Invention*, 92, also counters Colley's account of the post-Waterloo settlement

2. Boyd Hilton, *Corn, Cash, Commerce*.

3. Charles Lyell, "Scientific Institutions," 153. MacLeod, *Heroes of Invention*, discusses at length the campaign to erect a statue to the memory of James Watt.

4. Derby remained an active base for improvement even after the controversy over its support for Joseph Priestley in 1791. A Society for Mutual Improvement appeared in 1808, followed by a more ambitious Literary and Philosophical Society in 1811. Thomas Traill—an honorary member at Derby—seems to have adapted its rules for the Liverpool Literary and Philosophical Society. D5047/1, Derby Literary and Philosophical Society, journal, inc. minutes,1808–1816, D5047/1, Derbyshire Record Office (DRO). See also Elliott, *Derby Philosophers*, 69–162. In September 1811, the Literary and Philosophical Society of Preston invited Roscoe to give a paper, 920 ROS/4254, Liverpool Record Office (LRO). A society had begun in Bradford in 1808, but in 1814 it decided to focus on its book collection and become a library. Minute book 1808–1814, Add MS 204, Bradford Literary and Philosophical Society, York Minster Library.

5. Joseph Hunter, *Hallamshire*, 128. References to Hunter's book are given in the text from this point onward.

6. Edward Baines Sr. had been a printer on the Manchester reformer Thomas Walker's *Preston Review*; he crossed the Pennines to work on the *Leeds Mercury* in 1795. Soon afterward, he joined a "Reasoning society" and began associating with Dissenters who formed a set of "temperate but steady Reformers." See Edward Baines Jr., *Life of Edward Baines, late MP for the borough of Leeds*, 20–21, 26–30. The first issue of the *Mercury* after Baines took over made clear his opposition to the slave trade, his desire for peace, and support for "a large measure of Parliamentary reform" (*Life of Baines*, 45, 49). He became friendly with the Unitarian community in Leeds, including the minister William Wood, who had been the Leeds informant for John Aikin Jr.'s *Description of Manchester* and preached the funeral sermon for William Turner of Wakefield.

7. William Roscoe campaigned for Brougham in his unsuccessful attempt to become MP for Liverpool in 1812: Henry Roscoe, *Life of William Roscoe*, 2:3–49; William Roscoe, *Letter to Henry Brougham*. E. J. Clery's *Eighteenth Hundred and Eleven* gives an excellent account of Roscoe's leadership in these circles, including the campaigns against the Orders in Council. See also Trowbridge H. Ford, *Henry Brougham and His World*, 499–500, on Baines and Marshall in Leeds, and on Roscoe, 162–68.

8. *Cobbett's Political Register*, November 24, 1832, 457.

9. Robert Poole, *Peterloo*, 363–64, discusses the social and occupational composition of the crowd and the authorities at Peterloo.

10. Samuel Greg wrote to his nephew, Thomas Pares III, recently elected MP for Leicester, to inform him of Stanley's testimony: Samuel Greg to Thomas Pares III,

10 March 1820, 3/214/26, Pares Collection, DRO. Stanley's narrative is published in *Three Accounts of Peterloo*, 1–43. See also Poole, *Peterloo*, 323–24, 328.

11. Archibald Prentice, *Historical Sketches and Personal Recollections*, 73.

12. Hannah Greg to Elizabeth Rathbone, 23 August 1819, RP VI.1.130, Liverpool University Library (LUL) Special Collections.

13. E. Baines Jr., *Life of Baines*, 105; Poole, *Peterloo*, 218.

14. References to Roscoe's *On the origin and vicissitudes of literature, science and art* are given here in the main text. The speech was republished in the *Pamphleteer* 7 (1818): 507–36, and elsewhere, as well as being excerpted in many reviews. The younger Baines acknowledged its influence in his biography of his father (*Life of Baines*, 102). Charles Lyell noticed it in a note to "Scientific Institutions," 175.

15. William Roscoe, *Address, delivered before the Proprietors of the Botanic Garden*, 29–31.

16. The minute books of the early years of the Liverpool Literary and Philosophical Society are at 060 LIT/1/1, 2, and 3, Liverpool Record Office (LRO). Houlbrooke's death is recorded with regret at the meeting of January 2, 1824, at LIT/1/3, f. 2, wherein he is described as the society's first president. A list of officers of the Botanic Garden is given in Roscoe's *Address*, 53.

17. Details are given in "Unpublished papers read at the Lit & Phil," MS.3.62, LUL. The influence of Reid and Stewart in these Liverpool circles is discussed in Ian Sutton, "The Extended Roscoe Circle." Stewart was quoted in Roscoe's *Vicissitudes, 71-2.*

18. As recorded in Thomas Rickman's diary entry for December 5, 1817, RiT 2, "Thomas Rickman's personal journals, 1807–1834," RIBA Library Drawings & Archives, Victoria and Albert Museum. Rickman's journals provide a useful sidelight on the society up until he left for Birmingham in 1821. He and Aikin had competed against each other in the contest to design the Wellington Assembly Rooms in 1814. Once Aikin arrived in Liverpool, they became friends. Joseph Sharples, "From Rickman's Liverpool to Victorian Liverpool," 140.

19. Roscoe's son credited Traill with the original idea: H. Roscoe, *Life of William Roscoe*, 2:153. Other claims are discussed in Henry Ormerod's *Liverpool Royal Institution*, 9–10.

20. S. G. Checkland, *The Gladstones*, 28–34, 44; Trevor Burnard and Kit Candlin, "Sir John Gladstone and the Debate over the Amelioration of Slavery."

21. Gladstone offered to stand down in the interests of introducing new blood. Arline Wilson, *William Roscoe*, 94–95, suspects it reflected intensifying animosity between the two men. As it turned out, Gladstone accepted the nomination for vice president. Roscoe was replaced after a year in office by B. A. Heywood.

22. Henry Roscoe quoting from the report of the committee drawn up to carry the project into effect, *Life of William Roscoe*, 2:155. The Liverpool Philomathic Society Archive is at GB 141 LPS, LUL.

23. Ormerod, *Liverpool Royal Institution*, 29, notes that B. A. Heywood warned that its usefulness was put in jeopardy "by the variety and extent of its objects."

24. [Unknown] to William Shepherd, 7 February 1816, 920 ROS/4391A, Roscoe Letters and Papers, LRO.

25. William Dixon, "The Advantages of a Society whose object is the mutual interchange of Literary communication unclouded by Political animadversion or Sensual excess,'" LIT/1/1, 78–82; Edward Baines Sr., *History, Directory, and Gazetteer, of the County Palatine of Lancaster*, 1:198.

26. Sutton, "Extended Roscoe Circle," 447–51.

27. Aikin's letter is reproduced in H. Roscoe, *Life of William Roscoe*, 2:122. Charles Lyell, "Scientific Institutions," 175, refers to the productive "rivalry between independent republics" in Roscoe's *Leo the Tenth*. Although he was writing in the *Quarterly*, Lyell self-identified as a Whig. See Klancher, *Transfiguring the Arts and Sciences*, 140–41. On the flattering prospects Roscoe's speech opened out to local merchants, see Navickas, *Loyalism and Radicalism*, 163–64.

28. *Blackwood's* may also have praised Roscoe because he was related to John Wilson by marriage. William Blackwood told John Maginn in 1825 that the connection had "saved Roscoe oftener than once." Margaret Oliphant, *William Blackwood and His Sons*, 1:402.

29. Thomas Jefferson to William Roscoe, 27 December 1820, 920 ROS/2207. By the time he replied to Roscoe, Jefferson was starting fully to dedicate his energies to the University of Virginia. Roscoe had also sent Jefferson a treatise on penal jurisprudence.

30. Review, "On the Origin and Vicissitudes of Literature, Science, and Art," *Journal of Science and the Arts* 5 (1818): 22–23; Klancher, *Transfiguring the Arts and Sciences*, 213.

31. William Turner's "Tour through the North of England" was read at the Literary and Philosophical Society of Newcastle upon Tyne in the fall of 1797, shortly before it was published in the *Monthly Magazine*. Turner was effectively investigating Aikin's account in his *Description of Manchester*, to which he had subscribed, as had the Newcastle society. Turner saw the employment of pauper apprentices as a sign that there was little difference between the corrupt nature "either of the landed or commercial aristocracy" (256).

32. Dixon, "Advantages," f. 80.

33. Connell, *Romanticism, Economics and the Question of "Culture,"* 104–5.

34. Further discussion of Roscoe and Quarry Bank appears in chapter 4. The correspondence with Owen appears in H. Roscoe, *Life of William Roscoe*, 2:62–65.

35. "Index of the Minute Book from 1822 to 1843," LRI 1/2/2, f. 109, LRI Archive, LUL. Ormerod, *Liverpool Royal Institution*, 22, notes the relative paucity of lectures on political economy.

36. B. A. Heywood, *Address delivered at the meeting of the Proprietors 1825*, 30, 22. Describing McCulloch's topic as "abstract and difficult" didn't seem designed to win McCulloch an audience. Heywood did praise John Kennedy's account of advances in the cotton industry, discussed at length in chapter 6, in his earlier addresses. See B. A. Heywood, *Addresses 1822 & 1824*, 45.

37. The Liverpool venture had been inspired by a similar initiative in New York. Newspaper clippings that describe the opening are gathered at Add MS 27824, f. 28, Francis Place Papers, "Collections relating to schools, mechanics' institutions, etc." British Library.

38. "Extravagant romances and novels, which may vitiate the taste of youth and give it disrelish for the more solid food of the mind" were excluded. Liverpool Mechanics' and Apprentices' Library, *An Account of the Liverpool Mechanics' and Apprentices' Library*, 4, 7, 15.

39. *Address delivered by Thos. Stewart Traill*, [iii], ix, v. The Liverpool Mechanics' School of Arts's *Report and Proceedings on the Liverpool Mechanics' School of Arts*, 7, mentions the disappointingly irregular attendance. The report begins with J. A. Yates celebrating the "utility" of the institution and then complaining "that the people of Liverpool showed so much apathy for a subject of such vital importance" [3]. These

developments are discussed by Mabel Tylecote, *The Mechanics' Institutes of Lancashire & Yorkshire*, 55–56, 62, 108–9.

40. Cropper joined the Literary and Philosophical Society on March 13, 1812. See "Centenary Roll," 060 LIT 3/1, LRO. Cropper's daughter recalled that her father found political economy "a science which was most congenial to his taste, as depending so materially on facts and invoking so much arithmetical calculation"—that is, "not merely as a *speculative* science, but *as a matter* affecting his every day transactions of commerce and busy life." James Cropper, *Extracts from Letters of . . . James Cropper*, n.p. Bessy Rathbone's letters back to her mother mention her husband's collaboration with Cropper in an attempt to gain "a proper representation" for Liverpool in the 1818 election. RP VI.1.189, Rathbone Papers, LUL. Roscoe described the hopes for the 1807 abolition of the trade as an "empty sound." William Roscoe to James Cropper, 15 January 1823, 920 ROS/6016.

41. James Cropper to William Roscoe, 14 January 1823, 920 ROS1091. Roscoe initially declined the approach to join Cropper's new abolition society.

42. The exchanges between Cropper and Gladstone were gathered in *The Correspondence between John Gladstone, Esq. M. P. and James Cropper, Esq.* (1824). See also Burnard and Candlin, "Sir John Gladstone and the Debate over the Amelioration of Slavery." Hinch gave his paper at the meeting of December 2, 1825, 060 LIT 1/3, f. 43. Fletcher discussed his position in his privately printed *Autobiographical memoirs*, 124–25: "Without attempting to vindicate the system of slavery, my argument was that it was a system long established and which could not be suddenly changed without great danger; that the actual condition of the West India slaves had been much meliorated of late years, especially since the abolition of the African slave trade; and that it was in some respects better than that of the labouring population in the East Indies, and even in Ireland; and that the West India planters had a fair claim to the protection they enjoyed."

43. Checkland, *Gladstones*, 224.

44. "Memoir of Mr. Roscoe," transcribed at LIT/1/3, f.118–19.

45. Eric Williams, *Capitalism and Slavery*, 135. Williams quotes Cropper's celebration of the British manufacturing sector "unshackled by bounties, unaided by useless monopolies, thriving with unrestrained freedom," 187.

46. Smith is the central figure in Emília Viotti da Costa's *Crowns of Glory, Tears of Blood*. Thomas Harding's *White Debt* is critical of the tendency to focus on the white martyr over the brutally repressed enslaved people evident as early as Montgomery's poem "A Deed of Darkness," originally published in the *Iris* as "The Missionary's funeral." Montgomery's poem is discussed in John Holland's *Memoirs of the Life and Writings of James Montgomery*, 4:71. An argument for immediate abolition was made in Elizabeth Heyrick's *Immediate, Not Gradual Abolition*. See Clare Midgley, "The Dissenting Voice of Elizabeth Heyrick."

47. The *Directory, General and Commercial, of the Town and Borough of Leeds for 1817*, 41, acknowledged an earlier short-lived attempt "to establish a Society for the discussion of literary and moral subjects.'" Two societies followed: one "confined its attention solely to philosophical lectures and experiments," the other "embraced the whole round of philosophy and literature.'" See also R. J. Morris, *Class, Sect and Party*, 235.

48. See the account of Leeds in 1819 in Morris, *Class, Sect and Party*, 228–29, and Jacob, *First Knowledge Economy*, chap. 4. Gott built a massive factory at Ing Bean where he installed a steam engine as early as 1792. W. E. Crump, ed., *Leeds Woollen Industry*,

196–99. Politically Gott as a loyal Tory supporter of the constitution was a counterweight to John Marshall's Whiggism. The son of a linen draper, Marshall made a fortune during the Napoleonic Wars. His development of the machine-based factory system culminated in the edifice of the Temple Mill, opened in 1840, that still stands today. See W. G. Rimmer, *Marshall's of Leeds*, 203.

49. Morris, *Class, Sect and Party*, 123, discusses the elder Baines's reforms at the workhouse board.

50. Edward Baines Jr. is identified in Thomas Wemyss Reid's *Memoir of John Deakin Heaton*, 97. Heaton's father's bookshop provided an important resort for men such as Edward Baines Sr., Gott, Hey, and Marshall prior to the Philosophical and Literary Society.

51. Priestley described Hey as "a zealous Methodist, [who] wrote answers to some of my theological tracts; but we always conversed with the greatest freedom on philosophical subjects, without mentioning any thing relating to theology." Joseph Priestley, "Memoirs of Dr. Priestley," in *Works*, 1 pt. 1: 77. Hey published a paper describing the eye of a seal in *MLPSM* 3 (1790): 274–78.

52. E. Baines Jr., *Life of Baines*, 103.

53. On June 8, 1821, the sum of fifty pounds was set aside for buying books toward a permanent library, and "only Books, of high credit and respectability for Literature and Science were admitted:" E. Kitson-Clark, *The History of 100 Years of Life of the Leeds Philosophical and Literary Society*, 29. In November 1826, the society offered 150 guineas to Thomas Campbell for a course of lectures on modern literature, making it clear that the fee was nonnegotiable. The society was aware of a similar offer about to be made from the Royal Institution at Manchester and hoped he could combine the two commitments. William Osburn, Secretary, to Thomas Campbell, [1826] at LPLS/10/1/3, Letter Book relating to the Society's Lectures (1826–1835), Leeds Philosophical and Literary Society (LPLS) Collections, Brotherton Library, University of Leeds. The council had been pursing Campbell since July 1824; he is not recorded in Kitson-Clark's list of lecturers. Montgomery was a cheaper, more local proposition. Campbell—a star lecturer at this period—had delivered the inaugural series on poetry at the LRI in 1818. Zimmerman, *Romantic Literary Lecture*, 25–26. The LPLS approached Coleridge after the initial rebuff from Campbell and eventually got a refusal that insisted it was not a matter of the fee. Samuel Taylor Coleridge to Dr. Williamson, 10 [11] November 1823, in Coleridge, *Collected Letters*, 5:309–10. On November 9, 1832, the council formally acknowledged Scott's death as "a serious loss to our national literature." The following April, it resolved to accept a gift of Scott's works. Council Minute Book (1822–1840), LPLS/02/2/2/3, LPLS Collections.

54. Compare, for instance, the brief notice of the December 1818 meeting on January 4, 1819, in the *Intelligencer* with the much more enthusiastic account in the *Mercury* for January 9 that celebrated the "laudable and civic spirit of improvement in this Borough."

55. Derek Fraser, "Life of Edward Baines"; David Thornton, "Edward Baines, Senior."

56. Benevolus [pseud.], "Observations on the Formation of a Leeds Literary and Philosophical Society," *Leeds Literary Observer*, January 1819, 9, 10–11. The *Observer* ran from January to December 1819.

57. D. Fraser, "Life of Edward Baines," 214, and Ford, *Henry Brougham and His World*, 499–502. When Brougham vacated the seat soon after his election, John Marshall Jr. wrote to tell him of the "forlorn condition" in which he left the West Riding.

John Marshall Jr. to Henry Brougham, 23 November 1830, Brougham Papers, University College London (UCL) Special Collections.

58. T. B. Macaulay to Miss H. Macaulay, 16 December 1833, in Thomas Babington Macaulay, *Letters of Thomas Babington Macaulay*, 2:361. Derek Fraser ("Life of Edward Baines," 211) describes the *Mercury* as "the leading middle-class provincial journal of its day."

59. Benevolus, "Observations," 13.

60. Sadler's speech to the Pitt Club was reported in the approving *Leeds Intelligencer* on May 31, 1819. There is a partisan account of the 1832 Leeds election in E. Baines Jr., *Life of Baines*, 136–37. Morris, *Class, Sect and Party*, 236–38, presents the voting statistics of members of the Leeds Philosophical and Literary Society for the years 1829–34. He also notes that Unitarians and other nonconformists were proportionally overrepresented (240).

61. See E. Baines Jr., *Life of Baines*, 141; R. B. Seeley, *Life and Writings of Sadler*, 41–42. Baines dismissed Sadler as a man of "talent rather than judgment . . . all his speeches bespoke rather the rhetorician and poet than the statesman" (*Life of Baines*, 137).

62. This commitment was made as early as December 1818. The Hall was to accommodate lectures, meetings, and a library. The society's collections were to be housed in a purpose-built museum. R. D. Chantrell was declared the winner of the design competition in May. See the details in Christopher Webster, *R. D. Chantrell, Architect*. On the contingencies of the museum's development, see Mark Steadman, "History of the Scientific Collections."

63. Leeds, like Manchester, was a town from which the local gentry and aristocracy had largely withdrawn. William White's *History, Gazetteer and Directory of the West-Riding of Yorkshire* claimed "it has long been totally abandoned by the aristocracy" (1:496). Morris, *Class, Sect and Party*, 230, contrasts the Yorkshire Philosophical Society, an enterprise which welcomed the involvement of the local landowners.

64. Morris, *Class, Sect, and Party*, 236–37. Proprietary members held the hundred-pound shares which financed the building of the Philosophical Hall. Ordinary members paid an entrance fee of three guineas and an annual subscription of two. The society's affairs were governed by a small council elected by the whole membership at an annual general meeting. The Council Minute Book (1819–1822), LPLS/02/2/2/1, contains a list of both kinds of members. The society never paid off its initial debt and had to be bailed out by the major proprietors in the 1840s.

65. Marshall was part of a group that provided money for the foundation of the *London Review* in 1834. See John Stuart Mill to Thomas Carlyle, 22 December 1833, in Mill, *Collected Works*, 202. Jane Marshall, his wife, was a close friend of Dorothy Wordsworth's, as reported by Jacob, *First Knowledge Economy*, 129, and Kirsty McHugh, "Yorkshire Tourists."

66. John Marshall, *Economy of Social Life*, iii.

67. John Marshall Jr. to Henry Brougham, 4 September 1832, Brougham Papers.

68. Page references to Thackrah's *An Introductory Discourse delivered to the Leeds Philosophical and Literary Society* are given in the main text. Details of Thackrah's time in London are to be found in editor Thomas G. Wright's "Biographical Memoir," published in his revised edition of Thackrah's *Inquiry into the Nature and Properties of the Blood*, 9–25. Wright claims that on his return to Leeds, Thackrah "drew up a striking report of the miserable and pernicious state of the inferior class of lodging houses." Thackrah's reputation was tarnished in 1823 after it was revealed that he had fathered a child with a patient.

69. Leeds Philosophical and Literary Society, *Prospectus of Preliminary Laws of the Philosophical and Literary Society*, 6; General Minute Book of Transactions (1821–41), LPLS/02/3/2; Morris, *Class, Sect, and Party*, 228.

70. Morris, *Class, Sect, and Party*, 230. The Council Minute Book from May 6, 1827, shows that the Infant School was given permission to use the Philosophical Hall for its general meetings. Morris also notes that thirteen of the original twenty subscribers to the Mechanics Institute were also members of the LPLS (241). The Council Minute Books show that the LPLS gave assistance with rooms and apparatus. On Williamson, see R. V. Taylor, *The Biographia Leodiensis*, 415–16. A staunch ally of Baines and Marshall, Williamson also played an important early part in the career of James Phillips Kay, his fellow Congregationalist, discussed in chapter 7.

71. John Marshall Jr. to Henry Brougham, 1 January 1825, Society for the Diffusion of Useful Knowledge (SDUK) Papers, UCL Special Collections; Brougham, *Practical Observations Upon the Education of the People*, 24. The younger Marshall reported that a course of lectures on political economy had been agreed despite some opposition; Brougham had sent copies of a lecture series he had given in London from which Marshall chose "some of the earlier ones, on the division of labour, & rate of Wages," believing it better not to shock people's prejudices by giving the whole course at once. John Marshall Jr. to Henry Brougham, 23 October 1826, SDUK Papers.

72. E. Baines Jr., *Life of Baines*, 125–30, claimed that the idea of opening a library for mechanics was originally John Marshall's. The idea was only taken up in earnest after George Birkbeck had set up the London Institute with Brougham's help in 1823. Baines claimed that he had argued that the library should include "history, travels, and general literature" but that he withdrew, not wishing to run "the risk of alienating the most munificent benefactors of the Institution" (128). A newspaper account of the Bradford meeting is pasted into Add MS 27824, f71v.

73. Leeds Philosophical and Literary Society, *Transactions of the Philosophical and Literary Society of Leeds* (1837), viii.

74. The paragraph appeared in the *Leeds Intelligencer* December 10, 1821. The council directed the secretary to write to the editor, deciding it had to act against "such publicity and animadversions on the proceedings of the Society," otherwise "freedom of its Investigations" would be curbed. December 21, 1821, Council Minute Book (1819–22), LPLS/02/2/2/1.

75. *Leeds Intelligencer*, December 16, 1822.

76. Edward Baines Jr., "Rise of Art, Science, and Literature among the Athenians" and "History of Printing," WYAS 383/49 and WYAS 383/89, respectively, Papers of Edward Baines, Jr., West Yorkshire Archives.

77. *Address to the Unemployed Workmen of Yorkshire and Lancashire* was first published in the *Leeds Mercury* on May 13, 1826. E. Baines Jr., *Life of Baines*, 138.

78. "Report of the Retiring Council at the close of the Fifth Session," General Minute Book of Transactions.

79. "The Physiological Principles of Mr. Sadler's Work on Population," *North of England Medical and Surgical Journal* 1 (August 1830): 106. Macaulay's attack on Sadler appeared in *Edinburgh Review* 51 (July 1830): 297–321 and 52 (January 1831): 504–29.

80. A ballot at the general meeting of January 15, 1829, voted overwhelmingly in favor of Baines. Three members resigned at the February meeting. General Minute Book of Transactions (1821–41) and Council Minute Book (1822–1840).

81. *Leeds Mercury*, October 16, 1830; see also the account in Cecil Driver, *Tory Radical*, 46. There had been an earlier editorial that prepared readers for Oastler's letter by

casting doubt on some of its claims. The Baines-Oastler rift seems to have been widened when a subsequent letter was dismissed by the younger Baines in his father's absence. Driver, *Tory Radical*, 72. Oastler turned to the delighted editor of the *Leeds Intelligencer* with the rest of the correspondence.

82. Oastler, *A Well Seasoned Christmas Pie for "The Great Liar of the North,"* 36. See D. Fraser, "Life of Edward Baines," on the protests outside the newspaper offices.

83. Council minutes, October 1, 1829, Council Minute Book (1822–40). Kitson-Clark, *History*, 43, mistakes the year as 1830.

84. Thackrah's *The Effects of Arts, Trades, and Professions* discusses the flax industry in detail, 58–69, criticizing the hours of labor and the employment of children. The *Leeds Intelligencer*, March 22, 1832, gives a detailed account of Sadler's speech of March 16 to introduce the second reading of the bill to Parliament, including the reference to Thackrah.

85. Hunter had left Sheffield before these hopes were expressed, first to study at Manchester College, York, and then to Bath to take up a ministry. David Crook, "Reverend Joseph Hunter and the Public Records." Aikin's chief informant about Sheffield had been Benjamin Naylor, minister at Upper Chapel, where Hunter worshipped. Naylor's copastor was Joseph Evans, who fostered Hunter from 1787. See J. E. Manning, *History of Upper Chapel*. The archival source "Diary of Joseph Hunter, 3 March 1797–20 July 1799," BL Add MS24789, f. 6, "Collectanea Hunteriana": Papers of Joseph Hunter, British Library, celebrates Aikin's "very valuable book." Stephen Colclough, *Consuming Texts*, 96–117, shows that the Sheffield Subscription Library, founded in 1771, was the focus of the youthful Hunter's reading life.

86. *Prospectus of a new miscellany, to be entitled The monthly magazine*, 2. The minute book of the Sheffield Society for the Promotion of Useful Knowledge (SSPUK) is in the records of the Sheffield Literary and Philosophical Society (SLPS) at the Sheffield City Archives and Local Studies Library (hereafter SCA), SLPS/216, SCA. Ian Inkster's otherwise excellent "Development of a Scientific Community in Sheffield, 1790–1850" to my mind differentiates too sharply the society's scientific and literary interests.

87. "Thomas Ward's Pocket Diary 1804," November 8, 1804, SLPS/126, SCA. The society also had a reviewing committee, presumably in part to winnow out anything provocative.

88. Inkster, "Development of a Scientific Community," 114. The medical men included David Davis, physician to the infirmary, who later attended at the birth of the future Queen Victoria; John Favell; and Hall Overend, a Quaker who became a member of the SLPS and later set up the city's medical school.

89. Joseph Hunter, "Biographical Notices," BL Add MS 36527, f24. Sylvester was introduced to the society by Davis. Hunter remembered Sylvester as the only man he had ever heard declare himself an atheist. Ward was somewhat more positive in his diary entry of April 10, 1805 (SLPS/127): "Sylvester is a very entertaining companion, was formerly a plate-wire maker, and now supports himself principally by lecturing on Galvanism." Ian Inkster and Maureen S. Bryson's *Industrial Man: The Life and Works of Charles Sylvester* provides a useful account of his career.

90. "Minute book of the SSPUK," ff. 5, 7, 38, 39, 41–42.

91. Hunter comments on his absence in his "Biographical Notices," f13. The notice describes Montgomery as the first person Hunter knew who "cut any comfortable figure in the world" (f6). They were often in each other's company until Hunter left for York, and sometimes afterward.

92. Ward's diary entry for October 1804, SLPS 126. Ward started to attend Upper

Chapel in 1808 and seems to have effectively left the Church of England by 1809. Hunter, "Biographical Notices," 23-24.

93. Thomas Asline Ward to Joseph Hunter, September 1831, SPLS 52.

94. Samuel Bailey, *Essays on the Formation and Publication of Opinions*, 103-4. See the very useful discussion in Connell, *Romanticism, Economics*, 106-11. In the SLPS's first season, Bailey gave a paper "On the mutual Relations amongst the different Sciences, and the light which they reciprocally afford." Later in the same season, Montgomery spoke on "On the possibility of one Science attaining to a degree of Perfection while all the rest are disproportionately depressed." See Sheffield Literary and Philosophical Society, *First Annual Report of the Sheffield Literary and Philosophical Society*. The title page of Bailey's *Questions in Political Economy, Politics, Morals, Metaphysics, Polite Literature and Other Branches of Knowledge* describes it as intended "*for discussion in Literary Societies*" as well as "*Private Study*." Presumably, it is not coincidental that it was published shortly after the SLPS was founded. Ward's diary for 1822 (SLPS 144) records meeting with Bailey to discuss the rules on December 27.

95. "Minutes of the general meeting," January 1824, SLPS 192, f. 21, SCA.

96. Ward had described the SSPUK as "the Literary and Philosophical Society" in a diary entry for December 1804. He presented its minute books to the SPLS in 1840, thereby creating an archive to affirm this narrative. William Smith Porter, *Sheffield Literary and Philosophical Society*, 7.

97. Alison Twells's *Civilising Mission* provides an excellent study of these groups in Sheffield. For the parallel Leeds context, see Morris, *Class, Sect and Party*, 173-80.

98. Mary Anne Rawson, "Memorials of James Montgomery," MS69, Montgomery Manuscripts, Sheffield University Library; Twells, *Civilising Mission*, 111.

99. See Twells, *Civilising Mission*, 54. Roberts and Montgomery collaborated on the *Iris*'s campaign to improve the plight of chimney sweeps that culminated in *The Chimney Sweeper's Friend and Climbing-Boy's Album*, which included William Blake's "The Chimney-Sweeper." Montgomery and Roberts also collaborated on *The Negro's Friend, or Sheffield Anti-Slavery Album*. Roberts became a close ally of Oastler's and attacked missionary initiatives that ignored conditions in Britain and those domestic missions that were insufficiently Christian. See Twells, *Civilising Mission*, 155-56. Samuel Roberts, *Autobiography*, reproduces the dialogue poem "The Four Friends," 57-70, written as an exchange with Montgomery.

100. Twells, *Civilising Mission*, 84-86; N. B. Lewis, "Abolitionist Movement in Sheffield."

101. Twells, *Civilising Mission*, 55-56, 61.

102. Rawson, "Memorials of Montgomery." Bennet was traveling as a missionary for most of the 1820s. He started donating items to the museum in 1832. Roberts seems to have joined at the very beginning but remained largely inactive. See W. Porter, *Sheffield Literary and Philosophical Society*, 51, 41.

103. Joseph Hunter to Thomas Asline Ward, 5 April 1821, "Private Letters of Joseph Hunter (1815-1845)," Add MS 35162, f. 100. Hunter feared that John Holland, whose poem *Sheffield Park* (1820) he admired, was going the same way. Ward complained to Hunter that Montgomery and Roberts were spending time with a "busy Evangelical, who certainly does not improve their principles" (SLPS 52/37). The account of Montgomery in Hunter's "Biographical Notices," written in 1827, identified his more recent intimates as "evangelical zealots" (12v). Hunter's early letters home from York c. 1806, Add MS. 35161, reveal his enthusiasm for Montgomery's poems. Holland was the primary author-editor of *Memoirs of Montgomery*. A teacher at the Sunday School at Red Hill in 1813,

and later secretary of the Sunday School Union, Montgomery had published his early poetry in the *Sheffield Iris*. Holland took over this newspaper upon Montgomery's retirement in 1825. He was later appointed curator to the society's museum and corresponded regularly with Hunter on antiquarian matters: details can be found in William Hudson, *Life of John Holland*. Mary Anne Rawson feared that Holland would be an inappropriate biographer for Montgomery, too concerned with literary celebrity; see E. D. Mackerness, "Mary Anne Rawson and the 'Memorials of James Montgomery.'" James Everett, Holland's collaborator on Montgomery's memoir, was author of *Historical Sketches of Wesleyan Methodism in Sheffield*, published at the *Iris* office by Montgomery.

104. *Sheffield Iris*, August 9, 1814.

105. William St. Clair, *The Reading Nation in the Romantic Period*, 217–18; Matthew Sangster, *Living as an Author in the Romantic Period*, 72–75.

106. Connell, *Romanticism, Economics*, 108.

107. The phrase is from Hunter's "Biographical Notices," f. 7v. Holland, *Memoirs of Montgomery*, 2:331, recalls a riot in 1812 when a crowd threatened the newspaper office. When Montgomery appeared, someone called out, "Nay, nay, sir we won't hurt you—you were once our friend." For details of Montgomery's trial and imprisonment, see Albert Goodwin, *Friends of Liberty*, 382–83; Kenneth Johnston, *Unusual Suspects*, 66–71.

108. See Ward's diary entry of November 4, 1825 (SLPS 147) and Thomas Asline Ward, *Peeps into the Past*, 269, on Ward's role at the *Independent* and his hopes that his friendship with Montgomery would survive. Rawson claimed in her "Memorials of Montgomery" that Montgomery "almost hated politics": "He had shown in times past what his opinions were and had suffered for them more than most people—he thought he had done his share & did not see it was incumbent upon him to go on fighting. He was weary of the strife of tongues . . . His old friends and those who were on the Liberal side in politics, could not help wishing that he had avowed the sentiments his judgment approved."

109. Johnston, *Unusual Suspects*, 64.

110. The leader for January 16, 1810, was concerned that a "spirit of warfare" was taking hold of the government.

111. Holland, *Memoirs of Montgomery*, 4:142. Characteristically, Rawson regretted that Montgomery had not "felt able to introduce more of the Christian element." She did acknowledge that it might not have been appropriate at this "heterogeneous assembly" ("Memorials"). *The Bow in the Cloud* collection is discussed in Lewis, "Abolitionist Movement in Sheffield."

112. *Edinburgh Review* 9 (Jan. 1807): 347–54. Sangster discusses the review in *Living as an Author*, 260–63. On Jeffrey's criticism of Thelwall, see Mee, "Policing Enthusiasm in the Romantic Period."

113. C. R. Johnson, *Provincial Poetry 1789–1839*, vi, notes the importance of Montgomery and the *Iris* to provincial poetry. Holland, *Memoirs of Montgomery*, 2:81, suggests that John Aikin first contacted Montgomery through the local Unitarian minister H. H. Piper. John Aikin defended him in "To Mr. James Montgomery, on his Poems, lately Published," *MM* 21 (March 1806): 145. Lucy Aikin's "To Mr. Montgomery. Occasioned by an Illiberal Attack on his Poems," first published by her father in the *Athenaeum* 1 (1807): 399–400, was collected in her *Epistles on Women* (1810). Correspondence with Roscoe and Lucy Aikin is at SLPS 36, 37, 222, SCA. A letter from her father to Montgomery from January 1807 reveals that John Aikin and Roscoe discussed his poetry: Holland, *Memoirs of Montgomery*, 2:126–27. On Montgomery and Wordsworth, see Holland, *Memoirs of Montgomery*, 2:183–84. Hunter's "Biographical No-

tices," f. 12, remembered Montgomery as a supporter of *Lyrical Ballads* when everyone else mocked them.

114. Holland, *Memoirs of Montgomery*, 2:39; Roscoe to Montgomery, 13 April 1810, *Memoirs of Montgomery*, 2:258; L. Aikin, *Memoirs of Lucy Aikin*, 330, 209.

115. Joseph Hunter to James Montgomery, 9 January 1823, SLPS 36/443. Montgomery was elected vice president at the first general meeting in January 1823. *First Annual Report* (1824), 15. He was elected president the following year, and then twice more, the last in 1841. Bailey was vice president with Montgomery for the first year of the society, and president in 1826, 1832, and 1833.

116. George Gordon Byron, *Lord Byron: The Complete Poetical Works*, 1:242. In a later footnote, Byron claimed that "the Bard of Sheffield is a man of considerable genius," his volume worth "a thousand *Lyrical Ballads*" (1: 407n). The sarcasm needs picking out of these comments.

117. *Proceedings of a Public Meeting for the Purpose of Establishing a Literary and Philosophical Society in Sheffield*, 11–12. James T. Hodgson's *Memoir of Francis Hodgson*, 1:91–104, reproduces the Hodgson-Montgomery exchange.

118. Sheffield Literary and Philosophical Society, *Second Annual Report*, 11, reveals that Williamson of Leeds gave a lecture on Sir Francis Bacon in April 1824. Thackrah gave a paper on digestion and diet in December 1824: "Minutes," SLPS 192, f. 33. On February, 24, Montgomery had given the first of his lectures on modern literature, "A Sketch of the History of Literature from the Earliest Ages to the Close of the 13th century," to a large audience. See W. Porter, *Sheffield Literary and Philosophical Society*, 20–21.

119. Montgomery, *Lectures on Poetry and General Literature*, 393. From this point on, all references to the lectures are given in the main text.

120. Neil Ramsey, "James Montgomery's Waterloo," 361.

121. Shortly after publication of Wordsworth's *The Excursion*, Montgomery praised its "familiar and complete access" to the "human heart." However, Montgomery balked at its lack of any explicit religious framework: "The love of Nature is the purest, the most sublime, and the sweetest emotion of the mind . . . yet the love of Nature *alone* cannot ascend from earth to heaven." *Eclectic Review*, 2nd ser., 3 (1815): 19.

122. Reinhart Koselleck, *Practice of Conceptual History*, 126–27.

123. Montgomery gave his "Strictures on several modern poets" at the Music Hall in Sheffield in January1828, returning to the same topic in the last public lecture of the same year. Holland, *Memoirs of Montgomery*, 4:230 describes the 1828 lecture as the one "repeated with applause at the Royal Institution."

124. Montgomery had been interested in phrenology, but in a series of papers and lectures over 1825–26, he reacted against attempts to use it to distinguish between racial groups on the basis of inherent biological traits that placed a limit on the possibilities of improvement. Holland, *Memoirs of Montgomery*, 4:165–66.

125. Knight spoke on the topic on October 4 and December 6, 1833. Sheffield Literary and Philosophical Society, *Eleventh Annual Report*, 7–8. Montgomery was presiding and, according to Holland, *Memoirs of Montgomery*, 5:85–87, immediately after the paper was finished rose from his chair to condemn the idea. The effects of dry grinding were discussed in Thackrah's *Effects of Arts, Trades, and Professions*, 59–60.

126. James Montgomery, "Lecture on the British Poets," 113.

127. Montgomery, "Lecture on the British Poets," 117, 120.

128. "Minute Book of the Sheffield Mechanics and Apprentices' Library," MD187, ff. 156–59, SCA, contains a transcription of Montgomery's letter of October 17, 1831. The rules are pasted into the minute book.

129. Connell, *Romanticism, Economics*, 106.

130. Bailey, *Essays on the Formation and Publication of Opinions*, 250.

131. Connell, *Romanticism, Economics*, 111, quoting Roscoe's *Vicissitudes*, 70.

132. Holland, *Memoirs of Montgomery*, 5:13–14. Ward was also asked to serve but told Hunter that he declined "as [he was] not scientific," SLPS 52/46. Stephen Harbottle, *William Turner*, 133, discusses Turner's participation.

133. See William Henry, "An Estimate of the Philosophical Character of Dr. Priestley," in British Association for the Advancement of Science, *Report of the First and Second Meetings of the British Association for the Advancement of Science*, 60–71. W. Vernon Harcourt, "Address," in British Association for the Advancement of Science, *Report of the Ninth Meeting of the British Association for the Advancement of Science*, 15, dismissed the criticism of Henry and then hinted that Priestley's career might be a topic with "a tendency to excite feelings alien to our pursuits, and destructive to all social union."

CHAPTER FOUR

1. Alan Richardson, *British Romanticism and the Science of the Mind*, xiv.

2. L. Aikin, *Memoir of John Aikin*, 1:174–78.

3. Asa Briggs, *Victorian Cities*, 56, describes Manchester as the "shock city" of the 1840s. Romantic-period scholars might bring that date forward.

4. Robert Owen, *Life of Robert Owen*, 27–28. Chapter 6 provides a fuller account of Owen's career in the Manchester cotton mills.

5. Stevenson's *Remarks on the Very Inferior Utility of Classical Learning* argued that "man is the necessary creature of original formation and external circumstances; that the laws of the intellectual and moral world are as fixed and regular as those of the natural." Stevenson presented a copy of this pamphlet to John Dalton, part of Owen's group at the Manchester Academy. John Chapple, *Elizabeth Gaskell: Early Years*, 41. Chapple, *Elizabeth Gaskell*, 21–23, discusses the Stevenson-Winstanley relationship.

6. Owen, *Life of Owen*, 35–36. Owen is hazy on dates, but his account broadly fits with other sources. Dalton moved to Manchester to take up his post at the college in 1793 when Winstanley was there training to become a minister. Winstanley took up a position at Derby (1798–1803) and then trained as a doctor in Edinburgh. He returned to Manchester, predictably joining the congregation at Cross Street and then the Literary and Philosophical Society (1807). He was elected physician of the infirmary in 1808 and gave evidence to the parliamentary committee on child labor. See E. M. Brockbank, *Sketches of the Honorary Medical Staff of the Manchester Infirmary*, 241–45.

7. Owen, *Life of Owen*, 37–38, and E. M. Fraser, "Robert Owen in Manchester," 37. Fraser, who provides the date for the paper (38), wrote with access to the society's minute books, later destroyed in the Second World War.

8. W. C. Henry, "Memoir of Dr. William Henry," 105–6, praised Ferriar's invaluable "'Medical Histories'—the systematised records of his experience in our great public charities." His style he described as "simple, concise, and energetic, though not neglecting on suitable occasions (as in his moving essay on the 'Treatment of the dying') the warmer colouring suggested by deep feeling." William Henry trained under Ferriar at the Manchester Infirmary.

9. Ferriar wrote to Cullen from Manchester on March 10, 1786, asking for medical advice; the letter is at DEP/CUL/1/2/1815, Royal College of Physicians of Edinburgh. The letter is signed "your much obliged & obedient pupil." Cullen's reply of March 16 is at

CUL/1/1/19. Both may be accessed online via the Cullen Project (see note 54 to chapter 1) at 1786/RCPE. Arthur Gair had written to Cullen from Alnwick on February 9, 1786, reporting that Ferriar had moved to Manchester and asking Cullen for a recommendation on his behalf to be sent there: DEP/CUL/1/3/176. I am very grateful to Estela Ducan for sending me a copy of the last.

10. John Ferriar, "Of Genius," in Ferriar, *Illustrations of Sterne* (1st ed., 1798), 271, 287. Fraser gives the title as "Genius and Modern Prophets," presumably on the basis of the minute books, which points up the overlap with Ferriar's paper "Of Popular Illusions, and particularly of Medical Demonology" discussed subsequently.

11. Christopher Lawrence, "Cullen, Brown, and the Poverty of Essentialism."

12. Thomas Cooper, "Sketch of the Controversy on the Subject of Materialism," in *Tracts ethical, theological and political . . . Vol. 1*, 167. No second volume was published. Cooper emigrated to the United States with Joseph Priestley in 1794.

13. John V. Pickstone, "Ferriar's Fever to Kay's Cholera," 412, 421–32.

14. Kathryn Ready, "'And Make thine own Apollo doubly thine': John Aikin as Literary Physician," 70, 73, 74. See also Marten Hutt, "John Aikin."

15. Anna Laetitia Barbauld, "To Dr. Aikin," in *Poems*, 19.

16. John Aikin Jr., *Essay on the Application of Natural History to Poetry*, 10.

17. Lisbeth Haakonsson, *Medicine and Morals in the Enlightenment*, 200.

18. L. Aikin, *Memoir of John Aikin*, 1:11. Aikin's essay on the ligature of arteries was appended to Charles White's *Cases in Surgery*, 177–78.

19. Haygarth recalled his discussions with Aikin in 1777 on topics "medical, literary or philosophical." See his *Sketch of a Plan to exterminate the Casual Small-pox*, 1:214. See also L. Aikin, *Memoir of John Aikin*, 1: 16–17; Francis M. Lobo, "Haygarth, Smallpox, and Religious Dissent," 227.

20. Lucy Aikin notes her father's political differences with Haygarth in her *Memoir of John Aikin*, 1:17. John F. Fulton, "Warrington Academy," 68, identified ventilating hospitals to avoid contagion as the single greatest advance made by Aikin's group. John Howard acknowledges his "ingenious friend" Aikin in a note in *The state of the prisons in England and Wales*, 97. L. Aikin, *Memoir of John Aikin*, 1:31–2, reproduces part of a letter from Aikin to his sister from February 1777 reporting the printing of Howard's book on Eyres's Warrington press; they also worked together on the revised edition (33).

21. Michel Foucault distinguishes "power relations" from "relations of domination" in "Ethics of Care for the Self as a Practice of Freedom."

22. John Aikin Jr., *A View of the Character and Public services of the late John Howard*, 81.

23. Alison Twells, *Civilising Mission*, 166.

24. The essay on "True Heroism" in Aikin and Barbauld's *Evenings at Home*, 5:85–90, contrasts John Howard and the son of a journeyman bricklayer with martial heroes including Achilles and Alexander.

25. David Hartley, *Observations on Man*, 2: 453, and Joanna Wharton, *Material Enlightenment*, 68–71. For Lamb's phrase, see Charles Lamb and Mary Lamb, *Letters of Charles and Mary Lamb*, 2:82.

26. Barbauld, *Poems*, 27–28, and Anna Laetitia Barbauld, "What is Education?" as discussed in Wharton, *Material Enlightenment*, 34–35.

27. Lobo, "Haygarth, Smallpox, and Religious Dissent," 221.

28. L. Aikin, *Memoir of John Aikin*, 1:59–61, 131–32.

29. *Memoirs of Science and the Arts*, 2nd ed, 1 (1793): 511, printed a summary of Ferriar's paper. Derek Roper's *Reviewing before the Edinburgh* estimates that Aikin con-

tributed more than 100 main articles between 1793 and 1799, and Ferriar around 150 from 1799 until his death. Both gave equally of their attention to medicine and poetry. B. C. Nangle, *Monthly Review*, 1, 22, gives summaries of their respective careers.

30. William Cullen, *Works*, 1:9.

31. Wharton, *Material Enlightenment*, 28, drawing on Lambros Malfouris, *How Things Shape the Mind*.

32. Thomas Percival, "Speculations on the Perceptive Power of Vegetables," 143.

33. J. Aikin, *Thoughts on hospitals*, 81. See the discussion in Haakonsson, *Medicine and Morals*, 117, 150.

34. Thomas Percival, *Medical Ethics*, 169. Further references given in the main text. I'm grateful to Fuson Wang for discussions on this point.

35. Thomas Percival, *A Father's Instructions; adapted to different periods of life* (1800), 45.

36. Thomas Percival, *A Father's instructions; consisting of moral tales, fables, and reflections*, 4th ed. (1779), 212, xiii; M. O. Grenby, *Child Reader*, 244.

37. Thomas Percival, *Moral and Literary Dissertations*, 140.

38. W. F. Bynum's "Cullen and the Study of Fevers" notes that Cullen always resisted the schematization pursued by his pupils John Brown and Benjamin Rush: "The treatment of fever was complicated and must be related not only to the different stages of the fever paroxysm but to the identified causes of the complaint and to the peculiarities of the patient's constitution, temperament, and mode of life" (139). Bynum traces the role of these principles in the fever hospitals set up by his pupils (146).

39. Thomas Percival, *A Socratic Discourse on Truth and Faithfulness* (1781).

40. Percival, *Moral and Literary Dissertations*, 100, 106. Percival is critical of Diogenes's rudeness to Plato.

41. Percival, *Socratic Discourse*, 79, acknowledges Thomson.

42. The issue was debated between "Episcopus" and Edward Higginson, *Monthly Repository of Theology and General Literature*, 3 (February 1808): 66–67 and (July 1808): 368–73. Percival's son Thomas became an Anglican clergyman only after a struggle with his father's reservations. See also Haakonssen, *Medicine and Morals*, 27.

43. Percival, *Medical Ethics*, 5–6, says that he sent Gisborne a draft while Gisborne was writing *Enquiry into the Duties of Men*. A list of other recipients is given at Percival, *Medical Ethics*, 139–40. Gisborne acknowledged "my excellent friend" in his work. Gisborne, *Enquiry*, 383.

44. Edward Percival, *Memoirs of Thomas Percival*, ccvii. The memoir makes no mention of Gisborne in this or any other context. His son did publish the correspondence with James Beattie, primarily from the later 1780s, in relation to their efforts toward the abolition of the slave trade. Beattie was a noted opponent of Hume, popular with Rational Dissenters and latitudinarians, and a member of the Literary and Philosophical Society.

45. Percival's account in *Medical Ethics*, 1–2, claimed that the first chapter was written in 1792 at the request of Ferriar and the other physicians of the Manchester Infirmary.

46. Gisborne, *Enquiry into the Duties of Men*, 559–60. Karl Marx quoted approvingly from Gisborne on "the infamies of the factory system" in a note that also cited Aikin, *Capital*, 710. *Reports of the Society for bettering the Condition of the Poor*, 1:98–115 and 2:224–234, print positive accounts of the Board of Health and House of Recovery. Ferriar's "Advice to the Poor," discussed subsequently, was printed in the second volume's appendix (17–23).

47. Thomas Gisborne, "On the Benefits and Duties," 70.

48. See, for instance, Barbauld's *Remarks on Mr. Gilbert Wakefield's Enquiry* (1792).

49. John Ferriar, *Medical Histories and Reflections*, 3:193–94. All references to *Medical Histories* are to the three-volume first edition (1792–98) and given in the main text from this point onward unless otherwise indicated.

50. See Pickstone, "Thomas Percival and the Production of Medical Ethics."

51. *Palatine Note-book*, 4 (1884): 174, makes the claim based on an annotation in a presentation copy of the *Necessity of Reform*. By the time he was a baronet, Phillips was freely blaming his earlier radicalism on Cooper and Ferriar. See "Autobiography of Sir George Philips written circa1845," MI 247, Warwickshire County Record Office (WCRO), and David Brown, "From 'Cotton Lord' to Landed Aristocrat," 2.

52. John V. Pickstone, *Medicine and Industrial Society*, 11.

53. Gisborne's *Enquiry into the Duties of Men*, 400, echoes Percival's chapter "On the Conduct of Physicians towards Apothecaries" in urging physicians not to show contempt for apothecaries in front of their patients.

54. Liverpool set up its infirmary in 1745. Pickstone, *Medicine and Industrial Society*, 11.

55. Rules of the *Manchester infirmary* quoted in Pickstone, *Medicine and Industrial Society*, 15.

56. Charles Webster and Jonathan Barry, "Medical Revolution," 169. Webster and Barry provide a useful overview of medical reform over this period in Manchester, presenting Percival as the nodal point between "all the agencies of enlightenment" (167). John V. Pickstone and S. V. L. F. Butler's "The politics of medicine in Manchester, 1788–1792" suggests that the younger group associated with Cooper, Ferriar, and Walker provided the radical impetus.

57. Thomas Henry, "Observations on the Bills of Mortality for the Towns of Manchester and Salford," 161–62, 168.

58. Kevis Goodman, *Pathologies in Motion*, 45.

59. Pickstone, *Medicine and Industrial Society*, 18, and Webster and Barry, "Medical Revolution," 169–70.

60. Pickstone and Butler, "Politics of Medicine in Manchester," 230–31. Percival was briefly an honorary physician at the Infirmary, 1779–80, but resigned as a result of the pressure of business. Before he left, he introduced the idea of assistant physicians, who started the practice of attending patients in their own homes, fulfilling the role taken by dispensaries in most other towns.

61. Thomas White was to play a part in the loyalist backlash against Cooper and White from 1792. Prentice, *Historical Sketches and Personal Recollections*, 422–23.

62. Brockbank, *Sketches of the Honorable Medical Staff of the Manchester Infirmary*, 127, provides some details of Ferriar's background. He seems to have first worshipped at Cross Street when he arrived in Manchester, but he had his children baptized at Mosley Street Chapel between 1790 and 1794, RG4 / Piece 2856, Non-Conformist and Non-Parochial BMDs, National Archives, Kew. Thereafter he may have accommodated himself to Anglican respectability; at least his wife Barbara was buried at St. Mary's Church in 1800, where he was also laid to rest in 1815: *Registers of Manchester, St Mary Parsonage, 1754–1888*, 281, 319. Confirming his status in the community, a plaque was erected in his name at St. Mary's, now in St. Ann's Church: "St. Mary's Church, Manchester," *Transactions of the Lancashire and Cheshire Antiquarian Society*, 8 (1891): 141–42. Ferriar remained in friendly contact with his radical friends Thomas Cooper and Thomas Walker at least through the 1790s. He treated Walker for illness in 1799 but

refused payment on account of "the many obligations which you have conferred on me, & of which I must always retain the strongest remembrance." John Ferriar to Thomas Walker, 16 May 1799, Add MS 88955, f. 200.

63. Thomas Clarkson mentions a letter signed by Cooper, Ferriar, and Walker promising the assistance of Manchester in *History of the Abolition of the African Slave Trade*, 1:452–53. Ferriar's *Prince of Angola* was positively received in performance, according to the *Gentleman's Magazine* 58 (April 1788): 343. The *Monthly Review* 88 (1788): 522, thought it not worth considering in a "dramatic light" as it was "avowedly a political pamphlet." Ferriar appears as a subscriber to the committee for the abolition of the slave trade in 1787–88 in the newspapers, and his name also appears on the "Petition from the inhabitants of Manchester in support of the Foreign Slave Trade Abolition Bill, 1806" at http://webarchive.parliament.uk/20100423142445/http://slavetrade.parliament.uk/slavetrade/assetviews/documents/a50mancpetitionforabolition.html;jsessionid=15A60CA32C33F2F18F1B70CB38034A1E where the transcription mistakes "Ferriar" for "FARRAR."

64. A Constant Reader [pseud.], letter to the editor, *Manchester Mercury*, March 17, 1789.

65. Pickstone and Butler, "Medical Revolution," 245, note the role of Anglican evangelicals and Methodists in medical reform. Interestingly, Ferriar and Philips were apparently introduced to John Wesley when he visited Manchester in 1790, according to "Autobiography of Philips." Bew, a former apothecary, had held office at the Literary and Philosophical Society from 1781 to 1784.

66. Letter to the editor, *World*, November 27, 1789. Webster and Barry, "Medical Revolution," 174, identify Este, who had trained with the Whites in Manchester, as the author of these letters to the *World*.

67. Pickstone and Butler, "Medical Revolution," 237–38.

68. *World*, August 17, 1790.

69. Quarterly Board Minutes, December 22, 1791, quoted in Webster and Barry, "Medical Revolution," 171.

70. Julia Kristeva, *Powers of Horror*, viii.

71. Goodman, *Pathologies of Motion*, 24.

72. Edwin Chadwick, *Report on an Inquiry into the Sanitary Condition of the Labouring Population of Great Britain*, 441–42. Ferriar is also quoted, 149, 287, 359.

73. George Rosen's "John Ferriar's 'Advice to the Poor'" does concede that Ferriar's circular was unusual at the time for addressing the poor directly.

74. Maria Edgeworth, unpublished essay "On the Education of the Poor," c.1800, MS. Eng. misc. e. 1461, f. 81, Bodleian Library, Oxford. I am very grateful to Joanna Wharton for pointing this reference out to me.

75. Pickstone, "Ferriar's Fever to Kay's Cholera," 411, and Webster and Barry, "Manchester Medical Revolution," 177.

76. Ferriar served several terms as joint secretary of the Literary and Philosophical Society, including two years with James Watt Jr., whose physician he became, succeeding Percival. Watt wrote to his father explaining that they had become intimate friends after working together at the society: James Watt Jr. to James Watt Sr., 21 December 1790, MS 3219/4/12/47, James Watt and Family Papers, Library of Birmingham. If Ferriar did not publicly involve himself in the campaigns for parliamentary reform, his correspondence with James Watt Jr. in 1794—and later Thomas Walker—suggests his sympathy for the victims of Pitt's repression. On November 8, 1794, a few days after the acquittal of Thomas Hardy for treason, Ferriar told Watt: "I congratulate you on

the result of the political persecution which we have seen carried so far. After this disappointment, Ministers will find it difficult to keep up party rage to its late standard." John Ferriar to James Watt Jr., 8 November 1794, MS 3219/6/2/F/13. Hardy's trial lasted until November 5.

77. Cooper, "Sketch of the Controversy," 167. Percival later wrote to Benjamin Rush to introduce Cooper, whose *Tracts*, he claimed, "evinces a very uncommon degree of metaphysical acumen." In the same letter, he recommended Gisborne's *Enquiry into the Duties of Men*, even as he also wished to be remembered to Priestley. Thomas Percival to Benjamin Rush [nd], Volume 28, Rush Family Papers.

78. Thomas Barnes, "On the Influence of the Imagination," 377.

79. In "Sketch of the Controversy," Cooper defines "immaterialism" simply as the "opposite doctrine" to materialism (188)—that is, the idea that it is an essential property of "the soul that it acts upon the body, or upon matter" (192). He ends his paper by saying it was written to encourage the perusal of Priestley's *Disquisitions relating to Matter and Spirit*.

80. Cooper, "Sketch of the Controversy," 167,

81. Cooper, preface to *Tracts*, vii.

82. "Truth, whenever it be thoroughly discussed, will never fail to come like tried gold out of the fire." Cooper, preface to *Tracts*, xiv.

83. Cooper, "Sketch of the Controversy," 301–2, 200, 222–23.

84. Ferriar, "Observations on the Vital Principle," read on February 27, 1787, *MLPSM*, 3:216–17, 222. Cooper, "Sketch of the Controversy," 242, mocks Hunter and Monro, citing Priestley on the idea of "the soul of the world," 236.

85. Ferriar, "Observations on the Vital Principle," 222, 240, 239, 241.

86. See the definition in Goodman's *Pathology of Motion*, 57.

87. I adapt the term "soft materialism" from Neil Vickers, "Coleridge, Thomas Beddoes and Brunonian Medicine," 68, where it distinguishes between Beddoes and what he takes to be Erasmus Darwin's "harder" materialism. Beddoes believed that all the phenomena of life had a material basis but—like Ferriar—granted mental life a relative autonomy. My use of the phrase also owes something to Pickstone's suggestion that Ferriar's sensibility "softened the dualism of mind and body."

88. John Ferriar, "An Argument against the Doctrine of Materialism," 21, 44. I am very grateful to Professor Christopher Pelling for help with Ferriar's Greek.

89. [Thomas Cooper], "Of Dr. Priestley's Metaphysical Writing," 1:334–5. Cooper and Ferriar remained in friendly contact as least until 1794. On August 21, 1794, Ferriar wrote to James Watt Jr. about the apparatus his father had invented for Beddoes after a conversation with Cooper (MS 3219/6/2/F/11.4, James Watt and Family Papers). When Cooper left England for the United States, he asked Walker to send copies of his pamphlets and books recently published by Joseph Johnson to Ferriar, among others: Thomas Cooper to Thomas Walker, 14 and 16 August 1794, Add MS 88955, ff. 132–35.

90. *British Critic* 4 (December 1793): 364–67. Coleridge may have only been accepting the review's version of Ferriar's opinions when he told John Thelwall, "Dr. Beddoes, & Dr. Darwin think that *Life* is utterly inexplicable, writing as Materialists . . . Ferriar believes in a Soul, like an orthodox Churchman." Samuel Taylor Coleridge to John Thelwall, 31 December 1796, *Collected Letters*, 1:294–5. Coleridge's quotation of the lines from "The Eolian Harp" that use Monro's idea of "plastic nature" suggests that he may not have been aware of Ferriar's first paper, where Monro's Platonism is mocked, or of the wider debate with Cooper, although he may have heard of their exchange when he

visited Manchester earlier in 1796 to collect subscriptions for the *Watchman*. He certainly met Thomas Walker on this visit. Only in 1798 did Coleridge borrow the second volume of *MLPSM* from the Bristol Library. Apparently he knew the third volume by this stage, too, as he acknowledged Haygarth's essay on the Brocken Spectre as a source for his "Constancy to an Ideal Object." See George Whalley, "Bristol Library Borrowings of Southey and Coleridge"; Arthur Nethercot, *Road to Tryermaine*, 59–62; John Livingston Lowes, *Road to Xanadu*, 471, 500.

91. William Tattersall, *A brief view of the anatomical arguments for the doctrine of materialism*, 29. Tattersall, 6–7, claimed that Ferriar intended to "deter superstitious minds from free enquiry." Tattersall, originally a clergyman, had taught William Winstanley at his school in Preston before turning to medicine. Brockbank, *Sketches of the Honorary Medical Staff of the Manchester Infirmary*, 241. Beddoes reviewed Tattersall in *Monthly Review* 16 (March 1795): 341 and described his criticism as "unjustifiably severe."

92. Beddoes and Ferriar remained awkwardly aware of each other professionally. Beddoes reviewed Ferriar's essay on materialism in *Monthly Review* 13 (February 1794), concluding that the case histories did not disprove Cooper's theory because "as long as the sensorium shall continue, according to the immaterialist, in a condition to be the instrument, the materialist will contend, it may be the cause, of thought" (468). Beddoes used Ferriar's reports on conditions in Manchester in his *Essay on the Public Merits of Mr. Pitt*, 162–63, to argue that "the feelings of individuals during the same period" rather than shipping "tonnage" might be a better gauge of "the stock of public happiness."

93. Mike Jay, *Atmosphere of Heaven*, 97.

94. James Watt Jr. to John Ferriar, 19 December 1794, MS 3219/6/7ff 20–21, James Watt and Family Papers, discussed in Levere, "Dr. Thomas Beddoes (1750–1808)," 196.

95. John Ferriar to James Watt Jr., 21 August 1794, MS 3219/6/2 f11, James Watt and Family Papers. The reference seems to be to Beddoes's *Observations on Calculus* (1793), 265, where he had complained about "those rude hands that are ever ready to pluck up the tender plants of science, because they do not bear ripe fruit at a season when they can only be putting forth their blossoms."

96. James Watt Sr. to James Watt Jr., 2 September 1795, MS 3147/3/24, James Watt and Family Papers.

97. *British Critic* 12 (August 1798): 125.

98. Ferriar, *Illustrations of Sterne* (1798), 24; M. M. Bakhtin, *Rabelais and his World*, 27.

99. Goodman, *Pathologies of Motion*, 57–58.

100. John Ferriar, "Comments on Sterne," 47. Thomas Mallon, *Stolen Words*, 17, claims that Sterne scholars tend to see Ferriar as "a literalist in the funhouse" but—rightly to my mind—judges *Illustrations* reveals him to be "lacking in neither literary sophistication nor a sense of humour."

101. Ferriar, *Illustrations of Sterne*, 181, 273.

102. Cooper, "Sketch of the Controversy," 222.

103. John Ferriar, "Of Popular Illusions," 24, 103.

104. Leonard Smith, *Lunatic Hospitals in Georgian England*, 69. The Lunatic Hospital had been added to the infirmary in 1763. On Ferriar's work in the asylum, see also Roy Porter, *Mind-Forged Manacles*; Richard Hunter and Ida Macalpine, *Three Hundred Years of Psychiatry 1535—1860*.

105. Ferriar, *Medical Histories*, 2:112, 86, 109.

106. John Ferriar, *An Essay Towards a Theory of Apparitions*, 13–14. Subsequent quotations are given in the main text.

107. Goodman, *Pathologies of Motion*, 45.

108. See Michelle Faubert, "John Ferriar's Psychology," 84, on "readerly pleasure."

109. On Coleridge's interest in Ferriar's original paper, see Nethercot, *Road to Tryermaine*, 59–62, 90. Nora Crook's "Shelley and His Waste-Paper Basket" identifies a reference to Ferriar in Shelley's annotations. See also Ina Ferris, "'Before Our Eyes'"; Faubert, "John Ferriar's Psychology"; Terry Castle, "Phantasmagoria."According to his diary (viewable online), Godwin read the *Essay towards a Theory of Apparitions* over April 16–17, 1816, and may have returned to it in 1820. See William Godwin's Diary.

110. Helen Groth, *Moving Images*, vi.

111. John Ferriar, "Essay on the Dramatic Writings of Massinger." William Gifford reprinted the essay in Philip Massinger, *The Plays of Philip Massinger with notes critical and explanatory, by W. Gifford*. See Coleridge, *Notebooks 1808-1819*, 3445.

112. Ferriar, "Dramatic Writings of Massinger," 136, 125.

113. John Aikin Jr., "On the Impression of Reality Attending Dramatic Representations," 97–98, 101. The *Manchester Mercury* on October 4 advertised Aikin's paper as the first of the 1791–92 season.

114. Ferris, "'Before Our Eyes,'" 65.

115. The *Quarterly Review* 9 (1813): 31, insisted that such experiences had ultimately to be traced to a source "in the immortality of the soul: whether this be a traditional fragment of revelation, or an induction formed from dreams."

116. *Blackwood's Edinburgh Magazine* 3 (1818): 595. The comment appears in a comic review essay under the title "PHANTASMAGORIANA" written by J. H. Merivale. See A. L. Strout, *Bibliography of Articles in Blackwood's Magazine*, 63.

CHAPTER FIVE

1. "Collected Letters of Hannah Greg," quoted in Peter Spencer, *A Portrait of Hannah Greg*, 17. This chapter makes copious use of the archives at Quarry Bank Mill and the correspondence held at the Liverpool University Library (LUL) and Liverpool Record Office (LRO). Hannah Greg arranged 4 volumes of "Collected Letters" lost since Spencer prepared his *Portrait of Hannah Greg* and *A Portrait of Samuel Greg*. Wherever possible I have used the original manuscripts but quoted from Spencer's two volumes when necessary.

2. Joseph Priestley, "Reflections on Death" (1790), in *Works*, 15:419.

3. Winifred Faraday was elected an ordinary member in April 1900, *MLPSM* 44 (1899–1900): xx. The previous year she had given the paper "On the question of Irish influence on Early Icelandic Literature," *MLPSM* 44 (1899–1900): 1–22.

4. Helen Plant's *Unitarianism, Philanthropy, and Feminism* is a useful discussion of Cappe's philanthropic activism. See also Jane Rendall, "The Principle of Mutual Support: Female Friendly Societies in Scotland, c. 1789–1830." Cappe's *Account of two charity schools for the education of girls*, 69–70, adverted to John Ferriar's discussion of domestic violence caused by drunkenness in his *Medical Histories* (1st ed., 2:208).

5. On Rawson, see Twells, *Civilising Mission*. Wilberforce told Thomas Babington that "for ladies to meet, to publish, to go from house to house stirring up petitions—these appear to me proceedings unsuited to the female character as delineated in

Scripture." Robert Wilberforce and Samuel Wilberforce, *Life of William Wilberforce*, 5:264–65.

6. Joseph Hunter, "Biographical Notices," BL Add MS 36527, f. 51. Hunter's letters home from York mention Cappe regularly, including the pleasure he took in meeting with her the daughters of William Cullen, whom he found "entertaining conversers" with intimate knowledge of "almost all the Scotch literati" (Add MS 35161, f. 62). Cullen's daughters moved to York in 1798. Plant, *Unitarianism, Philanthropy, and Feminism*, 19.

7. Norma Clarke, *Ambitious Heights*, 6.

8. David N. Livingstone, *Putting Science in Its Place*, 78.

9. David Sekers, *A Lady of Cotton*, 143.

10. Ellen Melly, "Reminiscences, October 1889," "Memorials about the Family of Greg," QBA765.1/9/79/32, f. 31, Quarry Bank Archive (QBA), National Trust.

11. Thomas Gisborne, *An Inquiry into the Duties of the Female Sex*, 21, 23.

12. John Ferriar, *Prince of Angola*, viii.

13. Arianne Chernock, *Men and the Making of Modern British Feminism*, 23. William Shepherd of Liverpool was also a staunch defender of women's rights. See William Shepherd to Frances Shepherd, [summer 1798?], in William Shepherd, *A Selection from the Early Letters of the Late William Shepherd*, 74.

14. Thomas Cooper, "Propositions respecting the Foundation of Civil Government," 491; Thomas Cooper, *Reply to Mr. Burke's invective*, 81.

15. See the previous chapter on Philips's recantation and the evidence on Ferriar's role in writing the pamphlet.

16. John Aikin Jr., *Letters from a father to his son*, 341.

17. Ruth Watts, *Gender, Power and the Unitarians*, 66, 68, 123. William Turner to Mary Turner, 29 January 1812, notes that his daughter had "perused the strong and often coarse, though too often well-founded strictures, of Mrs Wollstonecraft," in Elizabeth Gaskell, *Private Voices*, 115.

18. Mary Robberds, "Recollections of a Long Life," in E. Gaskell, *Private Voices*, 109–10. Plant, *Unitarianism, Philanthropy, and Feminism*, 14, notes that her husband J. G. Robberds was studying at Manchester College York when Cappe was a regular visitor. Gaskell stayed with the Turners in Newcastle before her marriage. Chapter 7 of this book provides further details.

19. Harriet Martineau, *Autobiography*, 54, 104.

20. "Books Recommended to be Ordered," Newcastle Literary and Philosophical Society (NLPS). The new category of membership was confirmed at the annual meeting on March 15, 1799. See Literary and Philosophical Society of Newcastle upon Tyne, *A Historical Sketch of the Transactions of the Literary and Philosophical Society of Newcastle upon Tyne*, 1.

21. Livingstone, *Putting Science in Its Place*, 78.

22. Robberds, "Recollections of a Long Life," 110.

23. "Reports of the Monthly Meetings," July and August 1801, NLPS. Paul Gailiunas has pointed out to me that the monthly minutes show an increase in the participation of establishment figures from the summer of 1801 onward. Their appearance, suggests the growing desire for respectability that Eneas Mackenzie later complained about and perhaps helps explain why Barbauld and Hays were not elected as honorary members. See Gailiunas, "Women during the Early Years of the Newcastle Lit and Phil," 151–52.

24. The proposal was that "ladies be admitted to Lectures and public meetings by

subscribing for a sum of 8 guineas per annum." General meeting of May 16, 1828, "General Minute Book of Transactions (1821–41)."

25. "Hackney Literary Institution and Subscription Library: Minutes of the Proceedings of the Committee, Monthly & Anniversary Meetings," D/S/36/1, Hackney Archives, London.

26. On Elizabeth Lightbody's circle, see Sekers, *Lady of Cotton*, 43 and 47. James Currie was particularly close to Cropper, who helped him build up a client base when he first moved to Liverpool. See W. W. Currie, *Memoir of James Currie*, 1:66. On Hannah Lightbody's time in London, see Sekers, *Lady of Cotton*, 25–26.

27. Entry for April 6, 1787, "Diary of Hannah Lightbody 1786/1790," 49–50. R. Watts, *Gender, Power and the Unitarians*, 67, suggests that daughters "were often deliberately sent to visit relatives and friends within the tightly knit yet disparate intellectual and cultured Unitarian network in order to extend their education." Among Barbauld's visitors was Eliza Fletcher's daughter, who was invited to stay at Quarry Bank on the way south: Hannah Greg (HG) to Elizabeth Rathbone, 20 May 1815, RP IV.1.112, Rathbone Papers, LUL. See also Betsy Rodgers, *Georgian Chronicle*, 101–2.

28. Entries for June 11, 1788, and December 31, 1786, "Diary of Hannah Lightbody," 72, 1.

29. John Morley, "W. R. Greg: A Sketch," 111, claimed that the household's "taste was formed by Mrs. Barbauld and Dr. Channing." Morley seems to have had unprecedented access to the Greg family papers. From this point on, references to Morley's essay are given in the main text.

30. Her entry for June 4, 1788, "Diary of Hannah Lightbody," 72, records going to Manchester and "finding Dr & Mrs P always kind and friendly."

31. Melinda Elder, "The Liverpool Slave Trade," 122, 132–33. Hannah Greg records sitting up with Hodgson, Currie, and Roscoe until early the next morning on May 26, 1789. She spent the next day at Hodgson's and discussed "difficulties in Morals"; "Diary of Hannah Lightbody," 70. The following month, on June 10, she arrived home to find the household full of anxiety over the bankruptcy of one of Hodgson's partners in the trade, rather than its moral consequences.

32. The entry for March 2, 1788, "Diary of Hannah Lightbody," 63, refers to "The African" by the names of its protagonists "Marratan and Adela.". See the account of its origins in W. Currie, *Memoir of James Currie*, 1:109–37. Currie discussed Roscoe's *The Wrongs of Africa* with Hannah Lightbody on March 16.

33. Currie told Ann Duncan, "Of all society I must esteem that of men of sound sense and enlarged understandings; and next to that, I am fond of the company of women." He told Graham Moore that his Literary Club debated the question of female education. W. Currie, *Memoir of James Currie*, 1:58, 2:141.

34. "Diary of Hannah Lightbody," 11.

35. HG's comments on the Octonian were made January 3, 1787, "Diary of Hannah Lightbody," 9. The diary, 79, shows that she studied "Reid on the active Powers" in August 1788. Currie had reviewed Reid's book for the *Analytical Review* 1 (1788): 145–53, 521–29. The Seward-Reeve debate ran over several issues of the *Gentleman's Magazine* in 1786. Seward, another favorite author in these circles, defended the right of women. The diary shows that Currie took Christie to call on Hannah Lightbody on June 18, 1787, and entertained her at supper with Christie and Roscoe the next evening. After HG's death, William Smyth, Regius Professor of History at Cambridge, told Roscoe that he was "the last of a Triumvirate [with Currie and Rathbone] that she had been long accustomed to look up to," Smyth to Roscoe, 4 April, 1828, 920 ROS/4650. Shortly afterward,

Smyth sent Roscoe an epitaph he had composed for her; 920 ROS/1835. Roscoe and Smyth were regular house guests at Quarry Bank. See William Roscoe to Jane Roscoe, September 1817, 920 ROS/3566/22, and William Stanley Roscoe to William Roscoe, 6 April 1820, 920 ROS/4197.

36. Entries of February 13 and May 10, 1787, "Diary of Hannah Lightbody," 14, 23.

37. Dugald Stewart, *Account of Thomas Reid*, 108; Nigel Leask, "Robert Burns and Scottish Common Sense Philosophy," 70–87.

38. Entry of May 19, 1787, "Diary of Hannah Lightbody," 25, a week or so after she had been present at the argument between Currie and Godwin on materialism.

39. Mary Rose, *The Gregs of Quarry Bank Mill*, 8. For Samuel Greg's family background, see 13.

40. Samuel Greg continued to buy enslaved people after he inherited the Hillsborough estate from his uncle in 1795. See the inventory dated April 22, 1818, MS RCMS 266/4, Royal Commonwealth Society Library, Cambridge University, and "The Greg Estate Documents," *Royal Commonwealth Library Notes*, new ser., 90 (June 1986): 1–3. Thomas Greg, his eldest son, claimed for the loss of 210 enslaved people at abolition in 1833. See *Interim Report on the Connections between Colonialism and Properties now in the Care of the National Trust* and "UCL Legacies of British Slave-ownership," in the online database of the UCL Centre for the Study of the Legacies of British Slavery, https://www.ucl.ac.uk/lbs/person/view/10314. The Gregs also had strong family links with the Hibbert family of West India merchants discussed in Katie Donington's "Transforming Capital."

41. Rose, *Gregs of Quarry Bank Mill*, 9, 17, 19–23. Ewart, a member of the Literary and Philosophical Society, had trained with Boulton and Watt. A steam engine to supplement the waterpower was introduced at Quarry Bank in 1807.

42. She wrote imagining Samuel at Mosley Street but wanted his presence there to be "the consequence of your own inclination rather than a compliance with my opinion & desires." QBA765.1/9/6/5.

43. Sekers, *Lady of Cotton*, 89. Rose, *Gregs of Quarry Bank Mill*, 16, sees his membership primarily in terms of consolidating his commercial networks, 9.

44. Entries of March 11, 1787, and [nd] 1790, "Diary of Hannah Lightbody," 17, 117.

45. William Rathbone to HG, [nd], RP II.1 56, Rathbone Papers, LUL; Melly, "Reminiscences," 34.

46. HG to William Rathbone, 29 July 1794, RP II.1.62, Rathbone Papers, LUL.

47. Spencer, *Portrait of Hannah Greg*, 14, 15.

48. HG to William Rathbone, April 1798, RP II 1.65, Rathbone Papers, LUL.

49. Catriona Kennedy, "'Womanish Epistles?'" 660–61.

50. HG to Hannah Rathbone, April 1798, RP II.1.65. The same letter revealed the name of an informant—Robert Gray—active nearby. See Albert Goodwin, *Friends of Liberty*, 439–41; Emily Rathbone, *Records of the Rathbone Family*, 348–58.

51. HG to Thomas Pares III, 9 June 1823, D5336/3/214/30 Pares Collection.

52. Spencer, *Portrait of Samuel Greg*, 13. She told Hannah Rathbone that Samuel had deputed her to consult with her husband on the campaign of the Manchester textile merchants against the monopoly of the East India Company. HG to Hannah Rathbone, 18 December 1792, RP II.1.60, Rathbone Papers, LUL. She added a note: "I believe I have now done as a Woman of Business," before turning to a new book of poems by her cousin Samuel Rogers. William Roscoe acknowledged both husband and wife as experts on the state of manufacturing in the area. William Roscoe to HG [1809?], 920 RoS/1835.

53. HG to William Rathbone, 29 July 1794, RP II.1.62, Rathbone Papers, LUL; William Rathbone to HG, [1795], in Emily Rathbone, *Records of the Rathbone Family*, 346.

54. HG to William Rathbone, 1797, in Spencer, *Portrait of Hannah Greg*, 6–7; James Currie to HG, 27 March 1800, in W. Currie, *Memoir of James Currie*, 2:188.

55. HG described *A Collection of Maxims*, [i]–ii, as originally conceived as "an useful legacy to her children, gleaned from her reading and reflection," printed only because of difficulties in gaining enough copies for a large family, and "not intended for the public."

56. QBA765.1/9/6/6. She named her primary source as Joseph Ritson's *The Spartan Manual*.

57. HG, *Moralist*, 140, from Jebb's *Works Theological, medical, political, and miscellaneous*, 2:105.

58. HG, *Collection of Maxims*, 3, 49.

59. Jane Rendall, "Adaptations: Gender, History, and Political Economy," 144. See also her "'Elementary Principles of Education.'"

60. Dugald Stewart, *Elements of the Philosophy of the Human Mind*, 1:20.

61. Dugald Stewart, *Outlines of Moral Philosophy*, 8.

62. Greg told Rathbone that she had by her "both Reid and Stewarts large works from which I have formerly experienced more pleasure as well as improvement than perhaps from any books I ever read," but as she was unwell "'Outlines' will just suit us—and be a text book for conversation into which my reading generally subsides." HG to William Rathbone, 1 October 1806, RP II.1.69, Rathbone Papers, LUL.

63. Spencer, *Portrait of Hannah Greg*, 20.

64. Mary Ann to Robert Roscoe, 13 December 1807, 920 ROS/3625. I'm grateful to Mary Fairclough for suggesting Jeremiah Joyce's six volumes. Joyce was a close friend of William Shepherd.

65. HG, *Collection of Maxims*, iii. See Stewart, *Elements*, 1:40. HG's papers contain an exercise book addressed to her children's Duodecimo Society into which a passage from "Stewarts Philosophy of the Human Mind" is copied as a preface. QBA765.1/9/6/33.

66. HG, *Collection of Maxims*, iv.

67. Samuel Greg to Thomas Greg, 27 February 1814, QBA, on loan from K. Walker, L5180, no. 165.

68. HG to William Rathbone IV, 1 October 1806, RP II 1.69, Rathbone Papers, LUL. Underlining in the original. Greg described Edgeworth as "inimitable in telling a story, or drawing a character, but I question whether I should have read 'Leonora' to them had I not found that they had picked it up at L[. . .]pool last winter – It is rather too French I think."

69. She described the Edgeworths as "amiable, attached and most happy in each other," but complained that the father "talks so incessantly & in such a boastfully egotistical manner that we could scarce hear Miss E speak." HG to Tom Greg, 15 April 1813, QBA L5810. Edgeworth gave her own account to Charlotte Sneyd on April 19, 1813: 'While we were at Mr Holland's Mrs Gregg, wife to Mr Ewart's partner came from Manchester to spend a day with us. She is a particular friend of Mr Holland's & behold we found her to be the very lady with the 12 well behaved children at whose house. Mrs E Hamilton spent so much time. She described the family to us in one of her letters." I am grateful to Jane Rendall for providing this reference from the Edgeworth correspondence in the National Museum of Ireland, Dublin, MS 10166/7, no. 901.

70. HG, *Collection of Maxims*, 44. This passage was left out of the later collections. See David Sekers, "'The Cultivation of Mind and Refinement of Manners,'" 169.

71. HG to Tom Pares III, 10 July 1812, D5/336/3/214/6/2, Pares Collection. Robert Hyde Greg, who eventually took over the mill at Quarry Bank, did join the Literary and Philosophical Society in 1817, where he gave a paper on his travels. See Robert Hyde Greg, *Travel Journals of Robert Hyde Greg of Quarry Bank Mill*.

72. HG, "To the Duodecimo," QBA 765.1/9/6/33.

73. William Rathbone to HG, [1795?], in Emily Rathbone, *Records of the Rathbone Family*, 345.

74. HG, "The Art of Happy Living," QBA 1/9/6/47. This text is an exposition of HG's educational principles in the form of a lengthy letter of advice to Tom Greg. See Sekers, *Lady of Cotton*, 146–47. This is probably the "old letter" that she discussed several times with her daughter Bessy after Jane Roscoe had asked her to copy and circulate it. She comforted herself to think "that I may perhaps have occasionally touched their hearts (for my aim used to be to make from circumstances impressions) on subjects the most important." RP VI.1.120, Rathbone Papers, LUL.

75. HG, *Virtue made Easy*, iii.

76. Spencer, *Portrait of Hannah Greg*, 19.

77. HG, *Virtue made Easy*, iii–iv.

78. HG, *Collection of Maxims*, 97.

79. Samuel Greg built an Apprentice House in 1790, by which time Quarry Bank had about 90 parish apprentices, making up about half the workforce. Millowners received a premium for taking them. Numbers declined thereafter but remained an important part of the labor force until well into the 1840s. Other children worked under contract, often provided by parents receiving poor relief: Katrina Honeyman, *Child Workers in England*, 103; Rose, *Gregs of Quarry Bank Mill*, 31–32; Sekers, *Lady of Cotton*, 237.

80. William Turner, "Tour through the North of England," 256.

81. See Michael Meranze, *Laboratories of Virtue*. Meranze's brilliant study of the contradictions within liberal ideas of prison reform in the United States of this period touches on many of the themes raised in this book.

82. Rose, *Gregs of Quarry Bank Mill*, 2.

83. Alfred Kydd, *History of the Factory Movement*, 1:30–33; Rose, *Gregs of Quarry Bank Mill*, 134–37.

84. W. Currie, *Memoir of James Currie*, 1:456.

85. W. Currie, *Memoir of James Currie*, 1:456, 160–61.

86. HG to Elizabeth Rathbone, 2 October 1813, RP VI 1.109, Rathbone Papers, LUL. George Philips would have shared Greg's insider knowledge. In 1816, as the representative of the Manchester cotton lobby on the Committee on the employment of children in factories, Philips interrogated Owen so ferociously on his religious opinions that Henry Brougham, as chair, had the exchanges struck from the record, as chronicled in Robert Owen, *Life of Robert Owen*, 121.

87. [Edward Hyde Greg], "Memoranda of Quarry Bank from its commencement about 1784," Memorandum Book 1, f/2, QBA. Katrina Honeyman, "The poor law, the parish apprentice," 132–33, notes Samuel Greg's "careful supervision of the children," acknowledging the provision of decent nourishment, by the standards of the time, and access to a doctor (Peter Holland). However, in *Child Workers in England*, 188, she details cases of runaways such as Joseph Sefton, who complained of missing school because he was kept behind after work to clean machines.

88. Spencer, *Portrait of Hannah Greg*, 11.

89. HG to Thomas Greg, 15 April 1810, QBA Greg Letter Book 1.46. The torrent of

advice Hannah sent to Thomas Greg in preparation for his removal to London, where he worked in the family-owned insurance firm, was gathered into the manuscript book entitled "The Art of Happy Living," QBA 765 1/9/6/47. See note 74.

90. HG to Elizabeth Rathbone, [1805?], RP XXV 10.2 (2), Rathbone Papers, LUL.

91. HG, *Monitor*, 64.

92. "Sermons for the Apprentices" [1819–20], QBA 765 1/9/1/48. The text was: "To teach us to number our days" (Psalms 9:12).

93. HG to Elizabeth Rathbone, October 1813, RP VI I.109, Rathbone Papers, LUL.

94. HG, *Monitor*, 65.

95. HG to Elizabeth Rathbone, 23 and 24 August 1819, RP VI I.129 and 130, Rathbone Papers, LUL.

96. Morley's "W. R. Greg: A Sketch," 11, mentions the book being used in Carpenter's school.

97. Henry Holland to Lucy Aikin, 29 September 1809, MS 16087/3, Bodleian Library, Oxford. The letter reveals Holland had recommended Lucy Aikin's poetry to Hannah Greg. Henry Holland was the son of Peter Holland, physician to the family and to the apprentices at Quarry Bank. He was educated at William Turner's school in Newcastle from 1799, which he describes in his correspondence with his father, MS 16087/4, Bodleian Library.

98. Eliza Fletcher, *Autobiography of Mrs Fletcher*, 97. Samuel Greg asked to be remembered "to all the Fletcher family, to Mrs. Hamilton" when he wrote to Robert to give him advice on his studies: Samuel Greg to Robert Greg, 26 February 1814, QBA 765 1/9/5/2. Henry Holland also described his time with the Fletchers while studying at Edinburgh in his correspondence with his father. Jane Rendall discusses Fletcher's circle in "'Women that Would Plague Me,'" 327. Fletcher regularly visited Catharine Cappe in York. See Plant, *Unitarianism, Philanthropy, and Feminism*, 19.

99. HG to Elizabeth Rathbone, [1805?], RP XXV.10.2 (2), Rathbone Papers, LUL.

100. Samuel Greg to Thomas Greg, 27 February 1814. Sekers, *Lady of Cotton*, 138–49, provides details of the children's education.

101. HG to Elizabeth Rathbone, 21 May [1816?], RP VI.1.114, Rathbone Papers, LUL.

102. HG to Thomas Greg, 1 April 1814, QBA, on loan from K. Walker L5810.

103. HG to Thomas Greg, 1 March 1814, QBA765 1/9/6/17.

104. HG to Elizabeth Rathbone [1817?], RP VI I.120, Rathbone Papers, LUL.

105. Spencer, *Portrait of Hannah Greg*, 27.

106. John James Tayler to HG, 17 October 1820, QBA, on loan from K. Walker, L5810. Despite his sympathy for the idea of a national church, Tayler's "rational Christianity" precluded him from subscribing to its articles. Tayler's *On Communion with Unbelievers* argued against the exclusion of anyone from the chapel on the basis of any religious test.

107. Howard M. Wach, "Unitarian Philanthropy and Cultural Hegemony," 546.

108. Sekers, *Lady of Cotton*, 162–69, 188–93, details the educational roles of the Greg children at the mill.

109. "Journal of Elizabeth Greg," in Emily Rathbone, *Records of the Rathbone Family*, describes a visit "to see manufactures. Singeing, muslins, cutting fustians" (287) and later the violent reception of Roscoe on his return to Liverpool (289–91).

110. Elizabeth Rathbone to HG, 5 June 1818, RP VI.1.189, Rathbone Papers, LUL. Shortly afterward, Bessy also reported on a scheme for "collecting pennies on the same plan as the Bible ass. To save for coals & winter clothing." RP VI 1.191. Her mother's response to these schemes is at RP VI.1.124. For Bessy's later social activism, see Kitty Wilkinson, *Memoir of Kitty Wilkinson 1786–1860*; Eleanor Rathbone, *William Rath-*

bone, 50–51; Sekers, *Lady of Cotton*, 166–68, 235–37; Emily Rathbone, *Records of the Rathbone Family*, 171. Robert Owen gave Bessy a detailed account of his New Harmony experiment on his return from the United States: Emily Rathbone, *Records of the Rathbone Family*, 375–78.

111. James Martineau's description of Samuel Greg Jr.'s beliefs in Samuel Greg Jr., *A Layman's Legacy in Prose and Verse*, 59.

112. S. Greg Jr., *Layman's Legacy*, 3.

113. Samuel Greg Jr., *Two letters to Leonard Horner, Esq*, 22.

114. Elizabeth Gaskell to Lady Kay-Shuttleworth, 16 July [1850?], in Elizabeth Gaskell, *Letters of Mrs Gaskell*, 120.

115. Friedrich Engels, *The Condition of the Working Class in England*, 195.

116. Samuel Greg Jr. to Dr. C[arpenter], 16 May 1823, from the transcription made in 1963, MSS. Shorthand 2, HMCO. After Samuel Greg Sr.'s death, the estates passed to Thomas, and then—after his death five years later—to the other brothers. See UCL Centre for the Study of the Legacies of British Slavery. Samuel Greg Jr. sold his share of the plantation to his brother Robert in 1845.

117. John Seed, "Unitarianism, Political Economy, and the Antinomies of Liberal Culture," 9, discusses the stresses and strains caused in middle-class lives by these contradictions. Elizabeth Green Musselman, *Nervous Conditions*, explores similar territory, including the suicide of William Henry, friend of the Gregs and pupil of John Ferriar.

CHAPTER SIX

1. Frank Podmore, *Robert Owen*, 66. During the campaign to extend the act to all children after 1815, Peel acknowledged the help of Thomas Percival and "other eminent medical gentlemen of Manchester" with the 1802 Act. "Report of the minutes of evidence, taken before the Select Committee on the State of the Children Employed in the Manufactories of the United Kingdom." HC 397 (1816) 3: 133. Peel also cited the resolutions proposed by Percival for the consideration of the Board of Health in January 1796, 139.

2. William Wordsworth, *The Excursion*, 8:89–97. See Mary Wedd, "Industrialization and the Moral Law in *The Excursion*," and Philip Connell, *Romanticism, Economics and the Question of "Culture,"* 160–81.

3. See the discussion of Southey's *Quarterly* essays in Connell, *Romanticism, Economics*, 241–47. Most of them were collected in Robert Southey, *Essays, Moral and Political* (1832).

4. Margaret Jacob, *First Knowledge Economy*, 99.

5. See W. H. Chaloner, "Robert Owen, Peter Drinkwater, and the Early Factory System," and E. M. Fraser's account of Owen's involvement in the Literary and Philosophical Society discussed in chapters 1 and 4.

6. R. S. Fitton and A. P. Wadsworth, *The Strutts and the Arkwrights*, 192–93.

7. Kennedy described Owen and his employer Drinkwater visiting his business to inspect the mule he had adapted to "artificial power" in John Kennedy, "Brief Memoir of Samuel Crompton," 342–43. Kennedy's "Brief Notice of my Early Recollections," in his *Miscellaneous Papers on Subjects connected with the Manufactures of Lancashire*, 17–18, recalled that Owen bought rovings from his firm.

8. Robert Owen, *Life of Robert Owen*, 22. See also Chaloner, "Robert Owen," 80. Advertisements in the *Manchester Mercury* for January 18 and 25, 1791, show that Owen's

partnership was making water frames and mules. The surrounding newspaper columns contain multiple job opportunities for managers, as capitalists looked for people with the skills to integrate the labor and machinery necessary in the new cotton mills. For the general picture in Manchester at this stage, see A. E. Musson and E. Robinson, "Early Growth of Steam Power."

9. Chaloner, "Robert Owen," 87, speculates that Drinkwater's wish to keep his factory "sweet and wholesome" influenced Owen's innovations at New Lanark.

10. Owen, *Life of Robert Owen*, 56–57.

11. This mantra echoes through Owen's *Life of Robert Owen* and appears in the epigraph to the first essay in *A New View of Society*, in *Selected Works of Robert Owen*, vol. 1, *Early Writings*, 33.

12. "Queries submitted to Mr. Dale," *MM* 2 (July 1796): 458–60.

13. The origins of the monitor are discussed in Ian Donnachie's *Robert Owen: Social Visionary*, 81–82.

14. Robert Owen, *A Statement regarding the New Lanark Establishment* (1812) in *Early Writings*,18, 14.

15. Owen, *A New View of Society*, 27–30. References to *A New View of Society* are given in the text from this point onward.

16. Michael Ignatieff, *A Just Measure of Pain*, 146.

17. For Godwin's relationship with Owen, see Peter H. Marshall, *William Godwin*, 310–11. In Ferriar's "Dialogue in the Shades," *Illustrations of Sterne*, 295, Lucian debates with Neodictatus, a disciple of William Godwin's, who tells him, "Our only rule is the promotion of general good, by strict, impartial justice; whatever inconveniences may arise to individuals from this system we disregard them."

18. Edward Baines Jr., *Life of Baines*, 103–4, is careful to distance the deputation from ideas of any interest in socialism, noting that it was responding to local interest stirred by a talk Owen had given in Leeds on the problem of poor relief. Later John Marshall Jr. told Henry Brougham that the educational initiatives associated with the Mechanics' Institute in Leeds were a better prospect than the model at New Lanark: "I cannot help entertaining a hope that we shall be able be able to engraft on our little Holbeck Book Club, some plan of giving the children employed in the Mills some mental employment in the evenings, and that without so expensive a method as Mr. Owen's." John Marshall Jr. to Henry Brougham, 13 September [1826?] SDUK Papers.

19. See Hazlitt's review of *A New View of Society*, which first appeared in the *Examiner* in 1816, in William Hazlitt, *Complete Works*, 7:97–103. See also William Hazlitt, "People with one Idea," in *Complete Works*, 8:66–7.

20. See *Cobbett's Weekly Political Register*, August 2, 1817, 569–70, and the report of Wedderburn's interruption in the *Times*, August 22, 1817. Wedderburn was a proponent of Thomas Spence's radical land plan, from which the Literary and Philosophical Society of Newcastle upon Tyne was busily distancing itself at this time.

21. Robert Southey, *Journal of a Tour in Scotland in 1819*, 262–64. Tom Duggett provides an excellent discussion of the relationship between Owen and Southey in the introduction to his edition of Robert Southey, *Sir Thomas More: or, Colloquies on the Progress and Prospects of Society* (2018), 1:xxxvi–xliii.

22. Robert Southey, *Sir Thomas More: or, Colloquies on the Progress and Prospects of Society* (1824), 1:144–45, 177.

23. Anna Barbauld, "Thoughts on the Inequality of Condition," 15.

24. James Currie to W. W. Currie, 29 January and 19 February 1804, in W. W. Currie, *Memoir of James Currie*, 2:241–44.

25. Mitchell Dean, *Constitution of Poverty*, 93.

26. Karl Marx, *Capital*, 676.

27. Boyd Hilton, *The Age of Atonement*, 55–70, discusses the influence of Chalmers in England.

28. Thomas Chalmers, "Causes and Cure of Pauperism," 272.

29. Hazlitt, *Complete Writings*, 11:45; Hilton, *Age of Atonement*, 58; *Leeds Mercury*, November 3, 1827.

30. Thomas Malthus, *An Essay on the Principle of Population*, 394.

31. Dean, *Constitution of Poverty*, 84.

32. Owen remained in sufficient contact with M'Connel and Kennedy to ask them to enable visits to their factories. On February 19, 1807, for instance, Owen wrote to them introducing a partner in a Glasgow firm, "interested in the improvements presently in progress in weaving by power." He wrote "not knowing any who are better informed [of] the latest mechanical discoveries in Lancashire then yourselves." MCK 2/1/13, Papers of M'Connel and Kennedy, John Rylands Library (JRL), University of Manchester.

33. C. H. Lee, *A Cotton Enterprise*, 102–3, 105, 114. Kennedy acknowledged using a Savery engine to drive his mule in 1793 in Kennedy, "Memoir of Crompton," 341.

34. Jacob, *First Knowledge Economy*, 97–100.

35. Lee, *Cotton Enterprise*, 10–11, and Jacob, *First Knowledge Economy*, 87–94, discuss Kennedy's early life. For an account of the wider debate, see Maxine Berg's *The Machinery Question*.

36. Page references to Kennedy's "Observations on the Rise and Progress of the Cotton Trade" are given in the main text from this point onward.

37. Berg, *Machinery Question*, 195.

38. Mary Poovey, *Genres of the Credit Economy*, 1.

39. A point made by Jacob, *First Knowledge Economy*, 105.

40. Kennedy, "Early Recollections," 17. Jacob, 87, notes that Kennedy's father does seem to have gone to the university.

41. M'Connel and Kennedy to John Bell & co, 13 February 1816, MCK/2/2/5, Papers of M'Connel and Kennedy; Jacob, *First Knowledge Economy*, 106–7.

42. Adam Smith, *Wealth of Nations*, 2:367.

43. Andreas Malm, *Fossil Capital*, 93.

44. Dean, *Constitution of Poverty*, 95.

45. References to Kennedy's "Inquiry into the Effects Produced Upon Society by the Poor Laws" are given in the main text. The *Leeds Mercury*, February 4, 1837, accepted that "outdoor relief cannot be refused in these districts owing to the fluctuations in the amount of employment." See Derek Fraser, "Edwards Baines," 187.

46. B. A. Heywood, *Addresses 1822 & 1824* (1824), 45.

47. J. R. McCulloch, "Review of Charles Babbage," 323.

48. McCulloch, "Rise and Progress of the Cotton Manufacture," 135. McCulloch praised Kennedy as "one of the most eminent and intelligent cotton manufacturers in the Empire." Edward Baines Sr.'s *History, Directory, and Gazetteer* makes copious use of Aikin's *Description* of the canal system, "transcribed and enlarged by the description of subsequent extensions" (1:122–28), and the second volume used Kennedy's figures on the expansion of the cotton trade (2:134).

49. McCulloch voiced his encouragement in a footnote to his article on the "Present State of Manufactures," 46.

50. Edward Baines Jr., "History of Printing," WYAS 383/89, Papers of Edward Baines Jr., West Yorkshire Archives.

51. References to E. Baines Jr., *History of the Cotton Manufacture*, are given in the main text.

52. Malm, *Fossil Capitalism*, 213. The opposition Baines Jr. makes at length between Indian inertia and European inventiveness had an awkward time with the fact that the success of the British cotton industry had depended on taking various techniques from India and elsewhere, not to mention the general need to compete with the fine quality of Indian exports.

53. Giorgio Riello, *Cotton*, 228.

54. Malm, *Fossil Capital*, 140, describes the colony mill as a "laboratory" where "the capitalist and his managers could plan the living quarters, write the rules, patrol the streets, inspect the workers in their homes, keep records of their manners, oversee the instruction of reverence in the schools and through numerous other techniques fuse economic and social power in what took on a character similar to that of a totalitarian system." Much of his evidence is taken from the archives at Quarry Bank.

55. Erasmus Darwin, *The Botanic Garden*, 27ff, has an extended anthropomorphic description of a steam engine that is quoted in both Aikin Jr.'s *Description* (505) and Baines Jr.'s *History of the Cotton Manufacture* (186–87).

56. Baines reinforces his incorporation of the steam engine into the tradition of English Protestant liberty by incidental biographical comments—for example, the observation that Edward Cartwright, inventor of the power loom, was "brother of Major Cartwright, the well-known advocate of radical reform" (229).

57. On previous uses of the word "revolution" in relation to technical change rather than a notion of a decisive historical break, see Witt Bowden, *Industrial Society in England*, 71–72. D. C. Coleman, *Myth, History, and the Industrial Revolution*, 15, suggests that Baines's use of the word "revolution" is restricted to changes in manufacturing processes rather than any larger paradigm shift.

58. Andrew Ure, *Philosophy of Manufactures*, 15.

59. Dipesh Chakrabarty, "Climate of History," 208.

60. McCulloch, "Rise and Progress of the Cotton Manufacture," 17.

61. Jacob, *Knowledge Economy*, 109, notes John Kennedy's role on the board of the Manchester Mechanics' Institution in the 1820s, where he helped set the curriculum, buy apparatus, and invite speakers. She judges the institution "a resounding success for several decades, in large part because it attracted the participation of workers and manufacturers alike." It did eventually prove to be a durable part of the civic culture of Manchester without ever achieving the success for which its early supporters hoped. Early excitement, as Mabel Tylecote, *Mechanics' Institutes*, 87, more soberly describes it, was followed by rapid disillusionment, both with the teaching methods and with the subjects of instruction.

CHAPTER SEVEN

1. James Losh, *Diaries and Correspondence*, 2:59–60.

2. James Phillips Kay, *Moral and Physical Condition*, 2nd ed., 63. Page references from this point onward are made in the main text, unless the reference is to the first edition. James Phillips Kay took on his wife's surname when they married in 1842 to become James Kay-Shuttleworth. He later became Lord Shuttleworth for his sustained service to state-sponsored social reform. The surname Kay will be used throughout this chapter as it focuses on the period before his marriage.

3. Mary Poovey, *Making a Social Body*, otherwise influential on my analysis here,

does not look back beyond some general connections with Adam Smith's thinking and Sir John Sinclair's early statistical enquiries.

4. An advertisement in the *Manchester Guardian* for March 31, 1832, described the first edition as "the substance of a paper given at the Literary and Philosophical Society on Friday 23rd March." On the chronology, see R. J. W. Selleck, *James Kay-Shuttleworth*, 64–65. According to Selleck (52), Kay had joined the Literary and Philosophical Society in 1829.

5. The memory of Phillips Kay quoting Shelley is John Bright's. See Selleck, *James Kay-Shuttleworth*, 59.

6. John V. Pickstone, "Ferriar's Fever to Kay's Cholera," 408.

7. Selleck, *James Kay-Shuttleworth*, 1–20, provides details of Kay's early family life. Edward Baines Jr. mentions his time at school in Manchester in his *Life of Baines*, 253. Later in life, Kay and Baines were adversaries in disputes about state education. Baines defended the rights of Dissenters to maintain their own schools, fearing Anglican dominance in any state education system. See Selleck, *James Kay-Shuttleworth*, 205.

8. James Phillips Kay to Thomas Chalmers, 13 December 1837, CHA 4.265.62, Chalmers Collection, University of Edinburgh. See also the discussion in Selleck, *James Kay-Shuttleworth*, 151. Stephen Harbottle, *William Turner*, 134–38, notes that in 1838, Edward Maltby, Bishop of Durham, faced attacks in the *Times* and protests in the streets for subscribing to Turner's collected sermons.

9. William Gaskell, *Protestant Practices Inconsistent with Protestant Principles*, 36.

10. Henry admitted that the contest with Kay had not been "a contest of comparative professional merit, but of local interest, and my father, who had formerly filled the same office carried the election by a large majority in my favour." Quoted in W. V. Farrar, Kathleen R. Farrar, and E. L. Scott, "The Henrys of Manchester, Part 6," 2. Henry wrote to Kay in 1832 hoping that their "estrangement" would not degenerate into any public scene. Soon afterward, he drifted away into the life of a retired country gentleman. W. C. Henry to James Phillips Kay, 1832, GB 133 JKS/1/1/66, Papers of James Phillips Kay-Shuttleworth, John Rylands Library (JRL), University of Manchester.

11. By 1834, though, Williamson was worrying that his young friend was sacrificing his medical practice to "politics and political economy." James Williamson to James Phillips Kay, December 1834, JKS/1/1/150.

12. James Phillips Kay, "Physical Condition of the Poor," 220.

13. John K. Walton, *Lancashire*, 123.

14. Review of *Memoir of the Life of James Currie*, by W. W. Currie, *North of England Medical Journal*, May 1831, 511.

15. Edmund Lyon, "Medical Topography and Manchester," 135.

16. [James Phillips Kay ?], review of *Laws of Population*, by Michael Sadler, *North of England Medical Journal*, August 1830, 105. The review of Thackrah's *The Effects of Arts, Trades, and Professions on Health and Longevity* appears in the issue of February 1831, 394–95.

17. James Phillips Kay, *A Letter to the People of Lancashire*, 16, 14.

18. G. B. Hindle, *Provision for the Relief of the Poor in Manchester*, 78–89.

19. Pickstone, "Ferriar's Fever to Kay's Cholera," 409.

20. Poovey, *Making a Social Body*, 80. Pickstone's analysis pays more attention to the "otherness of the poor" ("Ferriar's Fever to Kay's Cholera," 408), than abstraction as such. He represents the shift away from Ferriar as a "transfer of attention from the mutuality of individual contact to the abstract, law-governed operations of an environmental system including and determining the conditions of men and women" (412).

21. Friedrich Engels, *Condition of the Working Class*, 61, 73.

22. John Ferriar, *Medical Histories and Reflections*, 1st ed., 3:49.

23. Baines, *History of the Cotton Manufacture*, 465, quoting from Kay's second edition of *Moral and Physical Condition*. The first edition had been stronger on the dangers of "the prolonged labour of an animal—his physical energy wasted—his mind in supine inaction" reducing workers to "sensual sloth" at home (11). Baines quoted Kay's favorable account of Thomas Ashton's factories at length (*History of the Cotton Manufacture*, 447–51).

24. James Phillips Kay, *Moral and Physical Condition*, 1st ed., 28.

25. Kay prefaced his second edition with a lengthy dedication to Chalmers, who had suggested changes to the first edition. See James Phillips Kay to Thomas Chalmers 4 June 1832 CHA 4.183.4, Chalmers Collection, University of Edinburgh. Selleck, *James Kay-Shuttleworth*, 77, provides a useful summary of the changes between the editions.

26. From the statement drawn up by the Board of Health to present to the king quoted in William Brockbank, *Portrait of a Hospital*, 56. *Moral and Physical Condition*, 1st ed., 44, describes the work of Henry and Percival as "the best calculations on the subject."

27. Kay to Chalmers, 4 June 1832; James Phillips Kay to Thomas Chalmers, 21 November 1832, CHA.4.183.4. Both letters are discussed in Selleck, *James Kay-Shuttleworth*, 73.

28. Selleck, *James Kay-Shuttleworth*, 82. Details of the protracted courtship are given in Selleck's third chapter.

29. Greg's papers were published in the sixth volume of the second series of *MLPSM*. He also published *Sketches in Greece and Turkey* as a separate pamphlet.

30. W. R. Greg to James Phillips Kay, 24 December 1831, GB 133 JKS/1/1/65.

31. William Rathbone Greg, *An Enquiry into the State of the Manufacturing population*, 24.

32. W. R. Greg, *Enquiry*, 2, 3. Robert Southey, *Sir Thomas More: or, Colloquies on the Progress and Prospects of Society* (1824), 2:96, describes the "new cottages of the manufacturers" as "upon the manufacturing pattern . . . naked, and in a row."

33. W. R. Greg, *Enquiry*, 28, 8.

34. W. R. Greg, *Enquiry*, 30.

35. Robert Hyde Greg, *The Factory Question*, 70.

36. John Doherty, *Misrepresentations Exposed*, 21–23. See R. G. Kirby and A. E. Musson, *The Voice of the People*, 396–97, and Mary Rose, *Gregs of Quarry Bank Mill*, 136.

37. W. R. Greg, "The Employment of Machinery," *Voice of the People*, February 5, 1831, 44. On the same page, Doherty replied to Greg's near-hysterical closing letter of the previous week by accusing him of shortening his workers' statutory breaks and suggesting he keep his future letters for his "kindred spirits" at the *Manchester Guardian*. The initial letter and Doherty's response appear in *Voice of the People*, January 22, 1831, 28, 30. See also Kirby and Musson, *Voice of the People*, 219.

38. *Analysis of the Evidence taken before the Factory Commissioners*, 31–32. Read before the society in March 1834, the printed version is in "Appendix to the Minutes of the Statistical Society," GB127.BR MS f 310.6 M5/Volume 1, Papers of the Manchester Statistical Society, Manchester Central Library (MCL).

39. John Morley, "W. R. Greg: A Sketch," 114.

40. *Analysis of the Evidence*, 11. The Statistical Society's committee seemed less than enthusiastic about any crusade, noting that it had been "unable to determine what some parties might call 'immoral' and 'irreligious.'" The hesitancy may indicate a Unitarian aversion to pushing too much on matters of freedom of worship. Instead they simply

reported on "those [publications] with greatest circulation," which included the *Poor Man's Guardian*; Thomas Paine's *Rights of Man*; and *Cobbett's Legacy to Parsons*. See GB127.BR MS f 310.6 M5/Volume 1/11/45. The idea for the enquiry was Kay's, probably betraying the influence of Chalmers. *Second Report of the Manchester Statistical Society* (1835), GB127.BR MS f 310.6 M5/Volume 1/11/50.

41. Richard J. Helmstadter, "W. R. Greg: A Manchester Creed," 188, describes Greg's *Creed of Christendom* (1851) as articulating in religious terms "that general orientation towards material progress and scientific rationalism that is associated with the emergence of industrial society." In December 1833, Chalmers had promised to send his *Christian Economy* for the Statistical Society but said he felt he might be "obtruding" upon them "matter which might be felt by some to be beyond the proper sphere of your society." Thomas Chalmers to James Phillips Kay, 14 December 1833, JKS/1/1/91. Possibly he was aware of tensions between his religious views and Unitarian feeling in the society. Howard Wach, "Unitarian Philanthropy," 547, discusses the Unitarian suspicion of "tract mongers" among other denominations.

42. References to Benjamin Heywood's *Addresses Delivered at the Manchester Mechanics' Institution* (1843) are given in the text.

43. Heywood added his name to the list of those calling for a public meeting to discuss raising a statue to Watt, published in the *Manchester Guardian* June 26, 1824.

44. The Statistical Society's papers contain a flyer for "Manchester Mechanics Institution: Outline of a Course of Lectures on Political Economy 1834," Papers of the Manchester Statistical Society, MCL, GB127.BR MS f 310.6 M5/Volume 1/4. The series was introduced by Heywood; Kay lectured on "Distribution-Wages" and W. R. Greg on "Interchange-Restrictions."

45. Thomas Heywood, *A Memoir of Sir Benjamin Heywood*, 47, and Henry Brougham, *Practical Observations*, 24. Mabel Tylecote, *Mechanics' Institutes*, 128, 137, discusses Detrosier's New Institution. Detrosier's *On the Necessity of an Extension of the Moral and Political Instruction among the Working Classes* (1831) was commended by Doherty, as discussed in Kirby and Musson, *Voice of the People*, 334–35.

46. Tylecote, *Mechanics' Institutes*, 120, sees Kay's more pessimistic sense of industrial development as increasing its influence on Heywood after 1830. Heywood's 1832 address blamed the low subscriptions on the failures of the working classes themselves—their "physical and moral condition," as he put it—rather than the "active rivalry" of Detrosier's institution. He acknowledged the role of "long hours of labour" in exhausting their leisure time but explicitly followed Kay in placing any hope of "lightening of the burdens which press upon the people" in "a liberal commercial policy" and the "termination of commercial monopolies" (Heywood, *Addresses*, 56).

47. Tylecote, *Mechanics' Institutes*, 149–89.

48. *First Report of the Manchester Statistical Society, July 1834*, 1, printed for circulation to the members. GB127.BR MS f 310.6 M5/Volume 1/11.

49. M. J. Cullen, *The Statistical Movement in Early Victorian Britain*, 108–9.

50. The manuscript version of the Statistical Society's report on "Institutions for the Promotion of Literature & Science in Manchester" (1834) began with the Literary and Philosophical Society, implicitly acknowledging its premier position within the town's cultural institutions, GB127.BR MS f 310.6 M5/37 f.1.

51. *First Report of the Statistical Society*, 1.

52. See the invitation from William Langton, secretary, at GB127.BR MS f 310.6 M5/Volume 1/27. The committee appointed to revise the rules of the Statistical Society discussed the financial difficulties it faced because members did not adopt the subscription

model. They recommended voluntary contributions be sought. See "Draft report of the committee appointed to revise the rules of the Manchester Statistical Society, 15 Oct 1834," GB127.BR MS f 310.6 M5/Volume 1/27, f. 3. Cullen, *Statistical Movement*, 110, notes that the rule restricting membership was finally rescinded in 1837.

53. Cullen, *Statistical Movement*, 107. See also Eileen James Yeo, *Contest for Social Science*, 69–70.

54. James Phillips Kay, *Defects in the Constitution of Dispensaries*, 10, 6, 4. On the broader movement against medical charities in the period, see Michael Brown, "Medicine, Reform and the 'End' of Charity."

55. Tuckerman had been shocked by conditions in the manufacturing districts when he visited Britain in 1816. His return visit in 1833 inspired a domestic mission movement on a national scale. Among Tuckerman's closest friends was William Ellery Channing, associated with the "deepening spirituality" of Unitarianism. Wach, "Unitarian Philanthropy," 539–40. Channing's disciple John James Tayler had important connections with the Gregs, as we have seen, and with the Unitarian domestic missions set up in Manchester and Liverpool in the 1830s.

56. R. H. Greg and James M'Connel were among the stewards. J. T. Rutt told the assembled company that an old letter from Priestley he had in his pocket showed that William Turner of Newcastle, who was also present, had long ago proposed "this multiform society, which we see so happily completed." British and Foreign Unitarian Association, *Report of the proceedings of a meeting of the British and Foreign Unitarian association*, 12.

57. Chalmers and Tuckerman met in 1834. See Mary Theresa Furgol, "Thomas Chalmers: Poor Relief Theories," 396.

58. Manchester Statistical Society, *Report of a Committee of the Manchester Statistical Society on the Condition of the Working Classes*, 7, 5.

59. Cullen, *Statistical Movement*, 115, notes the poor response of clergy across the denominations to the 1835 survey.

60. Kay, *Defects*, 24.

61. Cullen, *Statistical Movement*, 110.

62. The individual reports from the committee to the subscribers are bound together as *Reports of the Ministry to the Poor commenced in Manchester Jan. 1, 1833* at UCC/5/13/4/1 in the JRL. These reports supplied summaries of and reflections on the individual reports sent to the committee by John Ashworth and George Buckland. Buckland emigrated to Australia in 1838.

63. *Fifth Report of the Ministry to the Poor* (1839), 25, and *Fourth Report* (1837), 20.

64. *Sixth Report of the Ministry to the Poor* (1840), 9, and "Manchester Mission from the Poor," *Christian Teacher* 4 (1838): 308. John Seed, "Unitarianism, Political Economy and the Antinomies of Liberal Culture," 17, sees these reports as having an important influence back on liberal ideology. See also Wach, "Unitarian Philanthropy," 547; David Steers, "Origin and Development of the Domestic Mission Movement"; Martin Hewett, "Travails of Domestic Visiting."

65. John Chapple, *Elizabeth Gaskell: Early Years*, 139–41.

66. Chapple, *Elizabeth Gaskell: Early Years*, 42, 162, 145.

67. Chapple, *Elizabeth Gaskell: Early Years*, 71, 162.

68. P. J. Yarrow, "Mrs Gaskell and Newcastle upon Tyne," 66.

69. Elizabeth Gaskell to William Turner, 6 October 1832, in Elizabeth Gaskell, *Further Letters of Elizabeth Gaskell*, 21–22, speaks of her hopes of being "a useful friend" to

members of her husband's congregation and expresses her thanks for Turner's daughter's help.

70. Yeo, *Contest for Social Science*, 66–67.

71. Monica Correa Fryckstedt, *Elizabeth Gaskell's Mary Barton*, 90–97, prints the relevant passages from the reports. See also Anthony Burton and Diane Duffy, "Elizabeth Gaskell and the Industrial Poor."

72. Elizabeth Gaskell, *Mary Barton*, 58–59. Subsequent page references to Gaskell's novel are given in the text.

73. William Rathbone Greg, "*Mary Barton: A Tale of Manchester Life*," 407–8. Subsequent page references are given in the main text.

74. Unitarian Domestic Mission, *Eighth Report of the Ministry to the Poor*, 18. Gaskell wrote: "The most deplorable and enduring evil that arose out of the period of depression to which I refer, was this feeling of alienation between the different classes of society" (*Mary Barton*, 82–83).

75. Elizabeth Gaskell to Edward Chapman, 9 March 1849, in Elizbeth Gaskell, *Letters of Mrs Gaskell*, 72.

76. Poovey, *Making a Social Body*, 133, 150–51.

77. Morley, "W. R. Greg: A Sketch," 109. Subsequent page references are given in the main text.

78. Morley, "W. R. Greg: A Sketch," 117, notes that Greg married the daughter of William Henry.

79. On Eleanor F. Rathbone's contribution to a wide range of advances in social welfare, see Susan Pederson, *Eleanor Rathbone and the Politics of Conscience*.

BIBLIOGRAPHY

MANUSCRIPTS

Bodleian Library
    Letters from Maria Edgeworth to Peter Holland and letters from Sir Henry Holland
        to Maria Edgeworth, Lucy Aikin, and Peter Holland
British Library
    "Collections relating to schools, mechanics' institutions, etc.": Francis Place Papers.
    "Collectanea Hunteriana": Collections of the Rev. Joseph Hunter
    Letters Addressed to Thomas Walker, 1749–1817
Brotherton Library, University of Leeds
    Leeds Philosophical and Literary Society (LPLS) Collections
Carlisle City Library
    Diary of James Losh
Derbyshire Record Office (DRO)
    Derby Literary and Philosophical Society, 1808–1816
    Pares Collection
Hackney Archives
    Hackney Literary Institution and Subscription Library
Henry E. Huntington Library
    De Quincey Correspondence
Harris Manchester College Oxford (HMCO)
    MSS, Shorthand
John Rylands Library (JRL), University of Manchester
    Papers of James Phillips Kay-Shuttleworth
    Papers of M'Connel and Kennedy
Library of Birmingham
    James Watt and Family Papers
Library Company of Philadelphia
    Rush Family Papers: Correspondence.
Liverpool Record Office (LRO), Central Library
    Diary of Thomas De Quincey (1803)
    Holt and Gregson Papers
    Liverpool Literary and Philosophical Society
    Roscoe Letters and Papers

Liverpool University Library (LUL)
    Liverpool Philomathic Society Archive
    Liverpool Royal Institution (LRI) Archive
    Rathbone Papers
Manchester Central Library (MCL)
    Appendix to the Minutes of the Statistical Society
National Archives, Kew
    Non-Conformist and Non-Parochial BMDs
Newcastle Literary and Philosophical Society (NLPS)
    Papers of the Literary and Philosophical Society of Newcastle upon Tyne
Royal College of Physicians of Edinburgh
    Consultation letter books of William Cullen
Royal Commonwealth Society Library, Cambridge University
    Greg Estate Documents
Quarry Bank Archive (QBA), National Trust
Sheffield City Archives (SCA) and Local Studies Library
    Sheffield Literary and Philosophical Society (SLPS)
    Sheffield Mechanics' and Apprentices' Library
    Sheffield University Library Special Collections
    Montgomery Manuscripts
Shropshire Archives
    Diary of Katherine Plymley
University College London (UCL)
    Henry Brougham Papers
    Society for the Diffusion of Useful Knowledge (SDUK) Papers
University of Edinburgh
    Chalmers Collection
Victoria and Albert Museum
    "Thomas Rickman's personal journals, 1807–1834," RIBA Library Drawings & Archives
Warwickshire County Record Office (WCRO)
    Autobiography of Sir George Philips, written in 1845
West Yorkshire Archives Service (WYAS)
    Papers of Edward Baines Jr.
York Minster Library
    Bradford Literary and Philosophical Society, Minute Book, 1808–14

PRIMARY TEXTS, SECONDARY TEXTS, AND DISSERTATIONS

Adelman, Richard, and Catherine Packham. "Introduction: The Formation of Political Economy as a Knowledge Practice." In *Political Economy, Literature and the Formation of Knowledge, 1720–1850*, edited by Adelman and Packham, 1–20. London: Taylor and Francis, 2018.

Aikin, John, Jr. *Essays on song-writing: with a collection of such English songs as are most eminent for poetical merit*. London, 1771.

———. *Thoughts on hospitals, by John Aikin, surgeon*. London, 1771.

———. *Essay on the Application of Natural History to Poetry*. Warrington, 1777.

———. *Biographical memoirs of medicine in Great Britain from the revival of literature to the time of Harvey*. London, 1780.

———. "Remarks on the different success with respect to Health, of attempts to pass the Winter in High Northern Latitudes." *MLPSM* 1 (1785): 89–109.

———. "An Apology for the Literary Pursuits of Physicians." *Gentleman's Magazine* 56 (1786): 667–69.

———. *An Address to the Dissidents of England on their Late Defeat*. London, 1790.

———. *Poems by John Aikin, M. D.* London, 1791.

———. *A View of the Character and Public services of the late John Howard, Esq.* London, 1792.

———. "On the Impression of Reality Attending Dramatic Representations." *MLPSM* 4 (1793): 96–108.

———. *Letters from a father to his son, on various topics, relative to literature and the conduct of life. Written in the years 1792 and 1793*. London, 1793.

———. *A Description of the country from thirty to forty miles round Manchester*. London, 1795.

Aikin, John, Jr., and Anna Laetitia Barbauld. *Miscellaneous Pieces in Prose*. 3rd ed. London, 1792.

———. *Evenings at Home, or The Juvenile Budget Opened*. 6 vols. London, 1792–96.

Aikin, John, Jr., and William Enfield. *General Biography, or lives, critical and historical, of the most eminent persons of all ages, countries, conditions, and professions*. 10 vols. London: 1799–1815.

Aikin, Lucy. *Memoir of John Aikin, MD with a Selection of Miscellaneous Pieces*. 2 vols. London, 1823.

———. *Memoirs; miscellanies and letters of the late Lucy Aikin; including those addressed to the Rev. Dr. Channing 1826 to 1842*. Edited by P. H. Le Breton. London: Longman, 1864.

Allan, David. *Making British Culture: English Readers and the Scottish Enlightenment, 1760–1830*. London: Routledge, 2008.

Bailey, Samuel. *Questions in Political Economy, Politics, Morals, Metaphysics, Polite Literature and Other Branches of Knowledge*. London, 1823.

———. *Essays on the Formation and Publication of Opinions and Other Subjects*. 2nd ed. London: 1826.

Baines, Edward, Jr. *Address to the Unemployed Workmen of Yorkshire and Lancashire, on the Present Distress, and on Machinery*. London, 1826.

———. *History of the Cotton Manufacture in Great Britain with a Notice of its Early History in the East, and in All the Quarters of the Globe*. London, 1835.

———. *The Life of Edward Baines, late MP for the borough of Leeds*. London: Longman, 1851.

Baines, Edward, Sr. *History, Directory, and Gazetteer, of the County Palatine of Lancaster, with a variety of Commercial and Statistical Information*. Liverpool, 1824–25.

Baker, Thomas. *Memorials of a Dissenting Chapel*. Manchester: Johnson and Rawson, 1884.

Bakhtin, M. M. *Rabelais and His World*. Translated by Helene Iswolsky. Bloomington: Indiana University Press, 1984.

Barbauld, Anna Laetitia [neé Aikin]. *Devotional Pieces, compiled from the Psalms and Book of Job*. London, 1775.

———. *Remarks on Mr. Gilbert Wakefield's Enquiry into the expediency and propriety of public or social worship*. London, 1792.

———. "What is Education?" *Monthly Magazine* 5 (1798): 167–71.

———. "Thoughts on the Inequality of Condition." *Athenaeum* 2 (July 1807): 14–19.

———. *Poems of Anna Letitia Barbauld*. Edited by William McCarthy and Elizabeth Kraft. Athens: University of Georgia Press, 1994.

Bardsley, Samuel Argent. "Cursory Remarks, Moral and Political, on Party-prejudice." *MLPSM* 5 (1798): 1–27.

———. *Critical remarks on Pizarro, a tragedy, taken from the German drama of Kotze-bue, and adapted to the English stage by Richard Brinsley Sheridan. With Incidental Observations on the Subject of the Drama*. London, 1800.

Barker, Hannah. "'Smoke Cities': Northern Industrial Towns in Late Georgian England." *Urban History* 31, no. 2 (2004): 176–90.

Barnes, Thomas. *A Discourse Delivered at the Commencement of the Manchester Academy*. Warrington, 1786.

———. "On the Nature and Essential Characters of Poetry, as distinguished from Prose." *MLPSM* 1 (1785): 54–72.

———. "On the Influence of the Imagination and the Passions upon the Understanding." *MLPSM* 1 (1785): 375–95.

———. "A plan for the improvement and extension of liberal education in Manchester." *MLPSM* 2 (1789): 16–30.

———. "Proposals for establishing in Manchester a plan of liberal education for young men designed for civil and active life." *MLPSM* 2 (1789): 30–46.

———. "Constitutions and Regulations of the College of Arts and Sciences in Manchester." *MLPSM* 2 (1789): 42–46.

Beddoes, Thomas. *Observations on the Nature and Cure of Calculus, Sea Scurvy, Consumption, Catarrh, and Fever*. London, 1793.

———. *Essay on the Public Merits of Mr. Pitt*. London, 1796.

Behrendt, Stephen. "Barbara Hofland and Romantic-Era Provincial Poetry by Women." *Women's Writing* 20, no. 4 (2013): 421–40.

Bennett, Jane. *Vibrant Matter: A Political Ecology of Things*. Durham, NC: Duke University Press, 2010.

Berg, Maxine. *The Machinery Question and the Making of Political Economy 1815–1848*. Cambridge: Cambridge University Press, 1980.

———. *The Age of Manufactures, 1700–1820: Industry, Innovation and work in Britain*. 2nd ed. London: Routledge, 1994.

———. "The Genesis of 'Useful Knowledge.'" *History of Science* 45, no. 2 (2007): 123–33.

Berg, Maxine, and Pat Hudson. "Rehabilitating the Industrial Revolution." *Economic History Review* 45, no. 1 (February 1992): 24–50.

Bergstrom, Carson. "Literary Coteries, Network Theory, and the Literary and Philosophical Society of Manchester." *ANQ* 26, no. 3 (2013): 180–88.

Bewick, Thomas. *A General History of the Quadrupeds*. 4th ed. Newcastle, 1800.

———. *A Memoir of Thomas Bewick, written by Himself*. Edited by Ian Bain. Oxford: Oxford University Press, 1975.

Bigge, Thomas. *An Address to the Public from the Literary and Philosophical Society of Newcastle upon Tyne*. Newcastle, 1802.

Borgatti, Stephen P., Martin G. Everett, and Jeffrey C. Johnson. *Analyzing Social Networks*. 2nd ed. London: Sage, 2018.

Bowden, Witt. *Industrial Society in England towards the End of the Eighteenth Century.* 2nd ed. London: Frank Cass, 1965.

Braithwaite, Helen. *Romanticism, Publishing and Dissent: Joseph Johnson and the Cause of Liberty.* Basingstoke: Palgrave Macmillan, 2003.

Briggs, Asa. *Victorian Cities.* London: Penguin Books, 1963.

British and Foreign Unitarian Association. *Report of the proceedings of a meeting of the British and Foreign Unitarian Association, held in [. . .] Manchester, and of the speeches [. . .] in the town hall, Salford.* Manchester, 1830.

British Association for the Advancement of Science. *Report of the First and Second Meetings of the British Association for the Advancement of Science, at York in 1831, and at Oxford in 1832.* London, 1833.

———. *Report of the Ninth Meeting of the British Association for the Advancement of Science.* London, 1840.

Brockbank, E. M. *Sketches of the Lives and Works of the Honorary Medical Staff of the Manchester Infirmary from Its Foundation in 1752 to 1830.* Manchester: Manchester University Press, 1904.

Brockbank, William. *Portrait of a Hospital 1752–1948 to Commemorate the Bi-Centenary of the Royal Infirmary, Manchester.* London: Heineman, 1952.

Brougham, Henry. *Practical Observations Upon the Education of the People; Addressed to the Working Classes and their Employers.* London, 1825.

Brown, Bill. "Thing Theory." *Critical Inquiry* 28, no. 1 (2001): 1–22.

Brown, Christopher. *Moral Capital: Foundations of British Abolitionism.* Chapel Hill: University of North Carolina Press, 2006.

Brown, David. "From 'Cotton Lord' to Landed Aristocrat: The Rise of Sir George Philips Bart., 1766–1847." *Historical Research* 69, no. 168 (February 1996): 66–82.

Brown, Michael. "Medicine, Reform and the 'End' of Charity in Early Nineteenth-Century England." *English Historical Review* 124, no. 511 (December 2009): 1353–88.

Bruton, F. A., ed. *Three Accounts of Peterloo.* Manchester: Manchester University Press, 1921.

Budge, Gavin. *Romanticism, Medicine and the Natural Supernatural: Transcendent Vision and Bodily Spectres, 1789–1852.* Basingstoke: Palgrave Macmillan, 2012.

Bugg, John. "The Other Interesting Narrative: Olaudah Equiano's Public Book Tour." *PMLA* 121, no. 5 (October 2006): 1424–42.

Burnard, Trevor, and Kit Candlin. "Sir John Gladstone and the Debate over the Amelioration of Slavery in the British West Indies in the 1820s." *Journal of British Studies* 57, no. 4 (October 2018): 760–82.

Burns, Robert. *The Works of Robert Burns; with an account of his life, and a criticism on his writings. To which are prefixed, some observations on the character and condition of the Scottish peasantry.* 4 vols. Edited by James Currie. London, 1801.

Burton, Anthony, and Diane Duffy. "Elizabeth Gaskell and the Industrial Poor: How Did She Know About Them?" *Gaskell Journal* 34 (2020): 1–24.

Bynum, W. F. "Cullen and the Study of Fevers in Britain, 1760–1820." *Medical History* 25, Supplement No. 1 (1981): 135–47.

Byron, George Gordon. *Lord Byron: The Complete Poetical Works.* 7 vols. Edited by Jerome J. McGann. Oxford: Oxford University Press, 1980–93.

Cappe, Catherine. *An account of two charity schools for the education of girls: and of a female friendly society in York.* York, 1800.

———. *Thoughts on various charitable and other important institutions, and of the best mode of conducting them. To which is added an address to the females of the rising generation.* York, 1814.

———. *On the desireableness and utility of ladies visiting the female wards of hospitals and lunatic asylums. First pr. in the Pamphleteer.* York, 1817.

Carroll, Siobhan. "Dangerous Energies: Agency and Energy Regimes in the Waverley Novels." *Studies in Romanticism* 61, no. 2 (Summer 2022): 255–77.

Castle, Terry. "Phantasmagoria: Spectral Technology and the Metaphorics of Modern Reverie." *Critical Inquiry* 15, no. 1 (Autumn 1988): 26–61.

Chadwick, Edwin. *Report to Her Majesty's Principal Secretary of State for the Home Department from the Poor Law Commissioners, on an Inquiry into the Sanitary Condition of the Labouring Population of Great Britain.* London: Clowes, 1842.

Chakrabarty, Dipesh. "The Climate of History: Four Theses." *Critical Inquiry* 35, no. 2 (Winter 2009): 197–222.

Chalmers, Thomas. "Causes and Cure of Pauperism." *Edinburgh Review* 53 (1818): 261–302.

———. *Christian Economy of Large Towns.* 3 vols. Glasgow, 1821–26.

Chaloner, W. H. "Robert Owen, Peter Drinkwater, and the Early Factory System in Manchester, 1788–1800." *Bulletin of the John Rylands Library* 37, no. 1 (1954): 78–102.

Chandler, George. *William Roscoe of Liverpool 1753–1831.* London: Batsford, 1953.

Chapple, John. *Elizabeth Gaskell: The Early Years.* Manchester: Manchester University Press, 2009.

Checkland, S. G. *The Gladstones: A Family Biography 1764–1851.* Cambridge: Cambridge University Press, 1971.

Chernock, Arianne. *Men and the Making of Modern British Feminism.* Stanford, CA: Stanford University Press, 2010.

Claeys, Gregory. "Virtuous Commerce and Free Theology: Political Economy and the Dissenting Academies 1750–1800." *History of Political Thought* 20, no. 1 (January 1999): 141–72.

Clarke, Norma. *Ambitious Heights: Writing, Friendship, Love—the Jewsbury Sisters, Felicia Hemans, and Jane Welsh Carlyle.* London: Routledge, 1990.

Clarkson, Thomas. *The History of the Rise, Progress and Accomplishment of the Abolition of the African Slave-Trade, by the British Parliament.* 2 vols. London, 1839.

Clennell, John. *Thoughts on the Expediency of Disclosing the Processes of Manufactories being the Substance of Two Papers Lately read before the Literary and Philosophical Society of Newcastle upon Tyne.* Newcastle, 1807.

Clery, E. J. *Eighteen Hundred and Eleven: Poetry, Protest and Economic Crisis.* Cambridge: Cambridge University Press, 2017.

Colclough, Stephen. *Consuming Texts: Readers and Reading Communities, 1695–1870.* Houndmills: Palgrave Macmillan, 2007.

Coleman, D. C. *Myth, History, and the Industrial Revolution.* London: Hambledon Press, 1982.

Coleridge, Samuel Taylor. *Collected Letters of Samuel Taylor Coleridge.* 6 vols. Edited by E. L. Griggs. Oxford: Oxford University Press, 1956–71.

———. *Notebooks of Samuel Taylor Coleridge.* Vol. 3.1808–19. Edited by Kathleen Coburn. London: Routledge and Kegan Paul, 1973.

A Collection of Songs, Comic, Satirical, and Descriptive, chiefly in the Newcastle Dialect, and illustrative of the language and manners of the common people on the Banks of the Tyne and neighbourhood. Newcastle: John Marshall, 1827.

Colley, Linda. *Britons: Forging the Nation 1707–1837*. New Haven, CT: Yale University Press, 1992.

Connell, Philip. *Romanticism, Economics and the Question of "Culture."* Oxford: Oxford University Press, 2001.

Cooper, Thomas. *Tracts ethical, theological and political [. . . .] Vol.1*. London, 1789.

———. "Propositions respecting the Foundation of Civil Government." *MLPSM* 3 (1790): 481–510.

———. *A reply to Mr. Burke's invective against Mr. Cooper, and Mr. Watt, in the House of Commons on the 30th April, 1792*. Manchester, 1792.

———. "Of Dr. Priestley's Metaphysical Writing." In *Memoirs of Dr. Priestley to the year 1795, written himself, and continued by his Son, Joseph Priestley, [. . .] with Observations on his Writings by Thomas Cooper [. . .]. and William Christie*. 2 vols. Northumberland, PA, 1806.

The Correspondence between John Gladstone, Esq. M. P. and James Cropper, Esq. on the Present state of slavery in the British West Indies and in the United States of America. Liverpool, 1824.

Corrie, Jane Anne. "William Cullen's Exemplary Retirement: The Art of Aging in Enlightenment Scotland." PhD diss., University of Glasgow, 2017.

Costa, Emília Viotti da. *Crowns of Glory, Tears of Blood: The Demerara Slave Rebellion of 1823*. New York: Oxford University Press, 1997.

Crafts, N. F. R. *British Industrial Growth during the Industrial Revolution*. Oxford: Oxford University Press, 1985.

Crook, David. "The Reverend Joseph Hunter and the Public Records." *Transactions of the Hunter Archaeological Society* 12 (1983): 1–15.

Crook, Nora. "Shelley and His Waste-Paper Basket: Notes on Eight Shelleyan and Pseudo-Shelleyan Jottings, Extracts, and Fragments." *Keats-Shelley Review* 25, no. 1 (2011): 68–78.

Cropper, James. *Extracts from Letters of the late James Cropper, transcribed for his Grandchildren by their Affectionate Mother and Aunt, Anne Cropper*. [Liverpool, 1850?].

Crump, W. E., ed. *The Leeds Woollen Industry 1780–1820*. Leeds: Thoresby Society, 1931.

Cullen, M. J. *The Statistical Movement in Early Victorian Britain: The Foundations of Empirical Social Research*. Brighton: Harvester, 1975.

Cullen, William. *The Works of William Cullen, MD*. 2 vols. Edited by John Thomson. Edinburgh, 1827.

Currie, James. "Memoirs of the late Dr. Bell." *MLPSM* 2 (1785): 381–393.

Currie, W. W. *Memoir of the Life of James Currie*. 2 vols. London, 1831.

Daniels, Stephen, and Paul Elliott. "John Aikin's Geographical Imagination." In James and Inkster, *Religious Dissent and the Aikin-Barbauld Circle*, 94–125.

Darcy, C. P. *The Encouragement of the Fine Arts in Lancashire, 1760–1860*. Manchester: Chetham Society, 1976.

Darwin, Erasmus. *The Botanic Garden; a Poem, in two parts*. London, 1791.

Davies, Jeremy. "Introduction: Romantic Studies and the Shorter Industrial Revolution." *Studies in Romanticism* 61, no. 2 (Summer 2022): 187–202.

———. "Romantic 'Ghost Acres' and Environmental Modernity." *Studies in Romanticism* 61, no. 2 (Summer 2022): 203–27.

Davis, David B. "James Cropper and the British Anti-Slavery Movement, 1821–1823." *Journal of Negro History* 45, no. 4 (October 1960): 241–58.

Dean, Mitchell. *The Constitution of Poverty: Towards a Genealogy of Liberal Governance* London: Routledge, 1991.

Defoe, Daniel. *A Tour through the Whole Island of Great Britain*. Edited by Pat Rogers. Harmondsworth: Penguin, 1971.

DeLanda, Manuel. *A New View of Society: Assemblage Theory and Social Complexity*. London: Continuum, 2006.

De Polier, Charles. "On the Pleasure which the Mind receives from the Exercise of its Faculties; and that of Taste in particular." *MLPSM* 1 (1785): 110–34.

De Quincey, Thomas. *The Works of Thomas De Quincey*. Edited by Grevel Lindop. 21 vols. London: Pickering and Chatto, 2000–2003.

Detrosier, Roland. *On the Necessity of an Extension of the Moral and Political Instruction among the Working Classes: An Address Delivered to the Members of the New Mechanics Institution*. Manchester, 1831.

Dick, Alexander. "'A good deal of Trash': Reading Societies, Religious Controversy and Networks of Improvement in Eighteenth-Century Scotland." *Journal for Eighteenth-Century Studies* 38, no. 4 (December 2015): 585–98.

Directory, General and Commercial, of the Town and Borough of Leeds for 1817. Leeds, 1817.

Ditchfield, G. M. "The Early History of Manchester College." *Transactions of the Historic Society of Lancashire and Cheshire* 123 (1971): 81–104.

———. "Manchester College and Anti-Slavery." In *Truth, Liberty, Religion: Essays Celebrating Two Hundred Years of Manchester College*, edited by Barbara Smith, 185–224. Oxford: Manchester College, 1986.

Doherty, John. *Misrepresentations Exposed in a Letter addressed to the Right Honourable Lord Ashley M. P.* Manchester, 1838.

Donington, Katie. "Transforming Capital: Slavery, Family, Commerce and the Making of the Hibbert family." In *Legacies of British Slave-Ownership: Colonial Slavery and the Formation of Victorian Britain*, by Catherine Hall, Nicholas Draper, Keith McClelland, Katie Donington, and Rachel Lang, 203–49. Cambridge: Cambridge University Press, 2014.

Donnachie, Ian. *Robert Owen: Social Visionary*. Edinburgh: John Donald, 2000.

Driver, Cecil. *Tory Radical: The Life of Richard Oastler*. Oxford: Oxford University Press, 1946.

Dupree, Mary Helen, and Sean Franzel, eds. *Performing Knowledge, 1750–1850*. Interdisciplinary German Cultural Studies 18. Berlin: De Gruyter, 2015.

Elder, Melinda. "The Liverpool Slave Trade, Lancaster and its Environs." In Richardson et al., *Liverpool and Transatlantic Slavery*, 118–37.

Elliott, Paul A. *The Derby Philosophers: Science and Culture in British Urban Society, 1700–1850*. Manchester: Manchester University Press, 2009.

Enfield, William. *An Essay on the Cultivation of Taste*. Newcastle, 1818.

Engels, Friedrich. *The Condition of the Working Class in England*. Edited by David McLellan. Oxford: Oxford University Press, 1993.

Equiano, Olaudah. *The Interesting Narrative and Other Writings*. Edited by Vincent Carretta. London: Penguin, 2003.

Everett, James. *Historical Sketches of Wesleyan Methodism in Sheffield*. Sheffield, 1823.

Farrar, W. V., Kathleen R. Farrar, and E. L. Scott. "The Henrys of Manchester Part 1: Thomas Henry (1734–1816)." *Ambix* 20, no. 3 (1973): 183–208.

———. "The Henrys of Manchester, Part 6: William Charles Henry: The Magnesia Factory." *Ambix* 24, no. 1 (1977): 1–26.

Faubert, Michelle. "John Ferriar's Psychology, James Hogg's Justified Sinner, and the Gay Science of Horror Writing." In *Romanticism and Pleasure*, edited by Thomas H. Schmid and Michelle Faubert, 83–108. Basingstoke: Palgrave Macmillan, 2010.

Felski, Rita. "Latour and Literary Studies." *PMLA* 130, no. 3 (May 2015): 737–42.

——. *Limits of Critique*. Chicago: University of Chicago Press, 2015.

Ferriar, John. *The Prince of Angola, a tragedy, altered from the play of Oroonoko. and Adapted to the Circumstances of the present times*. Manchester, 1788.

——. "Of Popular Illusions, and particularly of Medical Demonology." *MLPSM* 3 (1790): 31–116.

——. "Essay on the Dramatic Writings of Massinger." *MLPSM* 3 (1790): 123–59.

——. "Observations concerning the Vital Principle." *MLPSM* 3 (1790): 216–41.

——. "An Argument against the Doctrine of Materialism, addressed to Thomas Cooper, Esq." *MLPSM* 4 (1793): 20–44.

——. "Comments on Sterne." *MLPSM* 4 (1793): 45–86.

——. *Medical Histories and Reflections*. 3 vols. Warrington, 1792–98.

——. *Medical Histories and Reflections*. 2nd ed. 4 vols. London, 1810–13.

——. *Illustrations of Sterne: with Other Essays and Verses*. London, 1798.

——. *Illustrations of Sterne: with Other Essays and Verses*. 2nd ed. London, 1812.

——. *An Essay Towards a Theory of Apparitions*. London, 1813.

Ferris, Ina. "'Before Our Eyes'": Romantic Historical Fiction and the Apparitions of Reading." *Representations* 121, no. 1 (Winter 2013): 60–84.

Fitton, R. S., and A. P. Wadsworth. *The Strutts and the Arkwrights 1758–1830: A Study of the Early Factory System*. Manchester: Manchester University Press, 1973.

Fletcher, Eliza. *Autobiography of Mrs Fletcher: With Letters and Other Family Memorials*. Edinburgh, 1875.

Fletcher, Thomas. *Autobiographical memoirs of Thomas Fletcher, of Liverpool*. Liverpool: privately printed, 1853.

Ford, Trowbridge H. *Henry Brougham and His World: A Biography*. Chichester: Barry Rose, 1995.

Foucault, Michel. "The Ethics of Care for the Self as a Practice of Freedom: An Interview." In *The Final Foucault*, edited by James Bernhauer and David Rasmussen, translated by J. D. Gauthier, 1–20. Boston: MIT Press, 1998.

Fraser, Derek. "Edward Baines." In *Pressure from Without in Early Victorian England*, edited by Patricia Hollis, 183–209. London: Edward Arnold, 1974.

——. "The Life of Edward Baines: A Filial Biography of the 'The Great Liar of the North,'" *Northern History* 31, no. 1 (1995): 208–22.

Fraser, E. M. "Robert Owen in Manchester." *MLPSM* 82 (1937–38): 29–41.

Fryckstedt, Monica Correa. *Elizabeth Gaskell's Mary Barton and Ruth: A Challenge to Christian England*. Uppsala, Swed.: Uppsala Universitet, 1982.

Fulton, John F. "Warrington Academy (1757–1786) and Its Influence on Medicine and Science." *Bulletin of the Institute of the History of Medicine* 1 (1933): 50–80.

Furgol, Mary Theresa. "Thomas Chalmers: Poor Relief Theories and Their Implementation in the Early Nineteenth Century." PhD diss., University of Edinburgh, 1987.

Gailiunas, Paul. "Women during the Early Years of the Newcastle Lit and Phil." *Archaeologia Aeliana*, 5th ser., 46 (2017): 147–55.

——. "John Marshall: Printer, Librarian and Radical." *Durham County Local History Society Journal* 84 (June 2020): 5–36.

Galloway, Alexander R., and Eugene Thacker. "Protocol, Control, and Networks." *Grey Room*, no. 17 (Fall 2004): 6–29.

————. *The Exploit: A Theory of Networks*. Minneapolis: University of Minnesota Press, 2007.

Gaskell, Elizabeth. *Letters of Mrs Gaskell*. Edited by J. A. V. Chapple and Arthur Pollard. Manchester: Manchester University Press, 1996.

————. *Private Voices: The Diaries of Elizabeth Gaskell and Sophia Holland*. Edited by J.A.V. Chapple and Anita Wilson. Keele: Keele University Press, 1996.

————. *Further Letters of Elizabeth Gaskell*. Edited by John Chapple and Alan Shelston. Manchester: Manchester University Press, 2003.

————. *Mary Barton*. Edited by Shirley Foster. Oxford: Oxford University Press, 2006.

Gaskell, William. *Protestant Practices Inconsistent with Protestant Principles: A Discourse delivered at Renshaw Street Chapel, Liverpool*. Manchester, 1837.

Gatrell, V. A. C. "Incorporation and the Pursuit of Liberal Hegemony in Manchester, 1790–1839." In *Municipal Reform and the Industrial City*, edited by D. Fraser, 16–60. Leicester: Leicester University Press, 1982.

Gidal, Eric. "Industrial Transport and Political Economy in *Blackwood's Edinburgh Magazine*." *Studies in Romanticism* 61, no. 2 (Summer 2022): 279–303.

Gisborne, Thomas. *The Principles of Moral Philosophy Investigated, and briefly applied to the Constitutions of Civil Society: together with remarks on the principles assumed by Mr. Paley*. London, 1789.

————. *An Enquiry into the Duties of Men in the Higher and Middle Classes of Society in Great Britain*. London, 1794.

————. *An Inquiry into the Duties of the Female Sex*. London, 1797.

————. "On the Benefits and Duties resulting from the Institution of Societies for the Advancement of Literature and Philosophy." *MLPSM* 5 (1798): 70–88.

Golinski, Jan. *Science as Public Culture: Chemistry and Enlightenment in Britain, 1760–1820*. Cambridge: Cambridge University Press, 1992.

Goodman, Kevis. *Pathologies of Motion: Historical Thinking in Medicine, Aesthetics and Poetics*. New Haven, CT: Yale University Press, 2023.

Goodwin, Albert. *The Friends of Liberty: The English Democratic Movement in the Age of the French Revolution*. London: Hutchinson, 1979.

Greg, Hannah [neé Lightbody]. *Virtue Made Easy; or a Tablet of Morality: being a Collection of Maxims and Moral Sayings*. [Liverpool], 1799.

————. *A Collection of Maxims, Observations, etc*. Liverpool, 1799.

————. *The Moralist: A Collection of Maxims, Observations &c*. Liverpool, 1800.

————. *The Monitor, or a Collection of Precepts, Observations, etc*. Liverpool, 1804.

————. *Practical suggestions towards alleviating the sufferings of the sick*. London, 1828.

————. "The Diary of Hannah Lightbody 1786/90." *Enlightenment and Dissent*, Special Supplement, 24 (2008).

Greg, Robert Hyde. *The Factory Question, Considered in Relation to Its Effects on the Health and Morals of Those Employed in Factories, and the "Ten Hours Bill" in Relation to Its Effects Upon the Manufactures of England, and Those of Foreign Countries*. London, 1837.

————. *The Travel Journals of Robert Hyde Greg of Quarry Bank Mill: Travels in Scotland, Spain and Portugal, Italy, and the Ottoman Empire, 1814–17*. Edited by Beryl and Allen Freer. Donington: Shaun Tyas, 2007.

Greg, Samuel, Jr. *Two Letters to Leonard Horner, Esq., on the Capabilities of the Factory System*. London, 1840.

————. *A Layman's Legacy in Prose and Verse*. London: Macmillan, 1877.

Greg, William Rathbone (W. R.). *An Enquiry into the State of the Manufacturing Population, and the Causes and Cures of the Evils Therein Existing.* London, 1831.

———. *Sketches in Greece and Turkey; with the Present Condition and Future Prospects of the Turkish Empire.* London, 1833.

———. "*Mary Barton: A Tale of Manchester Life.*" *Edinburgh Review* 89 (April 1849): 402–35.

Greg, W. R., and Samuel Greg Jr. *Analysis of the Evidence Taken before the Factory Commissioners, as far as it Relates to the Population of Manchester.* Manchester, 1834.

Grenby, M. O. *The Child Reader 1700–1840.* Cambridge: Cambridge University Press, 2011.

Griffin, Emma. *A Short History of the British Industrial Revolution.* 2nd ed. London: Palgrave Macmillan, 2018.

Groth, Helen. *Moving Images: Nineteenth-Century Reading and Screen Practices.* Edinburgh: Edinburgh University Press, 2013.

Guillory, John. *Cultural Capital: The Problem of Literary Canon Formation.* Chicago: University of Chicago Press, 1993.

Guthrie, Matthew. "Some Account of the Persian Cotton Tree." *MLPSM* 5 (1798): 214–20.

Haakonsson, Lisbeth. *Medicine and Morals in the Enlightenment: John Gregory, Thomas Percival, and Benjamin Rush.* Amsterdam: Rodopi, 1997.

Hailaire-Peréz, Liliane. "Technology as Public Culture in the Eighteenth Century: The Artisans' Legacy." *History of Science* 45, no. 2 (2007): 135–53.

Halifax Literary and Philosophical Society. *Centenary Handbook.* Halifax: Halifax Literary and Philosophical Society, 1930.

Hall, Samuel. "An Attempt to show that a taste for the beauties of nature and the fine arts has no influence favourable to morals." *MLPSM* 1 (1785): 223–40.

Harbottle, Stephen. *The Reverend William Turner: Dissent and Reform in Georgian Newcastle upon Tyne.* Newcastle: Northern Universities Press, 1997.

Harding, Thomas. *White Debt: The Demerara Uprising and Britain's Legacy of Slavery.* London: Orion, 2022.

Hardy, Alan. *The Origins of the Idea of the Industrial Revolution.* 2nd ed. Shepperton: Aidan Press, 2014.

Harley, C. Knick. Review of *The Enlightened Economy*, by Joel Mokyr. EH.net (Economic History Association), December 2010. https://eh.net/book_reviews/the-enlightened-economy-an-economic-history-of-britain-1700-1850/.

Harling, Philip. *The Waning of 'Old Corruption': The Politics of Economical Reform in Britain, 1779–1846.* Oxford: Oxford University Press, 1996.

Harrison, Ralph. *A sermon preached at the dissenting chapel in Cross-Street, Manchester, [. . .] on occasion of the establishment of an academy in that town.* Manchester, 1786.

Hartley, David. *Observations on man, his frame, his duty, and his expectations.* 2 vols. London, 1749.

Haygarth, John. "Description of a Glory." *MLPSM* 3 (1790): 63–67.

———. *A Sketch of a Plan to exterminate the Casual Small-pox from Great Britain.* 2 vols. London, 1793.

Hazlitt, William. *Complete Works.* Edited by P. P. Howe, 21 vols. London: Dent, 1930–34.

Heinzelman, Kurt. "The Last Georgic: Wealth of Nations and the Scene of Writing." In *Adam Smith's Wealth of Nations: New Interdisciplinary Essays*, edited by Stephen Copley and Kathryn Sutherland, 171–94. Manchester: Manchester University Press, 1995.

Helmstadter, Richard J. "W. R. Greg: A Manchester Creed." In *Victorian Faith in Crisis*, edited by Richard Helmstadter and Bernard Lightman, 187–222. London: Palgrave Macmillan, 1990.

Henry, Thomas. "On the Advantages of Literature and Philosophy in general, and especially on the consistency of Literature and Philosophy with Commercial Pursuits." *MLPSM* 1 (1785): 7–29.

———. "Observations on the Bills of Mortality for the Towns of Manchester and Salford." *MLPSM* 3 (1790): 159–73.

Henry, W. C. [Charles]. "A Memoir of the Life and Writings of the late Dr. William Henry." *MLPSM* 6 (1842): 99–141.

Hewett, Martin. "The Travails of Domestic Visiting: Manchester 1830–70." *Historical Research* 71, no. 175 (1998): 196–227.

Heyrick, Elizabeth. *Immediate, Not Gradual Abolition: Or, An Inquiry into the Shortest, Safest, and Most Effectual Means of Getting Rid of West Indian Slavery*. London, 1824.

Heywood, B. A. *Addresses Delivered at the Meetings of the Proprietors of the Liverpool Royal Institution . . . 27th February 1822 & 13th February 1824*. Liverpool, 1824.

———. *Address delivered at the meeting of the Proprietors of the Liverpool Royal Institution . . . February, 1825*. Liverpool, 1825.

Heywood, Benjamin. *Addresses Delivered at the Manchester Mechanics' Institution*. London, 1843.

Heywood, Thomas. *A Memoir of Sir Benjamin Heywood, Baronet*. Manchester: Thomas Fragie, 1888.

Hilton, Boyd. *Corn, Cash, Commerce: The Economic Policies of the Tory Governments 1815–1830*. Oxford: Oxford University Press, 1977.

———. *The Age of Atonement: The Influence of Evangelism on Social and Economic Thought 1785–1865*. Oxford: Oxford University Press, 1991.

Hindle, G. B. *Provision for the Relief of the Poor in Manchester 1754–1826*. Manchester: Cheetham Society, 1975.

Hodgson, James T. *Memoir of Francis Hodgson, Scholar, Poet, and Divine*. 2 vols. London: Macmillan, 1878.

Holland, John. *Sheffield Park: A Descriptive Poem*. Sheffield, 1820.

———. *Memoirs of the Life and Writings of James Montgomery; including selections from his correspondence, remains in prose and verse, and conversations on various subjects*. With James Everett. 7 vols. London, 1854–56.

Honeyman, Katrina. *Child Workers in England, 1780–1820: Parish Apprentices and the Making of the Early Industrial Labour Force*. Abingdon: Taylor & Francis Group, 2007.

———. "The Poor Law, the Parish Apprentice, and the Textile Industries in the North of England, 1780–1830." *Northern History* 64, no. 2 (2007): 115–40.

Howard, John. *The state of the prisons in England and Wales, with preliminary observations, and an account of some foreign prisons and hospitals*. Warrington, 1777.

Howman, Brian. "Abolitionism in Liverpool." In Richardson et al., *Liverpool and Transatlantic Slavery*, 277–96.

Hudson, William. *The Life of John Holland*. London: Longman, 1874.

Hume, David. *Essays and treatises on several subjects [. . . ;] Vol. IV. containing Political discourses*, 2nd ed. Edinburgh: 1753.

Hunter, Joseph. *Hallamshire. The History and Topography of the Parish of SHEFFIELD*. London, 1819.

Hunter, Richard, and Ida Macalpine, eds. *Three Hundred Years of Psychiatry 1535–1860: A History Presented in Selected Texts*. London: Oxford University Press, 1963.

Hutt, Marten. "John Aikin: Biographical Memoirs of Medicine in Great Britain (1780)." *TUHS* 21, no. 4 (1998): 302–10.

Huxtable, Sally-Anne, Corinne Fowler, Christo Kefalas, and Emma Slocombe, eds. *Interim Report on the Connections between Colonialism and Properties Now in the Care of the National Trust, Including Links with Historic Slavery*. Swindon: National Trust, 2020.

Huzzey, Richard. "The Moral Geography of British Anti-Slavery Responsibilities." *Transactions of the Royal Historical Society* 22 (2012): 111–39.

Ignatieff, Michael. *A Just Measure of Pain: The Penitentiary in the Industrial Revolution 1750–1850*. Harmondsworth: Penguin, 1989.

Inkster, Ian. "The Development of a Scientific Community in Sheffield, 1790–1850: A Network of People and Interests," *Transactions of the Hunter Archaeological Society* 10 (1973): 99–131.

———. "'Under the eye of the public': Arthur Aikin (1773–1854), the Dissenting Mind and the Character of English Industrialization." In James and Inkster, *Religious Dissent and the Aikin-Barbauld Circle*, 126–55.

Inkster, Ian, and Maureen S. Bryson. *Industrial Man: The Life and Works of Charles Sylvester*. Las Vegas, NV: privately printed, 1999.

Innes, Joanna. "'Reform' in English Public Life: The Fortunes of a Word." In *Rethinking the Age of Reform Britain 1780–1850*, edited by Arthur Burns and Joanna Innes, 71–97. Cambridge: Cambridge University Press, 2003.

An Inquiry into the Principle and Tendency of the bill now pending in parliament for imposing certain restrictions on Cotton factories. London, 1818.

Jacob, Margaret. *Scientific Culture and the Making of the Industrial West*. New York: Oxford University Press, 1997.

———. *The First Knowledge Economy: Human Capital and the European Economy, 1750–1850*. Cambridge: Cambridge University Press, 2014.

James, Felicity. "Religious Dissent and the Aikin-Barbauld Circle, 1740–1860: An Introduction." In James and Inkster, *Religious Dissent and the Aikin-Barbauld Circle*, 1–27.

James, Felicity, and Ian Inkster, eds. *Religious Dissent and the Aikin-Barbauld Circle 1740–1860*. Cambridge: Cambridge University Press, 2012.

Jay, Mike. *The Atmosphere of Heaven: The Unnatural Experiments of Dr. Beddoes and his Sons of Genius*. New Haven, CT: Yale University Press, 2009.

Jebb, John. *Works Theological, medical, political, and miscellaneous*. 3 vols. London, 1787.

Johnson, C. R. *Provincial Poetry 1789–1839: British Verses Printed in the Provinces; The Romantic Background*. Otley: Jed, 1992.

Johnson, Joseph. *The Joseph Johnson Letterbook*. Edited by John Bugg. New York: Oxford University Press, 2016.

Johnston, Kenneth. *Unusual Suspects: Pitt's Reign of Alarm and the Lost Generation of the 1790s*. Oxford: Oxford University Press, 2013.

Jones, Peter. *Industrial Enlightenment: Science, Technology, Culture in Birmingham and the West Midlands, 1760–1820*. Manchester: Manchester University Press, 2008.

Jonsson, Fredrik Albritton. "The Industrial Revolution in the Anthropocene." *Journal of Modern History* 84, no. 3 (2012): 679–96.

Jordanova, L. J. "Earth Science and Environmental Medicine: The Synthesis of the Late Enlightenment." In *Images of the Earth: Essays in the History of the Environmental Science*, edited by L. J. Jordanova and Roy Porter, 119–47. Chalfont St. Giles: British Society for the History of Science, 1981.

Kames, Henry Home, Lord. *Elements of Criticism*. Edited by Peter Jones. 2 vols. Indianapolis: Liberty Fund, 2005.

Kay, James Phillips. "Physical Condition of the Poor." *North of England Medical and Surgical Journal* 1 (November 1830): 220–30.

———. *A Letter to the People of Lancashire concerning further Representation of the Commercial Interest*. London, 1831.

———. *The Moral and Physical Condition of the Working Classes Employed in the Cotton Manufacture in Manchester*. Manchester, 1832.

———. *The Moral and Physical Condition of the Working Classes Employed in the Cotton Manufacture in Manchester*. 2nd ed. Manchester, 1832.

———. *Defects in the Constitution of Dispensaries, with Suggestions for their Improvement*. 2nd ed. London, 1834.

Keen, Paul. *A Defence of the Humanities in a Utilitarian Age: Imagining What We Know, 1800–1850*. Cham, Switz.: Palgrave Macmillan, 2020.

Kennedy, Catriona. "'Womanish Epistles?' Martha McTier, Female Epistolarity and Late Eighteenth-Century Irish Radicalism." *Women's History Review* 13, no. 4 (2004): 649–67.

Kennedy, John. "Observations on the Rise and Progress of the Cotton Trade." *MLPSM*, 2nd ser., 3 (1819): 115–37.

———. "An Inquiry into the Effects Produced Upon Society by the Poor Laws." *MLPSM*, 2nd ser., 3 (1819): 430–45.

———. "A Brief Memoir of Samuel Crompton; with a Description of his Machine called the Mule, and of the Subsequent Improvement of the Machine by Others." *MLPSM*, 2nd ser., 5 (1831): 318–53.

———. *Miscellaneous Papers on Subjects connected with the Manufactures of Lancashire*. Manchester: privately printed, 1849.

Kirby, R. G., and A. E. Musson. *The Voice of the People: John Doherty, 1798–1854, Trade Unionist, Radical and Factory Reformer*. Manchester: Manchester University Press, 1975.

Kitson-Clark, E. *The History of 100 Years of Life of the Leeds Philosophical and Literary Society*. Leeds: Jowry, 1924.

Kitteringham, Guy. "Science in Provincial Society: The Case of Liverpool in the Early Nineteenth Century." *Annals of Science* 39, no. 4 (1982): 329–48.

Klancher, Jon. *The Making of English Reading Audiences, 1790–1832*. Madison: University of Wisconsin Press, 1987.

———. *Transfiguring the Arts and Sciences: Knowledge and Cultural Institutions in the Romantic Age*. Cambridge: Cambridge University Press, 2013.

———. "Lecturing Networks and Cultural Institutions, 1740–1830." In Mee and Sangster, *Institutions of Literature*, 135–56.

Knight, Frida. *The Strange Case of Thomas Walker*. London: Lawrence & Wishart, 1957.

Koselleck, Reinhart. *The Practice of Conceptual History: Timing History, Spacing Concepts*. Translated by Todd Samuel Presner et al. Stanford, CA: Stanford University Press, 2002.

Kristeva, Julia. *Powers of Horror: An Essay on Abjection*. Translated by Leon S. Roudiez. New York: Columbia University Press, 1982.

Kydd, Alfred. *The History of the Factory Movement from the Year 1802 to the Enactment of the Ten Hours Bill in 1847.* 2 vols. New York: Burt Franklin, 1966.

Lamb, Charles, and Mary Lamb. *The Letters of Charles and Mary Lamb, 1796–1801.* 10 vols. Edited by Edwin W. Marrs Jr. Ithaca, NY: Cornell University Press, 1976.

Lancashire Parish Registry Society. *Registers of Manchester, St Mary Parsonage, 1754–1888,* transcribed by C. A. Hewitt and G. Hewitt, no. 77 (Preston: Lancashire Parish Register Society, 1939).

Langton, John. "The Industrial Revolution and the Regional Geography of England." *Transactions of the Institute of British Geographers* 9, no. 2 (1984): 145–67.

Lascelles, David. *The Story of the Rathbones since 1742.* London: James & James, 2008.

Latour, Bruno. *Pandora's Hope: Essays on the Reality of Science Studies.* Cambridge, MA: Harvard University Press, 1999.

———. *Reassembling the Social: An Introduction to Actor-Network-Theory.* Oxford: Oxford University Press, 2005.

Lawrence, Christopher. "Cullen, Brown, and the Poverty of Essentialism." In *Brunonianism in Britain and Europe,* ed. W. F. Bynum and Roy Porter, 1–21. London: Welcome Institute, 1988.

Leask, Nigel. "Robert Burns and Scottish Common Sense Philosophy." In *Romantic Empiricism: Poetics and the Philosophy of Common Sense, 1780–1830,* ed. Gavin Budge, 64–87. Cranbury: Bucknell University Press, 2007.

———. "'Penetrat[ing] the Gloom/Of Britain's Farthest Glens': A Response from the Highlands." *Studies in Romanticism* 61, no. 2 (Summer 2022): 305–25.

Lee, C. H. *A Cotton Enterprise 1795–1840: A History of M'Connel and Kennedy Fine Cotton Spinners.* Manchester: Manchester University Press, 1972.

Leeds Philosophical and Literary Society. *Prospectus of Preliminary Laws of the Philosophical and Literary Society of Leeds.* Leeds, 1819.

———. *Transactions of the Philosophical and Literary Society of Leeds, consisting of Papers Read before the society, Volume I – Part I.* London, 1837.

Levere, Thomas H. "Dr. Thomas Beddoes (1750–1808): Science and Medicine in Politics and Society." *BJHS* 17, no. 2 (1984): 187–204.

Levine, Caroline. *Forms: Whole, Rhythm, Hierarchy, Work.* Princeton, NJ: Princeton University Press, 2015.

Lewis, N. B. "The Abolitionist Movement in Sheffield, 1832–1833: With Letters from Southey, Wordsworth and Others." *Bulletin of the John Rylands Library* 18 (1934): 377–92.

Lindsey, Theophilus. *The Letters of Theophilus Lindsey (1723–1808).* Edited by Grayson Ditchfield. 2 vols. London: Boydell Press, 2012.

Literary and Philosophical Society of Newcastle upon Tyne. *Plan of the Literary and Philosophical Society of Newcastle Upon Tyne.* Newcastle, 1793.

———. *Rules of the Literary and Philosophical Society of Newcastle upon Tyne.* Newcastle, 1801.

———. *Proceedings relative to the Establishment of the Library of the Literary and Philosophical Society of Newcastle upon Tyne, 1793–4.* Benham, 1823.

———. *Transactions of the Literary and Philosophical Society of Newcastle upon Tyne.* Newcastle, 1831.

Livingstone, David N. *Putting Science in Its Place: Geographies of Scientific Knowledge.* Chicago: University of Chicago Press, 2003.

Liverpool Mechanics' and Apprentices' Library. *An Account of the Liverpool Mechanics' and Apprentices' Library.* Liverpool, 1824.

Liverpool Mechanics' School of Arts. *The Report and Proceedings on the Liverpool Mechanics' School of Arts*. Liverpool, 1828.

Lobo, Francis M. "Haygarth, Smallpox, and Religious Dissent in Eighteenth-Century England." In *The Medical Enlightenment of the Eighteenth Century*, edited by Andrew Cunningham and Roger French, 217–53. Cambridge: Cambridge University Press, 1990.

Losh, James. *The Diaries and Correspondence of James Losh*. 2 vols. London: Andrews and Quaritch, 1962–63.

Lowes, John Livingston. *The Road to Xanadu: A Study in the Ways of the Imagination*. London: Constable, 1927.

Lyell, Charles. "Scientific Institutions." *Quarterly Review* 34 (June 1826): 153–79.

Lyon, Edmund. "The Medical Topography and Manchester," *North of England Medical and Surgical Journal*, August and November 1830, 7–25, 133–48.

Macaulay, Thomas Babington. *Letters of Thomas Babington Macaulay*. 6 vols. Edited by T. Pinney. Cambridge: Cambridge University Press, 1974.

Macintosh, Charles. *A Biographical Memoir of the Late Charles Macintosh*. Edited by George Macintosh. Glasgow: Blackie, 1847.

Mackenzie, Eneas. *To the Ordinary Members of the Literary and Philosophical Society of Newcastle upon Tyne*. Newcastle, 1809.

———. *Descriptive and Historical Account of the Town and County of Newcastle upon Tyne*. Newcastle, 1827.

Mackerness, E. D. "Mary Anne Rawson and the 'Memorials of James Montgomery.'" *Transactions of the Hunter Archaeological Society* 8 (1962): 218–28.

MacLeod, Christine. *Inventing the Industrial Revolution: The English Patent System, 1660–1800*. Cambridge: Cambridge University Press, 1988.

———. *Heroes of Invention: Technology, Liberalism and British Identity, 1750–1914*. Cambridge: Cambridge University Press, 2007.

Malfouris, Lambros. *How Things Shape the Mind: A Theory of Material Engagement*. Cambridge, MA: MIT Press, 2016.

Mallon, Thomas. *Stolen Words: The Classic Book on Plagiarism*. Harmondsworth: Penguin, 1991.

Malm, Andreas. *Fossil Capital: The Rise of Steam Power and the Roots of Global Warming*. London: Verso, 2016.

Malone, Dumas. *The Public Life of Thomas Cooper, 1783–1839*. New Haven, CT: Yale University Press, 1926.

Malthus, Thomas R. *An Essay on the Principle of Population, as it affects the future improvement of society*. London, 1798.

Manchester Literary and Philosophical Society. *Complete List of the Members & Officers of the Manchester Literary and Philosophical Society, from Its Institution on February 28th, 1781, to April 28th, 1896*. Manchester: [Manchester Literary and Philosophical Society], 1896.

Manchester Statistical Society. *First Report of the Manchester Statistical Society, July 1834*. Manchester, 1834.

———. *Report of a Committee of the Manchester Statistical Society on the Condition of the Working Classes, in an Extensive Manufacturing District in 1834, 1835, and 1836*. London, 1838.

Manning, J. E. *The History of Upper Chapel*. Sheffield: Independent Press, 1900.

Marshall, John. *The Economy of Social Life for the use of schools intended to give just ideas of the constitution of society, and of the relative situation of the different classes of social life.* London, 1825.

Marshall, Peter H. *William Godwin.* New Haven, CT: Yale University Press, 1984.

Martineau, Harriet. *Autobiography.* Edited by Linda H. Peterson. Peterborough, ON: Broadview Press, 2007.

Marx, Karl. *Capital: The Critique of Political Economy.* Vol. 1. Edited by Friedrich Engels. Translated by Samuel Moore and Edward Aveling. London: Lawrence and Wishart, 2003.

Massinger, Philip. *The Plays of Philip Massinger with notes critical and explanatory, by W. Gifford* 4 vols. London, 1805.

McCulloch, J. R. "Rise, Progress, Present State, and Prospects of British Cotton Manufactures." *Edinburgh Review* 46 (June 1827): 1–39.

———. "Review of Charles Babbage, On the Economy of Machinery and Manufactures." *Edinburgh Review* 56 (1833): 313–32.

———. "Present State of Manufactures." *Edinburgh Review,* 58 (1833): 40–64.

McElroy, David. *Scotland's Age of Improvement: A Survey of Eighteenth-Century Clubs and Societies.* Pullman: Washington State University Press, 1969.

McHugh, Kirsty. "Yorkshire Tourists: The Beginnings of Middle-Class Travel in Georgian Britain." *Yorkshire Archaeological Journal* 90 (2018): 111–27.

———. "Northern English Travellers to Wales and Scotland 1790–1830: A Study of Manuscript Travel Accounts from Yorkshire and Lancashire." PhD diss., University of Wales, 2021.

McLachlan, H. J. *Warrington Academy: Its History and Influence.* Manchester: Frome, Butler & Tanner, 1943.

———. *Essays and Addresses.* Manchester: Manchester University Press, 1950.

Mee, Jon. "Policing Enthusiasm in the Romantic Period: Literary Periodicals and the 'Rational' Public Sphere." In *Spheres of Influence: Intellectual and Cultural Publics from Shakespeare to Habermas,* edited by Alex Benchimol and Willy Maley, 175–95. Oxford: Peter Lang, 2007.

———. *Conversable Worlds: Literature, Contention, and Community.* Oxford: Oxford University Press, 2011.

———. "'A Reading People?': Global Knowledge Networks and Two Australian Societies of the 1820s." *Australian Literary Studies* 29, no. 3 (2014). https://doi.org/10.20314/als.aofcfe8202.

———. "The Buzz about the *Bee*: Policing the Conversation of Culture in the 1790s." In *Before Blackwood's: Scottish Journalism in the Age of Enlightenment,* edited by Alex Benchimol, Rhona Brown, and David Shuttleton, 63–74. London: Pickering and Chatto, 2015.

———. "'Some mode less revolting to their delicacy': Woman's Institutional Space in the Transpennine Enlightenment, 1781–1822." *Journal for Eighteenth-Century Studies* 42, no. 4 (December 2019): 541–56.

———. "Raymond Williams, Industrialism, and Romanticism, 1780–1850." In *Raymond Williams and Romanticism,* edited by Jonathan Klancher and Jonathan Sachs. Romantic Circles Praxis series. November 2020. https://romantic-circles.org/praxis/williams/praxis.2020.williams.mee.html.

———. "'All that the most romantic imagination could have previously conceived': Writing an Industrial Revolution, 1795 to 1835." *Studies in Romanticism* 61, no. 2 (Summer 2022): 229–54.

Mee, Jon, and Matthew Sangster. *Institutions of Literature, 1700–1900: The Development of Literary Culture and Production.* Cambridge: Cambridge University Press, 2022.

———. Introduction to *Institutions of Literature*, 1–23.

Mee, Jon, and Jennifer Wilkes. "Transpennine Enlightenment: The Literary and Philosophical Societies and Knowledge Networks in the North 1781–1830." *Journal for Eighteenth-Century Studies* 38, no. 4 (December 2015): 599–612.

Meiklejohn, A. "The Life, Work, and Times of Charles Turner Thackrah." In *Charles Turner Thackrah: The Effects of Arts, Trades, and Professions on Health and Longevity*, edited by A. Meiklejohn, 1–50. Edinburgh: Livingstone, 1957.

Meranze, Michael. *Laboratories of Virtue: Punishment, Revolution, and Authority in Philadelphia, 1760–1835.* Chapel Hill: University of North Carolina Press, 1996.

Midgley, Clare. "The Dissenting Voice of Elizabeth Heyrick: An Exploration of the Links between Gender, Religious Dissent, and Anti-Slavery Radicalism." In *Women, Dissent, and Anti-Slavery in Britain and America, 1790–1865*, edited by Elizabeth J. Clapp and Julie Joy Jeffrey, 88–110. Oxford: Oxford University Press, 2011.

Mill, John Stuart. *The Collected Works of John Stuart Mill.* Vol. 12, *The Earlier Letters 1812–1848 Part I.* Edited by Francis E. Mineka. Toronto: University of Toronto Press, 1963.

Miller, Thomas P. *The Formation of College English: Rhetoric and Belles Lettres in the British Cultural Provinces.* Pittsburgh: University of Pittsburgh Press, 1997.

Mitchell, Robert. *Experimental Life: Vitalism in Romantic Science and Literature.* Baltimore: Johns Hopkins University Press, 2013.

Mokyr, Joel. *The Gifts of Athena: Historical Origins of the Knowledge Economy.* Princeton, NJ: Princeton University Press, 2002.

———. "Intellectual Origins of Modern Economic Growth." *Journal of Economic History* 65, no. 2 (June 2005): 285–351.

———. *The Enlightened Economy: Britain and the Industrial Revolution, 1700–1850.* New Haven, CT: Yale University Press, 2009.

Montgomery, James. *The Wanderer of Switzerland and Other Poems.* London, 1806.

———. *Lectures on Poetry and General Literature, delivered at the Royal Institution in 1830 and 1831.* London, 1833.

———. "Lecture on the British Poets delivered at the Royal Institution, 1837." *Metropolitan Magazine* 19 (1837): 1–7, 113–19.

Montgomery, James [arranged by]. *The Chimney Sweeper's Friend and Climbing-Boy's Album.* London, 1824.

———. *The Negro's Friend, or Sheffield Anti-Slavery Album.* Sheffield, 1826.

Morley, John. "W. R. Greg: A Sketch." *Macmillan's Magazine* 48 (June 1883): 109–26.

Morris, R. J. *Class, Sect and Party: The Making of the British Middle Class: Leeds, 1820–1850.* Manchester: Manchester University Press, 1990.

Morton, Timothy. "An Object-Oriented Defense of Poetry." *New Literary History* 43, no. 2 (Spring 2012): 205–24.

Multigraph Collective. *Interacting with Print: Elements of Reading in the Era of Print Saturation.* Chicago: University of Chicago Press, 2018.

Musselman, Elizabeth Green. *Nervous Conditions: Science and the Body Politic in Early Industrial Britain.* Albany, NY: SUNY Press, 2006.

Musson, A. E. "Early Industrial Chemists: Thomas Henry (1734–1816) of Manchester, and His Sons." In Musson and Robinson, *Science and Technology in the Industrial Revolution*, 231–51.

Musson, A. E., and E. Robinson. "The Early Growth of Steam Power." *Economic History Review* 11, no. 3 (1959): 418–39.

———. *Science and Technology in the Industrial Revolution.* Manchester: Manchester University Press, 1969.

Nangle, B. C. *The Monthly Review: Second series, 1790–1815.* Oxford: Oxford University Press, 1955.

Navickas, Katrina. *Loyalism and Radicalism in Lancashire, 1798–1815.* Oxford: Oxford University Press, 2009.

Nethercot, Arthur. *The Road to Tryermaine: A Study of the History, Background, and Purposes of Coleridge's "Christabel."* New York: Russell & Russell, 1962.

Nottingham, Lucie. *Rathbone Brothers: From Merchant to Banker 1742–1992.* London: Rathbone Brothers, 1992.

Oastler, Richard. *A Well Seasoned Christmas Pie for "The Great Liar of the North," prepared, cooked, baked and Presented by Richard Oastler.* Bradford, 1834.

Observations on the Woollen Machinery. Leeds, 1803.

Oliphant, Margaret. *William Blackwood and His Sons.* 3 vols. Edinburgh: Blackwood, 1897.

Orange, Derek. "Rational Dissent and Provincial Science: William Turner and the Newcastle Literary and Philosophical Society." In *Metropolis and Province: Science in British Culture, 1780–1850,* edited by Ian Inkster and Jack Morrell, 205–30. London: Hutchinson, 1983.

Ormerod, Henry A. *The Liverpool Royal Institution: A Record and a Retrospect.* Liverpool: Liverpool University Press, 1953.

Owen, Robert. *The Life of Robert Owen Written by Himself: With Selections from His Writings and Correspondence.* London: Effingham Wilson, 1857.

———. *Selected Works of Robert Owen.* Vol. 1, *Early Writings,* edited by Gregory Claeys. London: William Pickering, 1993.

Pederson, Susan. *Eleanor Rathbone and the Politics of Conscience.* New Haven, CT: Yale University Press, 2004.

[Percival, Edward]. *Memoirs of the Life and Writings of Thomas Percival, M.D.* London, 1807.

Percival, Thomas. *A Father's instructions; consisting of moral tales, fables, and reflections; designed to promote the love of virtue, a taste for knowledge, and an early acquaintance with the works of nature.* 4th ed. London, 1779.

———. *A Socratic Discourse on Truth and Faithfulness.* Warrington, 1781.

———. *Moral and Literary Dissertations.* Warrington, 1784.

———. "Speculations on the Perceptive Power of Vegetables." *MLPSM* 2 (1789): 114–30.

———. "An Inquiry into the Principles and Limits of Taxation as a Branch of Moral and Political Philosophy." *MLPSM* 3 (1793): 1–31.

———. *A Father's Instructions; adapted to different periods of life, from youth to maturity.* London, 1800.

———. *Medical Ethics; or a Code of Institutes and Precepts, adapted to the Professional Conduct of Physicians and Surgeons.* London, 1803.

Pickstone, John V. "Ferriar's Fever to Kay's Cholera: Disease and Social Structure in Cottonopolis." *History of Science* 22, no. 4 (1984): 401–19.

———. *Medicine and Industrial Society: A History of Hospital Development in Manchester and Its Region, 1752–1946.* Manchester: Manchester University Press, 1985.

———. "Thomas Percival and the Production of Medical Ethics." In *Medical Ethics and Etiquette in the Eighteenth Century,* vol. 1 of *The Codification of Medical Morality:*

Historical and Philosophical Studies of the Formalization of Western Medical Morality in the Eighteenth and Nineteenth Centuries, edited by Robert Baker, Dorothy Porter, and Roy Porter, 161–78. Dordrecht, Neth.: Kluwer, 1993.

Pickstone, John V., and S. V. F. Butler. "The Politics of Medicine in Manchester, 1788–1792: Hospital Reform and Public Health Services in the Early Industrial City." *Medical History* 28, no. 3 (July 1984): 227–49.

Plant, Helen. *Unitarianism, Philanthropy, and Feminism in York, 1782–1821: The Career of Catherine Cappe*. York: University of York Press, 2003.

Podmore, Frank. *Robert Owen A Biography*, 2 vols. in one. New York: August M. Kelley, 1968.

Polanyi, Karl. *The Great Transformation: The Political and Economic Origins of Our Time*. 2nd ed. Boston: Beacon Press, 2001.

A Political Litany, or People's Prayer to the Prince & Legislature for the Redress of Grievances. Newcastle, 1817.

Pomeranz, Kenneth. *The Great Divergence: China, Europe, and the Making of the Modern World Economy*. Princeton, NJ: Princeton University Press, 2000.

Poole, Robert. *Peterloo: The English Uprising*. Oxford: Oxford University Press, 2019.

Poovey, Mary. *Making a Social Body: British Cultural Formation, 1830–1864*. Chicago: University of Chicago Press, 1995.

———. *Genres of the Credit Economy: Mediating Value in Eighteenth- and Nineteenth-Century Britain*. Chicago: University of Chicago Press, 2008.

Porter, Roy. "Science, Provincial Culture and Public Opinion in Enlightenment England." *Journal for Eighteenth Century Studies* 3, no. 1 (1980): 20–46.

———. *Mind-Forged Manacles: A History of Madness in England, from the Restoration to the Regency*. Cambridge, MA: Harvard University Press, 1987.

Porter, William Smith. *Sheffield Literary and Philosophical Society: A Centenary Retrospective*. Sheffield: Sheffield Literary and Philosophical Society, 1922.

Prentice, Archibald. *Historical Sketches and Personal Recollections*. London: Gilpin, 1851.

Price, Richard. *Observations on the Importance of the American Revolution, and the Means of Making it a Benefit to the World*. London, 1784.

Priestley, Joseph. *The History and Present State of Electricity, with Original Experiments*. 2nd ed. London, 1769.

———. *Disquisitions relating to Matter and Spirit*. London, 1777.

———. *An History of the Corruptions of Christianity*. 2 vols. London, 1782.

———. *An appeal to the public, on the subject of the riots in Birmingham, part II*. London, 1792.

———. *Memoirs of Dr. Priestley to the year 1795, written himself, and continued by his Son, Joseph Priestley, . . . with Observations on his Writings by Thomas Cooper . . .* 2 vols. Northumberland, 1806.

———. *Theological and Miscellaneous Works*. Edited by J. T. Rutt. 25 vols. London, 1817–32. The first volume was issued in two parts, each with its own pagination.

Proceedings of a Public Meeting for the Purpose of Establishing a Literary and Philosophical Society in Sheffield. Sheffield, 1822.

Prospectus of a new miscellany, to be entitled The monthly magazine; or British register. London, 1796.

Rajan, Tilottama. *The Supplement of Reading: Figures of Understanding in Romantic Theory and Practice*. Ithaca, NY: Cornell University Press, 1990.

Ramsey, Neil. "James Montgomery's Waterloo: War and the Poetics of History." *Studies in Romanticism* 56, no. 3 (Fall 2017): 361–78.

Rathbone, Eleanor F. *William Rathbone: A Memoir*. London: Macmillan, 1905.

Rathbone, Emily A., ed. *Records of the Rathbone Family*. Edinburgh: Clark, 1913.

Rawson, Mary Ann, ed. *The Bow in the Cloud; or, the Negro's memorial. A collection of original contributions, in prose and verse, illustrative of the evils of slavery, and commemorative of its abolition in the British Colonies*. London, 1834.

Read, Donald. *The English Provinces c. 1760–1960: A Study in Influence*. London: Edward Arnold, 1964.

Ready, Kathryn. "'And make thine own Apollo doubly thine': John Aikin as Literary Physician and the Intersection of Medicine, Morality and Politics." In James and Inkster, *Religious Dissent and the Aikin-Barbauld Circle*, 52–69.

Reid, Thomas Wemyss. *Memoir of John Deakin Heaton M. D*. London: Longman, 1883.

Rendall, Jane. "'Women that Would Plague Me with Rational Conversation': Aspiring Women and Scottish Whigs, c. 1790–1830." In *Women, Gender and Enlightenment*, edited by Sarah Knott and Barbara Taylor, 326–47. Basingstoke: Palgrave Macmillan, 2005.

———. "Adaptations: Gender, History, and Political Economy in the Work of Dugald Stewart." *History of European Ideas* 38, no. 1 (March 2012): 143–61.

———. "'Elementary Principles of Education': Elizabeth Hamilton, Maria Edgeworth and the Uses of Common Sense Philosophy." *History of European Ideas* 39, no. 5 (2013): 613–30.

———. "The Principle of Mutual Support: Female Friendly Societies in Scotland, c. 1789–1830." *Journal of Scottish Historical Studies* 40, no. 1 (May 2020): 17–39.

Rhodes, Alice. "'Mechanic Art and Elocutionary Science': Speech Production in British Literature, 1770s–1820s." PhD diss., University of York, 2021.

Richardson, Alan. *British Romanticism and the Science of the Mind*. Cambridge: Cambridge University Press, 2001.

Richardson, David, Suzanne Schwarz, and Anthony Tibbles, eds. *Liverpool and Transatlantic Slavery*. Liverpool: Liverpool University Press, 2007.

Rickman, Thomas. *An Attempt to Discriminate the Styles of English Architecture, from the Conquest to the Reformation; preceded by a sketch of the Grecian and Roman orders*. London, 1817.

Riello, Giorgio. *Cotton: The Fabric that Made the Modern World*. Cambridge: Cambridge University Press, 2013.

———. "Cotton Textiles and the Industrial Revolution in a Global Context." *Past & Present* 255, no. 1 (May 2022): 87–139.

Rimmer, W. G. *Marshall's of Leeds, Flax-spinners 1788–1866*. Cambridge: Cambridge University Press, 1960.

Robberds, Mary [née Turner]. "Recollections of a Long Life." In *Private Voices: The Diaries of Elizabeth Gaskell and Sophia Holland*. Edited by J. A. V. Chapple and Anita Wilson, 108–13. Keele: Keele University Press, 1996.

Roberts, Daniel Sanjiv. *Revisionary Gleam: De Quincey, Coleridge, and the High Romantic Argument*. Liverpool: Liverpool University Press, 1996.

Roberts, Samuel. *Autobiography and Select Remains*. London: Longman, 1849.

Rodgers, Betsy. *Georgian Chronicle: Mrs Barbauld and Her Family*. London: Methuen, 1958.

Roper, Derek. *Reviewing before the Edinburgh, 1783–1803*. London: Methuen, 1978.

Roscoe, Henry. *The Life of William Roscoe*. 2 vols. London, 1833.

Roscoe, William. *Ode, On the Institution of a Society in Liverpool, for the Encouragement of Designing, Drawing, Painting etc.* Liverpool, 1774.

———. *The Wrongs of Africa, Part the First.* London, 1788.

———. "On the Comparative Excellence of the Sciences and Arts." *MLPSM* 3 (1790): 241–60.

———. *Life of Lorenzo do Medici called the Magnificent.* 2 vols. Liverpool, 1795.

———. *Address, delivered before the Proprietors of the Botanic Garden, in Liverpool, previous to opening the Garden.* Liverpool, 1802.

———. *The Life and Pontificate of Leo the Tenth.* Liverpool, 1805.

———. *A Letter to Henry Brougham on the subject of Reform.* Liverpool, 1811.

———. *On the origin and vicissitudes of literature, science and art, and their influence on the present state of society: a discourse, delivered on the opening of the Liverpool royal institution.* Liverpool, 1817.

Rose, Mary. *The Gregs of Quarry Bank Mill: The Rise and Decline of a Family Firm, 1750–1914.* Cambridge: Cambridge University Press, 1986.

Rosen, George. "John Ferriar's 'Advice to the Poor.'" *Bulletin of the History of Medicine* 11, no. 2 (February 1942): 222–27.

Rush, Benjamin. "Result of some Observations during his Attendance as Physician General of the Military Hospitals of the United States." *MLPSM* 2 (1789): 506–9.

———. "An Account of the Progress of Population, Agriculture, Manners, and government in Pennsylvania." *MLPSM* 3 (1790): 183–97.

Sampson, David. "Wordsworth and the 'Deficiencies of Language.'" *ELH* 51, no. 1 (Spring 1984): 53–68.

Sangster, Matthew. *Living as an Author in the Romantic Period.* Basingstoke: Palgrave Macmillan, 2021.

Saxton, Eveline B. "The Binns Family of Liverpool, and the Binns Collection in the Liverpool Public Library." *Transactions of the Historical Society of Lancashire and Cheshire* 111 (1959): 167–80.

Schofield, R. E. *The Lunar Society of Birmingham.* Oxford: Oxford University Press, 1963.

Scott, Rosalie. "Health and Virtue: or, How to Keep out of Harm's Way; Lectures on Pathology and Therapeutics by William Cullen c. 1770." *Medical History* 81, no. 2 (April 1987): 123–42.

Seed, John. "Unitarianism, Political Economy and the Antinomies of Liberal Culture in Manchester." *Social History* 7, no. 1 (1982): 1–25.

———. "Gentleman Dissenters: The Social and Political Meanings of Rational Dissent in the 1770s and 1780s." *Historical Journal* 28, no. 2 (June 1985): 299–325.

Seeley, R. B. *Memoirs of the Life and Writings of Michael Thomas Sadler.* London, 1842.

Sekers, David. *A Lady of Cotton: Hannah Greg, Mistress of Quarry Bank Mill.* Stroud: History Press, 2010.

———. "'The Cultivation of Mind and Refinement of Manners in the Midst of a Money-Making and Somewhat Unpolished Community': Hannah Greg's Legacy Reconsidered." *Enlightenment and Dissent* 26 (2010): 163–94.

Selleck, R. J. W. *James Kay-Shuttleworth: Journey of an Outsider.* London: Routledge, 1995.

Serres, Michel. *Conversations on Science, Culture, and Time.* With Bruno Latour. Translated by Roxanne Lapidus. Ann Arbor: University of Michigan Press, 1995.

Sharples, Joseph. "From Rickman's Liverpool to Victorian Liverpool." In *Thomas Rickman and the Victorians*, edited by Megan Aldrich and Alexandrina Buchanan, 133–49. London: Victorian Society, 2019.

Sheffield Literary and Philosophical Society. *First Annual Report of the Sheffield Literary and Philosophical Society delivered at the annual meeting Jan 2, 1824*. Sheffield, 1824.

———. *The Second Annual Report of the Sheffield Literary and Philosophical Society*. Sheffield, 1825.

———. *The Eleventh Annual Report of the Sheffield Literary and Philosophical Society*. Sheffield, 1834.

Shepherd, William. *A Selection from the Early Letters of the Late William Shepherd, LL. D.* Edited by Richard C. Scragg. Liverpool, 1855.

Smith, Adam. *An Inquiry into the Nature and causes of the Wealth of Nations*. 2 vols. London, 1776.

Smith, Frank. *The Life and Works of Sir James Kay-Shuttleworth*. London: John Murray, 1923.

Smith, Leonard. *Lunatic Hospitals in Georgian England, 1750–1830*. London: Routledge, 2007.

Society for bettering the Condition and increasing the Comforts of the Poor. *Reports of the Society for bettering the Condition and increasing the Comforts of the Poor*. 2 vols. London, 1798–99.

Southey, Robert. *Sir Thomas More: or, Colloquies on the Progress and Prospects of Society*. 2 vols. London, 1824.

———. *Essays, Moral and Political*. 2 vols. London, 1832.

———. *Journal of a Tour in Scotland in 1819*. Edinburgh: Mercat Press, 1972.

———. *Sir Thomas More: or, Colloquies on the Progress and Prospects of Society*. 2 vols. Edited by Tom Duggett and Tim Fulford. London: Routledge, 2018.

Spencer, Peter. *A Portrait of Hannah Greg 1766–1828*. 2nd ed. Styal: Quarry Bank Trust, 1985.

———. *A Portrait of Samuel Greg 1758–1834*. Rev. ed. Styal: Quarry Bank Trust, 1989.

St. Clair, William. *The Reading Nation in the Romantic Period*. Cambridge: Cambridge University Press, 2004.

Steadman, Mark. "A History of the Scientific Collections of the Leeds Philosophical and Literary Society's Museum in the Nineteenth Century: Acquiring, Interpreting and Presenting the Natural World in the English Industrial City." PhD diss., University of Leeds, 2019.

Steers, David. "The Origin and Development of the Domestic Mission Movement Especially in Liverpool and Manchester." *TUHS* 21 (1996): 79–103.

Stevenson, William. *Remarks on the Very Inferior Utility of Classical Learning*. London, 1796.

Stewart, David. "The End of Conversation: Byron's Don Juan at the Newcastle Lit & Phil." *Review of English Studies* 66, no. 274 (April 2015): 322–41.

Stewart, Dugald. *Elements of the Philosophy of the Human Mind*. 3 vols. London, 1792–1827.

———. *Outlines of Moral Philosophy. For the Use of Students in the University of Edinburgh*. Edinburgh, 1793.

———. *Account of the Life and Writings of Thomas Reid*. Edinburgh, 1803.

Stewart, Larry. "Experimental Spaces and the Knowledge Economy." *History of Science* 45, no. 2 (2007): 155–77.

Strout, A. L. *A Bibliography of Articles in Blackwood's Magazine, Volumes I through XVIII, 1817–1825*. Lubbock: Texas Technological College, 1959.

Sutton, Ian. "The Extended Roscoe Circle: Art, Medicine, and the Cultural Politics of Alienation in Liverpool 1762–1836." *British Journal for Eighteenth-Century Studies* 30, no. 3 (September 2007): 439–58.

Tattersall, William. *A brief view of the anatomical arguments for the doctrine of materialism; occasioned by Dr. Ferriar's argument against it*. London, 1794.

Tayler, John James. *On Communion with Unbelievers: A Discourse delivered in the Unitarian Chapel, Mosley-Street, Manchester*. Manchester, 1828.

Taylor, R. V. *The Biographia Leodiensis; or, Biographical Sketches of the Worthies of Leeds and Neighbourhood*. London: Simpkin, Marshall, 1865.

Thackray, Arnold. "Natural Knowledge in Cultural Context: The Manchester Model." *American Historical Review* 79, no. 3 (June 1974): 672–709.

Thackrah, Charles Turner. *An Introductory Discourse delivered to the Leeds Philosophical and Literary Society, April 6, 1821*. Leeds, 1821.

———. *The Effects of the Principal Arts, Trades, and Professions, and of civic states and habits of living, on Health and Longevity: with a particular reference to the trades and manufactures of Leeds*. London, 1831.

———. *Inquiry into the Nature and Properties of the Blood, in Health and Disease*. Rev. ed. Edited by Thomas G. Wright. London, 1834.

———. *The Effects of Arts, Trades, and Professions on Health and Longevity*. Edited by A. Meiklejohn. Edinburgh: Livingstone, 1957.

Thomson, Frances M. *Newcastle Chapbooks in Newcastle upon Tyne University Library*. Newcastle upon Tyne: Oriel Press, 1969.

Thomson, John. *An Account of the Life, Lectures, and Writings of William Cullen, M.D.* 2 vols. Edited by David Craigie. Edinburgh: Blackwood's, 1832–59.

Thornton, David. "Edward Baines, Senior (1774–1848), Provincial Journalism and Political Philosophy in Early-Nineteenth-Century England." *Northern History* 40, no. 2 (2003): 277–97.

Thornton, R. D. *James Currie: The Entire Stranger and Robert Burns*. Edinburgh: Oliver and Boyd, 1963.

Traill, Thomas S. *Address delivered by Thos. Stewart Traill . . . and Resolutions adopted at a General Meeting of the Inhabitants*. Liverpool, 1825.

Tuke, Ruby. "Gifts, Gratitude, Charity: Representing Indebtedness 1790–1834." PhD diss., Queen Mary, University of London, 2021.

Turner, William. "An Essay on Crime and Punishments." *MLPSM* 2 (1789): 293–325.

———. *Speculations on the Propriety of Attempting the Establishment of a Literary Society in Newcastle*. Newcastle upon Tyne, 1792.

———. "Tour through the North of England." *Monthly Magazine* 4 (September and October 1797): 173–77, 253–58.

———. *A Sermon Peached at the Chapel in Hanover Square, Newcastle, for the Support of the New College, Manchester*. Newcastle, 1800.

———. *A Historical Sketch of the Transactions of the Literary and Philosophical Society of Newcastle upon Tyne*. Newcastle, 1807.

———. *A Short Sketch of the History of Protestant Nonconformity, and of the Society assembling in Hanover Square*. Newcastle, 1811.

———. *Address to the Monthly Meeting of the Literary and Philosophical Society of Newcastle Upon Tyne*. Newcastle, 1814.

——. *Introductory Address at the First Meeting of the Literary, Scientific, & Mechanical Institution of Newcastle upon Tyne*. Newcastle, 1824.

——. *Resignation and Submission Under the Afflictive Dispensations of Providence. A Sermon . . . on Occasion of the Lamented Death of James Losh*. Newcastle, 1833.

——. *Warrington Academy 1757–1786*. Edited by G. A. Carter. Warrington: Library and Museum Committee, 1957.

Twells, Alison. *The Civilising Mission and the English Middle Class, 1792–1850*. Basingstoke: Palgrave Macmillan, 2009.

Tylecote, Mabel. *The Mechanics' Institutes of Lancashire & Yorkshire before 1851*. Manchester: Manchester University Press, 1957.

Tyson, G. P. *Joseph Johnson: Liberal Publisher*. Iowa City: University of Iowa Press, 1979.

Unitarian Domestic Mission. *Report of the Ministry to the Poor commenced at Manchester in 1833*. Manchester, 1834.

——. *Fourth Report of the Ministry to the Poor commenced at Manchester in 1833*. Manchester, 1837.

——. *Fifth Report of the Ministry to the Poor commenced at Manchester in 1833*. Manchester, 1839.

——. *Eighth Report of the Ministry to the Poor commenced at Manchester in 1833*. Manchester, 1842.

Ure, Andrew. *The Philosophy of Manufactures; Or, An Exposition of the Scientific, Moral, and Commercial Economy of the Factory System of Great Britain*. London, 1835.

Vickers, Neil. "Coleridge, Thomas Beddoes and Brunonian Medicine." *European Romantic Review* 8, no. 1 (1997): 47–94.

Wach, Howard M. "Culture and the Middle Classes: Popular Knowledge in Industrial Manchester." *Journal of British Studies* 27, no. 4 (October 1988): 375–404.

——. "Unitarian Philanthropy and Cultural Hegemony in Comparative Perspective: Manchester and Boston, 1827–1848." *Journal of Social History* 26, no. 3 (Spring 1993): 539–57.

Wahrman, Dror. *Imagining the Middle Class: The Political Representation of Class in Britain, C.1780–1840*. Cambridge: Cambridge University Press, 1995.

——. "National Society, Communal Culture: An Argument about the Recent Historiography of Eighteenth-Century Britain." *Social History* 17, no. 1 (1992): 43–72.

Walton, John K. *Lancashire: A Social History*. Manchester: Manchester University Press, 1982.

Walton, Mary. *Sheffield: Its Story and Achievements*. 4th ed. Wakefield: S. R. Publishers and Corporation of Sheffield, 1968.

Ward, Thomas Asline. *Peeps into the Past: Being Passages from the Diary of Thomas Asline Ward*. Edited by Alexander Bell. Sheffield: W. C. Leng, 1907.

Watson, Robert Spence. *The History of the Literary and Philosophical Society of Newcastle upon-Tyne, 1793–1896*. London: Walter Scott, 1896.

Watts, Isaac. *The Improvement of the Mind: or, a Supplement to the Art of Logic*. London: 1741.

Watts, Ruth. *Gender, Power and the Unitarians in England 1760–1860*. London: Routledge, 1988.

Webster, Charles, and Jonathan Barry. "The Manchester Medical Revolution." In *Truth, Liberty, Religion: Essays Celebrating Two Hundred Years of Manchester College*, edited by Barbara Smith, 165–83. Oxford: Manchester College Oxford, 1986.

Webster, Christopher. *R. D. Chantrell, Architect: His Life and Work in Leeds 1818–1847.* Leeds: Thoresby Society, 1992.

Wedd, Mary. "Industrialization and the Moral Law in Books VIII and IX of *The Excursion.*" *Charles Lamb Bulletin* 81 (1993): 5–25.

Welford, Richard. *Men of Mark Twixt Tyne and Tees.* 3 vols. London, 1895.

Whalley, George. "The Bristol Library Borrowings of Southey and Coleridge, 1793–8." *Library* 5, no. 4 (1949): 114–32.

Wharton, Joanna. *Material Enlightenment: Women Writers and the Science of Mind, 1770–1830.* Woodbridge: Boydell & Brewer, 2018.

White, Charles. *Cases in Surgery, with remarks. Part the First.* London, 1770.

White, Daniel E. *Early Romanticism and Religious Dissent.* Cambridge: Cambridge University Press, 2006.

White, William. *History, Gazetteer and Directory of the West-Riding of Yorkshire.* 2 vols. Sheffield, 1837.

Wilberforce, Robert, and Samuel. *The Life of William Wilberforce.* 5 vols. London, 1838.

Wilkes, Jennifer. "Transpennine Enlightenment: Literary and Philosophical Societies in the North of England, 1780–1800." PhD diss., University of York, 2017.

Wilkinson, Kitty. *Memoir of Kitty Wilkinson 1786–1860.* Edited by Herbert R. Rathbone. Liverpool, 1927.

William Godwin's Diary. *William Godwin's Diary: Reconstructing a Social and Political Culture.* http://godwindiary.bodleian.ox.ac.uk/index2.html.

Williams, Eric. *Capitalism and Slavery.* Chapel Hill: University of North Carolina Press, 1994.

Williams, Raymond. *Marxism and Literature.* 1977. Reprint, Oxford: Oxford University Press, 1985.

Wilson, Arline. *William Roscoe: Commerce and Culture.* Liverpool: Liverpool University Press, 2008.

Wilson, Kathleen. *The Sense of the People: Politics, Culture and Imperialism in England, 1715–1785.* Cambridge: Cambridge University Press, 1995.

Winner, L. "Upon Opening the Black Box and Finding It Empty: Social Constructivism and the Philosophy of Technology." *Science, Technology and Human Values* 18, no. 3 (1993): 362–78.

Wood, William. *Sermon Preached Sept. 7, 1794 on the Occasion of the Death of the Rev William Turner to which are added, Memoirs of Mr. Turner's Life and Writings.* Newcastle, 1794.

Wordsworth, Dorothy. *Journals of Dorothy Wordsworth.* Edited by Ernest de Selincourt. 2 vols. Macmillan: London, 1959.

Wordsworth, William. *The Prose Works of William Wordsworth.* Edited by W. J. B. Owen and Jane Worthington Smyser. 3 vols. Oxford: Clarendon Press, 1974.

———. *The Excursion.* Edited by Sally Bushel, James A. Butler, and Michael C. Jaye, with the assistance of David Gracia. Ithaca, NY: Cornell University Press, 2007.

Wordsworth, William, and Samuel Taylor Coleridge. *Lyrical Ballads, and Other Poems 1797–1800.* Edited by James Butler and Karen Green. Ithaca, NY: Cornell University Press, 1992.

Wrigley, E. A. *Continuity Chance & Change: The Character of the Industrial Revolution in England.* Cambridge: Cambridge University Press, 1988.

———. *Energy and the English Industrial Revolution.* Cambridge: Cambridge University Press, 2010.

Wykes, David. "The Contribution of the Dissenting Academy to the Emergence of Rational Dissent." In *Enlightenment and Religion: Rational Dissent in Eighteenth-Century Britain*, edited by Knud Haakonssen, 99–139. Cambridge: Cambridge University Press, 1996.

Yarrow, P. J. "Mrs Gaskell and Newcastle upon Tyne." *Gaskell Society Journal* 5 (1991): 62–73.

Yeo, Eileen Janes. *The Contest for Social Science: Relations and Representations of Class and Gender*. London: Rivers Oram Press, 1996.

Zimmerman, Sarah. *The Romantic Literary Lecture in Britain*. Oxford: Oxford University Press, 2019.

INDEX

Page numbers in italics refer to illustrations

appendages, 166–67; and Darwin's anthropomorphic description of steam engine, 242n55; defense of mechanical improvement, 83–84; editor of *Leeds Mercury*, 68; *History of the Cotton Manufacture in Great Britain*, 25, 84, 150, 163, 164–68, 178; on limitless future of technological advancement, 94, 150, 166, 169; and Mechanics' Institute, 82, 169; "Mule Spinning" engraved plate from *History of the Cotton Manufacture in Great Britain, 165*; and New Lanark innovations, 155, 240n18; papers given at Leeds Philosophical and Literary Society, 83–85; parallel between steam engine and printing press, 168; parallel between the Industrial Revolution and the Reformation, 164; and Peterloo Massacre, 69; and Reform Bill of 1832, 68; role in Leeds Philosophical and Literary Society, 68, 69, 77–78, 79–80, 164; and Sadler, 167, 219n61; and steam-powered factory as turning point in history of progress, 164, 165–68, 172, 242n56; on study of political economy for the working class, 84; on superiority of British manufacturing, 168, 242n52; techno-determinism, 167, 169; on "the moral influence of free trade," 85, 220n80; "Throstle, Mule and Self Acting Mule," from *History of the Cotton Manufacture in Great Britain, 151*; view as natural world as limitless resource, 9

Baines, Edward, Sr.: advocacy for improvement of Leeds, 77, 96; argument with Oastler, 85, 220n81; burned in effigy outside *Mercury* office, 85; editor of *Leeds Mercury*, 68, 69; *The History, Directory and Gazetteer of the County Palatine of Lancaster*, 164; and Leeds Philosophical and Literary Society, 69, 78; and Literary and Philosophical Society of Liverpool, 72; opposition to slave trade and support for Parliamentary reform, 214n6; and Reform

Bill of 1832, 68; on universal male suffrage, 69

Baines-Marshall alliance, Leeds, 32, 79, 80, 83, 85

"Bainesocracy," 88; commitment to political economy, 69, 84, 85; and Leeds Philosophical and Literary Society, 79; Sadler and, 80; and ten-hours movement, 84

Bakhtin, M. M., "the grotesque body," 121

Banks, Sir Joseph, 120

Barbauld, Anna Laetitia: and abolition of slave trade, parliamentary reform, and civic rights of Dissenters, 22; "Address to the Deity," 133; educational work with Aikin, 103, 105, 107, 124, 129–30, 140, 153; *Evenings at Home* (with John Aikin Jr.), 105, 140, 226n24; gift of poem to William Turner, 31, 54, 55, 105, 130; hosting of women visitors, 133, 234n27; as London agent for friends in transpennine area, 30, 34; "Mouse's Petition," 63; obituary and poem published by William Turner, 31, 54, 130, 210n44; and object-oriented pedagogy, 105, 106, 141, 153; poetry of, 30, 54, 55, 59, 138; "Thoughts on the Devotional Taste," 22, 203n32; "Thoughts on the Inequality of Condition," 157; "To Dr. Aikin," 103; "To Mr. S. T. Coleridge," 48; "Verses written in the Leaves of an Ivory Pocketbook," 31, 105; and Warrington Academy, 30, 127; "What is Education?," 105, 226n26; work praised by Cooper, 129

Bardsley, Samuel Argent, 52, 210n38

Barker, Hannah, 34

Barnard, Robert (of Sheffield), "On taste," 87

Barnes, Thomas: Arianism, 21, 48, 135; debating group on philosophical materialism, 44; and development of literary taste over profit making, 27; and difference between poetry and prose, 59; *A Discourse Delivered at the Commencement of the Manches-*

slavery/slave trade (*continued*)
derived from in Liverpool, 72, 133–
34, 204n39; wealth derived from
in transpennine enlightenment, 6,
26, 135, 147, 235n40; Yates's sermon
against, 50, 70, 134
Smith, Adam: and division of labor, 17,
161; and stationary state, 162; *Wealth
of Nations*, 75
Smith, John, death in prison on Demerara, 76, 217n46
Smith, Leonard, 122
Smyth, William, 234n35
"social body," 169–70; versus machine, 172
social inquiry and reform, tradition of in
transpennine enlightenment, 6, 81,
112, 146, 173
social networks, 28
"social reform," as site of state and government intervention, 17, 202n14
society as machine: Kennedy and, 163;
versus view of as organic body, 172
Society for the Betterment of the Condition of the Poor, 109, 115
"soft materialism," 118, 230n87
Southey, Robert, 34; analogy between
Owen's plans and slavery, 155–56;
*Colloquies on the Progress and
Prospects of Society*, 149, 156, 181,
244n32; and consequences of factory
system for the poor, 149, 155, 159,
161, 181; Montgomery on, 93–94;
Poems, 59
Spa Field Riots, London, 64
Spence, Robert, 60
Spence, Thomas, 64, 240n20
spinning jennies, 25, 152
spinning masters, 159
spinning mule, 17, 25, 152, *165*, 239n7
Stanley, Edward, rector of Alderley, 69,
214n10
Statistical Society, Manchester: digest
of report to Factory Commissioners,
183, 244n38, 244n40; Doherty's
critique of, 182; financial difficulties, 245n52; flyer for "Manchester
Mechanics Institution: Outline of
a Course of Lectures on Political
Economy 1834," 245n44; goal of

social improvement in manufacturing population, 185; "Institutions
for the Promotion of Literature &
Science in Manchester," 245n50; and
justification of factory system, 185;
labor defined as self-reliance, sexual
restraint, and frugality, 158; overlap
in membership with Literary and
Philosophical Society, 185; problems
of obstruction and resentment of
population under study, 186, 191;
survey of working population for
British Association for the Advancement of Science, 186; views
on political economy and poor law
reform, 180
steam engines: adapted to cotton production, 15, 152, 159, 162; Boulton
and Watt, 152, 159; introduction in
and around Manchester, 17
steam-factory system: Baines's view of as
turning point in history of progress,
164–69; emergence of, 5–6, 158, 159;
perceived ability to transcend limits
of growth, 94, 150, 166, 169, 172; and
social restructuring, 159. *See also*
factory system, machine-based
STEM (science, technology, engineering,
and mathematics), demands for, 8
Sterne, Laurence: Ferriar and, 121,
231n100; story of Le Fevre, 124
Stevenson, Elizabeth Cleghorn. *See* Gaskell, Elizabeth (née Stevenson)
Stevenson, William (father of Elizabeth), 100, 188; *Remarks on the Very
Inferior Utility of Classical Learning*, 225n5
stewardship: middle-class assumptions
of and working-class demands for
access, 5, 42, 193; of the privileged
over the non-privileged, 9, 144, 147–
48, 181, 183, 192–93
Stewart, David, 59
Stewart, Dugald, 29, 74, 145; "Common
Sense" philosophy, 29, 70; *Elements
of the Philosophy of the Human
Mind*, 138, 236n65; influence on
women activists, 138–39; *Outlines of
Moral Philosophy*, 138–39, 236n62

Turner, William (of Newcastle)
(*continued*)
at Hanover Square, Newcastle, 55,
130, 211n58; and Newcastle society
library, 60, 62; and New Institution,
60–62, 213n82; and *Oeconomist*,
63; organization of "Literary Club"
within the society, 62, 65; paper on
corporal and capital punishment in
MLPSM, 54–55; publishing of poem
and obituary for Anna Barbauld,
31, 54, 130, 210n44; receipt of poem
from Anna Barbauld, 31, 54, 55, 105,
130; and repeal of Test and Corporation Acts, 171; *Speculations*, 55, 56,
60; student of Warrington Academy,
54; support for education of women,
130; "Tour through the North of England," 216n31
Turner, William (of Wakefield), 31
Twells, Alison, 104, 128, 222n97
Tylecote, Mabel, 242n61
typhus outbreak, 7, 112, 113

Unitarian chapel, Hanover Square,
Newcastle, 55
Unitarian domestic mission, Manchester, 186; *Eighth Report*, 189, 247n74;
reports of Ministers to the Poor, 187,
189, 246n62, 246n64; *Sixth Report*,
187
Unitarianism: emphasis on personal
freedom, 160; evangelical view of,
89; in Manchester society, 44, 104,
174; "Unitarian ethos," 159; viewed
with suspicion by Anglican establishment, 174, 243n8. *See also* Cross
Street Chapel, Manchester; Mosley
Street chapel, Manchester
United States: raw materials from plantations, 19, 26; and slavery, 33
Ure, Andrew, 168–69
useful knowledge: disputes over constitution of and modes of communication, 3, 7, 18, 19, 42, 44, 47–48,
59–64, 212nn75–76; and Industrial
Revolution, 6; and the literary,
debates over, 2–3, 4, 6, 20, 27–29, 29,

194; and restricted idea of Manchester culture, 34

vernacular literary canon formation,
58–60
Vernon, Di., 131–32
Vickers, Neil, 230n87
vitalism, 117
Voice of the People, 187–88, 192;
exchange of Doherty and W. R. Rathbone, 182–83, 244n37; "Mr. Heywood
and the Working Classes," 188

Wach, Howard, 146
Walker, Thomas, 69, 136, 203n33,
230n90; and appointment of Ferriar
as honorary infirmary physician,
112; friendship with Ferriar, 228n62,
229n76; and Manchester Constitutional Society, 49; and Olaudah
Equiano, 26, 204n42; resignation
from Manchester Literary and
Philosophical Society, 51; trial and
acquittal of treasonable conspiracy,
51, 209n26, 229n76
Walpole, Horace, *The Castle of Otranto*,
133
Wang, Fuson, 227n34
Ward, Thomas Asline: analogy of freedom of discussion to free trade, 88;
*Essays on the Formation and Publica-
tion of Opinions*, 88; leadership role
in Literary and Philosophical Society
of Sheffield, 68, 88, 222n94; membership in SSPUK, 87–88, 221n89,
222n96; and Montgomery, 89, 90;
radical supporter of Francis Burdett,
88; and Reform Bill of 1832, 68; and
Sheffield Independent, 90, 223n108;
and Unitarianism, 87, 221n92
Warrington Academy: center for the education of Dissenters, 21; demise of,
105; exclusion of women, 127; most
important academic institution in
transpennine enlightenment, 29–
30; "self-organizing alumni, 30–31
water frame, 25
Waterloo, Battle of, 90, 93